German Literature

A CRITICAL SURVEY

German Literature

A CRITICAL SURVEY

Edited by Bruno Boesch

Translated by Ronald Taylor

METHUEN & CO LTD

II NEW FETTER LANE LONDON EC 4

First published as Deutsche Literaturgeschichte in Grundzügen
by Francke Verlag, Bern
© *1946 A. Francke AG Verlag Bern*
Third edition 1967
English translation first published in 1971
by Methuen & Co Ltd
© *1971 Methuen & Co Ltd*
Printed in Great Britain by
The Camelot Press Ltd,
London and Southampton

SBN 416 14940 5

Distributed in the USA
by Barnes & Noble Inc

Contents

Translator's Preface

This is a history of German literature of a somewhat unconventional kind. Instead of being a continuous narrative, with dates of authors and works, summaries of plots and other features of the encyclopedic method, it takes the basic periods and movements, from Carolingian to modern times, and treats each such section as a narrative with its own literary, intellectual and cultural cohesion. The nine contributors have sought to characterize the inner nature and historical significance of the individual epochs in terms of the most important works in that epoch. Chapters devoted to 'baroque' or 'realism', for example, are concerned, not to list and discuss a set of 'baroque' or 'realist' writers, but to explain the significance of these concepts as focal points of interest at certain moments in history, and to illustrate them from the work of individual poets, novelists and dramatists. Readers can thus perhaps grasp more quickly the 'feel' of a particular age or movement than in a 'conventional' history of literature laid out as a continuous chronicle of events.

The German original – *Deutsche Literaturgeschichte in Grundzügen*, edited by Bruno Boesch (Bern and Munich: Francke Verlag) – was first published in 1946. The text used for the translation is that of the enlarged third edition (1967).

To translate is to interpret, and to present to an English public a survey of German literature by a group of Swiss scholars forces the translator to make occasional modifications in the original text, above all in deference to the different background from which the new public will approach the work. I offer this professional apologia, especially to the authors of the individual articles, as a reflection of the spirit in which such modifications have been made.

A few dates have been added or revised, and a new bibliography compiled with the interests of English readers in mind. For her help in compiling this bibliography and preparing the index I am most grateful to Mrs Erika Poole.

I affectionately dedicate this translation to my parents.

Eusserthal,
Summer 1971   R.T.

The Literature of the Carolingian Age

HEINZ RUPP

Latin and German

European Literature and the Latin Middle Ages – the title of this well-known work by E. R. Curtius states basic premises about the age in which a vernacular German literature emerges, begins to develop, and flourishes. For this German literature emerges in the Latin Middle Ages: Latin is the language of the Church, of theology, indeed, of all learning, the language of politics and administration – and the language of literature. This is the language which, crossing all barriers between tribes and peoples, unites Western Christendom under a religious banner. But it was – as it still is – a learned language, the language above all of theologians and clerics. Thus everything committed to parchment down to the eighth century, and the greater part of everything recorded right down to the late Middle Ages, is in Latin – and this does not apply only to those areas in which German was spoken.

This literature is European and Western, because it is Latin and because it is Christian. 'National' characteristics are hard to detect, especially in the early Middle Ages. Theological literature, in the wide sense, follows the works of the Church Fathers both in content and in form: the models for early medieval theologians are the exegetic, homiletic and moral writings of Augustine, Gregory the Great, Saint Jerome, Saint Ambrose and others. The study of grammar was based on the curriculum used in the days of the late Roman Empire; similarly the remainder of the *septem artes liberales,* the seven liberal arts, followed what had been bequeathed to them, pagan and Christian elements alike, by classical and late antiquity. These are the roots of this European literature, and even where it out-grows these roots – as it does everywhere – it remains European, because the roots remain the same.

The situation with regard to poetry is not very different. It, too, is European, and in so far as it is Christian poetry, which it largely is, its models are to be found in early Christian poetry – the epics of Juvencus, Sedulius, Arator and Prudentius, and the hymns of Ambrose, Prudentius and Venantius Fortunatus. But the great poets of pagan Rome – Virgil,

Ovid, Horace, Terence and others – were also acknowledged and imitated, though with reservations. They were admired for their skill in language and poetic form; their styles were copied, and their felicitous turns of phrase appropriated.

One of the most important influences besides these was that of the Bible, which was not only the repository of Christian ideas but also a source of poetic influence, since many of its books – the Psalms, the Song of Songs, the Book of Job – were soon recognized as poetry and exerted their attraction as such.

These are the foundations of medieval Latin religious verse, and the situation with regard to secular verse, at least in the early Middle Ages, is not very different. New forms are added, such as rhythmic verse, and new types appear, such as the sequence, but the basis remains the same. And it remains despite 'national' characteristics, such as the Irish predilection for rhyme or the Germans' liking for the leonine hexameter, since these features are not sufficiently pronounced to destroy the basically European character of this poetry.

Since we are dealing here with written literature which was in Latin, its impact was bound to be limited – limited, in fact, to those who could read and write, and who could understand Latin. These were the *litterati*, i.e. as far as the early Middle Ages is concerned, the clerics and certain sections of the nobility. Latin poetry is thus the poetry of clerics and noblemen – and in this early period these two classes virtually coincide. The only impact of this poetry on wider circles was felt through certain parts of the liturgy, such as the hymns.

Vernacular literatures grew out of this medieval latinity – with different time-scales and sometimes with varying emphases – in France, England and Germany. As a result of the conditions created by the process of Christianization, vernacular literature developed very early in England, where the native tradition of alliterative verse lasted longer than in Germany. In France, on the other hand, vernacular literature took longer to emerge than in Germany; the main reason for this is that the French language derives directly from Latin and was therefore slower to achieve independence.

These newly emerging vernacular literatures inevitably lose part of their European character, and their sphere of influence is naturally more restricted, but they retain their European character at least by virtue of their religious subject-matter. The same is true of a good deal of the secular literature – poetic versions of the legends of Alexander, Aeneas and Troy, the Arthurian epics, and many *Schwänke* (comic anecdotes) and short narrative poems.

Compared with the Latin, German literature continued to be backward. Latin was *the* literary language for the early Middle Ages, for it was one of the three holy languages. Despite all the efforts of Charlemagne, German could never achieve such eminence; in the eyes of the *litterati* it remained an uncouth barbarian tongue of inferior quality. As a result vernacular German literature could not develop out of Latin literature but rather grew alongside it, and sometimes in opposition to it. It could not achieve the same eminence, and even had to struggle for its very existence – a struggle which can be witnessed in manuscripts right down to the twelfth century; only then did German literature establish its equal importance. This long struggle explains a great deal about the development of German literature which could not otherwise be appreciated.

It is precisely because of this slow development of a German vernacular literature between 800 and 1180 – a literature virtually ignored by the *litterati* and the leading men of the time, with the exception of Charlemagne, and restricted in its reception – that Latin literature has to be drawn into any history of German literature. Without a knowledge of this Latin literature one cannot properly understand German literature. A comparison of poetic forms shows clearly how German was trying to free itself from the powerful grip of its Latin forebears, and the amount of Latin poetry preserved reveals the paucity of the German material. And if one surveys the entire literary scene in the early Middle Ages, one will not make the mistake of overestimating the historical importance and intellectual influence of the German literature of the period, for from the eighth to the twelfth centuries it is but a sluggish stream compared with the broad river of Latin literature.

From when can we date the beginning of German literature? From the time when the forms of the German language were recorded on parchment. Without embarking on a discussion as to when the German Empire was founded, one can say that there has been a German language since the time when a number of continental Germanic tribes were drawn into a political union under the Emperor Charlemagne. The existence of written records in this language – which was not a unified language but an assemblage of related Germanic tribal dialects – derived from the need to codify the language for particular purposes, a need which accompanied the Christianization of the German parts of the Frankish Empire.

This early German literature is therefore liturgico-Christian, and there was neither need nor reason to record the Germanic poetry which had been orally transmitted through the generations. The only known attempt to commit this native poetry to writing – Charlemagne's collection of heroic lays – led to no extant manuscript. Such a manuscript would scarcely have been deliberately destroyed but may well have been lost because the *litterati* had no interest in it. Nor indeed is it certain that this so-called *Heldenliederbuch* really did consist of Germanic lays. The history of written German literature until well into the twelfth century is therefore only the history of religious literature. The history of early pagan German literature – and the existence of such a literature can be proved – cannot be traced, since there are no written records from the period. And when, in the *Nibelungenlied* and other works, this literary tradition emerges, it has changed so much that one can hardly draw conclusions about its earlier nature. Had the *Hildebrandslied* not been preserved by a stroke of good fortune, we could have no real idea of this pagan literature. The history of German literature is thus in the first instance the history of Christian German literature, and it is this that links it to the European literature of the Latin Middle Ages.

It has been said that the German ethos is compounded of Germanic, classical and Christian elements. This is only true of early medieval literature with reservations. The poetic genres governed by pagan Germanic values have not been preserved, and in the extant Christian literature Germanic elements are comparatively unimportant. The much-talked-of 'Germanization' of Christianity does not stand up to examination. It is, of course, evident that when a new religion replaces an old, it changes the modes of thought and feeling of its new converts. It is equally evident that, in penetrating new realms, a new religion itself undergoes changes, merely by virtue of the transference of its thoughts and writings to another language. But Christianity underwent no decisive change during its adoption by the Germanic tribes, although certain Christian concepts which were from the beginning close to Germanic modes of thought were more strongly emphasized, such as the notions, widespread since the time of Constantine, of the *militia Christi*, with its military terminology. The feudal system was seen as a parallel to the relationship of God to man; the Christian nature of the principle of service and reward was emphasized and there were other elements besides. But the heart of the Christian message was preserved with remarkable purity among the Germanic peoples, without regard to whether Christian concepts appeared to the lately converted tribes as familiar or totally new. The so-called 'Germanization' of Christianity went no further than the 'Latinization' or 'Romanization' of Christianity. A Germanic Christianity never existed, and early medieval German literature is essentially Christian literature.

The Beginnings of German Literature

The earliest German literary documents – excluding the runes – date from the second half of the eighth century. What are the circumstances?

There are two important figures from whom vital characteristics in Western Christendom and its culture stem, and from whom German literature, directly and indirectly, derived vital impulses, namely Benedict of Nursia (d. 547) and Charlemagne.

It is no accident that written German records start in the second half of the eighth century. In 744 Abbot Sturmi, a disciple of Boniface, founded the monastery of Fulda; twenty years earlier Pirminius had founded the monastery of Reichenau; in 747 the monastery at St Gallen, a hitherto unimportant cell living by the rule of Columba, adopted the Benedictine rule, thereby launching its rise to eminence in the intellectual and cultural sphere.

These are only a few examples of the rise of Benedictine monasteries in Germany with which the emergence of German literature is so closely associated. The efflorescence of the Benedictine order in Germany derives from the fact that the Anglo-Saxon missionaries, particularly those owing allegiance to Boniface, were Benedictines. The eastern part of the Frankish kingdom also received its liturgy from these missionaries, and gradually the Benedictine rule was adopted in all German monasteries.

The credit for the rise of an influential monastic culture, however, belongs fundamentally to St Benedict himself. Without him and his monastic rule the course of European history would have been very different. There were, of course, monastic orders and monastic rules before Benedict, but their concern was mainly with a strict asceticism which left little scope for cultural activity. The Columban rule is the best example of this, and as long as St Gallen, founded by a disciple of Columba's (St Gall), followed that rule, it remained insignificant: it was the Benedictine rule that brought about the change.

The importance and the effect of the Benedictine rule rest mainly on the fact that Benedict envisaged not only an ascetic monk but also a human being; he knew that very few men were capable of living a life of strict asceticism, and that exaggerated demands would do more harm than good to a community. He therefore reduced the ascetic requirements of his order to a minimum which was humanly tolerable, lessened the severity of punishments and penances, and made the liturgy the centre of monastic life.

Two of the requirements of his rule in particular have proved to be of cultural value. Monastic communities needed a certain stability for their continued existence; he therefore established the principle of *stabilitas loci*, which required a monk to spend his entire life in his chosen monastery unless there were pressing reasons why he should not. At the same time Benedict realized the need to offset the acts of worship and prayer with work. In the first instance he conceived of this as physical work, but intellectual and artistic work quickly found a place as well, such as copying manuscripts, writing new books, activities connected with the monastery school, and arts and crafts. Scribal activity was not confined to Christian works, for pagan Latin authors too were needed in the schools. There is thus a conscious humanistic element in the Benedictine order.

Without the activity of the Benedictine order Charlemagne could never have carried through his reforms. He both depended on, and supported, the monasteries. The majority of the scholars and theologians to whom he turned were Benedictines, and it was from Benedictine monasteries that the important works of Carolingian theology came.

Much has been written about the 'Carolingian Renaissance', but it would be more accurate to speak of 'Charlemagne's Renaissance', for it was the Emperor's purpose to restore generally accepted standards in all branches of national life, political, intellectual and religious. He was thus as concerned to record the old tribal legal codes as he was to obtain the original text of the *Regula Benedicti* and the authentic liturgical books. His plan for a German grammar is also part of this. Once the authentic texts had been laid down, education could proceed: Latin would become accurate classical Latin again, and Latin style would be modelled on the great authors of antiquity; the theological training of the clerics, hitherto sadly neglected, would be improved. The priests, however, would also preach in German, and the congregation would at least learn the Creed and the Lord's Prayer in German.

Charlemagne was active in all spheres, issuing decrees, making suggestions and ordering punishments, and succeeded in attracting to his court, or at least employing for his purposes, many of the most prominent men of the time. Alcuin, an Englishman from York, identified himself with Charlemagne's reforms and wrote theological works which served as practical and authoritative handbooks for the clerics. His works are not simply to be dismissed as compilations; rather they are concise summaries of the essential elements in the works of the Church Fathers. Besides Alcuin we find Paul the Deacon, a Langobard, Peter of Pisa, Einhard, the East Frankish biographer of Charlemagne, and many others, all of whom left their mark on the following generation.

Hrabanus Maurus, Abbot of Fulda and later Archbishop of Mainz, continued the work of his teacher Alcuin. He too is more than a mere compilator, for he wrote Bible commentaries, an encyclopedia called *De universo*, derived from Isidore's *Etymologies*, and works of dogma; all this activity entitles him to be ranged alongside those who have earned the title of *praeceptor Germaniae*. In the following generation come Walahfrid Strabo, poet and theologian, and Lupus of Ferrières, philologist and textual scholar, both pupils of Hrabanus. What Charlemagne had initiated was thus continued into the tenth century, the *saeculum obscurum*, and thence into the eleventh and twelfth centuries.

It is out of this background of Carolingian culture and Benedictine monasticism that the hesitant beginnings of vernacular German literature emerge. Initially it is a purely practical literature, tied to the monasteries, for these were the only places, together with episcopal and royal capitals, where the necessary technical and intellectual conditions existed.

In the monasteries the monks and the young novices first had to learn Latin, but there was no Latin grammar in German and no Latin-German dictionary: one might go so far as to say that Latin had to be learnt from Latin sources. The need was for dictionaries and aids to translation. Thus there arose collections of glosses, interlinear texts and translations from the Latin. Aids to the study of theology were also required: a monk had at least to understand the rules of the order within which he was supposed to live.

But it was not only the monasteries that required German texts: the Church as a whole needed them even more. A new convert was required to learn the stock baptismal phrases by which he renounced his pagan beliefs, and also the creed of the new religion to which he had pledged himself; he must know the Lord's Prayer in German and also the formal language of confession. But who was to produce these texts, if not the monks? This virtually exhausts the scope of the earliest German literature.

It is a laborious beginning. Even writing the words was a laborious business, for the sounds of the German language had to be reproduced by Latin letters – a state of affairs about which Otfrid von Weissenburg still complained in the ninth century. Today we can only wonder at how well and relatively uniformly this problem was solved in the various scriptoria.

Furthermore these Christian Latin texts contain words for which there are no German equivalents, or at most only vague ones. This forced the scribes to create new words, and they had to take great care to find the correct word for the new object or idea; a mistake over a word amounted to a mistake over the object or idea itself, which, since the subject-matter was predominantly religious, could amount to a sin.

These and many other problems made the preparation of glosses and translations a hazardous venture, and many errors were inevitably made. The view has been expressed that the German language was at this time not sufficiently well developed, not sufficiently subtle, to convey the new ideas. But this can hardly be the real reason for these cumbersome, error-ridden beginnings, for the Old High German translation of Isidore, as well as the *Hildebrandslied*, show that German could be a well-developed vehicle of expression, capable of considerable subtlety. The real reasons lie elsewhere.

On the one hand they are to be found in the difficulties referred to above, and on the other hand in the fact that the knowledge of Latin possessed by many of these translators and compilers of glosses was not all that great. But above all they are to be found in the general attitude towards the relative value of the two languages. German, a *lingua barbarica*, could only be a means to an end, not an end in itself. It had no proper orthography and no proper grammar, and was completely dependent on Latin, whose grammar and syntax gave the lead. Glosses and translations were not made for the sake of rendering them into German – at the most this could apply to liturgical texts – but so that the Latin originals could be understood. In the main, therefore, this early German material has the character of a mere means to an end, necessary but regrettable, and to be put aside as soon as possible. The few exceptions prove the rule.

These early German prose pieces should therefore not be overestimated. They have an undeniable value for the study of the German language, and are also important in that they show how Latin-Christian ideas were gradually taken over into German, but they have little value for the history of German literature or for the history of culture; the manuscripts of the time and the contents of libraries can tell us far more in these respects. Yet because these pieces are the earliest in the German language, they are bound to command our respect, testifying, as they do, to the efforts which paved the way for the achievements of the following centuries.

This German literature, designed for practical use, opens with two dictionaries which belong to the pre-Charlemagne era: the so-called *Abrogans*, compiled *c.* 765, probably in Freising, and based on Italian material, and the *Vocabularius Sancti Galli*, which was, however, not written in St Gallen but probably in Fulda, from where its Anglo-Saxon traits could have come. These two works thus represent two of the most important directions from which Christian ideas reached the Frankish kingdom – the one from Rome via Bobbio and Salzburg in the south, the other, more important, also from Rome, via England and entering from the north via Fulda.

The *Abrogans* – the name is taken from the first word – was an old-established alphabetical Latin dictionary of synonyms used in the study of rhetoric; alongside the standard Latin word it listed rarer synonyms and poetic usages. In Freising the Latin words were given German equivalents, possibly by Bishop Arbeo himself, though this is not certain. The *Vocabularius*, on the other hand, also a work with a long history, is arranged in subject-groups.

For centuries after these two works the activity of compiling glossaries went on without cease; important theological and poetical writings were provided with glosses, either between the lines of the Latin text or in the margins. The Bible, the writings of the Church Fathers, decretals, and the works of Virgil, Prudentius and others were treated in this way.

Complementary to these glosses are interlinear versions of texts, i.e. word-for-word translations. In Reichenau there were such versions of the Benedictine rule and of a few hymns by the end of the eighth century, and versions of the Psalms have been preserved from a number of monasteries. There are translations of the Creed and the Lord's Prayer (St Gallen, Freising, Weissenburg), of baptismal vows and confessions.

The most important and extensive translation of the period is the Old High German version of the sixth-century Latin translation of the *Harmony of the Gospels* written by the second-century Syrian Christian Tatian. This German translation was made in Fulda at the time of Hrabanus Maurus, and the continuous biblical narrative, drawn from the four Gospels, was probably produced by a community of monks, each contributing according to his ability. Whether Hrabanus himself worked on it is not known; at all events he makes no reference to it in his extant writings. The Tatian translation would in any case have been intended for educative purposes in the monastery school, and not as an independent presentation of the New Testament in German.

But by far the most outstanding of these translations is that of a treatise by Isidore of Seville. No other work of the period even approaches its standard, for its anonymous author trnaslated the theological subject-matter into a real German, not a Latinized German. This can be seen in the orthography, the vocabulary, the use of cases and tenses, and the syntax. The translator may have worked in a monastery in Alemannic, Alsatian or Frankish territory, probably around the end of the eighth century. The attractive notion has even been advanced that it was written during the adoptian controversy and recited at one of the councils in order to help the princes, most of whom knew no Latin, come to a decision. If this were so, it would explain why such pains were taken over the translation, and it would also be a rare example of a German translation standing in its own right and not merely as an adjunct to the Latin. At all events it was a long while before this level was reached again: the Monsee-Wiener fragments of a New Testament translation are the only work to approach it.

Latin Poetry

While there is a German prose literature from the second half of the eighth century, it is some time before we encounter a written poetic literature. On the one hand this is surprising, since the Carolingian Renaissance gave an unprecedented impetus to all aspects of intellectual and cultural life; on the other hand one must recall that, notwithstanding the existence of German prose writings, the language of literature was, and continued to be, Latin. Indeed Latin poetry, like theology, received a new lease of life in the Carolingian era. The pagan poets of classical Rome were read and praised, and their poetic form and style imitated; even more highly esteemed were the Christian poets of late antiquity, whose language and form were seen as the equal of those of the classics, and whose Christian subject-matter set them far above their pagan predecessors. Classical poetry, *monumentum aere perennius*, ceded pride of place to a literature that would live on after the Day of Judgement, for this literature dealt with the only eternal truth in the world, i.e. with God, to whose glory these poets composed their works. This was the principle from which Juvencus proceeded, and it was a principle shared by all the others.

The Latin poetry of the Carolingian era rests on these foundations. It was not original, and did not intend to be, for, like theology, it is based on reverence for authority. To compose poetry did not mean to write something new, but to show one's facility in language and metre, as in the classical schools of rhetoric. This has led to this poetry being called the poetry of epigones, and to the judgement that the greatest ability of the poets of the age lay in their pillaging of classical and late-classical authors.

But this misses the main point. Part of the poet's skill lay in incorporating at an appropriate point in his poem a classical turn of phrase, or perhaps an entire line from the *Aeneid* or other work, in order to show that he knew the classics and was adept in the *ars*, the τέχνη. The reader, for his part, would recognize which phrase came from Virgil, which from Statius, which from Prudentius, and so on.

Thus poetic activity flourished at Charlemagne's court. Particularly popular was the poetic letter; Alcuin, Peter of Pisa, Charlemagne himself and many others wrote such letters. Other small poetic genres – fables, epitaphs, historical poems, hymns, epigrams for various occasions – were also cultivated, but extended forms are rare. Some of these efforts are mediocre, some excellent; some are the laborious products of poetasters, some are accomplished literary achievements. Artificiality was reckoned a sign of great skill, so we find such features as acrostics and telestichs incorporated into poems, and so-called abecedaries, in which the first line or strophe begins with *a*, the second with *b*, and so on. The climax of such frivolities is reached in 'figure-poems', the most highly developed examples of which are probably those given by Hrabanus Maurus in his *Liber de laudibus sanctae crucis*.

Of the important Latin poets of the Carolingian age three should be mentioned, all from the East Frankish kingdom and of a later generation than Charlemagne. Two of them – the Swabian Walahfrid Strabo, later abbot of Reichenau, and the Saxon nobleman Gottschalk, whose knowledge of St Augustine and whose profound religiosity was to cause the great theological dispute over the question of predestination which was to prove his downfall – had been friends since their days in Fulda together. They both felt themselves to be *Latin* poets, and Gottschalk in particular would have nothing to do with his barbaric mother tongue. The few poems of his that have survived reveal, despite their linguistic ostentation and their decorative form, a more personal thought and emotion than is usual in this period, and his hymns and odes are imbued with his faith in the deity, his fear of God the Arbiter and his trust in God the Father. Of interest from the formal point of view is that, some years before Otfrid, he shows a predilection for rhyme – a feature with which he may well have become acquainted through the poems of Irish monks.

Walahfrid's poems are more straightforward, more serene, more human. He writes of his longing to return home to Reichenau, he composes odes, experiments with classical metres and also tries his hand at epic verse. His poem on gardens, *De cultura hortorum*, is still remembered; less well-known are his *Visio Wettini*, the first medieval treatment in verse of the Vision of Hell and a humble precursor of the *Divine Comedy*, and his *De imagine Tetrici*, a condemnation of Theodoric the Great, whose statue Charlemagne had ordered to be brought to Aachen but whose reputation had changed, during the time of Louis the Pious, from that of a hero to that of a servant of Satan.

The third of these important poets of the late Carolingian age is also, like Walahfrid, a Swabian, though of a later generation – Notker Balbulus. Notker, son of a Thurgau nobleman, was born about 850 and spent his life as a monk and a teacher at St Gallen in the years of its ascendancy. This attractive personality is, if not the actual inventor, then at least the first major practitioner of a new lyrical genre, the sequence, which later evolved into the Middle High German *Leich*. Irrespective of whether the first sequences were composed in Jumièges or St Gallen, and whether their origin is to be found in the coloraturas on the final vowel of the Halleluja in the gradual, it was Notker's great poetic gifts that brought this new form to its first and greatest climax.

The sequence may well have been born out of music, but Notker gave it independence and made it a formal poetic genre in its own right, to which music then came to be added to intensify the effect of the whole. In form the textual sequence is close to liturgical chants, above all to the Psalms, and is characterized by the use of antiphonal versicles arranged in equal pairs, each versicle having its own structure. Later there were variants to this pattern, as sequences became longer and more involved, but basically they retained the form given to them by Notker.

Another achievement of Notker's, though one not publicly attributed to him, is the *Gesta Caroli Magni*, a compilation of events from the life of the Emperor as related to him from various authoritative sources. In a pleasing, yet rhetorical and assured style he sets out these anecdotes as an act of homage to the already legendary figure of Charlemagne and at the same time as both a gift and an admonition to Charlemagne's great-grandson Charles III.

One final work must be mentioned in this context of Latin literature, since there are reasons for believing that it belongs to the Carolingian age. This is *Waltharius*, the epic tale of Walther and Hildegunde and of Walther's battles with Gunther and his warriors. Scholars of the Romantic period, following a statement by Ekkehard IV, took this epic, which is preserved without ascription, to be the work of Ekkehard I of St Gallen, but there are good grounds for disputing the authorship both of Ekkehard and of one Geraldus, whose dedicatory prefaces to *Waltharius* are preserved in a number of manuscripts. The only things we know about the author are that he was a monk and that he turned this Germanic legend into a Latin epic for the entertainment of his fellow brethren. There is nothing particularly surprising about this, for we know that a number of clerics appreciated being entertained in this way.

The author, whoever he was, was attracted by the story and set out to relate it in the form of a classical Latin epic. And he did indeed Latinize it completely, composing with great skill a polished Latin epic in hexameters. Moreover, he adapted the content to a monastic mentality, while leaving undisturbed the basic events of the legend.

Walther, blood-brother of Hagen, escapes with Hildegunde from the Huns. Gunther, Hagen and eleven other warriors, their eyes on the treasure that Walther and Hildegunde have taken with them, pursue the couple. Battle is joined, and the poet gives vivid descriptions of the fighting. At first Hagen holds back, but when his nephew Patafrid is killed by Walther he is forced to involve himself.

We are thus presented with the classic tragic situation of heroic literature: loyalty to one's people and the duty to avenge a relative are set against the fact of blood-relationship, and there is no way out. In Germanic lays both would have had to die, but this was no solution for the ninth-century monastic poet, who, having reached this climax, makes the wounded warriors Gunther, Hagen and Walther, by a kind of *salto mortale*, reconcile their quarrel, display scornful mockery of each other's wounds, and finally make their peace. And on this note of serene reconciliation, which in the context of Germanic heroic poetry can only be called grotesque, the epic ends.

German Poetry

Together with this new Latin poetry there arose a new German poetry, and it is something of a miracle that this poetry should open with two outstanding works, namely, the *Heliand* and Otfrid's *Evangelienbuch* (*Harmony of the Gospels*).

It is generally assumed that the *Heliand* was written about 820 or 830, and that since its author used in the main the Latin version of Tatian's *Harmony of the Gospels*, and also drew on Hrabanus' commentary on St Matthew's gospel, he had close links with Fulda, and may even have written the work there. But of the author himself we know very little, and all attempts to identify him, or at least the place in which he worked, have proved unconvincing. If one takes a Latin *Praefatio in librum antiquum*, discovered in the sixteenth century, as referring to the *Heliand* (it is very doubtful if Hrabanus himself wrote this *Praefatio*), then it appears that the work was composed at the instigation of Louis the Pious by a *non ignobilis vates de gente Saxonum* with the aim of overcoming superstition and making the *illiterati* familiar with the life and teaching of Christ.

The *Heliand* (the name was given to the poem by its first editor) tells the story of Jesus in the Saxon dialect and using the old alliterative *Langzeile* (a line divided into two halves, each consisting basically of four stresses, the two halves being linked by a common alliterative or assonant element). It is not unduly remarkable that such a work should have been written at this time in the territory of the Saxons, for there were close links between the Saxons and England, where Christian alliterative verse had long been known, and from the point of view of form the *Heliand* belongs to this Anglo-Saxon tradition. What is remarkable, however, is that only a few decades after the conversion of the Saxons, largely by force, to Christianity so profoundly Christian a work should be found whose author was unwilling to make any concessions in fundamental questions of Christian belief.

A good deal has been written about the 'Germanization' of Christianity by the poet of the *Heliand*, but it is only the external presentation that has been 'Germanized'. The author sees the figures of the New Testament as characters from his own age and surroundings, and there are traces of the Saxon countryside in his descriptions, but this is only what one would expect. It also reminds one of the practice of medieval painters. The outer layer may be Saxon-Germanic, but the core is completely Christian.

Following the broad outlines of Tatian, the poet tells simply and directly the life of Jesus, giving graphic descriptions of characters and events in a manner very different from the plain, dull style of much of Otfrid's *Evangelienbuch*. But the narrative is not there just for its own sake; it is intended to help the poet's compatriots become true Christians. The storyteller is at the same time a teacher, and one wonders which role was the more important. Since the poet knew that many Christian thoughts and commandments were not merely unfamiliar to his hearers but sometimes even offensive to them, he left certain things out, but only when they were not vital to the Christian message.

Thus he omitted Jesus' command to turn the other cheek but emphasized the command that one forgive and love one's enemies. He is particularly harsh on the rich and the powerful: whereas Otfrid does not have Christ's saying about the camel passing through the eye of a needle, or the parable of Dives and Lazarus, the *Heliand* stresses both. Similarly the *Heliand* poet warns of the wickedness of war and battle, staple ingredients in the Germanic way of life: *waldad* (rule by force) leads to hell, and, unlike Otfrid, he makes the story of Peter cutting off the servant's ear an occasion for pointing out the un-Christian nature of violence. Indeed, he even omits the Saviour's statement that he did not come to bring peace but a sword.

The poet of the *Heliand* thus expected a good deal of his listeners, but he helped them at the same time by expressing Christian concepts in homely terms. He portrays the relationship of Christ to his disciples and to mankind as a whole as a normal human relationship: Christ is the Master, and His disciples, like all men, are bound to Him by an oath of allegiance; the Lord cares for His servants and rewards their loyalty. But this bond of service between God and man is unique, since Christ is not one lord among many but Lord of all, and to be in His service makes unconditional demands; to fail in this service is to fail God, which is a sin. The poet thus explains this difficult concept in terms of the feudal relationship of master and serf, exemplifying it above all through offences like Judas' betrayal of Jesus and Peter's denial of Him – offences which were both sins in the Christian context and crimes in the Saxon social code. Peter's denial is presented as the consequence of his arrogance in asserting that he would lay down his life for Christ, for pride spells the forfeiture of God's grace, and by breaking his oath he shows that he has committed the still greater sin of *superbia* – man's urge to lift himself above his proper station.

In such ways the poet slowly but persistently brings home the significance of the new Christian concepts of *superbia*, *gratia*, *humilitas*, etc. To do this he is often forced to give new meanings to old words. For instance, *mannes hruom* (manly pride) is no longer a virtue but receives the pejorative meaning of *superbia*, the cardinal sin; *wurd* (destiny) ceases to be blind fate and becomes *providentia Dei*. With considerable skill, and using the techniques of variation and repetition, the poet puts these old words into new contexts which convey the new meaning, and thus, slowly but surely, allows the Christian content to establish itself.

This is where the remarkable quality of the *Heliand* lies. The story and its message were not primarily aimed at conveying to the public the facts of Christian dogma but rather at showing how man should conduct his life as the servant of the Lord of creation. While carrying a warning of the consequences of sin, the Christian message should also encourage a spirit of cheerful service and tell man that God will be merciful if he recognizes his sinfulness, so that he can follow the path which will bring him the just rewards of faithful service.

As the meaning of old words was changed by new ideas, so also the old poetic line changed, for the involved trains of Christian thought could not be accommodated in the traditional short line. The poetic line became extended, and even in its extended form was not always capable of containing a complete idea. Thus arose a poetic technique which extends a particular thought or idea over a number of lines and often concludes the sentence in the middle of a line.

This new principle of versification also appears to have its counterpart in the structure of the work as a whole. For as Hrabanus employed acrostics, and as medieval and late-classical poets used symbolic numbers in the construction of their works, so the poet of the *Heliand* seems to have used such numbers to determine the form of his work down to the very last line. If this is so, it raises again the question of the authorship of the poem, for only a very considerable intellect would have been capable of planning so ingenious a structure. But, whoever he was, he shows himself to have been a man imbued with the true spirit of Christianity, an accomplished storyteller and poet, and above all a great educator.

With Otfrid von Weissenburg the situation is different. He comes from an area with a Christian tradition stretching back for generations, and it would not be surprising if he too were to have used numerological principles of poetic form. He had no need to explain the basic elements of the Christian message, for sin, humility and grace had become familiar and accepted concepts, and he could thus move on a different plane. The remarkable thing about the *Evangelienbuch* is that it exists at all as a poem, for unlike the author of the *Heliand*, Otfrid had no poetic tradition on which to draw, and his work was a bold new undertaking.

It was as a monk at Weissenburg, in Alsace, that Otfrid compiled his *Evangelienbuch* at the instance of his fellow brethren and of a certain noble lady. Its purpose was to help drive out the secular *cantus obscenus*, and from the introductory epistles we can conclude that it was written in the 860s at the time of Louis the German, to whom one of these epistles is dedicated.

Otfrid knew that German was not one of the three holy tongues but a *lingua barbarica et inculta* not amenable to grammatical rules. His first question was, therefore, whether this *lingua barbarica* could express the Christian truths of salvation which he wanted it to express, and his second concern was to avoid choosing the wrong word ('in themo wahen thiu wort ni missifahen'; I,2,16). To justify his undertaking he therefore set out the situation, in terms derived from Charlemagne and from the usage of the age, in an epistle to Archbishop Liutbert of Mainz and in the first chapter of his work. God, he says, can be invoked in any language, and although German is an uncouth tongue, it has a proper simplicity and directness ('thia rihti in sconeru slihti'; I,1,36); the Frankish *edilzunga* is therefore as suitable as Latin for preaching the message of Christian salvation; moreover, there is a historical justification for his work in that the Franks are a brave, bold and loyal people of God, who have taken over the leadership of Christendom from the Romans and thus become their legitimate heirs in literature as well as in politics. As Christian poets like Juvencus, Prudentius and Arator had inherited the pagan tradition of Virgil, Ovid and Lucan, so Otfrid sees himself as the heir of the Christian Latin tradition, and asks why the Franks should not, like all other peoples, sing the praise of God in their native tongue.

With an awareness of the tradition to which he belonged, and of the responsibilities that this entailed, Otfrid established Christian German poetry. Even the external features of his work show the care he took. The *Evangelienbuch* is the best-preserved work of this early period; in the principal manuscript the lines are arranged in pairs, with the second line inset; accents are marked to aid correct recitation of the text, and Otfrid himself corrected the entire manuscript. The poetic line he employs is new also: his allegiance to the classical tradition made it impossible for him to use the old alliterative line, so he evolved the *Langzeile* with internal rhyme, each half-line having four stresses, and this poetic line was destined to live on for centuries.

This *Langzeile* is sometimes held to have been drawn from the metre of the Ambrosian hymns, but it may be objected that, in view of Otfrid's position *vis-à-vis* the Latin tradition and the fact that he was composing a didactic epic, he would hardly have adopted a lyric metre; he himself, moreover, only names epic poets as his models. The only appropriate metre in existence was the hexameter, which had acquired a certain sacred symbolic meaning by virtue of its six feet, and Otfrid may have adapted this metre to German; the result could have been interpreted as a hexameter in the same way as Jerome and Arator interpreted the Psalms as being in hexameters. But this still leaves the problem of how Otfrid came to introduce rhyme at the caesura – whether it came from the leonine hexameter with internal rhyme, which was popular at this time, particularly in the East Frankish kingdom, or whether, as perhaps with Gottschalk also, it came from the Irish. It is at least certain that one can date from this period the initial triumph of rhyme in poetry, and Otfrid has his part to play in this triumph.

Otfrid, like the poet of the *Heliand*, sets out to tell the story of the life of Christ, but he is concerned to explain as well as to describe, and he sets his narrative against a background of the salvation of mankind, from the Creation and the Fall to Redemption and the Day of Judgement, drawing for his material above all on the Gospel of St John. Wherever he considers it necessary, he interposes explanatory phrases or whole sections, following the traditions of the Church Fathers, who not only treated the Bible in its own context but applied its wisdom to wider issues, past and present.

The story of the return home of the Three Wise Men, for instance, is used to show man that he must flee from the world as the Magi fled from Herod, and must find his way to Heaven, his true home. Otfrid's aim, in a word, is to give a reasoned theological interpretation of the life of Christ.

Otfrid's approach to the task of interpretation shows how different he is from the poet of the *Heliand*, for where the latter emphasizes his conviction of salvation, Otfrid dwells on the sins of man. Sin, for Otfrid, is not just a sinful act that can be redeemed but denotes the basic sinfulness of man. His negative view of the world is of a perilous stage in man's quest for God ('dal zaharo, unmezzigaz ser'), a transition to something better, and he shows his scorn for the world in harsher terms than the religious poets of the eleventh and twelfth centuries.

He is also gentler, more sensitive than the *Heliand* poet. It is no accident that his favourite character is John, Christ's favourite disciple, and although he sees Jesus as king he can still share His sufferings, and the lament of Mary Magdalene is his own lament. Such personal elements are unusual at this time; thus he portrays God as the Lord, but He is also a loving Father to whom one can turn: 'wis fater mir joh muater, thu bist min druhtin guater' (III,1,44).

But as well as an antipathy to the world and a willing submission to God Otfrid shows other, somewhat conflicting qualities. He is proud of being a Frank and proud of the Franks' achievements, seeing his people as destined to convert the world to Christianity. His tone is sometimes aggressive, and where the author of the *Heliand* had omitted Christ's assertion that He did not come to bring peace but a sword, Otfrid omits Christ's warning to Peter that he who lives by the sword shall perish by the sword, and sees Peter's attack on the servant, not as a warning against violence, but as an example of how a disciple should fight on behalf of his master. Thus we find in Otfrid a paradoxical contrast between *contemptus mundi* and pride in Frankish domination, between pious resignation and an emphasis on the *militia Christi*; yet, like many medieval figures, he manages to combine these apparently conflicting attitudes in his mind.

One can hardly claim that Otfrid's *Evangelienbuch* is a great poetic work, and although there are chapters and sections of considerable quality, a great deal of it is longwinded and clumsy and markedly inferior to the *Heliand*. Nevertheless Otfrid may be seen as the virtual founder of German poetic literature, whose influence lasted on where his *Evangelienbuch* itself was quickly forgotten, and the conflicts in his personality make him one of the more attractive figures in German literature.

The *Heliand* and Otfrid's *Evangelienbuch* are by far the longest extant poems of the ninth century, whether German or Latin. The other German poems have survived more or less by chance, whether on fragments of manuscript or to fill up space on the pages or covers of Latin codices. A fragmentary Old Saxon *Genesis* is preserved in this manner, a work which was later proved to be – as had been already suspected – the source of the Anglo-Saxon *Genesis*. This Old Saxon poem – which is unlikely, though it has been suggested, to have been written by the poet of the *Heliand* – only covers the story of Cain and Abel and the fall of Sodom and Gomorrha, but it can be seen that its author had considerable talent and mastery in the field of alliterative verse.

Two further alliterative poems have been preserved from South Germany – the *Wessobrunn Prayer* (*Wessobrunner Gebet*) and the *Muspilli*. The few alliterative lines of the former suggest an Anglo-Saxon provenance and evoke, in short, staccato phrases, a picture of chaos in which there was no one but God and the angels; this vision is followed by a prayer, in prose, for God to grant the supplicant faith, goodness, wisdom and strength to withstand the Devil and perform God's will, thus making him a true servant of the Lord.

The word *Muspilli* (Day of Doom) occurs in line 57 of the incomplete poem, and has come to be used as the title. The poem is recorded in the margins and on empty spaces in a manuscript presented to Louis the German. The beginning and the end are missing, but it is clear that the poem as it stands is the product of a good deal of revision and extension.

The subject is the fate of the soul after death – the happiness of the blessed and the torments of the damned; the battle between Elias and the Antichrist then leads to the end of the world, the resurrection of the dead and the Last Judgement. In vivid language the poet describes these events as though he had seen them with his own eyes, yet at the same time, at least in the form in which it has come down to us, the poem is also a penitential sermon: the description of the end of the world is meant to warn man of eternal damnation and to induce him to lead a righteous life on earth. In particular the rich and the ruling classes are exhorted to live and rule righteously, for on the Day of Judgement no one will help them and they will be judged by their deeds alone.

The *Wessobrunner Gebet* was certainly written before Otfrid's *Evangelienbuch*; the date of the *Muspilli* is uncertain. Both were without successors, however, for alliterative verse was dying out, while the future lay with Otfrid's rhyming lines, as the remaining Old High German poems show. With the exception of the *Ludwigslied* they all belong to the Bavarian-Alemannic area and were written in the second half of the ninth century or in the first decades of the tenth.

From Bavaria come the *Petruslied* and an accomplished paraphrase of the 138th Psalm. The *Petruslied*, a prayer to St Peter, is a hymn in three simple strophes, each of which consists of two rhyming *Langzeilen* and the refrain 'Kyrie eleison'. It was composed for use in church or in processions, and above the words in the manuscript are neumes which record the melody.

From the Alemannic realm come *Christ and the Woman of Samaria* (*Christus und die Samariterin*), the *Lay of St George* (*Georgslied*) and the *Lay of St Gall* (*Galluslied*). The first of these, written in a simple, direct style, was probably composed in Reichenau, as was also, in all probability, the *Georgslied*. This strophic lay, recorded in an unusual orthography, praises St George for so valiantly surviving all his trials and torments with the help of the Lord, and may have been written as an anthem to be sung at the consecration of the Georgskirche in Reichenau. The *Galluslied* is a hymn to the founder of the monastery of St Gallen and was written by Ratpert, a monk and teacher there. Ekkehard IV of St Gallen, wishing to see this work of Ratpert's – whom he greatly admired – preserved for posterity, translated it into literary Latin – a significant moment – and this is the form in which it has come down to us, but it is not difficult to sense behind the Latin text the internal rhymes of the original German *Langzeilen*.

The *Ludwigslied*, the most significant of these smaller Old High German poems, was written in Rhine-Franconian territory by an anonymous author to celebrate the victory of Louis III over the Normans at Saucourt in 881. The style is concise and objective, but the poet's skill in describing and interpreting the events of his story is very striking. The young Louis, left fatherless, is to be tested by God, and the Franks are to be punished for their sins; the Normans attack, and Louis is told by God to take up arms; he collects his forces, raising their spirits for the battle and promising them rewards for success, and leads them forward to victory with the words 'Kyrie eleison' on his lips. Both the content and the language are reminiscent of the Germanic panegyrics preserved in later Norse sources, but if the poet did in fact model his poem on such lays, he has made its spirit completely Christian. At the same time the *Ludwigslied* comes close to similar battle-scenes described in Latin poems, such as the lay of Pippin's victory over the Avars, or that of the Battle of Fontanetum.

The Christian German poetry of the Carolingian era is monastic literature, and we owe to two monks the preservation, albeit in an imperfect state, of one piece of traditional pagan literature, the *Hildebrandslied*. From what we know of Germanic heroic legend and Germanic verse, it would appear that the *Hildebrandslied* belongs to a late period, and its name also suggests a Langobardic origin. However, we cannot recast the original form of the lay with certainty and have to restrict ourselves to the evidence of the manuscript itself, which, despite its fragmentary nature and its confused linguistic state, is an impressive document.

The poem tells how, many years earlier, Hildebrand, honouring his oath of loyalty, had followed his lord, Dietrich, into exile, leaving his wife and child behind; now he has returned at the head of an army and finds himself confronted by a rival army, whose leader challenges him publicly to a duel. When he asks the name of his opponent, the father finds that he is face to face with his own son. Hadubrant, the son, however, has been told that his father is dead, and he does not believe that it can be his father who now stands before him, since when he had fled, Hildebrand had been but a poor refugee, whereas the man now calling himself Hildebrand stood at the head of an army and was offering presents of golden bracelets. Suspecting treachery, Hadubrant calls his father a coward and a traitor (the text is incomplete at this point). After this insult, uttered before the assembled armies, there is no turning back, and father and son are forced to fight each other. Fate thus follows its ineluctable course: the combat between father and son begins. The poem breaks off before the end, but other versions of the story leave no doubt that the father kills his son and regains his honour; thereafter, life having lost its value for him, he must have killed himself by the side of his son's dead body.

The story is not discursively told, for the poet has no time for super-fluities. It opens with the confrontation of the two heroes, and step by step, in a blunt, alliterative style that highlights the key-words, the speeches of the two men, separated by brief descriptive phrases, drive the action onwards to its climax, which is reached with the word 'arga' ('cowardly'); from here to the end is but a short step. The *Hildebrandslied* speaks the harsh, blunt, gripping language of the pagan German heroic tradition, and together with the two *Merseburg Charms* (*Merseburger Zaubersprüche*) reveals something of the native poetry of which historical circumstances have denied us further knowledge.

Literature in the Pre-Courtly Age (900 – 1170)

HEINZ RUPP

The Ottonian Period

Otfrid's attempt to establish a national literature failed, and from 900 to 1060 we know nothing of any German literature. What literature there was perished with the Carolingian empire, and the Ottonian age brought no revival. But even if there is no literature in the accepted sense, work on the German language itself went on: important texts continue to be glossed, while sermons, confessions and a number of important prose works have also been preserved.

The work of Notker the German belongs in this context. Born around the middle of the tenth century, he worked in the famous monastery of St Gallen, where he died in 1022. His aim as a teacher was to provide his pupils with model translations of, and commentaries on, difficult basic texts in order to facilitate the study of the *septem artes liberales*. Among these texts were Boethius' *De consolatione philosophiae*, Martianus Capella's *De nuptiis philologiae et Mercurii* – the most important medieval manual on allegory – Virgil's *Bucolics,* Terence's *Andria,* Aristotle's *Categories* and *Hermeneutics* in Boethius' Latin translation, and a number of others. His principal work is his translation of the Psalms, and shortly before his death he completed a commentary on the Book of Job.

Not all his work has survived, but what we do have shows him to have been one of the greatest masters of the German language and an important medieval stylist. He himself modestly regarded his work as being for the benefit of his pupils, and called it *res paene inusitata* (a thing hardly used) – rightly so, for it was a long while before he found successors, and his writings reached only a limited public. Nevertheless they are far superior to all other German prose works of the time, including Otloh's *Prayer* (*Gebet*) and Williram's paraphrase of the Song of Songs.

Latin Poetry: Tenth to Twelfth Centuries

For a century and a half after the year 900 there was no German literature. The situation was different with Latin literature, of which there was a great deal more, but it too was affected by the decline and fall of the Carolingian Empire, and it was not until the eleventh and twelfth centuries that it regained its former status.

In the tenth century there was not a great deal of Latin literature from the German Empire. The anthology known as the *Cambridge Songs*, preserved in an eleventh-century manuscript, is largely composed of short poems written in Germany in the tenth century: religious sequences, panegyrics, historical poems, satirical poems such as the Swabian farces of the snow-child and of Heriger von Mainz, together with love-poems, a number of which, however, have been erased in the manuscript. This varied collection is a precursor of the *Carmina Burana*.

Very different are the works of the aristocratic nun Roswitha from the monastery of Gandersheim, family monastery of the Ottonian line. She is remembered not only for her two historical poems and her verse-legends but also, and chiefly, for her efforts to substitute Christian drama for the morally dubious dramas of Terence, which continued to be read for their stylistic value. Her dramatized legends, however, sound but uninspired like her other works, were not equal to this task and hardly penetrated beyond monastic circles.

In St Gallen Ekkehard IV assembled a varied collection of his poems under the title *Liber Benedictionum*, and Tutilo, a renowned artist and craftsman, composed tropes. For a long while Tutilo was considered the inventor of this literary genre, and his Easter trope was held to mark the beginning of medieval religious drama, but although he cannot now be held to be its inventor – any more than Notker der Stammler can be held to be the inventor of the sequence – he had a decisive influence on its development and dissemination.

The eleventh century brings us a far greater number of works and poets. Froumund von Tegernsee, lyric poet and writer of epistles, flourished at the turn of the century; about 1020 Egbert of Liège, a monk of German descent, composed his *Fecunda ratis*, a collection of secular and religious moral verse for school use; around 1045 an anonymous German or French monk told of his escape from the monastery in the allegorical form of a beast-fable, *Ecbasis cuiusdam captivi per tropologiam*, one of the first extended beast-epics of the Middle Ages, written in a difficult Latin style.

Around the middle of the century Warnerius von Basel composed a number of allegorical theological poems, Arnulf wrote an ethical treatise,

Deliciae Cleri, for Henry III, and Wipo, chaplain to Conrad II and Henry III, wrote his proverbs, historical works and poems, among them the famous Easter sequence *Victimae paschali laudes*. Hermann the Cripple (Hermannus Contractus), equally famed as historian, musician and poet, died at Reichenau in 1054; around 1060 Williram von Ebersberg composed Latin poems and a paraphrase of the Song of Songs in Latin hexameters, appending to it, for practical reasons, a prose paraphrase in German. Around the year 1070 there appeared Heinrich von Augsburg's *Planctus Evae*, followed a few years later by the anonymous *Carmen de bello Saxonico*, on Henry IV's Saxon campaign, and around 1080 by the odes of Gottschalk von Limburg.

These are only a few of the surviving Latin works, but they serve to illustrate by comparison the paucity of contemporary German literature.

One further work must be mentioned which, though without influence in Latin literature, is extremely interesting for the history of German poetry. This is *Ruodlieb*, the first courtly medieval romance, written in leonine hexameters by an anonymous monk, possibly from the monastery of Tegernsee, and preserved in a very imperfect state. This remarkable mixture of the typical and the individual, the schematic and the realistic, the crudely erotic and the earnestly Christian, is intended both to instruct and to entertain, a work far in advance of its time and imbued with a true sense of Christian chivalry and humanism.

This rise of Latin poetry in the eleventh century, which is even more noticeable in France and Italy than in Germany, became more marked still in the twelfth century, when France again led Germany, which had little of interest to show. Every conceivable subject was given poetic treatment but the result was not always poetry. We have a versification, for example, of the work of Martianus Capella and even of Priscian's grammar; there is a mass of historical verse and large-scale mythological poems on subjects such as Leda and the swan; beast-epics and fables are popular – an example is the *Isengrimus* of Nivardus von Gent – so also are proverbs in verse and the *Streitgedicht* (poetic altercation) of Carolingian times: all manner of disputes are treated in verse form – between summer and winter, between animals, between ladies arguing about who is the best lover and between the daughters of God.

Religious and secular poems, including love lyrics, are found in abundance, and many of the best love-poems are by clerics. As to hymns and sequences, they are too numerous to mention. In addition the twelfth century brings the poetry of the *vagantes*, the wandering scholars, the best-known being the 'Primas' of Orléans and the Archpoet.

Scholarship, particularly theology, also flourished in the eleventh and twelfth centuries. From Lanfranc de Bec and Anselm of Canterbury the line leads to Bernard of Clairvaux, Abelard and the other great thinkers of early scholasticism.

This is the world of Latin literature which, slowly but surely, German literature begins to penetrate.

German Religious Poetry of the Salian and Early Hohenstaufen Periods (1060–1170)

GENERAL

German literature re-emerged late and established itself through a number of large collective manuscripts written in the second half of the twelfth century. The Vorau, Milstätt and Vienna manuscripts belong to the same period and the same area – Austria – in which the early Minnesang flourished; only the Strasbourg-Molsheim manuscript belongs to the west. From critical investigations and historical references, however, it is clear that the works in these manuscripts belong to an earlier period, and that the oldest of them date from the mid-eleventh century. The actual number of works is not great, but from this period onwards the number of German poems extant steadily increases.

Two related questions arise at this point. Why are the manuscripts that contain these eleventh- and twelfth-century German poems so late? And why, in view of the encouraging beginnings in the Carolingian age, do we find no German literature again before about 1160?

German religious poetry from 1050 and 1170 has been called the literature of the ascetic Cluniac period, the product of an age which denied the world, to be followed by the Hohenstaufen age which embraced the world. But this is to over-simplify the situation. The Cluny and Gorze reforms did not lead to a general withdrawal from the world, nor were tenth- and eleventh-century reformers any more antagonistic to the values of civilization than were their predecessors or their successors: the effects of the Cluny reforms on politics, on architecture, on literature and on education make this clear. Monastic reforms certainly had a lasting influence on religious life and thought, and even in Germany, where the Cluniac movement made little impact, they contributed at least indirectly to an intensification of Christian awareness. But not even the clerics and the educated classes were induced thereby to adopt rigid anti-world attitudes. The same is true of the Hirsau reforms, which had a brief, if widely felt, effect on personal and political life but lasted only a few decades and did not radically change the character of the German monasteries. These reforms cannot therefore be held directly responsible for the growth of German literature at this time. Moreover the chronological sequence argues against it, for the Cluniac reforms reached their climax in Germany in the tenth century and lost their force, except in Hirsau, in the eleventh, whereas the literature of which we are talking only came into its own at the beginning of the twelfth century. The most ascetic works in this context, the bitter satires of Heinrich von Melk, belong not to the eleventh century but to the second half of the twelfth, i.e. to the Hohenstaufen era.

Of the seventy or so religious German poems extant from this period – and quite apart from secular poems handed down by word of mouth–only a very few are ascetic in character. Certainly most of them are unyieldingly Christian, but there is nothing from the point of view of either asceticism or the affirmation of life to set them apart from the Christian verse of other centuries. This can easily be seen by comparing them with Otfrid or, even more obviously, with medieval Latin literature as a whole.

But why is there no German literature between 900 and 1050? A single, straightforward answer is hardly possible. One reason, which also applies to Carolingian times, is the attitude of the *litterati* to things German, for they continued to regard the cultivation of Latin, the only true literary language, as a sacred duty, and to see German as a barbaric tongue, with German 'literature' as no true literature at all. The fate of Ratpert's *Galluslied* shows this.

And why should the *litterati* be interested in German literature? Apart from themselves hardly anyone could read, and they had their Latin. It was pointless for them to record works in German until the ability to read became more widespread, as it did during the Crusades. For one reason or another the odd passage of German might have been written on a spare piece of parchment or in an empty space in a Latin codex, but not until the second half of the twelfth century did German poems begin to be collected and written down.

In the first instance, naturally enough, these were only religious poems, for the scribes were as yet not concerned with poems that only survived in an oral tradition: this latter stage was reached in the age of courtly civilization, when a steadily growing number of people were able to read. To start with, therefore, attention was paid to any surviving religious poems, and the oldest that could still be found dated from about 1060. Whether there actually were any before this, or whether none happened to be found, we cannot tell; in any case, there cannot have been many.

If the interest of the *litterati* in German literature was slight, that of the secular aristocracy began to grow. The nobles were increasingly concerning themselves with religious matters but wanted them presented in an artistically pleasing form, and not just in sermons. Latin literature, however, was in general a closed book to them. The secular priests, therefore, if they were not to surrender to the German secular tradition, had to meet this need. Besides this, the vernacular language, in Germany as in other countries, was bound to take over eventually from Latin, and as interest in literature grew, together with the ability to read and write, vernacular literature was bound to expand and take its place alongside the Latin – a process which was encouraged by the general development of religious, intellectual and cultural life after the passing of the millennium. These and many other factors contributed to the rise of German literature at this time, a rise which was now to proceed without interruption.

Of the actual poets we know very little. Most works are preserved anonymously, and even where there are names, they remain just names. Not one of the great minds of the time is to be found among the authors of German poems. Most of these unknown authors would have been secular priests rather than monks, and both the names and the works indicate this. This is new; and the secular priest is soon followed by the layman – Heinrich von Melk, Der arme Hartmann, Frau Ava.

These developments influence the poems themselves, which deal in a variety of ways but in a straightforward spirit with the basic facts of the Christian faith. There is little theological speculation, its place being taken by a didactic element derived from the sermon. The influence of contemporary early scholastic theology – Anselm, St Bernard, Abelard – is virtually non-existent, and thought remains within the traditional framework of approved knowledge inherited from the Church Fathers. In their content, therefore, the poems show little originality, while their authors neither could nor would have had it otherwise. Their aim was to present the fundamental truths of Christianity in an attractive and universally comprehensible form.

Thus here too one must beware of overestimating the quality of the literature. Because there is hardly any originality of thought in it, it is difficult to find changes in religious attitudes, and one is as likely to find new and apparently progressive thoughts in early works as to be confronted in later poems with ideas which had long been superseded.

The talents of these poets show themselves in the treatment of the chosen subject, in the ways in which they select and arrange familiar material. Occasionally we find works of considerable poetic ability which give us an insight into the religious world of the medieval poet. Because these works arose in a different tradition from that of Latin poetry, they retain a formal independence of the latter's powerful influence and follow the line established by Otfrid, thereby preserving the freedom that was linguistically necessary though by no means historically inevitable.

Thus alongside the *Langzeile* there developed, in the late twelfth century, the four-stress rhymed couplet, which reached its apogee in the great epics of the Hohenstaufen age. The *Langzeile*, in an adapted form, lived on in the *Nibelungenlied*, in Wolfram's *Titurel* and in other works.

In spite of their individual characteristics the religious poems of the eleventh and early twelfth centuries also have a certain unity from the formal point of view, in that their blunt, terse style reflects a concern, not with elegance, but with accuracy. Like Otfrid, the poets are worried that they might choose the wrong word and thus give the wrong impression. In time their plain, unadorned language becomes more expansive, and their syntax more involved, but only in the twelfth century, perhaps under the influence of the rhyming couplet, does their harsh, often crude style give way to a subtler, more flexible approach.

This poetry is not drawn equally from all parts of the German-speaking realm. Bavaria and Austria are the main areas, followed by the Rhineland, whose share may well have been larger than the manuscripts suggest. Regions which later became important, such as the Alemannic area, contribute only few works.

EARLY RELIGIOUS POEMS

There are six important works surviving from the eleventh century, all of them of different types: (1) the Vienna *Genesis*, a biblical poem; (2) the *Ezzolied*, a hymn; (3) *Memento mori*, a penitential sermon; (4) *Himmel und Hölle* (*Heaven and Hell*), an eschatological work; (5) the *Annolied*, a religious legend; (6) the so-called *Merigarto*, fragments of a description of the earth, arranged as a kind of manual, which as poetry is the merest doggerel but which is interesting as an attempt to use German for conveying current notions about physical science.

The Vienna *Genesis*, written by a Bavarian or Middle Franconian cleric, tells its story in a direct, almost un-epic style, shortening here and expanding there. By telling the story of the Fall and by relating Jacob's blessing to Christ's act of redemption, the Antichrist and the Last Judgement, the poet turns the Genesis narrative into an epic of man's salvation, from the creation and the Fall to Redemption and the Day of Judgement. And by emphasizing, forcibly but not fanatically, certain ethical and religious principles in the practical manner of the village priest, the poet draws the listener directly into his story.

The salvation of man is also the subject of the *Cantilena de miraculis Christi*, a strophic hymn written around 1060 by Ezzo, canon of Bamberg, for use on crusade. In style it has something of the aristocratic spirit of the court of the bishops of Bamberg. Its preservation is very imperfect: of the older of the two versions (the Strasbourg manuscript) only a few strophes have survived, whilst the later version (the Vorau manuscript), though complete, is a much garbled work; but it is still possible to gain from this latter source a fair idea of Ezzo's intentions. *Miracula Christi* meant for him the works of Christ from Creation to Redemption, i.e. the whole of human history, and he praises these 'marvels' in his hymn. The Fall is followed by a period of darkness which patriarchs and prophets can hardly illumine, until, after the rise of John the Baptist, the Morning Star, Christ, the Sun, sheds His light upon the earth. The life of Christ is described in heavily allusive language only fully intelligible to theologians; then figures from the Old Testament appear, showing that the whole process of redemption was planned by God; finally, after Christ has died to save mankind, God keeps his word and receives his *dienestman*, his servant, into Heaven; and the poem ends with a paean of praise to the Trinity.

Of a different nature is the *Memento mori* of an otherwise unknown poet bearing the name of Notker. For some time this work was thought to be a mere reflection of the Hirsau reform movement, but this is neither demonstrable nor plausible, for its themes are as old as the Bible itself and occur so frequently that it is impossible to regard this particular poem as a model just because it happens to be the first of its kind in German. In a series of expressive strophes Notker tells of the world, of life and of his death: many foolish men think that life will stay with them for ever, but death can snuff out life like a candle; man must always have death in mind, must keep the goal of life in view and not dally over his pursuit of it. This is the message that Notker gives to the rich and the mighty, who all too readily forget it. But he is not a gloomy ascetic, for although he realizes the dangers confronting man, he also trusts his *selbwala*, his power of free will. Like St Augustine he could say: 'Praedicare cogor: territus terreo. Timete mecum, ut gaudeatis mecum.' ('I am bound to declare that I tremble in fear. Share my fear, that you may share my joy.')

The short work known as *Himmel und Hölle* does not fit into the framework of the other works of the period from the formal point of view, for it is in prose – the first such work in German. There is nothing remarkable about its content: the first part describes the heavenly heights, the second part the torments of hell, in familiar, conventional scenes drawn from the Psalms, the Apocalypse, the Apocrypha and other eschatological writings.

But there is a certain splendour to the language in which this familiar material is presented. The poet is not just a narrator; his work breathes a philosophy. Noun follows noun, one bold image or expression follows another, and practically the only verb used is 'to be'. It has been shown that the isocolic construction of the sentences, with their alliteration and their homoeoteleuta, follows classical prose style, such as that found, in a Christian context, in Augustine. At the same time this late-classical prose may itself have been modelled on the Psalms, which could have then been the direct model for the German. This style is also related to the couplets and paratactic constructions of the native tradition. Thus classical, Christian and national pagan elements combine in this work to form a remarkable unity. It was composed about 1080 and is in the same manuscript as the Bamberg *Creed* and the Bamberg *Confession*. Although it may have some connection with the monastery of Hirsau, it is more likely that, with the nobility of its tone and the self-consciousness of its language, it was written at an episcopal court, perhaps that of the Bishop of Bamberg, like the *Ezzolied*.

The *Annolied* was written in the monastery of Siegburg, near Cologne, towards the end of the eleventh century. Its hero is Archbishop Anno of Cologne (d. 1075), a somewhat sinister figure in German history, although by passing over his contentious policies during the minority of Henry IV and his quarrel with the Pope over the question of investiture (the *Investiturstreit*), and by glossing over his disputes with the town fathers of Cologne, the anonymous poet keeps this side of Anno's character out of sight.

The poem does not follow the usual pattern of such legends but starts with a historical sketch of the salvation of man through the stages of Creation, Fall, Redemption and the spread of Christianity by the Apostles and the martyrs, and leads up to the saints of Cologne, the latest of whom is Anno, described in Strophe 7 as the seventh in the line (cf. also line 573 of the poem).

This *historia spiritalis* is followed by a *historia mundana* in which, proceeding from the Vision of Daniel, the poet gives an account of the four great kingdoms of the world – the Babylonian-Assyrian, the Persian, the kingdom of Alexander and the Roman Empire: the last victory was won by Caesar with the help of the German tribes – Swabians, Bavarians, Saxons and Franks – each of which is assigned a genealogical link with one of the four great kingdoms; chief among these links is that between the Franks and the Romans, who are both seen as descended from the Trojans. The Germans, therefore, and in particular the Franks, are the rightful heirs of the Roman Empire.

This *historia mundana*, with its forthright, typically medieval interpretation of history, is also given its link with Cologne, and in Strophe 33 Anno is named as the thirty-third bishop of the city, thus representing the course both of secular and religious history. The remaining strophes of the poem are devoted to Anno himself, who is portrayed both as an ascetic and as a man of action, bishop and secular prince, a man who combines the *vita contemplativa* with the *vita activa*, and who enjoys the favour both of God and the world ('gotes und der welt hulde') – a concept that can be traced back to the *Heliand*. He is the servant both of the *riche* – the Empire – and of the Church, and the poet emphasizes the former almost more than the latter, his conception of the *riche*, the repository of spiritual and secular power, being that held by Charlemagne, Otto the Great and Henry III.

Anno ends his exemplary life by proving himself in God's final test and becoming a saint, testifying to his beatification by performing miracles after his death and standing as a paradigm of virtue for the edification of all Christians. At the same time the poem itself, as the prologue points out, stands as a piece of Christian historiography *vis-à-vis* the uncommitted, secular view of history.

TWELFTH-CENTURY RELIGIOUS POETRY (1100–1170)

Religious poetry continued to dominate German literature well beyond the era of the Salian emperors and the four-year reign of Lothar von Supplinburg. The first Hohenstaufen ascended the throne in 1138, and the overwhelming majority of these religious poems therefore belongs to the Hohenstaufen age.

Biblical poetry remained popular, but the attitude towards it changed. The blunt style of the Vienna *Genesis*, for instance, was no longer considered satisfactory, and at the beginning of the twelfth century this work was revised and brought up to date: the result is the so-called Milstätt *Genesis*. At the same time it was felt necessary to continue the story of Genesis. The first fifteen chapters of Exodus, with the deliverance of the Jews from the hand of Pharaoh, prefigured Christ's deliverance of man from Satan, and a Bavarian or possibly Rhine-Franconian cleric composed around 1120 an *Exodus* poem of considerable narrative skill. His main concern was with the story itself, and it is only in the epilogue that its significance for the history of man's salvation is dwelt upon.

The Vorau manuscript also has its own versions of Genesis and Exodus, the *Vorauer Bücher Mosis*. The *Exodus* has particular interest in that it gives considerable space to the interpretation of the events; the various explanatory interpolations, even those that start by repeating dogma, almost all end with exhortations to avoid the sin of *superbia*, to eschew the pursuit of worldly success, to be humble and to love God and one's neighbour; special censure attaches to any attempt to seek vengeance for a personal wrong. These features suggest that the poem, written about 1140, was addressed to an aristocratic public, for the poet contrasts with the life of the nobility his ideal of a pure monastic life and lays even greater weight on *contemptus mundi* than does the poet of the eleventh-century *Memento mori*.

The twelfth century also sees the poeticization of other Old Testament subjects. The story of Judith, for instance, survives in two versions. One of them is a short, strophic, ballad-like poem with stylistic features of apparently native origin which reappear in *König Rother*, *Orendel* and the heroic epics of the thirteenth century. The other version is a Christian heroic poem in epic style, like the poems, popular in this and later periods, on the revolt of the Maccabees. Following the Bible story closely, the poet tells the story of Judith and Holofernes, accompanying it with a sequence of ideas drawn directly from the narrative. Like the *Nibelungenlied*, this sequence runs thus: *ere* (honour) – *leit* (suffering) – *rache* (vengeance) – *ere* – with the difference that in the *Judith* poem the sequence is resolved in a

Christian manner: true *ere* only exists where man is with God, and vengeance is only justified when brought about by God Himself through His believers, since to offend these believers is to offend God, as in the altercation between Holofernes and Nebuchadnessar and between Judith and the Jews. It is conceivable that the poet thought of his work as a means of denouncing the un-literary, un-Christian heroic poetry of his day, and of offsetting by the Christian Judith the pagan Krimhild as she later appears in the *Nibelungenlied*.

The first half of the twelfth century also sees the first poetic account of the life of Jesus since Otfrid's *Evangelienbuch*. It is the work of a woman, Frau Ava, who is probably the 'Reclusa Ava' mentioned in historical records. As one would expect, she sets her *Life of Jesus* in a broad context, opening with a poem on John the Baptist and concluding with a poem on the Last Judgement.

In its religious attitudes there is little new in Ava's poem, and no sign of scholasticism, mysticism or pious subjectivism. It does, however, show touches of gentleness as the authoress expresses her compassion for the suffering Christ, and is noteworthy for the selectivity of its approach. Thus all the teachings and parables of Christ are omitted, even the Sermon on the Mount; only the events are related, and here too in a selective spirit, so that the miracles quoted are chiefly those which make direct demands on faith, and the events described at greatest length are those in which women are involved – the sinner Mary Magdalene is Ava's favourite character – and which deal with man's love of Christ.

This choice of subjects shows of itself what mattered most to Frau Ava – unquestioning faith in God, sincere love of Christ and preparedness to follow the *imitatio Christi* in one's life on earth. This is why her biography of Jesus is followed by the account of the Last Judgement, when it will be revealed who was an *imitator Christi* and who was not. It is also why the biography concludes with an extensive moral treatise on the good Christian life, some of Christ's teachings that had been omitted from the biography being included here instead. Frau Ava thus appears as a practical cleric in the best sense, seeking to help her people appear before the Saviour whom she loves above all else in the world. By not making rigid demands, she shows that she realizes man's weaknesses, and she holds up to his mind the meaning for us sinners of the life and death of Christ.

Dogmatic and theological poems are also preserved from this century. One such strophic poem, probably written in the Rhineland, is the *Summa Theologiae* – a misleading title, because it does not set out to be a *Summa* but, like the *Ezzolied*, gives a summary of the doctrine of salvation, though in a more dogmatic manner than the *Ezzolied*. The events in the story of man's salvation are described merely as links in the chain of redemption, one following inevitably upon the other. The freedom of the angels leads to the defection of Lucifer, which in turn leads to God's decision to create man to replace the fallen angel; Lucifer vents his rage on man by tempting him and driving him into the clutches of the Devil; Christ fights the Devil and delivers man by His death, as a result of which man receives his earthly obligations and is judged at the Last Trump by the way he has fulfilled them. The poet decorates his story with a mass of complicated theological allusions but it retains a certain impressiveness by virtue of the lucidity of its thought.

An aristocrat calling himself Der arme Hartmann, who renounced the world for a life of penance in the monastery, has left an extensive *Rede vom Glauben* (*Discourse on Faith*) written, not in the old strophic form of *Langzeilen* but in the new four-stress rhyming couplets. He composed his treatise as part of his own penance and in order to arouse the conscience of his fellow noblemen, following the old tradition of giving a commentary on the individual articles of the Creed, but in a free, independent style. His guiding principle is stated in the prologue, namely, that man's first duty is to believe in God; faith leads to obedience, through which man learns to live the good and just life; and through his love of God man finds his way to Heaven.

By relating to this unifying principle all the individual sections of his poem, Hartmann, whose work contains no new ideas, produces an original digest of established theological truths, infusing it with a grave spirit of absolute faith in Christ, the *lieber herre*.

Alongside works which treat in comprehensive terms the central problems of Christian philosophy we find shorter poems, generally in strophic form, which deal with individual questions. Such are the *Loblied auf Salomon* (*In Praise of Solomon*), the *Beschreibung des Himmlischen Jerusalem* (*Description of the Holy City*), poems on the Babylonian Captivity, the Last Judgement, and so on. In all of these the subject is treated not as an end in itself but for its symbolic significance.

The thought relationships in these poems become particularly revealing when works are constructed on the basis of symbolic numbers. This is not a matter of a play on numbers, or simply of a partiality for numerical associations. The Bible tells us that God arranged everything according to size and weight and number; man must therefore discover these indwelling relationships in order to be able to understand the nature of the world and praise God the *artifex*. This view dates from the time of the Church Fathers, of Isidore of Seville, Hrabanus Maurus, Honorius Augustodunensis and many others.

A particularly illuminating example is a twelfth-century poem on the Lord's Prayer. This is based on the divine number seven: the seven articles of the Lord's Prayer are set against the seven seals as the seven stages in the life of Christ (Revelation V), the seven beatitudes, the seven gifts of the Holy Spirit and the seven patriarchs of the Old Testament: however dissimilar individual phenomena appear, they form part of a meaningful whole, and it is man's task to find this original meaning.

This subject of the pattern of life and the world underlies two poems either composed or revised in the Austro-Bavarian area: *Vom Recht* (*On Propriety*) and *Die Hochzeit* (*The Marriage*). The core of both these mediocre works is the word *reht*, which means not only rights and duties but also the God-given *ordo* which it is man's obligation to observe. Again it is not the subject that is new but the manner in which it is treated – by means of images, examples and concepts drawn from the everyday life of the nobility for whom these works were intended.

In *Vom Recht* three basic conditions are laid down: all men must observe what is *reht* (just, proper, dutiful), for all men are equal before God, and the poor man has an equal claim to *reht* with the rich man – these are thoughts already familiar from the *Memento mori* and other works; all men must be *getriuwe* (loyal) and preserve God's *ordo*; and all men must be *gewaere* (truthful). A man who does not observe *reht* is arrogant; a man who is not *getriuwe* destroys the order of things; and a man who is not *gewaere* is a slanderer who will fall into *avaritia*, the *grundveste aller übele*.

The author of this poem is not a social reformer, as has sometimes been maintained, for these three basic principles can be realized within the framework of the existing social order, with God at its head. God is the *meister*, mankind are his *knehte*; on a lower level the priest is the *meister* and the people are the *knehte*; to the servant classes the lord and his lady are the *meister*, and in marriage the man is *meister* over the woman. Each class has its own rights and its own duties, but over and above these are the basic rights and duties which everyone has to God: any infringement of these rights and duties is an offence against the order that God has created.

The notion of *reht* is also paramount in the poem called *Die Hochzeit*, which starts with a brief description of a wedding and proceeds to give it a twofold allegorical meaning. The Lord, the Holy Spirit, marries the Virgin, man, and the stages in the wooing and the marriage are interpreted in the framework of a philosophy which explains to man his position and his moral obligations. The second meaning derives from the relationship between this moral philosophy and the history of man's salvation: the Lord, the Holy Spirit, marries Mary, Mother of God; Her Son, *deus humilis*, completes the work of salvation – the final *brutlouft* (nuptial ceremony) when God takes man unto Himself; but the *brutlouft* is open only to the man who has followed the ethical code and is humble like God Himself.

The remaining religious works that need to be mentioned belong to the second half of the century; their authors are therefore contemporaries of the early Minnesinger and epic poets of the Hohenstaufen age.

The so-called *Anegenge* (*Beginning*), the work of an anonymous cleric, tells of God, of the Creation, of the two Falls and of Redemption. The poet was not, however, primarily concerned with the story or with its practical applications but with a critical theological account of the problems, albeit not yet in a scholastic sense. But since he could not take too much for granted in his listeners, he had to simplify his complicated material, and because he was no great artist, he produced a strange but interesting mixture of theological exegesis and simple narrative. He concerned himself with the most problematical questions, such as: What is the Trinity? How can one understand man's fall and salvation? Is there a *visio Dei*? What is the meaning of divine prescience? Despite his efforts he rarely succeeds in giving clear explanations and often returns to his narrative without having completed his argument. His work must have appeared as laboured to the Middle Ages as it does to us.

Of a very different kind are the two works of Heinrich von Melk, the *Priesterleben* (*Life of the Priests*) and the *Erinnerung an den Tod* (i.e. *Memento mori*), written at the same period and preserved in the same fourteenth-century manuscript. They are moral penitential poems of an intolerance not hitherto met with in German literature, and their bitter satirical tone is directed against the Minnesang and other manifestations of courtly life in the Hohenstaufen era. No one is spared: the world and mankind are portrayed as wicked and corrupt, the clerics and the nobility as apostates living only for the pleasures of the flesh, and by holding up before their eyes a warning vision of the transience of life, Heinrich summons them to a radical *contemptus mundi*. If they do not repent, God will punish them – and Heinrich's God is not a God of mercy and compassion but a God of vengeance whom one must obey in the only way possible – by denying the world.

Heinrich's predecessors had always followed their admonitions with a call to trust in God's mercy, for the sinner should not fall into despair, but Heinrich cajoles and threatens mercilessly. It is possible to see his works as the last and most violent in the line of eleventh- and twelfth-century *contemptus mundi* poems before the exhilaration of courtly literature. But there is such poetry in every century, and the thirteenth and fourteenth centuries contain far more than the eleventh and twelfth; indeed, Heinrich's works are in form rather the precursors of thirteenth- and fourteenth-century moral and satirical verse than late examples of an earlier tradition, and it is scarcely an accident that they came to be recorded as late as the fourteenth century.

The same is true of other religious poems of this period, which form a transition between the Christian poetry of the twelfth century and that of the thirteenth. Of particular importance in this context are two related literary genres which, with a few precursors, begin to flourish in the second half of the twelfth century and come to full fruition in the thirteenth and fourteenth – Christian legends, and poems in praise of the Virgin Mary.

Not a great deal of poetic literature on the legends of the saints has survived from the twelfth century, but that from later centuries shows something of what its beginnings must have been, and its growing popularity accords with a partial recession of the dogmatic, didactic elements in favour of an increased emphasis on narrative and biographical features.

Mariendichtung begins with lyrics which are closely modelled on Latin poems, but it is not long before we meet the first epic on the life of Mary – the *Driu liet von der maget* (*Three Lays on the Virgin*) by Wernher, a Swabian or Bavarian priest, completed in 1172.

The cult of Mariolatry became firmly established in the course of the twelfth century, and Rupert von Deutz – the first to give a complete interpretation of the Song of Songs in terms of the Virgin – St Bernard and many others testify to its growth. *Mariendichtung* develops both directly and indirectly from this Mariolatry, which in another field has its effect on the worship of woman in chivalric literature, and Wernher's poem is the first large-scale German work in this field, looking both backwards and forwards in time, like the satires of Heinrich von Melk and the legends.

Following to a large extent his apocryphal source, the so-called Pseudo-Matthew – the first time that we find an apocryphal source being used extensively in German literature – Wernher tells the story of Mary and her parents. This use of an apocryphal gospel anticipates the thirteenth century, when the Apocrypha is drawn upon to supplement the brief New Testament records and thus make the biblical poems more interesting and more congenial. In style too Wernher's poem is progressive, for not only the two later revisions but even the surviving fragments of the original version have courtly features.

Yet in spite of this a relaxed narrative atmosphere is not yet present in Wernher's work: Mary is not primarily the mother whose suffering arouses our pity but an important character in the history of human redemption, the royal mother of God, the woman who makes amends for the sin of Eve. She is also a paragon of virtue, of *kiusche*, and exhorts men to follow the paths of righteousness by turning away from the world and trusting in God, not by harbouring doubts like Joachim and Joseph. These features, a blend of the old and the new, are what makes Wernher's poem a significant document of the twelfth century.

An important and unusual poem of the time is the anonymous *Himel-riche*, *c.* 1160/70, which describes the Kingdom of Heaven and the life of the blessed as the goal towards which man should strive. The content is conventional but the powerful language, the bold imagery and the strange, ponderous poetic style, appropriate to the subject, are highly original.

Prose too gains in importance. It is no longer a *res paene inusitata*, as in Notker's time, or a simple appendage to a Latin poem, as with Williram, but achieves an independent importance which grows in the succeeding centuries.

One work which, in addition to the various German versions of the *Physiologus*, a zoological textbook with Christian explanations and interpretations, should be mentioned here is the St Trudpert *Song of Songs*, a prose commentary of unexpected excellence, intended for nuns and probably written in the second half of the twelfth century. It is, however, much more than a commentary, and its formal structure, apparent already in the prologue, together with its skilful and powerful rhetorical language, lifts it out of a purely practical context and sets it, with its traces of Bernardine thought – seemingly the first to be found in German literature – among the more considerable works of the period.

Secular Poetry of the Early Hohenstaufen Period

It is not only religious poetry that shows developments and achievements in the mid-twelfth century, for this is the time when German secular poetry also comes into its own. Important as this fact is, one must not overestimate it; indeed, such traditional terms as pre-courtly literature and minstrel poetry (*Spielmannsdichtung*) dissuade one from doing so. For the age regarded the *Alexanderlied*, the *Kaiserchronik* and the *Rolandslied* in the first place as religious poems, and it was as such that the first two of these were included in the Vorau manuscript. And Alexander was also part of the history of redemption: poems about Alexander and poems about Judith or the Maccabees are closely related, while the *Kaiserchronik* consists of a history of the world, i.e. of the redemption of man, with overtones of Christian legend, as the *Annolied* is a Christian legend based on the history of the world, i.e. of redemption.

That the secular element could swamp the religious element was in the nature of the subject-matter, and there are many reasons why purely secular subjects came to receive literary treatment – reasons which had already played a part in the emergence of German religious poetry. Now came the rise of courtly-chivalric culture, above all in France, and the fact that France already possessed a rich secular literature in the vernacular had long since wiped out the Germans' lead in this respect.

It is therefore not surprising that a number of the earliest secular German works owe their existence to French models: the source of the *Alexanderlied* is the poem by Alberich de Besançon, and that of the

Rolandslied is the *Chanson de Roland*. The time was ripe for the rise of secular literature, but many of these early secular works cannot conceal their fundamentally religious spirit.

The *Kaiserchronik*, probably the work of a Regensburg cleric, is the first large-scale German historical chronicle in verse to have reached a wide public and to have found a number of continuators. In its earliest form it covered the history of the Roman Empire from Caesar to Conrad III – more precisely, to the year 1147, for the poet (or the scribe) stopped in the middle of a sentence at this point. The title is appropriate, for the history of the Empire is treated as the history of its emperors, but the work differs from the other poetic chronicles of the time in that it is not based on a familiar pattern such as that of the four kingdoms, or the six ages of the world, or Augustine's two states in his *De civitate Dei*, but apparently on straight chronological principles.

Yet only apparently. There is no particular call for surprise in the fact that the order of the emperors is not always accurate, or that historical emperors are left out and legendary emperors put in. The remarkable thing is what the poet says about the emperors, and the way he says it. At the end of each biography he gives, not always accurately, the dates of each emperor's reign, down to the day, with the result that a total of approximately 409 years accrues to the Roman emperors and a similar total to the German emperors. But whereas the 409 Roman years take up 14,239 lines in the poem, the 409 German years cover only 3,002 lines, and this disproportion betrays the poet's intentions. He is not concerned with history but with stories, and he seeks wherever possible to embroider his biographies, particularly those of the Romans, with sagas and legends, until in some cases these legends almost completely obscure the historical material. Where there is no such legend, the biography is usually brief and inadequate, particularly those of the German emperors; among these only Charlemagne is fully treated, and here there was already a good deal of legendary material to draw on, such as the legend of Aegidius and that of Charlemagne and Pope Leo.

The interpolated stories themselves are highly instructive. It is true that some of them, such as the Bavarian story of Adelger, derive from Germanic sagas, and that on the other hand the poet takes account of the new chivalric ideals, as in the love dialogue in the biography of Tarquin. But the vital point is that all these stories have an ethical or religious message, and as they were not originally included for their own sake, so too the emperors are not primarily treated as historical personages.

The emperors themselves are divided into two groups, good and bad, and a pagan emperor like Trajan could just as well be good as a Christian emperor like Henry IV could be bad. The two criteria for this division are, firstly, true Christian conduct and, secondly, service to the Empire as the political structure in which God has preserved the Christian ethic. History is thus an ethical force: the Empire is a religio-worldly unit (there is no mention of the Investiture Struggle), and the Emperor is the God-appointed lord of this Empire, which is not German but Roman. Theodoric the Great (Dietrich von Bern) is therefore condemned because he destroyed the Empire and was not, as the saga presents him, a true national hero. It is the poet's conception of the Roman emperors that determines his view of the *riche* in the *Kaiserchronik*, a conception also found in the *Annolied*, in *König Rother*, in Walther von der Vogelweide and in the *Lohengrin* epic.

Between 1130 and 1150 Pfaffe Lamprecht, from the Moselle area, composed an *Alexanderlied* in imitation of a French poem by Alberich de Besançon. This is the first occasion that Alexander, a popular figure in literature since late-classical times, appears in a German work, albeit not as a historical figure but as the hero of a romance.

Lamprecht's poem does not cover the whole of Alexander's life but only down to the death of Darius. He is portrayed as an exemplary ruler but with two faults: he is not a Christian, and he inclines to *superbia*. But neither in the prologue to the poem, where he talks of his poetic approach, nor in the poem itself does Lamprecht state it as his intention to set his story in the context of the salvation of man. It is possible that, like his predecessors, he broke off with the death of Darius because this is the point, as in the vision of Daniel, at which the third kingdom of the world begins; in this case Lamprecht's interest in Alexander would have been not as a world conqueror but only as the initiator of this third kingdom. This interpretation would also explain the presence of the poem in the Vorau manuscript, but the poem itself contains nothing to support this notion.

Around 1170 an anonymous cleric set about refining and extending Lamprecht's work. This so-called Strasbourg *Alexander* has become a courtly epic which is in style and content close to Veldeke's *Eneit*. In it Alexander is shown as the perfect ruler – even the accusation of *superbia* is withdrawn and levelled only at Darius; he is wise and bold, just and merciful, a proven knight – in fact, a paragon of virtue, until he decides to add Paradise to his conquests. Now God shows him his limits, teaching him humility and showing him that man, being mortal, must curb his arrogant desires. Alexander learns his lesson and becomes a humble ruler. At this point the courtly poem turns into a religious poem, and in the epilogue the poet warns his listeners to remember death and lead a true Christian life. Thus in the end courtly poetry and religious poetry blend, as in so many later poems of the courtly age.

The *Rolandslied* of Pfaffe Konrad, possibly composed around 1170, is an epic of the crusades. It is dedicated to a certain Duke Heinrich, and there has been much discussion over whether this means Heinrich der Stolze or Heinrich der Löwe.

Konrad follows the French *Chanson de Roland* but converts its national, patriotic character into an ethos in which Christian and pagan forces oppose each other. Charlemagne, the *voget* (lord) of the Roman *riche*, fights against the heathens in the name of God and Christendom, and the climax of the dramatic action is reached with the enmity between Roland, the Christian warrior, and Ganelan, the traitor. The action is described in a remarkably one-sided manner: Charlemagne, the great ruler, labours under the weight of his power and, like David, needs God's help to overcome the superior forces of Paligan; his knights are bold warriors who die a martyr's death in battle against the pagan foe who are fighting only for their own *ere*, whereas the Christians are fighting for their *sele*, for the *ere* of God and the preservation of His kingdom from the forces of the devil. God Himself has commanded them to act thus, as is seen most strikingly in the episode when the dying Roland gives back to the Angel the gauntlet which is the symbol of God's command.

Because it is a struggle between God and the Devil, no quarter is given: for the pagans, however brave they are, there is only conversion or death. Between the two sides stands Ganelan, who does not see that his desire to avenge himself on Roland is a betrayal of God Himself. The *Rolandslied*, one of the most significant poems of the time, is thus a poem about the Christian *riche* and a noble Christian martyr descended not from the Germanic warrior but from David.

Finally mention should be made of two poems, *König Rother* and *Herzog Ernst*, which, together with the legends of *Orendel* and *Oswald* and the poem *Salman und Morolf*, belong to the class of so-called *Spielmannsdichtung*. These last three poems, however, may well be later than twelfth-century, and the term *Spielmannsdichtung* (minstrel poetry) is problematical, for we do not know much about what these minstrels composed and performed, or whether it really was the minstrels that recorded such orally transmitted poems. Before these questions have been answered, it may be wiser to avoid the term.

König Rother, badly preserved in a late-twelfth-century manuscript and probably written by a cleric only slightly earlier, has charm, excitement and humour, and may well be called the first secular narrative poem in German literature. It tells of the eventful courtship of the daughter of the King of Constantinople by Rother, of the loyalty of Rother's warriors, of the savage giants who help him and of Constantine's deceit and treachery. Rother himself is the embodiment of a perfect Christian knight, and the antithesis of the cowardly, tyrannical Constantine. He is just, loyal, wise and generous, and *zuht* and *ere* reign in his kingdom. Piety informs all his actions, and when he has performed all his tasks on earth and is ready to bequeath his kingdom to his heir, he retires from the world to devote himself to the service of God.

König Rother is, however, not only an entertaining story but also a political poem, and it has been suggested that the hero is based on Roger II of Sicily, or even on the Emperor Henry VI. Be this as it may, the political nature of the poem is clear from the story itself: Rother is made the grandfather of Charlemagne; he wins the daughter of Constantine, who renounces his right to sovereignty over a Christian kingdom by planning to sell her to the pagans; Rother thus becomes the legitimate heir to the Eastern Empire, but because in the poem Rother is the grandfather of Charlemagne, it is proved that in reality the only legitimate Emperor is that of the Western Empire. In other words, the legitimacy of the German Empire of the West, which various medieval rulers and statesmen set out to demonstrate, is taken in the poem, by a piece of wishful thinking, to be a long-established fact.

The tendentious view of history presented by *König Rother* accords with that found in other poems, from the *Annolied* to *Lohengrin*. In form it bears similarities to the Old French *chansons de geste*.

Herzog Ernst is also derived from recent history, in that its basis is the quarrel between Conrad II and his stepson Ernst. Again it is not a work that keeps within historical bounds but branches out into the adventurous world of the crusades, telling of Ernst's exploits in distant lands in the manner of the Hellenistic romances. It is only preserved in fragmentary form but the story lived on and underwent a number of revisions in the following centuries – a fortunate, or unfortunate, fate that also befell the *Rolandslied* and many other works. Thus these poems, together with Christian legends and other religious works, form a natural link between the literature of the twelfth century and that of the thirteenth, and provide the basis on which the great poetry of Hartmann, Wolfram, Gottfried and Walther arose.

Courtly Literature
(1160 – 1250)

FRIEDRICH RANKE

The literature of the Early Middle High German period (mid-eleventh century to about 1160) is literature on religious themes by religious writers and served to extend and intensify the reception of the Christian message as well as to encourage piety. It ranges from the inculcation of fear and a sense of sin to the joyful affirmation of faith, and even where worldly beauty and the material concerns of life are at stake, the poet's primary concern is clearly with the religious interests of his public.

But soon after the middle of the twelfth century there is a change. The body of knights, who had evolved their own culture and mode of life in the service of the Hohenstaufen Emperor Frederick I (Barbarossa), turned to literature in order to give expression to their new-found sense of beauty and joy in life and to their ideal of nobility, and this literature was intended for the enjoyment of court circles and the general enrichment of life.

From obscure native roots and under the stimulus of the Provençal lyric of the troubadours, the courtly Minnesang arose in Germany, to be shortly followed by the courtly epic in the form of adaptations of French verse-romances. Minnesang, like all medieval lyric poetry, lives as song; the Minnesinger is poet, composer and performer in one, and *Spruch-dichtung*, with its more didactic tone, was also sung. The epic, on the other hand, is book-poetry – though the still very limited ability to read in lay circles meant that such works were still generally recited, and the epic poet envisaged his work as being declaimed before gatherings of the court rather than being read by individuals.

Minnesang and chivalric epic are both by their nature unrealistic, and the truth with which they deal – a reality of thought and idea – is of a higher order than visible reality. The Minnesinger, whether he be from a poor family of the *ministerialis* class, or a free knight, or the son of the Emperor himself, devotes his service to the lady of his choice, a married woman, praising her in the terms of *hohe Minne*, while she remains deaf to his entreaties.

We are not supposed to enquire about the lady's real life, for the poet sees her *in abstracto* as an ideal of womanhood and fills his poems with delicate and passionate expressions of yearning for his unattainable goal. To be allowed to serve his lady enriches his spirit and raises his stature, and the very thought of her gives him strength to ennoble himself. The transforming power of love gives him the chivalric virtues of *staete* (steadfastness), *triuwe* (loyalty), *zuht* (good breeding) and *ere* (honour), the *vröude* (happiness) with which to perform his social service, and above all the *hoher muot* (confidence) with which to embark on new, higher quests and conquer his sluggishness of spirit.

As the Minnesinger achieves his ideal frame of mind in the agonizing tension between desire and renunciation, the courtly epic poet paints his ideal of life as a reality within an unreal, ideal world which yet had the character of a magnified reflection of the real world. The figures in his works are real men and women, accessible to all, living in a free world of riches and splendour in the style in which the common man would wish to live, and revealing their innermost thoughts and feelings in a way that illuminates and purifies his own thoughts and feelings. The formative power of literature thus finds its way into the courtly life of the time.

It is hardly possible to explain, from the point of view of German literature, how, in contrast to the religiosity of the previous period, the phenomenon of Minnesang and courtly love arose and swept like a flood across the chivalric society of Europe. It is clear, however, that it came to Germany from France, as the vocabulary of German courtly civilization alone shows: *schevalier, garzûn, massenîe, cumpanîe, kastêl, palas, erkaere; turnei, turnieren, tjoste, tjostieren, walopieren, banier, lanze; note, melodîe, danz; amîs, amîe, kurteis, kurtôsîe, fîn, moraliteit*, etc. etc. The path of this influence from Northern France to Lower Franconian/Dutch territory and thence up the Rhine (i.e. from Flanders to Cologne) can be traced through a number of basic courtly terms in a West Low German form: *wâpen, ors, dörper, ritter* (for High German *rîter* or *riter*). In Hartmann's *Gregorius* the knights of Brabant and the Hennegau are taken as the ideal, while from Neidhart von Reuental onwards the aping of Flemish modes of speech by peasants pretending to be knights is a favourite object of scorn (cf. also Low German forms like *pardrîsekîn* and *schapelikîn* in Wolfram and Gottfried).

But stimulus and influence do not mean slavish imitation, and the Minnesang is not troubador lyric poetry in German, nor is German epic poetry the same as French. In the Middle Ages, as in any other period, each country sings with its own voice in the chorus of the nations. The distinguishing features of the German voice are its relative lack of originality, its more marked subjectivity, its more precise formulation of concepts and its emphasis on the didactic.

The high period of courtly literature in Germany embraces three generations – that of the founders (1160–90), that of the perfecters (down to *c.* 1220), and that of the preservers (to *c.* 1250). This period coincides with the rise of Hohenstaufen power under Barbarossa and its sudden collapse; with the death of Frederick II the knight lost his position of leadership, and in the transitional period of the latter part of the thirteenth century the burgher's concern with the sober and the realistic, the critical and the satirical, the edifying and the didactic moved into the ascendancy.

The Early Generation

In the mid-twelfth century the Austrian religious satirist Heinrich von Melk refers to love-songs (*trûtliet*) composed by the knights, and it is scarcely an accident that the earliest German poet of such lyrics known to us by name appears to have lived in Austria at that time – the Kürenberger, of a family of Lower Austrian *ministeriales*, the lords of Kürenberg.

The Kürenberger's poems show nothing of the despairing wooing and service, or man's self-ennoblement through love, of the courtly Minnesang. On the contrary, the poet presents himself as an experienced lover much sought-after by women and maidens, and in so doing, gives a remarkably varied series of portraits: the woman hungry for love, the chaste maiden, the naïve girl, and – his particular favourite – the abandoned, love-sick woman (as in the song of the falcon). The Kürenberger is a master of the art of saying a great deal in a few words. Within the narrow scope of a strophe of four *Langzeilen* (virtually the strophe of the *Nibelungenlied*), and often by hinting rather than stating, he can create a whole world of emotions.

Related to the Kürenberger are a number of separate anonymous strophes (the *Falkenlied* of Pseudo-Dietmar, etc.) which show nothing of Romance influence. Also from this period is the wandering *Spruchdichter* Herger, sometimes known as 'Der ältere Spervogel', who has left a number of independent seven-line strophes, each dealing with a single idea. His subjects – the praise of generous patrons and the principles of Christian morality and experience, sometimes treated in the form of a fable or proverb – are the same as those of the later, somewhat more sophisticated *Spruchdichtung* (gnomic poetry) but in Herger the extremely simple form considerably restricts the content.

This is also the moment when we observe the emergence of a German lyric poetry under Romance influence. Following Provençal and French models, the Minnesinger composed multi-strophe poems, decorating and refining their strophic forms by introducing a greater regularity of metre, a larger number of lines and subtler rhyme-schemes, and filling these new forms with a more self-conscious but also more fluently expressed sequence of thoughts from the world of courtly love and service. This courtly Minnesang arises above all in western areas – from the Lower Rhine (Heinrich von Veldeke) to the area around Worms (Friedrich von Hausen), Upper Alsace (Ulrich von Gutenberg) and Lake Neuchâtel (Rudolf von Fenis).

The acknowledged master among these is Friedrich von Hausen, a noble confidant of Barbarossa, who died on the same crusade as his Emperor (1190). He took over motifs and strophic forms from the troubadours, and some of his poems can in fact be sung to identifiable troubadour melodies, but he used this foreign stimulus to release his own poetic emotions, and his lyrics show the new art in a vigorous stage of development.

In poems of four or six strophes, each strophe having nine or ten lines and frequently-recurring rhymes, he uses antithesis and parallelism to build up extended expressions of his feelings. With a blend of urgency and deliberation his rhythm and sentence-structure reveal the passionate, yet controlled personality of a man who, like a true aristocrat, would rather give up being close to his lady than see everybody have the opportunity to speak to her. On his journeys to distant lands in the service of his Emperor he sings to her of his longings, letting his dreams lift him out of reality and thanking God for this agony of yearning which threatens to drive him out of his mind. Finally, like so many of his contemporaries, he experiences on crusade the meaning of love for God and love for his lady, solving the conflict between them by saying: 'First God – but then my lady'.

Compared with the work of Hausen, that of most of his contemporaries – including the waggish pedant Heinrich von Veldeke, whose passionless poems, mostly of only one strophe each but in a variety of forms, treat individual themes from the world of *Minnedienst*, and Rudolf von Fenis (d. 1196), the embodiment of the Provençalizing Minnesinger – pales into insignificance. There are, however, a few exceptional moments, such as the charmingly direct strophes – including a *Tagelied* (dawn-song) of doubtful authorship – of the Austrian nobleman Dietmar von Aist, which reveal a delicate blend of nature and love and whose allusive style recalls the Kürenberger. There is also the large *Minneleich* of Ulrich von Gutenberg, a masterpiece of metrical and musical construction; the crusading *Leich* of Heinrich von Rugge, who, on learning of the death of Barbarossa, calls on the nobility to send reinforcements for the crusade and, like Hausen, warns the ladies against the coward who stays at home; and the poems written by Henry VI, probably at the time of his *schwertleite* (investiture as a knight) in 1184, at the age of twenty, which include a four-strophe 'love-greeting' in a lively dactylic rhythm – a poem in which the young man's imagination will not permit him, despite the yearning and the happiness he expresses, to forget the thought of his future crown.

Whereas the Minnesang, both in content and as a literary genre, was something completely new, the courtly epic, in rhymed couplets, continued an old German tradition, albeit in a new style. Here too the new way came from the west, from northern France, where around 1160 the eroticization of literature that had started in the Provençal lyric led to large-scale narratives dominated, not by heroism or piety but by love in its varied manifestations. A bare decade later the Germans followed the Romance example, and the earliest acknowledged, though probably not the first, master of the genre was Heinrich von Veldeke, of whom Gottfried von Strassburg wrote: 'er impfete daz êrste rîs/in tiutischer zungen' ('he grafted the first branch on to the bare trunk of German poetry').

Veldeke belonged to a family of *ministeriales* from the border-lands between Germany and the Netherlands. He composed his *Eneide* on the basis of the Anglo-Norman *Roman d'Eneas* (*c.* 1165), taking over its substance faithfully but treating its form with a certain freedom. He started his work about 1170, but in 1174 or 1175 his manuscript was stolen, and it was not until nine years later that he was able to resume work on it. It was finally completed shortly after Barbarossa's *Hoffest* in Mainz at Whitsun 1184, an event which Veldeke recalls with enthusiasm.

In order to understand the lasting reputation of this longwinded and somewhat ungainly work, we must realize that it contained just what the age required – a famous love-story, taken from the ideal world of the Roman nobility, a world naturally portrayed in contemporary medieval style. The action lies between the two main pillars of the story – Dido's fatal passion for Aeneas, and the growth of Aeneas' love for the simple and charming princess Lavinia. The heroic adventures, such as the voyage to the underworld; the detailed descriptions of battles, festivities, courtly splendour and courtly conduct; and above all the elaborate account of the love-relationships: these are the qualities which gave the work its attraction for contemporary audiences and its popularity as a model.

This reception, however, depended on its language. For in his *Eneide*, unlike his lyrics, Veldeke was at pains, with his eye on an audience of knights from all parts of the Empire, to keep his work free from elements of his Limburg dialect. He therefore used the 'Rhenish literary language', took care to keep his rhymes pure, so that the work could be recited without difficulty in any German-speaking area and clothed the whole in a flowing poetic style through the technique of *Reimbrechung*, the extension of the syntactical construction beyond the limit of the rhyming couplet.

Another early courtly romance, of which only fragments have survived, is the *Trierer Floyris*, the earliest German version of the epic of Flore and Blanscheflur and their childhood love. Also from this period is the strange poem from Hesse called *Graf Rudolf*, which combines in a semi-archaic, semi-modern style an adventurous love-story with a topical story of the crusades. In addition there is the *Tristrant* of the Low German *ministerialis* Eilhart von Oberg, the oldest version of the Tristan story in German, which is also written, despite its author's provenance, in a kind of High German literary language. But the love-story is not yet fully realized, and a few decades later Eilhart's work was overshadowed by Gottfried's, at least for the duration of the courtly era.

Such religious poetry as there is from this period also shows the new modes of feeling and the new objects of attention. This is seen above all in the *Marienleben* (*Life of Mary*) of Priester Wernher (written 1172 in Augsburg), in which the more delicate emotions introduced by early lyric poetry, together with a delight in the idyllic, are couched in an expressive language which sings the praises of the Mother of God. It is also seen in the *Münchner Morgensegen*, which conveys in a particularly successful way the noble mentality of the pious Christian knight.

Other religious poems reveal a taste for fantastic adventures (Alber's *Tundalus*) and for fanciful pictures of the fate of man (the *Albanuslegende*). Didactic poetry also reveals a greater understanding of the needs and propensities of the knights than it did before (Wernher von Elmendorf), but it leads to no work of importance at this time.

'High' Chivalric Poetry

The new generation built on the foundations laid by its predecessors: 'high' epic poetry would not have been possible without Veldeke's *Eneide*, nor 'high' Minnesang without Hausen and his contemporaries. In the thirty years between 1190 and 1220 almost everything was written that can lay claim to be of lasting greatness in medieval German literature. Even more precisely, it is around the year 1200 that we find the seven great names assembled: Hartmann, Wolfram, Gottfried, the poet of the *Nibelungenlied*, Heinrich von Morungen, Reinmar and Walther.

The relationship of these poets to each other shows the extent to which they were aware of belonging to a common culture. Reinmar and Walther compete in Vienna for the title of leading Minnesinger; Wolfram chaffs Walther, alludes to the *Nibelungenlied*, has a critical word to say about Hartmann's ideal characters whose conduct strikes him as morally inadequate, and defiantly rejects Gottfried's criticisms; the poet of the *Nibelungenlied* borrows names from the beginning of Wolfram's *Parzifal*;

Gottfried von Strassburg decks out his work with a survey of the epic and lyric poetry of his day and shows himself to be an acute literary critic, mourning the lately deceased Reinmar and proclaiming Walther as his successor as leader of the 'nightingales'; he praises Hartmann as his master and gives a spiteful caricature of the 'unrefined' poetic style of his great rival Wolfram, with the intention of holding him up to ridicule.

The German literary language becomes a refined medium of expression in the hands of these masters, capable of conveying every nuance of mood, from solemnity to triviality, from lighthearted mockery to passionate anger. Literature acquires the 'classical' balance of form and content which corresponds to the harmony between 'God and the world' which Hartmann assumes and Wolfram posits as the goal of human striving; even Gottfried, led by his devotion to the world to put Love in the place of God, conveys through his perfect lovers the resolution of the conflict between the real and the ideal.

In the courtly epic Harmann von Aue, a refined *ministerialis* from the Thurgau, brought to Germany the Arthurian romances which, drawn from the world of Celtic myth, had been infused with the values of the contemporary chivalric world in France, above all by Chrétien de Troyes.

In *Erec* Hartmann portrays the conflict between honour and pleasure. Erec is so devoted to his beautiful wife Enite that he neglects his duties as lord and knight until, roused by her reproaches, he overcomes his inertia and sets out with her on a series of ever more challenging adventures in order to prove his bravery; she, for her part, shows her utterly unselfish love for him by sharing the dangers that befall him, and at the end of the story the harmony between love and honour is restored.

A counterpart to *Erec* is *Iwein* (shortly after 1200), in which the hero, with Erec's example as a warning, indulges in an excess of knightly exploits, loses his wife's affection thereby, and has to win it back again. Both these romances are governed by the rule of *mâze* (moderation, harmony), which is at the root of Hartmann's philosophy. He is the poet of harmony, serenity and classical purity.

In the decade between *Erec* and *Iwein* Hartmann, deeply affected by the death of his feudal master, turned away from secular court literature and devoted himself to religious poetry. In *Gregorius*, one of his two poems on religious legends, he takes from his French source the story of the knight who, having committed the sin of Oedipus, does not despair but undertakes the severest penance and shows himself worthy of God's grace. Yet this is not the dualism of the pre-courtly period. Gregorius purges his crime with harsh acts of self-denial, but his worldly life is not thereby utterly condemned, for under God's guidance he now achieves complete fulfilment: as he had been the best novice in the monastery, so he becomes the bravest knight, the most affectionate husband, the wisest and most just master to his servants, and finally the severest penitent and most pious Pope, who pronounces God's mercy on his beloved mother and wife.

Hartmann's masterpiece, the charming legend *Der arme Heinrich*, is a warning against surrendering oneself to the values of the world. Heinrich von Aue, a knight totally absorbed in the virtuous conduct of his own prosperous life, forgets to thank the Lord for his blessings and is punished by being stricken with leprosy; the willingness on the part of a young girl to sacrifice herself in pity for him brings home to him the truth of his position, and after his miraculous recovery he lives a pious life with his young redeemer, in harmony with God and the world. The philosophy of *Der arme Heinrich* makes it natural that Hartmann should have returned, with *Iwein*, to the secular courtly epic.

In medieval eyes the development in poetic technique between *Erec* and *Iwein* signified a further step forward: the rhythm has become more regular, the rhymes are freer from dialect forms, the syntax is more relaxed, the language has come even closer to the refined speech of courtly society, the narrative is quieter and more relaxed, and the spiritual significance of the events is brought out in a clearer manner – tense, yet natural and controlled.

A few years after Hartmann a greater poet took up the religious problem of *Der arme Heinrich*. Wolfram von Eschenbach, a Franconian *ministerialis*, had a far profounder conception of the destruction and ultimate restoration of the harmony between man and God. About the year 1204 he took up the unfinished *Perceval* of Chrétien de Troyes and produced, in his German version, the first *Entwicklungsroman* in European literature.

Parzival, brought up in the wilds as a child of nature, is drawn by his noble blood to the life of chivalry. He leaves his mother and receives instruction in chivalric deportment but unwittingly offends by concealing his pity – as the chivalric code requires – when confronted in the Gralsburg with the suffering of Anfortas, King of the Grail. Thus on the one hand he is praised by the Arthurian knights as a true chevalier, while on the other the curse of the Grail plunges him into despair. Thinking that God has deserted him, he renounces His service ('hât er haz, den wil ich tragen!' – 'if he hates me for it, I will bear it') and wanders disconsolately from country to country as an unhappy jouster. In these lonely years it is only his love for his faithful wife Condwiramurs and his determination to find the Grail once more that give him the strength to go on living. Matured by his years of loneliness, he comes one Good Friday upon a noble hermit called Trevrizent, who acquaints him with the secrets of the

Grail and with the 'sweet message' of God's merciful love and explains to him the offence he has committed. In the devout serenity of Trevrizent's cave Parzival finds his way back to God. After further combats, all of which he abandons as pointless before the outcome can be decided, he returns to the Arthurian circle, where the wonderful news reaches him that God has chosen him as King of the Grail in succession to Anfortas. With the blessing of Trevrizent, who again urges humility upon him, he makes his way to the Gralsburg, asks the question that he had failed to ask before and, happily reunited with Condwiramurs, becomes King of the Grail.

In the Grail and the semi-religious order of knights who guard it Wolfram symbolizes the union of Christianity and chivalry, the total infusion of chivalric life with Christian devotion and preparedness for suffering. The road to the Grail, the Stone of Humility, leads via the recognition of human sinfulness and the sharing of the sufferings of the Saviour, through which man comes to share the sufferings of his fellow men. Wolfram's *Parzival* is a warning to his age to apply itself in earnest to the realization of the ideal of Christian chivalry. At the same time life itself is not thereby to be degraded, for the man who finds the Grail will receive *der sêle ruowe* (spiritual peace) and *des lîbes vröude* (material contentment), since the Kingdom of the Grail is the symbol of the harmony between God and the world.

This ethico-religious message is embedded in an excessively involved plot, made the more so by the addition of the story of Parzival's friend Gawan. Gawan, a cheerful, uncomplicated Arthurian knight of the Hartmann type, inhabits a world which Wolfram portrays with an affectionate, slightly humorous regard for its adventures and *Minne* problems. But it is a second-class world, to be left behind by the true Christian hero whose eyes are set on the Grail.

One of the other figures in his *Parzival* concerned him to such an extent, however, that he intended to devote a whole epic to her – Sigune, the young widow and recluse, who remains faithful to the memory of the fiancé who had laid down his life in her service, with whom she retains a mystic union until they are united in death. In the so-called *Titurel* fragment, which was to have told of her suffering, Wolfram intended to depict the ultimate fusion of love and religious devotion – true love as the way to God. From the strophic form of the heroic epic he evolved, with striking originality, his own lyrico-epic strophe – a form better suited, in fact, to the more passionate parts of the story than to the smooth-flowing narrative. But only two sections of the work were completed.

Wolfram's other large-scale epic, *Willehalm* (1212 onwards), begins where *Parzival* left off, for its hero is from the outset an exemplary Christian knight who, despite his piety, is firmly based in the material world.

Following the French *Bataille d'Aliscans*, a heroic Christian poem of the pre-courtly period, Wolfram relates the story of the Margrave William of Orange and his wife Gyburg, a converted Saracen, and of the two bitter battles between the Christians and the heathens who set out to recapture Gyburg, but he radically changes the nature of his source and gives his poem a new ethical meaning.

Unfortunately the end of the work is missing, but we may assume that the humane Christianity which Wolfram introduced in place of the religious hatred of the French poem would have brought about an ultimate reconciliation. Gyburg's splendid speech before the second battle, in her distraction at the thought of another carnage among her relatives, shows this, as does also the attractive figure of her brother, the young giant Rennewart, who fights on William's side, is captured by his fellow Saracens and finally, Wolfram implies, marries the charming Alyze, princess of France, and becomes King. But it is shown above all by William himself, who grows to maturity through the immense suffering of the two battles and makes the gesture of reconciliation through which the prisoners are exchanged, Rennewart returns and a happy ending is brought about. Wolfram's *Willehalm*, the German epic of humanitarianism, breathes the spirit of the chivalric generation of Saladin and Frederick II.

The independence and originality of the action and the intellectual content show themselves also in the language. Wolfram is not interested in the process of refinement and intellectualization started in *Erec* and continued in *Iwein*, or in pleasant euphony, facile smoothness and 'normal' practice, but in personal, original expression. Many of his lines are archaic and metrically too long, his constructions are often awkward and ungrammatical, his thoughts unconnected and sometimes obscure – it is easy to believe him when he says that he knows nothing of the linguistic discipline of Latin. Yet everything he writes has an original, inimitable poetic power and is full of intuition and true life. His creativity is natural, untutored; abstract concepts become concrete images, and his expressiveness depends on animated observation, on symbols and on the action. Parzival is distinguished from Hartmann's Arthurian knights by the richness and profundity of his nature and by the uniqueness of his destiny, and all Wolfram's characters are individuals, not types. His narrative is eccentric and sometimes bizarre, often with a close personal involvement and with a highly subjective humour. No other German medieval poet lives so intimately with his characters.

Where Wolfram is the *homo illiteratus*, Gottfried von Strassburg is the most highly educated of the German poets of the time; where Wolfram, a Franconian knight, jokes about his poverty, Gottfried appears as a member of a well-to-do Alsatian burgher family; where Wolfram deals in characteristic traits, Gottfried conveys the Romance values of euphony and symmetry; where Wolfram praises marriage, Gottfried writes of adultery; where Wolfram is the serious Christian, Gottfried merely flirts with religious ideas like a humanist. Small wonder that neither could understand or appreciate the work of the other.

Gottfried's unfinished epic *Tristan* was written before 1210 rather than after. He follows the *Roman de Tristan et Iseut* of the Anglo-Norman cleric Thomas, who composed his story about 1180 for the highly cultured English royal court. His novel of adultery suited the taste of early courtly society, and love, from being an uncontrollable, mysterious force of nature, became the agent of a calculated earthly happiness.

But Gottfried went even further, and gave love a new, irrational, devotional, religious quality. The love of Tristan and Isolde is a *unio mystica* based on suffering ('wir zwei sîn iemer beide / ein dinc ân underscheide' – 'may we two become one and indivisible'). In the grotto in the forest the two lovers, cut off from the world like hermits, live their carefree life in the service of their goddess ('si sâhen beide einander an: / dâ generten si sich van' – 'they gazed at each other and grew well again'). Gottfried emphasizes the meaning of their ideal love by the allegory of the love grotto, to which he gives a symbolic meaning like that of a church. He uses the same religious terms throughout his description of their life, their suffering and their death, celebrating their experience as the true spiritual sustenance of 'noble hearts', the chosen few who are capable of identifying themselves with the fate of the two lovers and for whom happiness and suffering have become one.

With a Bernardine mystical language Gottfried has taken the worldly subject and turned it, through the lovers' self-sacrifice, into a religion of love. Gottfried did not appear to worry about the incompatibility of this with Christianity. As a poet he fervently believed in the 'heathen' goddess of love, and as the mystic knows both despair and ecstasy, so Gottfried descends from the realm of ideal love to the painful realization of its remoteness from real life and real love, and laments at length on this in a moralizing tone.

He also decks out his romance with a variety of reflections on the nature and effect of true and false love, thereby softening the offensive impact of the scenes of deceit and adultery that occupy the centre of the poem and furnishing them with a philosophical meaning. At the same time he gives his work a surface brilliance through the virtuosity of his poetic style, derived from that of Hartmann, the Minnesinger, Romance and Latin poets, with the result that the attractiveness of the form causes one to forget the controversial nature of the content.

At the same period (*c.* 1200–1204) a great anonymous poet in Vienna or Passau was working on the *Nibelungenlied*. The very fact that he concealed his name shows the difference between his tradition and that of the poets of the courtly epic, for as it is only natural for poets in the subjective tradition, French and German, of the courtly epic to put their names to their works, it would be equally inappropriate and stylistically disturbing to find the same in the native heroic epic.

The indigenous strophic form of the *Nibelungenlied* makes quite different demands on the poet from those of an unbroken succession of rhyming couplets. The style has to be broader and more deliberate, the *Langzeile* has to be intensified, and the independence of each strophe demands a definite pause at the end. The strophic epic retains the older, more solemn manner, the archaic vocabulary, the simpler sentences, the conciser, clearer dialogue, the greater objectivity. Yet at the same time the poet of the *Nibelungenlied* shows the deep influence of chivalric culture and poetry, and one could well call his work a 'courtly heroic epic'.

The subject-matter is taken in the main from two sources. From a comparatively short lay, the so-called *Jüngeres Brünhildlied*, the poet took the story of Siegfried and Brünhild, the trickery over Gunther's wooing, the quarrel between the two women and Brünhild's terrible revenge; and from a pre-courtly heroic epic, the so-called *Älterer Nibelungennot*, he took the story of the destruction of the Burgundians at the court of the Huns as Kriemhild's vengeance for the murder of Siegfried. From these two originally independent poems he compiled his great two-part fate-epic of Kriemhild's happiness, suffering and revenge.

In the first part he uses chiefly elements from the courtly world of his own background, and his affection centres on Siegfried and Kriemhild, whose love he portrays, in so far as the subject-matter permits, in the new, refined terms of his age. The story starts like a romance. The report of Kriemhild's beauty draws Siegfried from the Rhineland to Worms, and in tones reminiscent of the early lyric the poet describes the stirring of their love – secret glances, guilty blushes, silent hand-clasps and Siegfried's long years of devotion, including his fateful journey to Isenstein.

In the scenes dealing with the quarrel between the two women in Worms the emphasis is on explaining the irresistible change that comes over Kriemhild: how, from being the embodiment of gentleness and love, proud and happy with her noble consort, she comes to claim in Brünhild's presence his superiority over her brother Gunther, and how, not understanding Brünhild's replies, she makes her taunting remarks which lead to their public quarrel over precedence at the door of the cathedral and to the mortal insults that follow.

From this point onwards the destructive fate which the poet had allowed to overshadow the earlier events is seen to be irreversible. By revealing to Hagen – out of concern for her husband's safety – the secret of Siegfried's vulnerability, Kriemhild once again shows the power of this fate, but after Siegfried's death she feels only a suffocating pain and a savage hatred against the assassins. This Kriemhild has nothing more to do with the ideal figures of the chivalric epic whom she resembled at the beginning, nothing in common with the world of love and *mâze*, beauty of form, harmony and happiness. Transformed by the cruelty of her fate, she waits only for the hour of vengeance.

The second half of the story tells how she plots and eventually achieves her revenge, stopping at nothing in her cunning and her ferocity. She entices her brothers into the country, making sure that Hagen is with them; trying in vain to get the Huns to attack, she sends Blödel, Iring and Rüdiger to their death in a fight against her brothers. Hers is the insane act of setting fire to the castle hall, an act which is a mockery of courtly conduct. And when finally she dangles the head of her brother Gunther in front of the manacled Hagen and kills him with her own hand, it is only her own death that makes the gruesomeness of the scene tolerable. Yet at the end the image of the vengeful Kriemhild remains untarnished in the listener's memory: she is a legendary heroic figure who, instead of becoming a mourning widow, sets her iron will to the task of bending fate to her own purposes.

Hagen, the hero who knowingly advances towards his death from the very beginning, is of the same steely quality and fights to his last breath. Even when he stands in chains before Kriemhild as the last survivor, his will is not broken: 'den schaz den weiz nu niemen wan got unde mîn; / er sol dich vâlandinne iemer wol verholen sîn!' ('No one knows where the treasure is but God and me. It will always remain hidden from you, you witch!') Even at the moment of death his hatred is victorious, and he dies affirming his faith in himself, defiant to the end.

The same sense of heroism fills the other Nibelungen, who perish rather than concede any infringement of what they consider to be the binding principle of their honour: that they cannot be parted from one another, even by the threat of death. They all die without complaint, without appeal to God and without thought of an after-life. The hall of Attila's castle is filled with the odour of death – but at the same time with the unyielding affirmation of the will to live.

Only one of the characters lives in the gentler atmosphere of more modern times – Rüdiger von Bechelarn. Wherever he appears, there is a breath of Hohenstaufen courtliness. And when he too is drawn into the maelstrom of destruction, he is the only one who does not instinctively know what he has to do, and who is worried in Christian terms about the fate of his soul. He is bound by oath to fulfil Kriemhild's request, but as the Burgundians' escort he cannot break the peace; thus, however he decides, he will incur guilt. When the battle starts, it is therefore not only his life but also his honour as a knight and the salvation of his soul that are at stake. The poet rescues him from this conflict by having him give his shield to Hagen in a symbolic gesture of true chivalry. The more we come to feel how much of the poet's own sensitive spirit has found its way into the character of Rüdiger, the more we come to admire the artistry and the humanitarianism of the man who at the same time showed how vividly and how strikingly in advance of his time he could portray the more-than-life-size figures of the old Germanic world.

The central question in the best of the chivalric epics is that of the perfection of human nature as seen by courtly civilization: perfection through *mâze* in Hartmann; perfection through love in Gottfried; perfection through Christian humility in Wolfram's *Parzifal* and Christian humanitarianism in *Willehalm*. But the *Nibelungenlied* does not belong to this exemplary company. It tells a gripping human story from a past age, and only the scenes of the destruction of the Burgundians rise to the level of exemplary values in the sense of the old heroic poetry – the sense in which human perfection is achieved by a death in the name of the two heroic virtues of loyalty and strength of will.

In the realm of lyric poetry 'high' Minnesang continues in the first instance the direction given to it by Friedrich von Hausen, i.e. the love-lament continues virtually unabated. By generation Heinrich von Morungen (d. 1222), a Thuringian *ministerialis* of the Markgraf Dietrich von Meissen, almost belongs to the earlier group, for he still has close links with the troubadour lyric and still lives in the world of *hohe Minne*. At the same time he lavishes on what appears to be a narrow subject an extravagant range of strophic forms (*Töne*) and a remarkable wealth of poetic imagery.

He is given to sudden outbursts of emotion. Thus he calls on his friends to help him fight his lady: help me to sing, so that she will listen to me, he cries, and so that my pain will pierce her heart; she has been tormenting me too long! When he meets her alone on the battlements, he imagines that his passion will set the whole world on fire. His lady is to him as the sun – unattainable and far above him: she inflames him as the fire consumes the tinder, and a kind word from her sends him into a flight of rapture.

His love is shot through with strands of visionary experience and almost religious fervour. His lady is a miracle-worker who is not only for ever before his eyes when he is alone, and for ever in his heart, but comes to him through closed doors, as the angel comes to the imprisoned martyr, and leads him to Heaven. His yearning leads him to imagine his own death: his song is like the cry of the dying swan, and he begs her to speak a comforting word; he composes his own epitaph, which will proclaim that it is she who was responsible for his death, and he wishes his son to avenge him by ensnaring her with his beauty. Yet he knows that even after death he will not be free: 'Waenet ir, ob ir mich toetet, / daz ich iuch danne niemer mê beschouwe? / nein, iuwer minne hât mich des ernoetet, / daz iuwer sêle ist mîner sêle vrouwe.' ('Do you think that by killing me you will never see me again? It is not so – for my love has forced me into the position where you have become mistress of my soul.') By promising to be her servant in the life to come, he expresses in the most extreme form the eternally unfulfilled yearning of *hohe Minne*.

Morungen surpasses all his German predecessors in formal subtlety. His language, like Wolfram's, is rich in intuitive vision, and his strophic forms abound in beauties of sound and rhythm. Moreover he is himself very aware of his artistic vocation: 'wan ich durch sanc bin zer werlde geborn' ('for I was born to be a poet'). Perhaps the best of his poems is the short *Tagelied*, the only poem in which he stepped outside the world of *hohe Minne*.

In the judgement of his contemporaries, however, it was not Heinrich von Morungen who embodied the ideal of *hohe Minne* but Reinmar von Hagenau, whose songs are today far less easy of access. Originally from Alsace, Reinmar carried the art of 'high' Minnesang from the western frontiers of the German realm to Austria – though he was perhaps not the first to do so – and established it, and with it his own position as court poet, in Vienna.

All his many songs (written before and after 1195) are in one and the same minor key of lamentation (*Minneklage*) and despair: 'Waz ich nu niuwer maere sage, desn darf mich nieman vrâgen: ich enbin niht vrô' ('Let no one ask me what new subject I am going to sing about: it is the old song – I am not happy'). In vain does he try to escape to the realm of joy to which even unrequited love is said to lead. To be sure, on one occasion he does lift his voice in praise of the ideal of the Noble Lady – 'O wol dir, wîp, wie reine ein nam!' ('Hail to thee, Woman, how pure thy name!') – and Walther von der Vogelweide praises this poem as being Reinmar's greatest contribution to *hohe Minne*, but in the next breath he returns to his lament that he receives none of the *hoher muot* with which she inspires the rest of the world, and that his whole life depends on her: 'stirbet si, sô bin ich tôt' ('if she dies, then I too shall be dead'). But as she will never be his, there is nothing left for him save to seek the perfect expression of his suffering: 'des einen und deheines mê wil ich ein meister sîn, die wîle ich lebe: daz niht mannes sîniu leit sô schône kan getragen' ('I seek to surpass all others in only one thing as long as I live – that no one should sing of his suffering with greater artistry').

Reinmar can indeed lay claim to this artistry, and his poetry, in which the intellect is more prominent than the heart, and in which there is not the slightest trace of reality, represents the *ne plus ultra* of courtly

Minnesang. It had only taken a few decades to reach this climax, and, however foreign the whole movement may appear to us today, we cannot but admire the sensitivity of the lords and ladies who listened to these songs with a fine appreciation of the refinements of emotion expressed within the conventions of courtship and lamentation, of the subtlety of the thoughts and the delicacy of the feelings.

But it is more than mere chance that in the rarefied atmosphere of the Viennese court there arose a young poet who was to break through the restrictions of 'high' Minnesang – Walther von der Vogelweide (born *c*. 1170). Like the young Goethe in Leipzig, Walther started with lyrics of courtship and unrequited love in the conventional 'artificial' style, yet already one seems to sense his dissatisfaction, and more personal, more optimistic notes find their way surreptitiously into his poems, until, at first playfully, he begins to oppose the attitudes of Reinmar, the established master. Rejecting the exaggerated terms in which Reinmar had extolled his lady at the expense of all others, Walther paints a realistic picture of an attractive woman, giving signs of the poetic mastery that was to come. Who knows what would have happened if he had stayed at the Viennese court? But his destiny led him elsewhere.

In 1198 his patron, Duke Frederick of Austria, died, and Walther, a *ministerialis* without fief, was forced to leave the sheltered conditions of Vienna, moving restlessly from court to court for many years and even finding himself from time to time among the wandering minstrels. Under their influence he became a *Spruchdichter*, and by bringing to *Spruchdichtung* his aristocratic attitudes and his superior poetic skill, he became a great political poet.

It is possible to trace with some certainty the course of Walther's wanderings. In the main he sought out the highest men in the Empire: for a time he was in the retinue of Philipp von Schwaben, then, after Philipp's death, in that of Otto IV; later he was in the service of the Emperor Frederick II; between times we find him in Eisenach with Landgraf Hermann von Thüringen, then with Markgraf Dietrich von Meissen, Bishop Wolfger von Passau, on a few occasions at the Duke's court in Vienna again, and with a few other identifiable patrons.

In his *Spruchdichtung* Walther preserves the monostrophic tradition (cf. Herger) but develops subtler, more artistic patterns and deals with the great political issues of the day. After the confusion in 1198, when rival factions elected two kings, he urged the princes to restore peace by crowning Philipp, praising him as the rightful wearer of the crown but openly warning him at the same time not to omit to display the royal virtue of generosity towards the princes.

Time and again Walther was roused by the intervention of the Pope in political affairs. He championed the Hohenstaufen conception of Empire as upheld by Philipp, Otto and above all by Frederick, and a contemporary complained that by the power and passion of his *Sprüche* against the Pope he had turned the heads of countless citizens. His attacks were always aimed, however, at the Pope in person, never at the Church – though he certainly wished to see it give up its earthly possessions and composed a poem in which a noble hermit, spokesman of a pure, spiritual Church, complains that the Constantine Donation is the root of all evil in Christendom.

Walther also composed a great number of didactic *Sprüche* of a general ethical nature, stressing the virtues of a harmonious life, urging young people to reflect on the old chivalric values of honour and decorum, preaching the ideal of Christian humanitarianism, scorning those who rack their brains over the secrets of God and writing a prayer in which a knight expresses his devotional thoughts and hopes at the beginning of the day.

For himself Walther besought his noble masters to reward him for his services by putting an end to the insecurity of his existence, and around the year 1220, when he received his long-desired fief, he thanked Frederick II in a *Spruch* of fulsome happiness for permitting him at long last to 'warm himself at his own hearth'.

Never before had the life of the time been reflected in such variety and such objectivity in German poetry as in the *Sprüche* of Walther. Quick to anger and to hate, but also spontaneous in affection, he found words and forms for every subject, and his confidence grew with the applause to which he was accustomed from kings and princes.

But at no time in his life was Walther just a *Spruchdichter*. Wherever he found a sympathetic audience, he would also write love-songs, and his Minnesang, too, gained in range and power of emotion during the years of his vagrancy. It is generally impossible to tell at which courts he wrote his love-songs, though a few suggest that he returned to Vienna around 1203 and renewed his poetic feud with Reinmar. But his tone has now changed. In deliberate contrast to Reinmar's admission that he is only singing an old song (cf. p. 55 above), Walther emphasizes that he is going to sing something new, and embarks with characteristic whole-heartedness on his well-known panegyric on German womanhood and on the country where its virtues reign.

On another occasion he becomes more aggressive towards Reinmar. The latter had made his life dependent on that of his lady ('stirbet si, sô bin ich tôt'; cf. p. 55 above); Walther, seeing that the poetic existence of the lady depends on the poet, makes the parodistic riposte: 'stirbet si, sô ist si tôt!' Reinmar had lamented that his unrewarded service of his lady had given him grey hair; Walther retorts mockingly that the lady is not getting any younger either, and he invites the young man whom she probably prefers to this elderly admirer to take vengeance on her by smoothing out her wrinkles with a whip.

This is no longer courtly poetry. But Walther could count on the support of his audience against his old rival; he had learnt how to use the aggressive power of language, and he used this power to parody the formulae of the Minnesang and carry its concepts *ad absurdum*. In his more serious poems too he shows that he considers the assumptions behind the Minnesang to be played out. What is *minne*, he asks, rejecting in his answer the restriction of the concept to the love-sick knight, for a one-sided love is worthless: 'minne ist zweier herzen wunne' ('love is two people's rapture'). He knows that, for all the praise lavished upon it, it is not beauty that brings real happiness but *liebe* (affection, charm), and that it is he himself who has exalted his lady by his songs, and that in her haughtiness she is denying him his rightful reward.

So he now changes the object of his praise to 'wîp diu kunnen danken' ('women who know how to reward a man'), thereby opening up a path to a new kind of song – the song of a natural, sensuous, happy love instead of *hohe Minne*, a song at whose birth the Latin poems of the wandering scholars and early German lyric poetry were also present. Now he sings of the red lips of his 'herzeliebez vrouwelîn', whose cheap ring with coloured glass in it is more precious to him than the gold ring worn by a queen. He moves among the girls at the dance, looking for the one who had charmed him in his dream, and describes in the most graceful terms an imaginary meeting with her under the shade of a tree. The girl too he has recall, wistfully and with the romantic memory of the nightingale, the time they lay together 'under der linden'. Nature and love have intertwined in a moment of supreme bliss.

But Walther goes even further, and in his search for the essence of *Minne* and *Liebe* he arrives at a compromise between *hohe Minne* and *niedere Minne*, a middle path between the unrealistic pursuit of an illusory ideal and the descent to a common, unworthy level. This middle path represents true love, the ideal relationship between man and woman: the man as 'vriunt und geselle' ('lover and companion'), the woman as 'vriundin unde vrouwe' ('lover and lady').

Walther's last poems, which must have been written when he was about sixty, show the wisdom of age, but there is no lessening of poetic power – quite the contrary. In one poem he takes leave of 'Frau Welt' in a half-regretful, half-teasing tone, while retaining his fundamentally religious attitude to life. In another, more solemn poem he combines with his farewell to 'Frau Welt' his final word to society, which he calls upon to testify that to the very end he had persistently striven after *werdekeit* (chivalric honour) and true, divine love. In a series of *Sprüche* connected with Frederick II's preparations for the crusade of autumn 1227 he laments, again on behalf of the world at large, his wasted years on earth and sees only one way for man to redeem himself before the Day of Judgement: 'nu sul wir fliehen hin ze gotes grabe!' ('Let us now make our pilgrimage to the Saviour's tomb.')

The Emperor's crusade of 1227 also stands as a symbol of salvation in Walther's famous Elegy. He visualizes himself waking from a long sleep: he sees the transience of all earthly life, above all in terms of the changes that have taken place since his youth – the fields are neglected, the woods have been burnt down and only the stream is flowing as it did before; young people have become lax, knights and ladies no longer live by the standards of chivalry; and the world has been plunged into mourning by the Pope's excommunication of the Emperor. The world is a fraud, says Walther: on the outside it is attractive but its heart is false; so leave it alone and find salvation by taking up arms in the defence of Christianity, as I would do, were I not too old; I would then no longer be saying 'Alas!' but 'All hail!'

Thus in what was probably his last poem, reminiscent of the *Nibelungenlied* in the broad solemnity of its rhythm, the ageing Walther, for all his weariness, sends out a clarion call to his fellow knights, a call which carries at the same time a note of divine forgiveness and consolation.

The three great epic poets of the 'classical' middle High German period also wrote lyric poetry, most of it probably in their youth. Hartmann stands mid-way between Hausen and Reinmar with his love-laments; his lord's death stirs greater depths in him, and in 1189 he goes on crusade in his memory, praising the virtues of this, the true love, and looking askance at his contemporaries who have not acquired a true sense of values.

Wolfram goes his own way. Stimulated by Provençal models, he becomes a master of the *Tagelied*, a genre particularly suited to his skill in vivid description, seen in the epic motifs of the breaking dawn and the final embraces of the lovers, as well as in the dramatic dialogues between the watchman, the knight and the lady. His most original poem is his 'Farewell to the *Tagelied*', in which the young husband tells how much greater is married bliss than the dangerous delight of the *Tagelied* situation.

Gottfried does not appear to have written courtly love-songs, but we have two possibly authentic *Sprüche* of his, written in the style of Walther, which consist of moral precepts based on Latin proverbs and presented in a harmonious, graceful strophic form. But Gottfried's real contribution to literature, like that of Hartmann and Wolfram, lies in the field of the epic.

Late Chivalric Poetry

The generation of poets born around 1190 learnt its art from its great predecessors. Problems of technique were therefore virtually non-existent: questions of metre and rhyme solved themselves. But these poets had been born into a changed world, the 'joyless world' of which the ageing Walther had written.

The last few decades of Frederick II's reign were a period of political, ecclesiastical and social confusion and instability in Germany, and the self-confidence of the nobility of Barbarossa's time, which had still been influential during his grandson's early career, was beginning to falter in the face of the changes that they could see coming. The poets of this generation thus succumbed to the fate of all *epigoni*: the great themes of the age had already received perfect formal expression, and, try as one may to emulate one's masters, art does not consist of mere repetition. The new values which were seeking expression could no longer be contained in the old forms.

At first sight there appears to be a flourishing literature during these years but it is lacking in real power and in a sincerity of devotion to the highest goals. There are Arthurian epics (Heinrich von dem Türlin) and love-romances (Konrad Fleck), and while some works have a certain charm and liveliness, others are dry and lifeless. Chivalric values are nothing but a veneer, and there is no question of seeking a new path to human perfection. Ulrich von Türheim felt moved to complete *Tristan* and *Willehalm*, but in the former there is nothing of Gottfried's spirit, and in the latter hardly anything of Wolfram's.

Religious epic – the 'heroic poetry of the Church' – which had filled the literary scene with its pious martyrs in the period before 1160 and almost completely died out by 1190, gradually began to reassert itself. Following the example of Konrad von Fussesbrunnen's *Kindheit Jesu* (*Childhood of Christ*) (*c.* 1210), Konrad von Heimesfurt told the story of Mary's death and ascension and Christ's agony, death, resurrection and descent into hell, after the manner of Hartmann; Reinbot von Dürne (*c.* 1240) wrote an epic on Saint George as a counterpart to Wolfram's *Willehalm*, using the elements of Wolfram's imagery, but without Wolfram's conviction and intellect, to turn the Christian martyr into a chivalric figure.

The most substantial epic poet of this generation is Rudolf von Ems (*fl. c.* 1220–shortly after 1250), a *ministerialis* of the lords of Montfort. His courtly religious legend *Der gute Gerhard*, telling of a noble, generous merchant of Cologne, whose unselfishness and humility put the proud Emperor's self-conscious piety to shame, is derived stylistically from the direct manner of Hartmann, with a number of disturbingly obtrusive features taken from Gottfried in order to heighten the emotional content. The emphasis in this first of Rudolf's religious epics is entirely on the description of festive ceremonies and the emotional tensions of shared joys and sufferings. His legend of *Barlaam und Josaphat*, on the other hand, rests on theological precepts, above all that of self-denial, and it is stylistically disturbing to find chivalric praise of women in a story whose express nature is in opposition to the values of the world.

In his *Alexander* Rudolf is concerned, as a learned compiler from all the 'historical' sources available to him, to produce the complete truth about the life and deeds of the great King of Macedonia, but this striving after truth does not prevent him from inserting a virtually unconnected but highly contemporary list of chivalric virtues in his account of Alexander's education, or turning Alexander's encounter with the Queen of the Amazons into a miniature courtly love story. The unfinished work amounts to some 22,000 lines, and Rudolf has lavished on it all the poetic skill at his command: the cross-rhymed quadrameters, with their acrostics and further rhyme-subtleties, at the beginning of each of the four 'books' have an ingenuity that surpasses even Gottfried.

Rudolf's courtly romance *Wilhelm von Orlens*, telling the love-story of William and Amelie, daughter of the King of England, is based on a French source which he expands with motifs from *Tristan*, *Parzival*, *Willehalm*, *Eneide*, *Gregorius*, *Floire*, and even from the *Nibelungenlied*, as well as with items of his own invention, to produce a large-scale epic. At the same time he leaves out all fanciful adventures of the kind found in Arthurian epic and gives the work as a whole the character of a historical novel.

Rudolf's last work shows that it was ultimately as a historian that he saw himself. In this huge *Weltchronik* in rhyme he was to have written the history of the six ages of the world from the Creation to the present. The work is dedicated to King Konrad IV but the 33,000 lines that Rudolf wrote before his death only cover his narrative down to the Book of Kings.

The work of Rudolf von Ems is both characteristic of his generation and points beyond it. Its content, a blend of the courtly and the religious, of history and courtly romance, is typical of his age and of the age that follows, for the future lay with religious poetry and the poetry of realism; its formal skill is as remarkable as Rudolf's knowledge of German literature, which he shows in his *Alexander* and his *Wilhelm von Orlens* by quoting long lists of poets: what Gottfried knew from actually participating in the literary life of his day had become for his successors an item to be ostentatiously displayed as part of one's education. Yet at the same time the later sections of the *Alexander* and long stretches of the

Weltchronik are written in the flat, dry style which was to replace the formal richness of the 'classical' period.

In the heroic epic, which remains restricted to the Bavaro-Austrian area, the *Nibelungenlied* is the unchallenged model. A fragmentary epic, *Walther und Hildegund* (possibly *c.* 1220), uses a modified form of the *Nibelungen-*strophe and tells its story in an attractively painstaking, if somewhat colourless, classicistic style. The poet of the strophic epic of *Kudrun* (1230–40) constructed his long, two-part work on the basis of a tradition whose precise nature and extent we cannot ascertain. He evolved his strophe from the *Nibelungenlied* and the *Titurel* fragments, producing a somewhat smoother, rounder pattern well suited to his heroic romance in which there is no real heroism; at the same time a number of strophes in the *Nibelungen* metre itself have found their way into his work. There is a similar carelessness in the way he tells his story, for he is often obscure and contradictory, lacks a clear sense of time and place, and has no definite picture of the course of the action as a whole.

His strength, which really only shows itself in the second part, lies in his description of states of mind, particularly of the two chief characters, Kudrun and Hartmut. Hartmut has a genuine love for Kudrun, whom he has abducted, and he therefore cannot bring himself to force her to yield to him, however much her unbending attitude pains him; he encourages his mother in her intention to break down Kudrun's obstinacy, because it corresponds to his deepest wish, yet he cannot bear to see her treated harshly. The result is a state of mind abounding in unfulfilled promises and frustrated developments. Kudrun herself, noble in her determination in the face of suffering and humiliation, is not a true heroic character but an intensely feminine, understanding person. It is not love that sustains her – there is no trace of affection for her betrothed – but *hêrheit*, an inner nobility of soul, a feeling that, because of her royal rank, stronger demands are made upon her than upon others. She has been abducted against her will, her father has been killed, and she is already betrothed to another man – this more than suffices to make her repel any advance.

Unforgettable is the scene after her encounter with her brother and Hartmut on the shore. She knows that the moment of her release is near and that any pretence of innocence is now over. It is her *hêrheit* which, after her pretence of reconciliation with Gerlind, makes her first demand that a bath be prepared for her – a symbol of the cleansing of her soul of the impurities in her life of bondage. Then comes the triumphant laughter which again threatens her release; and the next morning she is once more prepared, as a true woman, to save all who seek her protection, even her arch-enemy Gerlind, whom she grants and denies protection in one and the same breath.

It is no service to *Kudrun* to range it alongside the *Nibelungenlied* – where the poet no doubt hoped it would find its place. It lives in a different world and at a lower level; but there are also traces of true artistry in it.

In the field of the lyric the work of Neidhart von Reuental – the name is most likely a symbolic pseudonym – is something quite new, in content, form and spirit. His career can be traced from 1217, when he was at the Bavarian court in Landshut, to 1237, when he was at the ducal court in Vienna. His poems clearly reveal a thorough knowledge of the work of Reinmar, Morungen, Walther and other Minnesinger, but from the beginning they go their own way.

At the beginning of his career, Neidhart, possibly stimulated by Walther's 'natural' love-poems and by the Latin lyrics of the wandering scholars, wrote *Sommertanzlieder* for his courtly audiences – joyful songs telling of the amorous village maiden who, feeling the call of spring and enchanted by the appearance on the scene of Neidhart, the noble Minnesinger, is eager to join her companions in the dance on the village green; her mother, partly out of jealousy, tries to keep her from doing so, and the poem ends in argument, sometimes even with physical consequences, wittily described in an infectious atmosphere of jollity, delight in nature, pleasure in the gaily dressed girls at the dance, and the joy of love.

Neidhart's *Wintertanzlieder* are very different. Some of them strike a similar note to the *Sommerlieder* in their descriptions of the light-hearted, sometimes abandoned behaviour of the lads and girls dancing at the inn, but in most of them Neidhart views the world of the peasants with a certain bizarre hostility and no longer with tolerance. He mocks the stupid village yokels who ape the dress and mode of speech of their lords, and resents in particular their successes with the village maidens.

Nor does he stop here, for into his caricatures of the peasants he inserts strophes in the manner of 'classical' Minnesang, producing a jarring incongruity of style both in content and in language. And when, as he does, he makes the object of this *Minne* a village girl, he is exposing both the world of the peasants and the world of *hohe Minne* to the mockery of his audience. With these songs, a strange, incongruous mixture of nature-poetry, parody and scorn, Neidhart became the spokesman of a society which, tired of the old ideals yet without a new faith to put in their place, took refuge in laughter.

Also of an original cast of mind was Tannhäuser (born *c.* 1200), a nobleman from the Nürnberg area. His *Tanzleiche*, which consist of a straightforward narrative section followed by a short, lively conclusion, represent a new courtly dance-form in which, characteristic of the time, the measured steps of the courtly dance give way to the free and lively style of popular dances. The texts of his poems too – a confusion of seriousness, parody, bravado, technical facility, arrogance and lamentation – reflect the confusion of his age.

The rest of the considerable body of lyric poetry from the late courtly period shows no originality. Ulrich von Singenberg, Truchsess von St Gallen, followed the paths laid down by Walther, his revered master; a circle of Swabian noblemen in the entourage of Heinrich, son of Frederick II, composed songs of *hohe Minne* together with 'natural' love-songs, dance-songs in the style of Neidhart's cheerful *Sommerlieder* and *Tanzleiche* in the manner of Tannhäuser.

Mention may also be made of Ulrich von Lichtenstein (*fl.* 1222–55), a man of importance in the political and military life of Styria, who composed attractive, if somewhat affected songs of *hohe Minne* and nobility of mind. His autobiographical *Frauendienst* is a perfect example of how a man who was so closely identified with the public life of his time could yet affect to live according to the courtly ideals enshrined in literature, ideals to which, unlike many of his contemporaries, he remained faithful throughout his life.

In the field of *Spruchdichtung* Walther's line is continued by Reinmar von Zweter, Bruder Wernher and others, none of whom, however, can be compared with Walther in poetic ability.

The marked didactic quality of courtly civilization with its aesthetico-moral demands had virtually exhausted itself in the realms of epic and lyric poetry, which had been concerned to depict characters that were models of ideal conduct and also to press home the point with exhortatory speeches by these characters or with didactic, theoretical excursuses in Minnesang and *Spruchdichtung*. The late courtly period developed large-scale didactic poetry in its own right, seeking either to preserve the courtly heritage or to generalize its significance – though on the other hand certain poets turned away from it altogether.

Thus a poet known as Der Winsbeke, a nobleman from the East Franconian lineage of Windesbach, wrote a moral treatise (1220–30) in the form of a pattern of advice given by a father to his son on how to conduct his life. With a true medieval sense of values he starts with love of God and respect for the clergy, proceeds to the chivalric service of women through which a knight is made worthy of higher things, then arrives at the heart of his message, which he summarizes in the three concepts love of God, honesty and noble bearing – an attractive example of the medieval belief in the harmony of 'God and the world'.

Only a few decades later, however, Der Winsbeke's poem was continued by an anonymous poet who made the son urge his father to join him in withdrawing from the world and devoting his life solely to the pursuit of salvation. The new age completely obliterated the ideal picture of the medieval knight, a figure who rejoiced in life but was yet devoted to God.

Thomasin von Zerkläre (b. 1187), an Italian canon of Aquileja under Bishop Wolfger, a patron of Walther's, compiled a German manual of ethics 'for brave knights, noble ladies and wise clerics' under the title *Der wälsche Gast*. In the first book he puts out a code of etiquette for young noblemen, recommending them to read the courtly epics, and follows this with a discussion of *Minne* and the ideal of service for the lords and ladies of the court, thus incorporating the principles of chivalry – which had already lost a good deal of their superficial attractiveness under his practical gaze – into the pattern of his universal Christian ethic.

In the years leading up to 1229 a middle-class poet named Freidank wrote his *Bescheidenheit* ('Wisdom', 'Experience'), a work which, no longer part of the courtly age, subsequently became very popular. Freidank worked on a small scale, using two- and four-line strophes and an epigrammatic style rich in images; his words were no longer addressed specifically to the knights but to a general public, and his message is universal. The model that he held up to his age was of a serene trust in God, against which, without distortion but also without flattery, he viewed the virtues and vices of man.

Another poet who takes us into the following age is Stricker (*c.* 1220–40), whose didactic epics reveal an interesting personality. Stricker, probably a native of the Nürnberg area, arrived at his philosophy of life during his years of vagrancy, when he discovered poetic subjects congenial to his temperament. His first work was a reworking of the early Middle High German *Rolandslied* (Stricker's *Karl*); this was followed by an unsuccessful chivalric epic (*Daniel von dem blühenden Tal*) and then by an epigonal work in praise of courtly women, which he intended to work on throughout his life but which breaks off after a few thousand lines and is his final tribute to the chivalric ideal. Then, partly in response to the public desire for something new, but equally as an expression of his own nature, he turned to writing short realistic narrative poems and didactic verse – parodies, anecdotes, fables, parables and rhymed epigrams. Among his main subjects are scorn of a world which so easily allows itself to be deceived (the cycle called *Pfaffe Amis*); scorn for the triumph of cunning over lasciviousness and stupidity; lamentation over the moral degradation prevalent in all classes; sermons on lying, false flattery, quarrelling, fornication and superstition, and on the virtues of piety, prayer and repentance. His approach is that of critical objectivity and devotion to religious values; from the point of view of form his works are conventional.

As Stricker describes the scene, the exaggerated concern of the aristocracy with the ideals of the chivalric code has led to the very opposite, namely to dishonour and moral laxity. Thus the Minnesinger are to him the apostles of adultery, and if one of these versifying womanizers should find his way into someone's house and ask for shelter, the master of that house should fob him off with blossoms, leaves and grass, and with the song of the nightingale under the linden tree – for that is what the Minnesinger is always singing about.

The age of courtly literature ends on the note of Neidhart's scornful laughter and Stricker's mockery, and a world disappears which had striven, in its highest moments, to present in art a harmonious ideal of the fine, good, pious man. God and the world had now parted company, and when around the year 1300 Stricker's poems, a number of strophes by Freidank and some anonymous verses were strung together in a didactic anthology entitled *Die Welt*, it meant that man had lost his illusions and was now looking at the world with realistic eyes.

Late Medieval Literature
(1250 – 1500)

BRUNO BOESCH

The New View of Life

There is scarcely a period in German literature that so obviously lacks a focal point of attraction as the two centuries of the late Middle Ages. One's attention is first caught by the so-called 'autumn' of the Middle Ages, the period of decline and decay, the incomprehension, or levelling-down, of what the courtly age had brought to perfection. The interregnum only served to emphasize the change, and people became painfully aware how far their achievements lagged behind those of the past.

There was more to this feeling than the familiar praise of the 'good old days', for while old values were vanishing, few ventured to commit themselves to the new values that were emerging. Yet the situation was not one of utter disintegration, for the national spirit of the *Volk* was sufficiently strong to overcome these conflicts and contradictions, seeing in each such moment a trial and a challenge. Only in this way can one explain how the sixteenth century witnessed the rise of a new world in which people became aware of the forces that had long lain beneath the surface. Intellectually and formally the age looked backwards; but from the thirteenth century onwards the forces of life itself had been moving in new directions.

Seen from the modern point of view, the late Middle Ages have an air of apathy, of confusion, of purposeless agitation about them. We can sense the new age, but although many now utterly rejected the Catholic medieval view of the world, few were prepared to acknowledge the new attitudes. Men came to feel that this conflict was central to the nature of their age, an inevitable tension which it was their task to bear, and the earthly pleasures which they had succeeded in laboriously extracting for themselves from a life lived out in the shadow of death were perpetually threatened by the awesome question: where is this uncertainty and insecurity driving us?

The more varied, the more hectic life became, the more intensely its transience was felt. The paradox is already expressed in Walther von der Vogelweide's Elegy. Gone is the uplifting happiness of *hoher muot* and of being part of a chivalric community; the burden of care and worry settled on men's minds, and instead of gratefully accepting one's given share of life, one strained for a larger share, setting the pursuit of material things above spiritual values. The joy and confidence that come with knowing that one is beyond the reach of temptation and the devil only returns in the Reformation period and in particular in Luther, while the joy of living shown by the late Middle Ages springs from the release of pent-up sensuous forces, accompanied by feelings of anxiety and apprehension. Only in the blissful mysticism of a man such as Johannes Tauler does one find a true, heartfelt joy.

The age is preoccupied with the thought of death. Konrad von Würzburg, in his poem *Von der Welt Lohn* (*The World's Reward*), tells how an attractive woman ('Frau Welt') appears to the poet Wirnt von Grafenberg, who in his poem *Wigalois* had devoted himself to the praise of the world: when she turns her back to him, it is seen to be eaten away by vipers and repulsive vermin; so shattered is he by his experience that he goes on crusade and finds salvation. Such a mood enabled sermons and religio-didactic poems to have a profound effect on the age.

The plastic arts show the same contrasts: there are sculptures of 'Frau Welt' in the cathedrals of Worms and Basle, and of the vain libertine in the Sebalduskirche in Nürnberg; a readiness to be shocked and then to repent exists side by side with an urge to power and the pursuit of pleasure; a strong feeling of community in the rising towns is countered by a desire for personal wealth and influence and a determination to live in one's own way; and the age itself begins to feel the insolubility of the problem it has posed.

In the twelfth century Heinrich von Melk had summoned a courtly lady to the bier on which the body of her husband lay rotting, and the vision of the horror of death reappears in this late period, as, for example, on a gravestone of Count de la Sarraz in the Waadtland, who is depicted lying in his coffin, his body eaten away by toads and worms, while his wife and daughter gaze down upon him. This was the late medieval view of death, seen in mystic visions, in discursive sermons, in public displays of torture and execution, and in the self-inflicted chastisement of penitents. How different is the picture in Wolfram's *Willehalm*, where the lament over the dead Vivianz turns into an expression of yearning for the sweetness of death (60, 24ff.)! And how dignified, how full of *mâze* is the tombstone of the Minnesinger Otto von Botenlauben in Frauenrode, who lies serenely by his lady's side as though in sleep!

But the late Middle Ages knew no such reconciliation with death, and the mystics, for whom death as *exitus vitae, introitus melioris* had lost its terrors, found life empty, even perverse, compared with the shining beauty of a life in union with God. In Chapter 21 of his *Büchlein der ewigen Weisheit* Seuse talks of the art of dying a proper, gentle death and describes the cold sweat of the man who has not prepared himself for dying.

This is not the place to follow the decline of established institutions as manifested in historical developments, but the *Spruchdichtung* of the thirteenth century makes it clear that even the *ministerialis*, the most resilient class within the nobility, fell victim to the new power politics of the princes. Some of Walther's successors among the *Spruchdichter* felt called upon to defend the cause of justice: the principle of *triuwe* applied only as long as the lord was just; otherwise rebellion was not only a right but a duty, and many of the numerous disputes and feuds of the time conceal a brave determination to uphold chivalric ideals.

But the only victor in the struggle to preserve order was the strong personality, like the city merchant, who worked his way into key positions in urban life and introduced a new set of attitudes into a class-bound society. The peasant, too, gradually emerged from his inferior position – witness the defeat of well-equipped knightly armies by organized bands of peasants. Wherever one looks, in fact, one sees cracks in the existing order and forces ready to burst out in the exuberance of a new-found independence.

Yet there were also counter-forces at work, seeking to maintain the divine order of the world as it stood. Neither the clerics nor the monastic orders had complete answers to the layman's questions, and the rapid growth of heretical groups shows that people were enquiring into the nature of their faith and that the Church itself was in need of spiritual renewal and a greater attention to its pastoral duties. Dominicans and Franciscans followed vows of poverty and went among the people preaching; indeed the whole of the priesthood deepened its spiritual awareness through the power of mysticism. In this time of plague and physical danger urban communities developed a sense of solidarity, and this new spirit found expression in Gothic cathedrals. More profoundly and personally than ever before, yet with a confident sense of community, the layman confronted the demands of his Christian religion and allowed himself to be overwhelmed by such eloquent preachers as Berthold von Regensburg. What the Church lost in political power, it gained in spiritual influence. It could not restore the old order, and various councils showed the uselessness of trying to do so, but the ground was being prepared to receive the seeds of the Reformation.

The move towards mystic inwardness was matched by a remarkable change in attitude to the external, objective world. For although their view of the world, as far as its expression in art was concerned, was still confined in typical and allegorical schemes, with no trace of 'real experience', people were beginning to feel the meaning of personal existence, a personal spiritual life. The force of traditional national customs, for example, which had no place in courtly literature, began to show itself – not, it is true, for its own sake, but, as in the humour, the dance-scenes, the formal games and the *joie de vivre* of Neidhart's poems, still a force of which the poet willingly took account.

In Wittenwiler's *Ring* the chapters on the Christian ethic have almost a mocking quality, for the poet's undisguised delight in a world simmering with sacrilegious pleasures shows how powerless the ethic was. The comic interludes in the middle of dramas concerned to proclaim the message of Christian salvation have their place alongside scenes depicting the holiest of truths, thus pandering to man's proclivity for effect and variety and showing what concessions have to be made to 'real' life – as Shrove Tuesday is an officially acknowledged moment of 'real' life.

The juxtaposition of spirituality and naturalism can also be observed in the plastic arts. In a corner of Strasbourg Cathedral, that proud Gothic monument to the power of mind over that most intractable form of matter, stone, there is a small, realistically carved figure of a carouser about to take a deep draught from his glass of wine. The inscription bears the name 'Steimar' – perhaps the poet Steinmar, famed during his lifetime for his *Herbstlied* and for his commitment to a philosophy of realism and *joie de vivre*.

New Views of Literary Form

The change in attitude to aesthetic form is a reflection of a change in the external circumstances of literary life. The harmony between the court poet and his public no longer existed, and the unity of spirit that had informed 'classical' Middle High German literature was broken. A poet who preserved the courtly spirit or was himself a knight lacked a ready-made audience and became the continuator of a formal tradition that was sometimes more appreciated in upper-class burgher circles than among the aristocracy. He had to create a new public for himself, whether from the nobility or from the middle class, and satisfy the most varied tastes.

One thing demanded of literature by all classes was entertainment and novelty. Some poets complained of such fickleness and of a lack of public sympathy, sulkily regarding themselves as misunderstood geniuses, like Konrad von Würzburg. But such attitudes are not to be taken particularly seriously, for we may find that the poet who at one moment proclaims the divine origin of his muse admits in the next breath that he is concerned for economic reasons to write what people want to hear.

In the courtly period the concept of artistic skill was inseparable from the ethos of the age in whose interests this skill was deployed. There was a complementary relationship between being a knight and being a poet, and Wolfram, for one, realized that, divorced from the active pursuit of chivalry, his art would degenerate into a mere practical job and call into question its true role in society.

An inseparable part of the background of the court poet is his learned education from the monastery school, an education which Hartmann and Gottfried, for instance, regarded as vital to their chivalric concerns. The next step is the incorporation into this education of the art of poetry itself, so that the poet becomes a professional, a *Meister*. The intellectual aspect of poetry asserts itself more and more in this later period, whether by the blunt, 'un-artistic' presentation of subject-matter or by the ever-increasing decoration of the purely formal elements, whereby the content becomes obscure or even insignificant. The former tendency attaches itself to Wolfram, with his typically German love of the circuitous, the whimsical and the bizarre, but his imitators are without warmth of emotion and dissipate their energies in empty and derivative showiness. The latter movement, which proceeds from Gottfried, concentrates on verbal artistry and leads to dull, uninspired exaggerations, lacking the passionate intensity which sets its seal on the richness of Gottfried's own style.

The summit of this intellectual formal skill is reached with Frauenlob, the founder of Meistersang, in whom the tendencies meet. His learned, esoteric content is couched in highly sophisticated language and form and represents a final break with the courtly world; the middle-class pursuit of knowledge led to more and more abstruse subject-matter, much of which is unintelligible to the layman without a commentary, and an accurate, detailed assessment of Frauenlob's art has yet to be given. Meistersang itself, developing from such beginnings, was an art for initiates, and its exclusivity quickly led to its petrification.

The future lay, however, neither with the 'last of the knights' nor with the busy Meistersinger but with the 'sub-literary' popular art of the despised *Spielleute*, who, from being the propagators of what we call folksong, became a very varied social and artistic group in the late Middle Ages. Their poems may not show a consciously developed blend of content and poetic form but they do reveal a simplicity and a clarity of narrative reminiscent of the courtly *Tagelied* and *Pastourelle*, and acquire a quaint charm through this juxtaposition of contrasting courtly and *Volk* elements.

Between the formless assemblage of narrative events and the empty sophistication of formal conceits lies the 'middle path' of vivid, epic description exemplified above all by *Meier Helmbrecht*, as well as by Stricker and *Moriz von Craûn*. In works of this kind, as in some of the religious prose of the period, there are signs of an emerging style based on a true, objective reference to the subject-matter.

Urban Life and Gothic Piety

According to Freidank there were only three real classes in society: 'gebûre, ritter unde pfaffen' ('peasants, knights and clerics'); a fourth class owed its existence not to God but the devil: 'daz leben ist wuocher genant, daz slindet liute unde lant' ('this mode of life is called profiteering, and it devours everybody') (Freidank, 27, 1). In this respect a court poet like Rudolf von Ems, in his *Guter Gerhard*, shows himself well disposed towards the merchants, though his hero's virtues are unmistakably portrayed as deriving from his courtly qualities. In general, however, the literature of the age is severely critical of the contemporary lust for wealth; no less bitter is the general scorn, from nobles and burghers alike, for the peasants who try to rise above their proper station. At the same time, from Freidank onwards true nobility was seen to lie not in the nature of one's ancestry but solely in personal virtues and efforts. This is a universal classical/Christian standpoint, but there is little sign to start with that it was applied in a class-conscious sense. In Der Teichner and Konrad von Ammenhausen, however, it is repeated not simply as a general moral statement but with a sympathetic glance towards the peasant and the virtue that he earns with the sweat of his honest brow. Praise of the peasants becomes particularly frequent in the fifteenth century, and is even found in Shrovetide Plays.

That middle-class writers no longer set themselves up in favourable contrast to the much-scorned peasants but sing the praise of work in general is an indication of their growing self-confidence, for they too live by the work of their hands and can establish their own middle-class values without recourse to the chivalry of the past.

Of particular power in this age was the doctrine of the equality of all men before God. Rich and poor alike are to be found taking part in the Dance of Death, and visions of hell show the highest and the lowest languishing side by side. Man's only permanent possession, the only part of him which death cannot conquer, is his soul. In the *Ackermann aus Böhmen* the common man sets out to oppose death, and even though he has to bow to death's power, he preserves the honour of the man who strives with all the strength at his command to save his soul for God.

A common man, the Thuringian chaplain Johannes Rothe, wrote a *Ritterspiegel* (1412–16) in which he gave a significant answer to a nobleman's complaint that, while he was having to suffer restrictions in his own mode of life, a poor peasant's son could acquire a fortune. The condition for the knight to regain his position in society was *der gemeyne nutz* (the common weal); the traditional trappings of chivalry, such as tournaments, coats of arms, titles, rules of etiquette and the rest of the pomp and circumstance, count for little with Rothe, but he sees in the aristocratic merchant a possibility of preventing the utter impoverishment of the knights as a class and of saving them from sinking to the level of robber barons.

Spruchdichtung and other non-aristocratic poetry give us but a pale reflection of the religious agitation of the period. Sombre, fatalistic sentiments emerge from the songs of the Flagellants, from Dances of Death and from poems on the Day of Judgement; the sibylline prophecies are revived, and the message of doom is preached; the inspiration of the new monastic orders takes root; the efforts put into building of all kinds testify to the townsman's sense of community. A comparable sense of intense religious devotion – except in mysticism – does not emerge in literature, which seems to be more concerned with the practical expression of dogmas. These townsmen had, however, a considerable knowledge of the Bible, the Church Fathers and current dogmatic writings, and even secular literature stood under such religious influences.

The role of middle-class religious poetry may be compared to the art of the stained-glass window: the artists in this latter field worked within the broad context of the cathedral and designed allegorical, often bizarre pictures whose interpretation depended on a detailed knowledge of the Bible, and which testify to a close concern with Church dogma, often appearing as a kind of counterpart to the Meistersang. For the Meistersang itself the Church, as a religious musical community, was also a force in the background, though today the world of the Meistersinger is foreign to us, and its products appear merely as arid pseudo-religious exercises almost completely devoid of the colour of a stained-glass window. The paramount urge is to instruct, to make men better, whether by exhortation, by parable or by cautionary tale. Here are the roots *inter alia* of the *Narrendichtung* which reaches its peak in the sixteenth century. Here too lies the reason why the art of the late Middle Ages so rarely achieves the symbolic power of images like Neidhart's broken mirror or Meier Helmbrecht's cap. The characters and images of late medieval art have no life of their own; they exist only for a purpose, and when that purpose has been fulfilled, their existence ceases, crushed under the weight of the didactic intent.

Thus Reinmar von Zweter's ideal man has the eyes of an ostrich, the neck of a crane, the ears of a pig, the heart of a lion, etc. – in short, a bizarre, unreal creature as described but whose individual characteristics are chosen for their symbolic value. This allegorical mode of thought shows the extent to which art was conceptualized at this time, and it is no surprise that such intellectualization should continue into the sixteenth century – witness, for example, Ulrich von Hutten's poem beneath the woodcut of the *vir bonus*.

Mysticism could have freed art from the dangers of such abstractions, but in fact it had little effect on literature. Mystical prose, such as that of Mechthild von Magdeburg and Heinrich Seuse, became extremely beautiful, but there is no mystic poetry, notwithstanding a few works like the *Song of the Trinity* (*granum sinapis*), that can be compared with that of the baroque age.

Narrative and Didactic Genres

To review works and writers in terms of genres, i.e. in a series of longitudinal sections, is probably the most convenient way of following literary developments in this period. At the same time it becomes increasingly difficult to distinguish between the various genres, many of which are in a state of flux.

It is only to a limited extent true, for example, that the heroic epic, in the strict sense, is in strophic form, and the romance in rhymed couplets, for heroic subject-matter, its emphasis now on the excitement of the story, is sometimes found in couplets – the external expression of the break with a centuries-old tradition, for from the mid-thirteenth century all feeling for the tragic heroism derived from the age of the Great Migrations was lost. The *Hürnen Seyfrid* (earliest version *c.* 1300) is no longer concerned with fate but only with the adventures of the young Siegfried, and the chap-book of *Gehörnter Siegfried* (sixteenth century) follows in the same tradition. Similarly the old *Hildebrandslied* takes on a completely different nature in the course of the thirteenth century and becomes a popular ballad with a happy ending. Narrative poems, of a variety of lengths and subjects, make their influence felt in the fields of sung folk poetry and of written epic, and once the sequence of the adventures has become the only unifying principle, there is no formal limit to the length of such poems. As the romance *qua* form has virtually become a series of independent episodes, the *maere*, the individual tale, becomes the most fruitful narrative genre, and from an assemblage of such tales new larger-scale narrative forms can in their turn develop.

The successors of the courtly romance are characterized by a delight in the content for its own sake, the absence of a central problem derived from the realm of chivalry, an often crude mixture of the most heterogeneous elements, and in particular a fusion of historical and legendary material with supernatural, fairy-tale motifs. Writers could not resist completing works left unfinished by earlier poets: there were continuations of Gottfried's *Tristan*, while the *Jüngerer Titurel* (*c.* 1270) of Albrecht von Scharfenberg is a sombre elaboration of the story of the Grail in which Wolfram's own *Titurel* fragments are incorporated, albeit in an inferior, quite different role from that in Wolfram's uncompleted original. An interesting moment in this confused, obscure and generally unrewarding work is the description of the Temple of the Grail, which reminds one of a Gothic cathedral. Also in the wake of Wolfram stands the *Lohengrin* epic, written at the end of the thirteenth century.

These and other romances come together in Ulrich Füetrer's immense *Buch der Abenteuer*, compiled towards the end of the fifteenth century for the Duke of Bavaria. Füetrer's interest in his work, like that of Püterich von Reichertshausen in his *Ehrenbrief* (1462), is historical: chivalry has become a subject for romantically minded amateurs. In the period between these works and the epigonal epics of the thirteenth century there is very little of originality, and one is left wondering about the relationship between such works and the real life and ideals of the knights. At the height of the courtly period the 'chivalric adventure', however 'unrealistic' it was, reflected ideal values, and was therefore as 'real' as chivalry itself. With the decay of courtly civilization tales of chivalry became just attractive stories, in the same way that allegory became an escape into an ideal world beyond the reach of crude reality. Here belong Wirnt von Grafenberg's *Wigalois*, Heinrich von dem Türlin's *Krone* and Stricker's *Daniel von dem blühenden Tal*.

Alongside such works we meet attempts to preserve, or re-create, the relationship between the 'real' and the 'poetic' worlds. Ulrich von Lichtenstein did so by writing a fictional autobiography; to have written a factual one would have been to renounce all courtly illusion, for Lichtenstein was in fact a practical, hard-headed man, a real precursor of the Habsburgs. He thus wrote a stylized life-story based on courtly models, and may even have lived at times in the manner of these models so as to be able to describe such episodes in the course of his epic. Some of the more fantastic stories, such as his experiences in the guise of the Goddess Venus, were in fact acted in dramatic form at the time, rather as certain present-day ceremonies follow procedures described in literary sources or portrayed in painting. The refinement and subtlety of the language of Middle High German literature, with its highly developed vocabulary for describing spiritual and psychological circumstances, was of inestimable value in preserving something of the values and splendours of the age of chivalry. Such were its associations with the noble and the elevated that it long delayed the emergence of prose as the obvious vehicle for the narrative art of the time with its emphasis on events themselves.

Very different from Ulrich von Lichtenstein is Konrad von Würzburg (d. 1287), a middle-class poet from Basle, who counted foreign nobles, urban dignitaries and clerics among his patrons – a small, patrician circle, but Konrad still boasted that the majority of people misunderstood him. His style, modelled on Gottfried's, is skilful and refined, and he cultivates all the classical Middle High German genres. In his two large-scale courtly romances he pursues Veldeke's ideal of a fusion of classical mythology with the spirit of courtly chivalry: *Partonopier*, for instance, is a courtly fairy-tale derived from the story of Amor and Psyche. Of the *Trojanerkrieg*, his last work, left unfinished at his death, he wrote some 40,000 lines, greatly expanding his source, the *Roman de Troie* of Benedict de Sainte-Maure, particularly in descriptions of battles and tournaments and in the dialogue. This unfettered elaboration of the incidental gives his works a baroque quality which is particularly in evidence in the ornamental arabesques of his smaller poems such as *Die goldene Schmiede*, yet he was also capable of considerable achievements in the straightforward style of Hartmann.

In his romance *Wilhelm von Österreich*, completed in 1314, Johannes von Würzburg turned for his subject to recent history, only to embroider it with material from all kinds of sources, including his own invention. In this strange mixture of the real and the imaginary the author appeared to attach the greatest importance to his display of historical knowledge, yet in order to make the whole work a courtly romance of the kind his patrons wished to see, he added imaginary material and employed decorative artifices of style in order to supply the links to the courtly world which the bare narrative lacked.

Heinrich von Neustadt, a Viennese doctor, sets about gaining the ear of his time in a different way. His *Apollonius* (early fourteenth century) is equally rich in Oriental adventures, but at the same time the trappings of external reality are colourfully described in great detail. He achieves a further contrast by introducing into a world of incredible escapades a personal note of concern for the fate of each individual character.

Shorter narrative poems, sometimes known as *maere* (Stricker), had already emerged during the courtly age. Their subject-matter is often Oriental, drawn from collections of tales brought to Europe by returning crusaders and preserved in Latin or French sources. In the forefront is the narrative itself, but in contrast to the fairy-tale, which moves in a world of its own, the *maere* has a didactic purpose, namely, to show the selfishness and folly of man. Thus as in *Moriz von Craûn* the countess denies her knight the reward due to him for his love, she is portrayed as foolish and sinful, and made to suffer for it. In Konrad von Würzburg's *Herzmaere* the jealous husband gives his wife the heart of her lover to eat.

There is no firm dividing-line between *maere* and *Schwank* (anecdote), the latter being a story intended to arouse laughter, while the former promotes contemplation and may even use tragic subjects, as do the Old French *lais*, as opposed to the *fabliaux*.

Meier Helmbrecht, the work of a minstrel of the second half of the thirteenth century who called himself Wernher der Gärtner, is a particularly accomplished achievement. As Neidhart had poked fun at the headgear worn by Hildemar, the farmer's boy, so Helmbrecht's remarkable cap, with its courtly decoration, becomes here the mocking symbol of the urge to rise beyond one's proper station in life. At the end of the poem the young Helmbrecht, who no longer wants to be a country lad but whose career as a would-be knight is held up to the reader's scorn as that of a mere plunderer, stands before us as a blind, mutilated wretch ripe for the gallows: the man who betrays his origins meets the same fate as the robber baron, for the rule of law, in the form both of *ordo* and of the justice by which order is restored, is inviolable and incorruptible.

> gesagt ich nie iht wâres,
> doch sult ir mir gelouben
> daz maere von der houben,
> wie kleine man sie zarte.

(Even if I had never spoken a word of truth in my life, you would have to believe my story of how they ripped his cap to shreds.)   (1892 ff.)

Wernher der Gärtner is telling us a true story; he has seen such things for himself. But to reduce it to a concept, or even to embody it in a typical series of actions, is not enough: it has to be given topical reference in time and place, and, whatever the moral message, there has to be a central factual truth – that Helmbrecht's cap really was torn to pieces. *Helmbrecht* is also full of warm, human touches, such as when the mother gives Helmbrecht a piece of bread after he has been turned out of the house.

In spite of the extent to which the real life of the time is mirrored in the poem – and this is the source of its educative purpose – we do not find a 'realistic' view of the world in it. As everything is subservient to the action, so the action is governed by what is typical and exemplary. The only moments of 'free' reality occur in incidental descriptive episodes.

As time goes on, the *Schwank* tends to displace the *maere*. The transition is marked by omnibus collections of tales – like those in Stricker's *Pfaffe Amis* – centred on a single character – Reynard the Fox, Neidhart, Kalenberger, etc.; these are then joined by typical, anonymous characters – the wandering scholar, the wicked old woman, etc. The development of character- and situation-types in these stories runs parallel to that in the folksong; of such situations that of adultery is the most popular, and the crudity and indecency of some of these poems beggar description.

Related to this shorter narrative verse is didactic poetry. Education is most effective when combined with entertainment, and the *bîspel*, the short anecdote, of Stricker is an example of an introductory story to a moral message. The *Predigtmärlein* ('sermon tale') used by preachers in their sermons is another case. Pure didactic poetry follows the lead given by Thomasin von Zerklaere and Freidank, but such works no longer treat fundamental issues like that of the union of the Christian and the chivalric life but deal with external matters of conduct, particularly at the dinner-table, in love (*Der Minne Regel*, thirteenth century) and in the relationship between social classes. Thus in Heinzelin von Konstanz's *Von dem Ritter und von dem Pfaffen* two women discuss the relative virtues of priest and knight as lovers; the decision was to have been given by Frau Minne herself, but the end of the poem is missing. Hugo von Trimberg's *Renner* (*c.* 1300) is a moralizing poem of over 24,000 lines which discusses the qualities of all the social classes: Hugo has little sympathy for courtly poetry, for example – indeed, the whole work, confused and formless except for its class-structure, has an air of somewhat elderly disapproval about it; there are endless personal digressions, and by calling his work the *Renner* Hugo seems to have realized that his diffuse sermon would not have the power to cure human weaknesses through its content of Christian knowledge and morality.

Poems of this kind bear the appropriate title of *Spiegel* – they hold up a mirror in which the various classes are meant to recognize themselves. Johannes Rothe, for instance, a canon at Eisenach, wrote a *Ritterspiegel* shortly after 1410. The game of chess, interpreted by one Jacobus de Cessolis towards the end of the thirteenth century in a Latin prose work translated into German in 1337 by Konrad von Ammenhausen, a Swiss lay-priest, provides a framework for a brief, effective description of the social classes, with a few words of blame or praise in each case.

In the satire *Des Teufels Netz,* from the same area (Thurgau) – which is also that from which Wittenwiler's *Ring* comes – the allegorical framework is the trap in which the devil catches man: the devil tells a hermit of all the victims he has caught in the net, the result being a catalogue of vices, with little poetic value.

Of an utterly different quality is the deservedly famous and popular satire *Das Narrenschiff*, by Sebastian Brant, printed in 1494 in Basle. This too has the typically medieval allegorical framework (the ship going to Narragonia with a cargo of fools (*Narren*)), and proceeds by listing all the passengers on the ship like the items of an inventory and exposing them to mockery. The idea of treating a particular vice as an inborn human folly had already been found in the medieval *Schwank* and in the Shrovetide Play, but Brant's work is remarkable for the breadth and perceptivity of its observation, even down to the slang used by the rogues of Basle.

Allegory, fable and satire are particular forms of didactic literature.

Allegorical personification was widespread in the Middle Ages – Frau Minne, Frau Welt, Frau Kunst, etc. A figure such as Wolfram's Frau Aventiure, however, is not symbolical, since she is simply a spokesman for her creator; in Gottfried's love-grotto, on the other hand, it needs to be explained – through the *Minnelehre* – that what we see stands for something else which cannot be presented in visible form. Thus whereas the symbol stands for what it is *and* for what it means, the allegory has no meaning of its own but is purely a figment of the poetic imagination. There is a connection between this and the nominalistic mode of thought common from the fourteenth century, according to which the world of ideas cannot be apprehended through individual physical objects.

This is the source of the vision of an ideal world which is only accessible to the poet who withdraws from everyday reality. From the poetic point of view there is a certain attractiveness in such allegorical presentations, but it is a chilling contrast to discover that such elaborately constructed figures are there only in order to convey a moral message. Allegorical meaning was what mattered, and every gesture, every colour had to have its hidden meaning.

Love-allegories were particularly popular, as was the theme of the law-court. In Konrad von Würzburg's *Klage der Kunst* a charge has been brought against feigned affection, and in the allegorical poem *Der Minne Gericht* (1449) the court consists of nine tents, above the entrances to which are plaques with inscriptions which are explained one by one, and with coats of arms on which the gem-stones are called the Grail. Painstakingly the poet explains the significance of all this, for no part of the meaning must be omitted. In other poems we encounter an Academy of Love where instruction in love is given, a Hospital of Love where the love-sick are healed, and a Monastery of Love where the doctrine of love is put into the form of a monastic rule.

The animal-allegory, the fable, is more entertaining. Ulrich Boner's *Edelstein* (mid-fourteenth century), for example, tells in a plain, unassuming manner its stories drawn from Aesop and other sources, without allowing the moral to become too obtrusive.

The didactic tendency is at its liveliest and most topical, however, in the satire. One such work is *Seifrid Helbling*, a series of fifteen satirical poems written around 1300 by an anonymous minstrel and named after one of the characters in the poems. Drawing on the circumstances of his own native area, the poet, a man of experience, rails against the immorality of the times, against the neglect of the courtly virtue of *triuwe* and against the vices of the individual classes of society, though admitting with the wisdom of maturity that he himself also stands in need of God's mercy.

The most striking work, however, in which biting yet amusing scorn is combined with the Christian message is Heinrich von Wittenwiler's

Ring (*c.* 1400), based on a witty and sometimes obscene *Schwank* in the Neidhart tradition called *Von Mayr Betzen*. From this anecdote of a village wedding Wittenwiler develops a large-scale epic, with full-blooded descriptions of real life, imaginative episodes, a satirical intent yet a pleasure in life as it is.

Interspersed in the main narrative are various *Spiegel*, small manuals of Christian behaviour, which contain a message of their own. The poet, who may well have derived his knowledge and experience from having been a lawyer at the court of the Bishop of Constance, has also marked with coloured lines in the margin which parts are serious and which parts belong to the wedding story – for life is just such a mixture of seriousness and frivolity. The mirror of Christian virtue is continually held up before the lewdness of common life but has little effect, and although they have been warned, the people pick a trivial cause for making war, and the village of Lappenhausen is razed to the ground.

Yet this spells neither the debasement of the Christian message nor the ultimate victory of man's animal nature. Far from passing judgement, the poet is concerned to present the conflict of irreconcilables, and as in the discussion on the pros and cons of marriage, he shows the lawyer's concern to enable both parties to give an honest account of themselves. Only in this way can the contrast be maintained, as everything the Christian message stands for is destroyed in the merciless reality of peasant life, culminating in the battle in which the demons, symbols of human senselessness, fight side by side with the soldiers of the Confederation and the troops from the towns.

Significantly, however, this tension does not lead to truly realistic description; the style is exaggerated, bizarre, powerful, but there are only occasional moments of genuine sympathy for human weakness and the suffering caused by human folly. We also find symbolic characters like old Helmbrecht, characters to whom a combination of positive and negative qualities give a certain human warmth. But however much understanding the poet seems to have for the common world and its faults, the narrative itself allows no reconciliation. Bertschi Triefnas, who has successfully defended his folly to the end, leaves the ruins of his home and becomes a penitent hermit in the loneliness of the Black Forest. Yet this decision too has the note of folly about it; it is only the moral principle itself, *in abstracto* and free of human application, that retains a serious meaning. The artistic unity of the work is thus based on the pessimism of the age, and the most vigorous characters that works such as Wittenwiler's *Ring* present are made to suffer for their realization of the duality of life.

As a whole, religious literature in the 'high' Middle High German period was overshadowed by courtly literature but without disappearing completely. Around 1300 and later it reappears, to be absorbed in the fourteenth and fifteenth centuries in prose, like the courtly epic. In the form of religious legends it had been cultivated by court poets themselves, and Konrad von Würzburg continues Hartmann's tradition in *Silvester*, *Der heilige Alexius*, *Pantaleon* and above all *Engelhard*, which may be compared in some respects to *Der arme Heinrich*. Like the *maere*, the religious legend satisfied the urge for something strange and miraculous. Konrad von Würzburg employs his technical skill to the full in his *Goldene Schmiede* (= *Geschmeide*, jewellery), a sophisticated poem in praise of the Virgin Mary, elaborately decorative, probably written in order to attract contributions towards the resumed construction of Strasbourg Cathedral between 1250 and 1275 and to encourage the faithful to join the Fraternity of the Holy Mother.

Like epics, legends began to be assembled in collections (*Väterbuch* (*c*. 1280); *Passional* (*c*. 1300)). A late follower of Konrad von Würzburg is Kuonze Kistener, an Alsatian, whose pilgrim legend *Die Jakobsbrüder* (*c*. 1350) was set in contemporary times. Poetic works also served to transmit a knowledge of biblical stories before the appearance of the first complete prose translations of the Bible. One of the last such works, a *Summa* in which the biblical narrative is supplemented by explanations of the principal tenets of Catholic dogma, is the Middle German poem called *Die Erlösung* (*c*. 1300). Its flowing style, its strophic prologue and its verbal ingenuity show its indebtedness to Gottfried; in form it is simply an assemblage of scenes from the Old and New Testaments – Creation, Paradise, Fall and Redemption.

These epic works are remarkably close to drama; construction in terms of self-contained scenes comes from religious plays, which were in their turn influenced by the epic narrative manner. Above all the proximity of the two genres is seen in the popularity of dialogue as a means of serving their didactic purpose. A popular formal framework for the dialogue was also the court trial.

Prose, as opposed to poetry, comes into its own in the most important work of around 1400, the *Ackermann aus Böhmen*, in which Death is prepared to embark on the dispute with the peasant only because the latter agrees to dispense with rhetorical 'poetic' devices and maintain a sober, reasonable tone. The author presents himself as an honest country labourer; at the same time, by setting out to oppose the omnipotence of Death, he also reveals his simpleminded folly. In rejecting his *superbia*, his attempt to go beyond man's proper limits, the work is entirely medieval in character: only when Death scorns man as such (Chapter 24) is the much-abused Ackermann, who had just presumed to change the divine order of things, permitted in the name of that same divine order to refute the charge. For through this upright, hardworking countryman the work also presents the image of a noble humanity – the Franciscan teaching that even the poor man is close to God and that the soul takes on the nature of God. In His judgement God makes both parties, the Ackermann and Death, aware of their limitations: 'Der claget, das nicht sein ist, diser rumet sich herschaft, die er nicht von im selber hat. Jedoch der krieg ist nicht gar one sache: ihr habt beide wol gevohten; . . . Darum, clager, habe ere! Tot sige!' ('The one complains about what is not his; the other usurps an authority that belongs elsewhere. Yet the struggle has not been without purpose. You have both fought well . . . So, plaintiff, all honour to you. And death, be victorious!')

The author of *Der Ackermann aus Böhmen* is Johann von Tepla, who was born about 1350, was Rector of the Lateinschule in Saaz from 1383 and also town-clerk, and died in Prague-Neustadt as notary public before 1415. The humanity which expresses itself in the concluding prayer infuses the entire work, whose language is as polished as its meaning is vital. Its rhetorical devices are derived from the so-called *geblümter Stil* of writers such as Heinrich von Mügeln, and are certainly not free from affectation. Its syntax shows the influence of the legal language of the time in the use of tripartite sentence-constructions and in the rhythmic pattern of the cadences; the influence of early humanism in Prague is also apparent.

At the same time the encomium of man and woman which the much-abused Ackermann is allowed to give is already foreshadowed in late-medieval literature, particularly in convivial social lyrics in which the qualities of the noble countryman and his virtuous wife are sung – the latter being seen as the people's equivalent of the courtly lady of the Minnesang. Death's tirade against women is modelled on the Shrovetide Plays and *Schwänke* on the subject of 'the bad woman'.

Thus the influence of contrasts is again decisive in the formation of the work: the disputation has both a learned and a popular source; there are popular poems in which the seasons struggle with each other for priority as there are Meistersinger poems which argue the relative virtues of the terms *wip* and *vrouve*. There are in the *Ackermann* linguistic and stylistic features which are derived from early humanism, but in general it is its medieval character that predominates. In the words of Huizinga: 'Novelty of form precedes novelty of spirit'.

Prose literature can be traced back to Old High German times, but in general it had been restricted to practical items – legal documents, sermons, treatises – and the mystics and great preachers of the late Middle Ages were the first to give it literary status; before this, in religious and secular literature alike, only poetry (despite occasional ecclesiastical suspicion) had been granted literary status. But it was a long while before poetry was deliberately laid aside. Even with the decay of a feeling for metre, the poetic line was retained, though now with the cadences of prose, so that the prose romances of the fifteenth century do not come as something completely new. Indeed we even have a few fragments, chiefly of the Lancelot story, which show that the change to prose had in a few places already taken place in the thirteenth century.

The primitive nature of the language in early prose works shows that the authors were solely concerned with the content, and the conscious development of a prose style occurs, not in 'literature as art' but in areas where the use of prose, written and spoken, had long been other than literary, such as religious treatises, letters, legal documents, contracts, public proclamations, interrogations, disputes; even verse-sermons use the spoken cadences of everyday usage. From the thirteenth century onwards all those affairs for which Latin had been used, or in which dealings had been oral, gradually came to be recorded in the written vernacular, but only in a few rare cases where an unusually creative mind was at work do we encounter a prose which betrays a deliberate artistic intent.

The influence of preachers such as Berthold von Regensburg (d. 1272) must have been considerable. Here for the first time we hear the living sounds of the Middle High German spoken language, an everyday language intensified in the courtly style with a dramatic, vivid power of expression which even a modern transcription can convey. To this newly released power of expression is now added the intense spiritual experience of mysticism. Mysticism is an expression of spiritual desire in time of trouble, and the schisms of the late twelfth century make it easy to understand the emergence of a longing for unity, for spiritual union with God and the state of grace in which to receive Him. The visions of Mechthild von Magdeburg (*Das fließende Licht der Gottheit* (post-1250 and originally Low German but preserved in an Upper German version by Heinrich von Nördlingen, *c.* 1340)) bring a great enrichment of the language as she strives to capture the intensity of her experience of the divine and express the fervour of her emotions. Without the language of the Bible, particularly the Song of Songs, together with the introspective vocabulary cultivated in the Minnesang and by Gottfried, her task would surely have proved insuperable.

Also of vital linguistic importance is Meister Eckhart's development of conceptual vocabulary, either in the form of new words or of existing words invested with figurative meanings which they have retained to this day, such as *Eindruck, Eigenschaft, Einkehr, Wesen, Zufall, innig, eigentlich, wesentlich, begreifen, fühlen, einleuchten, entrücken.* Similarly Heinrich Seuse (d. 1366 in Ulm) expressed his mystical experience in a style that recalls both the delicacy and decorativeness of the late Minnesang and the objectivity of Hadlaub's descriptive poems, a style that inspires and at the same time affords insight into the secret recesses of a soul dominated by the thought of God. The tone of the sermons of Tauler, on the other hand, is earthy, practical and more varied in its moments of contemplation.

Lyric and Gnomic Verse

The turning-point for the courtly lyric came with Neidhart, in whose lyrics the tone of mocking laughter fell both on the peasant who affected a mode of life above his station and on courtly manners themselves. Particularly in the south, however, the conventional Minnesang continued to be cultivated, and around 1300 it experienced something of an Indian summer in Swiss aristocratic and prosperous middle-class circles. An important result of this interest was the collection and preservation of *Minnelieder* in sumptuous manuscripts, the largest and most famous being the so-called Manesse Song-Book. Chief among these South German poets were three Swabians – Burkhart von Hohenfels (d. 1255), who followed Walther's *niedere Minne*; Schenk Ulrich von Winterstetten (*c.* 1280), whose dance-songs are reminiscent of Tannhäuser, and Gottfried von Neifen (mid-thirteenth century), whose song about his lover's rosy lips achieved proverbial popularity.

This late efflorescence of Minnesang shows an ingenious blend of the old and the new, and Konrad von Würzburg, for one, drew certain motifs from it for his own courtly lyrics, which were universally dedicated to the 'fair sex'. But some of Neifen's songs no longer belong to this world. In his poems of 'The Girl at the Spinning Wheel' and 'The Flax Weaver' the rural background seems to exist in its own right, and the genuine ballad-like opening creates an atmosphere of folk-poetry far removed from the courtly world. His gentle 'Lullaby' also has the allusive tone of the folksong: the central idea is not expressed but merely hinted at, and the mood of the whole is conveyed by the refrain.

The *Tagelied* shows the same development: in that of Steinmar, for example, the individual stages in the action acquire greater independence, and what had been a genre dealing with a typical, undifferentiated situation has become an original blend of *pastourelle* and folksong. An *Abendlied* by Hadlaub also describes in simple narrative terms how the lover made his way into the castle to meet his lady, while other similar poems bring the Watchman into the foreground, characterizing him as a miserable coward instead of leaving him, as in the conventional *Tagelied*, as a shadowy figure in the background.

Steinmar was of noble birth but towards the end of the thirteenth century he renounced his title and lived as an ordinary citizen in Waldshut. This decision is reflected in his poetry. In his *Herbstlied*, for instance, he does not parody village life as an outsider, like Neidhart, but becomes part of it, taking over the inn after the death of the landlord and joining the inner circle of carousers. To be sure, this is to a large extent play-acting, but it is significant that the poet is stimulated by popular poetry to give himself over so completely to a life of revelling and pleasure-seeking.

The originality of Hadlaub (early fourteenth century), a burgher of Zürich, emerges from his first six poems. They are based on personal experience but are also informed by a faith in the educative power of traditional courtly Minnesang; they are basically narrative in style but with attractive scenes from everyday life, particularly in the poem 'Ach ich sach si triuten wol ein kindelîn'. His other poems, too, retain a wistful, elegiac tone, even where, following Steinmar, he allows the forces of realism to make themselves felt. Both as an unhappy lover and as a citizen he sees himself as an outsider, an onlooker, and the realistic, everyday scenes are only there in order to emphasize his loneliness – though the contrast becomes crude when he is required to prove the constancy of his love by refusing to eat a dish of pig's trotters and sausage. There was nothing deliberately comic about this: he was simply using real-life situations instead of the conventional nature-scene to offset his elegiac mood.

If one were looking for progressive moments in the lyric poetry of the time one would find them in Tannhäuser, or in the poem 'Hie bevor do wir kint waren' by Der wilde Alexander, a wandering minstrel, in which the pleasure of two children playing in the wood is described in a remarkably modern manner.

Very different is Hugo von Montfort (1357–1423), who writes in his poems of his own aristocratic world in which his courtly lady is at the same time his own wife. He affects a decorative style but his content is dry and uninspired, and his four-line strophes have an awkwardness which betrays a technical insecurity. Artistic skill at this time is to be found not in the aristocracy but in the middle classes. Interest attaches also to the fact that Hugo did not compose the music to his poems but had it written by one Burk Mangolt.

The most gifted lyric poet of the period is Oswald von Wolkenstein (1377–1455), a man whose adventurous life is reflected in the remarkable range of his poetry – poems of travel and personal experience, love-songs, nature songs, pastoral idylls, confessional poems, political and moral *Sprüche*. In all the remarkable events that he describes he himself is always at the centre, and he conveys his reactions in a rich language characterized by a somewhat undisciplined expansiveness and vividness of image and allusion. 'Ich Wolkenstein!' he cries, making himself the focal point of his rich mosaic of events and impressions, composed of elements chosen at random – a true medieval characteristic.

Yet he is also a split personality and can only contain the doubts and sufferings that torment him by adopting an attitude of humorous irony. Thus although, as he admits, he easily gives way to the temptations of sin, he is also desperately concerned for his salvation; or, having been persuaded to go on pilgrimage, he suddenly changes his mind.

Wolkenstein is a typical late-medieval character, the first poet to portray himself in his work as we know him to have been in life. But he is a lone figure – he even bears traces of the Italian Renaissance – and he seeks to collect the scattered remains of the past at a time when the disintegration of the Minnesang is beyond recall. As a relic of a bygone culture, the concept of *Minne* outlived the forms that it created; Oswald destroyed the cultivation of these forms, using whatever weapons he could lay his hands on – not least those available in the national popular tradition – leaving only detached, empty words.

It is not true to say, however, that Minnesang merges into the anonymous folksong, for it was preserved in the bourgeois genres of *Spruchdichtung* (gnomic verse) and Meistersang. Convivial community songs attracted many of the elements of the decaying Minnesang and have a stronger artistic element in them than the folksong.

So-called historical folksongs are different in kind, as different from true folksongs as the chronicle is from the chap-book. The most important such collection, the *Liederbuch* of Clara Hätzerlin, was compiled in Augsburg in 1471, and also contains love-songs, *Tagelieder* and poems by Muskatblüth, Wolkenstein, Suchensinn, Suchenwirt and others. Like song-books from other towns, that of Clara Hätzerlin also includes melodies and testifies to the co-existence of popular song and learned Meistersang.

The greatest effect of bourgeois morality was felt in the *Spruch*. Little was now left of the noble religious, moral and political concerns of Walther and Reinmar von Zweter, the great names in this field. However, in Hardegger's *Spruch* 'Ich bin ûf einer verte, da mich niht erwenden mag' we still find the sense of honour of the man who is committed to the truth of his message and uses his talents in the service of particular patrons. And, as always, the poet's approval or disapproval of a patron depends almost entirely on the generosity or otherwise of the poet's treatment. Moreover the fact that they all made a livelihood suggests that their role was rather like that of journalists, and that they were not without influence. Many called themselves *Meister* and had had a learned education, and with a certain pride they set about the task of impressing their fellow citizens, who were anxious to improve themselves, with moral utterance and scholastic wisdom.

Friedrich von Sonnenburg (*fl.* 1247–75), for example, showed how, solely on the basis of a mastery of the gentle, decorative style, one could present a glowing picture of the Christian miracles and of the elevated nature of art; at the same time he had no qualms about writing poems openly demanding money from his patrons.

One of the most learned of these *Spruchdichter* was Marner, who frankly admitted that he had picked up the imagery and the other refinements of his art from the works of the great masters of the past. The modern notion of plagiarism was unknown in the Middle Ages, but lyric poets were expected to show originality in melody and strophic form. On the other hand the Meistersinger, at least down to Hans Folz, based the rules of their art on the strophic forms of the so-called Twelve Old Masters (the list does not remain constant), and all aspirants to the rank of Meistersinger had to compose in these forms.

The founder of the Meistersinger art was Heinrich von Meissen, called Frauenlob (d. 1318 in Mainz), who claimed to be able to teach the knowledge of theology, rhetoric and metrical form, which were the basic requirements of this art. The song-contest, the roots of which lie in the activities of religious lay choirs, led to the songs, having been assessed by the experts, being sung in church and thus acquiring a religious significance, while the poets began to see themselves as high priests of the Goddess of Art. In Frauenlob this feeling shows itself in an undisguised pride in his own verbal facility; then, using the theological analogy, he seeks to get to the 'essence' of his subjects and find a 'profound meaning', thereby linking his decorative style with an argumentative rationality.

The 'middle-class' quality of this poetry lies only in the fact that it is the product of a class which, feeling the lack of an independent tradition of its own, sought to work its way up by learning – more through impression then by intellect – from the masters of the courtly tradition and from theological scholasticism. Abstraction and preciosity go hand in hand, and such is the obscurity of his thought that he weaves a web of words in which one easily becomes entangled. Modern lyric poetry may well be a more appropriate point from which to approach Frauenlob's ecstatic, flamboyant language.

A more profitable, if soberer, line of development was that followed by Teichner, an Austrian poet who died around 1377. Using the words that Wolfram had used, he introduces himself as a member of the unlearned laity, and his generally uninspired verse virtually belongs to the category of didactic literature. The same is true of Suchenwirt, Rosenplüt and Folz (the latter two citizens of Nürnberg who flourished at the beginning of the fifteenth century), who, however, also indulged in experiments in a florid style and in crude, sometimes indecent subjects.

Drama

The origin of religious drama lies in the church celebration of Easter and Christmas. In the simplest manner clerics dramatized episodes from the Bible, accompanying them with texts drawn from liturgical hymns as a kind of commentary on the action, and subsequently recasting the biblical narrative in dialogue form in such scenes as Mary buying oil and spices on her way to the tomb, or Mary Magdalene's encounter with Jesus as a gardener, or the race between Peter and John to Jesus' tomb. The greater the extent to which such scenes are introduced, the more frequent become the opportunities to use everyday language, such as that of the pedlar of oils and spices in the market place, and eventually the plays were transferred from the church to the square in front of the church, and thence to the market place, where they turned into enormous spectacles which lasted for days and spurred the troupes of actors to great feats of dramatic performance and production.

The oldest fully developed German Easter Play, the *Osterspiel von Muri* (mid-thirteenth century), already has this juxtaposition of religious poetry (particularly impressive in the lament of Mary Magdalene) and realism (the pedlar, or the violent behaviour of the watchmen at the tomb).

It is only in drama that the transition from Latin to German coincides with the newly released power to express personal experience and feeling. In Passion Plays this takes the form of a personal confession of one's need for salvation, and it is a feature which persists from the twelfth-century *Mariensequenz aus Muri* to the fifteenth-century Low German *Bordesholmer Marienklage* – this latter being the most considerable achievement in a genre which is related to the Passion Play but has its roots in the *Planctus ante nescia* of Gottfried von St Viktor (d. 1194). The *planctus* as a form, with its simple folk-like piety, managed to preserve itself from the secularization which befell other religious plays. The stylistic features of the *Osterspiel von Muri* derive in part from Early Middle High German religious verse and in part from Hartmann, while the realistic episodes point forward to the use of contrasts which is characteristic of the following period.

The purpose of these plays is to alarm and to instruct, and to this end the forces of evil, especially the devil, are conjured up, so that, by means of both laughter and fear, the audience shall be made all the more receptive to the religious message which the plays contain. As in contemporary paintings of the Passion and Crucifixion, there is a precision of detail in the depiction of cruelty and suffering which is almost unbearable. Nothing was omitted, even things which today strike one as comical – such as when the cock that warns Peter is hung up on a pillar while a boy is given the job of crowing. No one doubts the victory of goodness, so there need be no limit to the portrayal of evil, and the greater the extent to which the forces of evil are made fearful by grotesque exaggeration or made ridiculous by mockery, the greater the ultimate triumph of divine truth.

The realism of these productions contrasts with the artificiality of erecting and dismantling a stage as the troupes move from place to place. This peripatetic existence also underlies the epic character of the plays themselves, the stringing together of scenes each complete in itself, the links between the scenes being either in the pattern of the familiar religious narrative itself or provided by an interpreter who was one of the characters. The *Rheinisches Osterspiel* (*c*. 1460), on the other hand, reveals a certain ability to distinguish the essential from the incidental and thus arrive at a balanced dramatic construction, but in general the speeches in these plays are addressed more to the audience than to the other characters (who are themselves more types than individuals), and the works as a whole have little dramatic quality about them – often less, indeed, than can be found in dialogues in various epic poems.

Virtually the only form of secular drama at this time is the Shrovetide Play. The influence of religious and didactic literature is clearly apparent in the revue-like assemblage of scenes and dialogues, but its real source lies, as the name alone conveys, in folk customs. Ghosts of earlier generations appear in disguise and pronounce judgement on the virtues and vices of the present; when disguised, a man is transformed and acquires the right to give unfettered expression to his dark instincts and his hitherto suppressed urges. The change of the seasons is also connected with this: the *Neidhartspiel von St Paul* (beginning of the fourteenth century) is built on the Viennese custom that the lord, in the company of his entire retinue, greets the first violet as a sign of spring.

The central elements in the Shrovetide Play are a newly discovered *joie de vivre* and the merciless revelation of human follies; only the setting changes. All disguises are dropped, and a subject taken from a *Schwank* or similar source is put into the form of dialogue. A particularly popular setting was that of the court-case.

The earthiness and obscenity associated with Shrovetide dominate the scene, and the Shrovetide Play never achieved a really high artistic standard. A particular tradition was introduced by Folz and Rosenplüt in Nürnberg, where the famous entertainment called the *Schembartlaufen* was exploited for dramatic purposes by the guilds. Here as elsewhere the late Middle Ages provided the starting-point for subsequent developments – in particular in the person of Hans Sachs, also from Nürnberg. It was, indeed, the age of the Reformation which took the secular drama on to a new, higher level.

DGL

The Age of Humanism and the Reformation

LEONHARD BERIGER

To follow the development of literature in Germany at the time of humanism and the Reformation is to follow how there arose from the chaos left by the collapse of the medieval pattern of life a new order of things which was then expanded, modified and consolidated in the age of the Counter-Reformation and baroque.

Jacob Burkhardt, dazzled by the classical perfection of Leonardo, Raphael and Dürer, saw the Renaissance – the 200 years from the mid-fourteenth to the mid-sixteenth century – as an essentially harmonious period. But modern research has tended to see it as a chaotic age of disturbances and uncertainties in which, according to one's point of view and according to the nature of the contemporary documents on which one bases one's case, one can emphasize either the symptoms of decay or the signs of revival. Günther Müller, author of one of the most vivid and informative works on the period, speaks of 'the chaos of the Renaissance', and as earlier scholars had taken Raphael's Sistine Madonna to be the essence of the Renaissance, so modern writers have cast the sixteenth-century Faust legend in this role. Whichever view one takes, the Renaissance does not embody a single, unified concept, or even the movement towards one.

With the terms humanism and Reformation it is different. They represent firmly delineated movements within this 'chaos of the Renaissance', attempts to arrive at a self-sufficient philosophy and to recast the principles of human life. The man who fought the most determinedly to overcome the chaos and establish a new foundation was Martin Luther, whose role is not merely that of a reformer in the religio-confessional sense but who was a man with a historical vocation, a man of destiny, who succeeded, where so many of his great contemporaries failed, in finding something permanent to hold on to, and to build upon, in the midst of this chaos. And although his religious philosophy did not do justice to all the tendencies, or fulfil all the needs, of the age, all intellectual movements had to take account of his work in arriving at their own related, or different, conclusions.

Sein Geist ist zweier Zeiten Schlachtgebiet:
Mich wundert's nicht, daß er Dämonen sieht.

(His mind was a battleground between two ages: I am not surprised that he
saw devils.) (C. F. Meyer)

The history of German literature in the age of humanism and the
Reformation is thus the story of the various attempts – successful,
half-successful and failed – to find order in this 'chaos of the Renaissance',
and the investigation of the effects of these efforts on the three main
literary genres – drama, lyric poetry and epic. The early reform movement
within the Catholic Church is represented by Thomas Murner, Christian
humanism by Erasmus, national humanism by Hutten, the Protestant
Reformation by Luther, and independent religious trends by Sebastian
Franck and Paracelsus.

As this list of names alone shows, and as Wolfgang Stammler's pioneer
study *Von der Mystik zum Barock* (1927) made clear, we have to deal with
a literature both in Latin and in German. In variety and intellectual content the former is almost the equal of the latter, while from the point of
view of literary form it is far superior. The German literature and Latin
literature of the Middle Ages may be treated separately, but such a
separation is not possible in this later period because the two are so
intimately linked: according to circumstances an author may write in
German at one moment and in Latin at another, and a particular subject
may be treated by one writer in German and by another in Latin. A study
of the literature of the period must therefore concern itself with both
languages.

The Early Reform Movement: Thomas Murner

The Franciscan monk Thomas Murner (1475–1537) stands at the transition
between old and new. His roots lie in the religious and literary traditions
of the late Middle Ages, yet he is not without sympathy for the failings
of his age, especially those of the Church, and he felt intensely the need
for reform, without realizing, however, what was ultimately at stake.
Although he was close enough to humanism for the authors of the
Epistolae virorum obscurorum (*c.* 1517) to regard him as one of their own
number, the literary forms he used – the sermon and the satire – belonged
to the late Middle Ages and had proved inadequate for dealing with the
crisis of the age. His subsequent involvement in the Reformation struggle
was involuntary rather than determined and took the form, first of
theological pamphlets, then of powerful satire in the shape of *Von dem
großen Lutherischen Narren*. This work aroused more resentment than

approval, however, and made Murner an object of derision to his more powerful opponents; as a result he quickly lost his popular appeal and after an abortive attempt to thwart the advance of the Reformation in Switzerland he ended his days in oblivion in his birthplace of Oberehnheim in Alsace.

The intensity of his conviction sprang, however, from a true sense of religious devotion and responsibility, as is evidenced by his passionate lament *Vom Untergang des christlichen Glaubens* and his inspired praise of Strasbourg Cathedral – one thinks forward to Goethe's *Von deutscher Baukunst* – and of the Virgin Mary, to whom the Cathedral is dedicated, at the end of his poem *Ein geistlich Badenfahrt*.

Murner's most important literary works are not those written in Latin during his early career, many of which are lost, but the German rhymed poems of his middle and later periods. In these he continues the medieval form of the 'satirical catalogue' in which human vices and follies are listed and illustrated by examples from life. The most famous work of this type, Brant's *Narrenschiff* (1494), was Murner's model, as the title of his first essay in this manner – *Die Narrenbeschwörung* (1512) – betrays, and his attitudes scarcely differ from those of Brant. He too sees no conflict between the demands of religion and the demands of middle-class morality, between the Christian commandments and the wisdom of the classical authors. Evil is conceived of as folly, not as some demonic, metaphysical power, and the arch-fool is the devil.

The difference between Murner and Brant is one of temperament: where Brant is dry, pedantic and even-tempered, Murner is lively, natural and agreeably pugnacious. Brant's manner is clearer, more penetrating, his style more direct and lucid, while Murner's language is more colourful, more down-to-earth, his style looser and less careful. The motif of exorcism is Murner's invention: imitating the ecclesiastical process of exorcizing devils by flogging, strangling, dousing in cold water and other methods, he assumes the role of exorcizer himself, introducing a satirical dramatic dialogue between exorcizer and fool in the manner of the Shrovetide Play.

A further novel feature of Murner's work is that each section is headed by a proverb or popular saying, and in this lies the interest of the work from the historical, cultural and folkloristic aspects. Among these sayings are some familiar ones like 'den Brand schüren', 'das Gras wachsen hören' and 'das Kind mit dem Badwasser ausschütten', while others – 'den Affen scheren' (to show one's weaknesses), 'Heuschrecken und Flöh sonnen' (to keep an eye on a woman), 'von blauen Enten predigen' (to swindle people into parting with their money) – have virtually died out. The woodcuts that illustrate the text are an integral part of Murner's works and almost give them the character of picture-books like those of

Wilhelm Busch – though without the latter's power of perception and expression.

The *Narrenbeschwörung* was followed by two similar satires, *Die Schmelmenzunft* (1512) and *Die Mühle von Schwindelsheim* (1515). *Die Geuchmatt* (1519) is of a different kind: it deals with a single subject, the folly of infatuation, and is more consistently and tautly constructed than his other works. Its particular historical interest lies in the fact that it virtually sums up the whole movement of courtly love and chivalric literature. In the *Epistolae virorum obscurorum* Murner is mocked for the uncritical length of his works in the phrase 'in omnibus aliquid in toto nihil', but *Die Geuchmatt* is in fact a complete entity, even if negative in its intention. According to his own statement he worked through 120 'histories' concerning classical and medieval love-poetry, so as to hold up to ridicule the attitude that love is a moving force in life. In his parodistic presentation of the three meanings of the word 'Gauch' in the title of his work, i.e. cuckoo, fool and lover (cf. cuckold), and in the manner in which he parades his cuckoos and has them make themselves ridiculous, he shows himself to be at the height of his powers. It marks a significant shift of emphasis when, a few years later, Murner's rejection of love gives way before Luther's *Vom ehelichen Leben*, a work in praise of love as a bond in life.

It is appropriate that Murner should use his heaviest armament in his work directed against Luther's reform movement, *Von dem großen Lutherischen Narren, wie ihn Doktor Murner beschworen hat* (1522). The 'fool' in this work is not Luther himself but an allegorical figure who embodies the disastrous social and political effects which Murner claimed that Luther's teaching would have. The work is difficult to follow because of its lack of logical construction and because it assumes a familiarity with the polemical literature of the Reformation. The first part, with the actual exorcism of the giant 'fool', is the most entertaining, while the end degenerates into a domestic comedy, obscene and objectionable rather than witty, and full of the most vulgar insults of Luther.

Murner's work as a whole, while reflecting a struggle to bring a new spirit of morality into life, lacks a firm philosophy and shares the shortcomings of its age, above all the sense of chaos and confusion, seen in its lack of linguistic and artistic discipline. Thus no work of Murner's has become part of the German literary tradition, although the historical and intellectual interest of his achievement remains.

Christian Humanism: Erasmus

Erasmus of Rotterdam (1466–1536), the very essence of a European, cosmopolitan mind, belongs to the history of German literature by virtue of his many years spent in German-speaking parts (from 1514 to 1536 he lived, with interruptions, in Basle and Freiburg) and of his relationship to his great German contemporaries Reuchlin, Hutten, Luther, Zwingli and Dürer. But first and foremost he stands as the embodiment of humanism, one of the most powerful philosophical, intellectual and educative forces of the time. As Murner attempted to restore intellectual and moral order in the spirit of the late Middle Ages, i.e. through the reform of the Church as a body and by means of satirico-didactic sermons, so Erasmus evolved the concept of 'Christian humanism' – *philosophia Christi,* as he called it.

Erasmus's goal was to unite the wisdom and humanity of antiquity with the teaching of Christ. The spirit of the classics was to him the spirit of the Sermon on the Mount; Socrates and the saints belonged side by side, and he even said in his prayers: 'Sancte Socrates, ora pro nobis' (*Convivium religiosum*). This conviction, however limited his realization of its implications, and however uncertain the value of his own efforts to apply it, is what gives Erasmus his intellectual importance in the history of European culture.

In all three fields of his activity – as scholar, religious thinker and poet – Erasmus served this unifying ideal. His chief works of scholarship are (1) his *Adagia* (1500), a collection of 5,251 proverbs and sayings from classical and modern writings and from the popular wisdom of the time, a work intended for linguistic and moral instruction; and (2) his edition (1516) of the original Greek text of the New Testament with parallel Latin translation and notes, a work which paved the way for the emphasis on the pure word which was to become so fundamental a feature of Reformation teaching.

His most lucid, most intensely felt religious work is his *Enchiridion militis Christiani* (1502), a handbook of Christian thought which had a considerable influence on Zwingli, Bucer, the Spiritualists and the Anabaptists, the Spanish mystics of the sixteenth and seventeenth centuries and the thinkers of the Enlightenment, and also inspired Dürer's famous engraving *Ritter, Tod und Teufel*. Similar importance attaches to his *De libero arbitrio* (1524), his great defence of free will against the doctrine of Luther, who retaliated with his own most substantial theological work, the *De servo arbitrio* (1525).

But the liveliest, most modern of Erasmus's works, however, are his *Encomium moriae* (1509) and *Colloquia* (1524). Like Brant's *Narrenschiff* and Murner's *Narrenbeschwörung*, the *Encomium moriae* exposes and mocks human weaknesses, not as evils but as follies, and folly appears as a character who, vigorously defending his presence and his power, may owe his existence to the influence of the German Shrovetide Play. Of the many meanings which the concept of folly acquires, three are predominant: folly as the unconscious, irrational feeling in man, as opposed to his conscious, rational acts; folly as presumptuousness, exemplified and pilloried in the form of the arrogance and depravity of the priests; and folly in the elevated sense of inspiration and religious ecstasy – for as Paul himself said, the Gospel is folly to the heathen.

The attractiveness of the work lies in its ironical tone, which is such that the reader continually finds himself wondering whether the praise is serious or in jest; at the same time this light, playful attitude can sometimes turn into fierce indignation. The weakness of the work is that of all humanistic writings – the endless use of quotations and a longwindedness in which an initial idea is pursued to inordinate lengths.

Erasmus's *Colloquia*, his wittiest and most personal work and the liveliest, most comprehensive presentation of sixteenth-century life, are free from these weaknesses. In a series of elegant and amusing dialogues on matters of Christian experience and ecclesiastical life, on love and marriage, education (including that of women), birth and death, health and sickness, living, eating, drinking, etc., he reveals the breadth and depth of his intellect, achieving in the dialogue on the death of his friend Reuchlin a true moment of poetic vision.

National Humanism: Hutten

As Erasmus's ideal of *philosophia Christi* consisted of the suffusion of the spirit of the New Testament with the spirit of classical antiquity, that of Ulrich von Hutten (1488–1523) lay in the utter supremacy of the values of classical humanism, added to a burning patriotism which puts him in the company of Walther von der Vogelweide and Heinrich von Kleist as a stimulator of the German national consciousness. Like Walther he carried on a feud with Rome, but whereas Walther opposed the Pope's political policies, not the Church as such, Hutten fought against the political control of Germany by the Church of Rome.

His concern was not simply with the eradication of abuses, and his path was not that of peace and inner purification but the path of violence, of revolt. *Perrumpendum est* is his slogan; *jacta est alea* – 'ich habs gewagt' – is his motto as he throws down his challenge to Rome, calling on the whole German people to throw off the Roman yoke and discover through their revolt against the enemy their true national unity.

He had little practical idea of how to achieve either his religious or his political aim. His links with Luther were chance, not the result of pursuing a common purpose, and there was something utopian and unreal about his hopes for a revival of the medieval Empire. But he struck a new note in his act of self-commitment, his determination to venture all, even his life, for his cause. The most striking testimony of this determination is his unforgettable poem 'Ich habs gewagt', in which, after the Edict of Worms in the spring of 1521, he renounces his allegiance to the Emperor and prepares to accept banishment.

This one short poem counts for more than all Murner's works put together, for it expresses in compelling terms one of the major issues of the time. Its imagery and the rhythm of its language – notwithstanding the clumsiness of the syntax, which betrays the Latin-trained humanist struggling to express himself in German – are infused with the intensity of his emotion, and the basic elements in his nature show themselves in it: the humanist's self-confidence ('Ich habs gewagt mit Sinnen / Und trag des noch kein Reu'); his patriotism ('Nit eim' allein, dem Land zugut'); his insistence on truth ('Von Wahrheit will ich nimmer lan'); his sense of justice ('Ich hätt das Recht gelitten'); his determination ('Es muß gan oder brechen'); and his sense of fraternity with the common people ('Auf Landsknecht gut und Reiters Mut, / Laßt Hutten nit verderben!').

Hutten was thirty-three when he wrote this stirring poem and already a dying man, but he had by then written Latin works which had brought him fame both in and outside Germany and given him influence in intellectual circles. Important among these are the *Epistolae obscurorum virorum*, his dialogues and the famous letter to Wilibald Pirckheimer.

The *Epistolae obscurorum virorum*, written by Hutten in collaboration with his friend Crotus Rubeanus (Johannes Jäger) from Dornheim and a few others, is a brilliant satire on the decadence of the monks and the small-minded pedantry of learned scholars, 'one of the most splendid pamphlets ever written', as David Friedrich Strauss called it, and indirectly both a bold affirmation of the formative ideals of humanism and a defence of the freedom of scholarship. The occasion of the work was the trial for heresy of the great Heidelberg philologist Johann Reuchlin, who had acquired fame for his edition of the Old Testament in the original Hebrew. A Jewish convert to Christianity named Pfefferkorn, from Cologne, had stirred up opinion against the Jews and demanded that the writings of the Jewish faith should be burned. Asked for his expert opinion, Reuchlin defended the Jewish writings as being a valuable source of knowledge about the Hebrew language. This led to his being accused of heresy by the Dominicans in Cologne, whereupon he published a series of letters from distinguished contemporaries who had sprung to his defence and supported, with him, the freedom of scholarship; this collection of letters Reuchlin called *Epistolae clarorum virorum* (1514).

A year later there appeared an anonymous riposte under the title *Epistolae obscurorum virorum*, which took the form of a number of letters ostensibly written by monks in all parts of Germany to Ortvinus Gratius, head of the Dominicans in Cologne, supporting the opposition to Reuchlin and the humanists but in fact, through their stupid prattling and their smug accounts, in dog-Latin, of their degenerate monastic life, making themselves the laughing-stock of the educated world. Crotus, the principal author of the first part, shows himself a master of caricature and also, in his penchant for short, self-contained episodes, of narrative; Hutten, whom we can take to be the author of the majority of the letters in the second part, published in 1517, writes in a harsher tone and sometimes goes from indirect satire and mimicry to open attack. He also strengthens the polemical character of the work by introducing well-known humanists and Dominicans by name, giving keenly observed portraits of Erasmus, Murner and others.

Hutten's *Colloquia* had an even greater effect than the *Epistolae*. Like Erasmus he started from the dialogues of Plato, Lucian and Cicero. Erasmus had breathed new life into the form by introducing contemporary issues and drawing on the circumstances of everyday life but, peaceful by nature, he had refrained even in his satires from making too specific allusions to events and personalities, since they might have put him in a difficult position. Hutten, however, had no such reservations and went straight into the attack. The characters in the dialogues are himself, his friends – Sickingen, Luther – and his enemies – Cajetan, the papal legate and others. In addition he introduces allegorical figures – Fortune, the Bull of Excommunication, Fever, German liberty, etc. – who not only speak but also take part in the action at the Mainzer Tor in Frankfurt, at the Reichstag in Augsburg in 1518 and elsewhere. Thus the dialogues have virtually become plays, and long stretches of them could be performed on the stage.

Hutten's friend Mutianus Rufus described Hutten's language as being like lightning, and of no work is this truer than two of the most brilliant of the *Colloquia* – the powerful attack on the Roman Catholic Church called *Vadiscus seu Trias Romana*, and the *Inspicientes*, in which he gives a character study of the German people and utters warnings which anticipate the ideas expressed in Goethe's *Götz von Berlichingen*. By translating these and a few other dialogues into German, or having them translated by others, Hutten secured a wider public and at the same time created a new literary genre, the polemic *Gesprächbüchlein*, large numbers of which now spring up to form what have been called 'the storm-troops of the Reformation'. Among the best-known examples of the genre are *Karsthans*, a witty dialogue formerly erroneously ascribed to Vadian, a Protestant reformer at St Gallen; Hans Sachs's *Gespräch zwischen einem Chorherrn und einem Schuhmacher*; and Niklaus Manuel's biting satire *Krankheit der Messe*.

The final testimony to Hutten's importance that should be mentioned is his great letter of October 1518 to the Nürnberg humanist and friend of Albrecht Dürer, Wilibald Pirckheimer, a letter which aroused Goethe's enthusiasm in Strasbourg and which he quotes in Book 17 of *Dichtung und Wahrheit*. It is a manifesto on his philosophy and on the career he planned for himself: Pirckheimer had urged upon him the *vita contemplativa* devoted to scholarship, but Hutten counters this with his own ideal of the *vita activa*, fashioned to contemporary needs and built on the principles of honour, glory and nobility of mind. The letter ends with a review of the great minds of the age and with the rallying-cry of humanism: 'O saeculum! O literae! Juvat vivere, etsi quiescere nondum juvat, Bilibalde! Vigent studia, florent ingenia!' ('O spirit of the age! O scholarship! This is not a moment for rest, Wilibald, but a moment to enjoy life. May the human mind arise! May learning flourish!')

The Protestant Reformation: Luther

As Murner, Erasmus and Hutten found the impulse for their literary work in the human failings of the age and in the urge for spiritual regeneration, so too did Martin Luther, who set himself the task of resolving the Faustian conflict in man between the forces of nature and the forces of the spirit, between the will to live and the desire to be saved. One has thus to approach Luther's own works and all post-Lutheran literature from his spiritual experience and from what was his profoundest concern. What lifts this experience beyond the personal realm and gives it its universal importance is its new conception of man and its new social message. The basis of Luther's anthropology lies in the Epistles of St Paul, and that of his sociology in the text of the biblical writings as the source of divine revelation.

The basis of Luther's view of man is St Paul's distinction between man as an animal and man regenerated by Christ, the man of the flesh and the man of the spirit, or, as Luther also put it, between the outer and the inner man. This distinction is quite different from that between the instinctive and the rational, between feeling and thought, which is of Greek origin, was re-expressed in the age of humanism (Erasmus) and remains a central issue in German idealism (Kant, Schiller). For Luther's whole conception assumes the essential oneness of man *vis-à-vis* his creator: feelings, instincts, reason, senses, will – all, without distinction or exclusion, make up what he calls the man of the flesh.

In his *Vorrede zum Römerbrief*, for example, he states that the flesh does not simply stand for unchastity but for 'everything which is born of the flesh, the whole man, body and soul, with his reason and all his senses'. Therefore man cannot but live in sin, since he is descended from Adam; sin is existential, and sinfulness is the natural condition of man. The inner man, on the other hand, the man of the spirit, is man redeemed by Christ – again, man in his entirety – man in a state of grace, free Christian man.

Luther's strict distinction between these two knows of no compromise. Natural man is depraved and 'seeks only evil'; he has no choice, as he energetically argued in his *De servo arbitrio* against Erasmus. The man of the spirit, on the other hand, is 'Lord of all things and subject to no one', even though he has to struggle ceaselessly not to relapse into his former state of bondage. Whatever view one takes of it, this implacable rejection of man in his natural state and unconditional acceptance of man in a state of grace is the most original and most impressive feature of Luther's faith. All man's attempts to achieve his salvation by 'good works', or even to come some way towards achieving it, let alone to improve the world, are doomed, and all the teachings of the Church which put this hope into men's hearts are false – indeed, the indispensable condition for grace and redemption is the realization of the hopelessness of one's own efforts, and the purpose of the Commandments 'is merely to make man aware of his inability to achieve goodness and to teach him to despair of doing so' (*Freiheit eines Christenmenschen*, 8). Salvation requires faith from man, and God rewards this faith with grace. 'All faith is a sign of the divine presence in us which causes us to be reborn in God, which destroys the old Adam, which changes our hearts and minds and all our power, and which brings the Holy Spirit upon us.' (*Vorrede zum Römerbrief.*) Through grace God 'fills us with His spirit . . . making us fit to stand before Him' (loc. cit.). 'Good works' are now no longer a means to salvation but the expression of a grateful soul for the justice and grace that God has bestowed upon it.

Luther's view of man is thus, like that of the late Middle Ages, dualistic, but the dualism is no longer the irreconcilable antagonism between the affirmation and the denial of life but a dualism beyond the reach of human influence, to be resolved on a transcendental plane under the shadow of the Cross.

Spiritual man does not, however, as is often the case among the mystics, become separated from material man and from the world but acts directly upon them: outward man, man as flesh and as nature, like physical nature itself, is transformed by inner man, man inspired by faith and by the grace shared by all believers. This transformation must needs be imperfect, for the struggle between the spirit and the flesh cannot be concluded in this life, but this imperfection can no longer make man in his new-born state despair. This is the difference between Luther's teaching and that of the Anabaptists and the Spiritualists, who considered themselves to have been made free and perfect by the spirit and sought to establish the kingdom of God on earth.

What makes Luther's teaching of supreme intellectual importance is that it holds the individual alone responsible for his relationship to God, to the absolute, and does away with the intermediate role of the Church. One may describe the Renaissance as marking the end of the medieval collective spirit and the birth of the individual, but neither Petrarch nor the mystics nor Johannes von Tepla shows a fundamental personal outlook: the autonomy of the individual conscience is established only by Luther – autonomy *vis-à-vis* the collective conscience of society, the rule of the Church or the laws of men. Conscience is subject to God, to Christ, to the Word, and the ultimate authority in issues of conscience is the Bible – Luther admits of no other form of revelation. He thus opposed Sebastian Franck, for example, who claimed that there was a revelation in history as well as a revelation through the scriptures.

The centrality of the word is also the reason why Luther's teaching was not just a personal experience but led to the establishment of a new Church and a new social order. For as he called on each individual to renew his spirit in Christ, so also he sought to reform the entire pattern of collective spiritual and social life: the offices of the Church and the furnishing of church buildings, now seen as part of the concept of a common priesthood; society organized in terms of marriage, family, classes and professions; economic and political problems; reform of scholarship and education – such questions and many others are drawn into his programme of reforms. His tract *An den christlichen Adel deutscher Nation von des christlichen Standes Besserung* gives the best idea of the extent of his vision and his field of activity. The culture that he founded on these principles was to last over 200 years.

Luther's significance in the history of literature, apart from the new content which his movement introduced, lies above all in his relationship to language. In the entire late-medieval, pre-Lutheran period language was primarily a tool, an instrument: works of literature were 'shaped', 'made' (the *Meistersinger*, Oswald von Wolkenstein). Luther's axiom that the 'inner' renewal of man must lead to a renewal of 'outer' reality also means that, from being a means to an end, language becomes its own end – a feature observable in all Luther-inspired sixteenth-century literature and the beginning of a development that reached its climax in Goethe and Hölderlin. According to Günther Müller (*Deutsche Dichtung von der Renaissance bis zum Ausgang des Barock* (Potsdam, 1927)), the fact that Catholic literature did not share in this development created a duality in German literature that lasted down to the time of the Romantics: in the sixteenth-century context one may think of the passionate language of Gryphius's Protestant dramas on the one hand, and the Latin dramas of the Jesuits, in which the language is more functional, on the other. This dualism was only resolved by the Romantic fusion of the Catholic and the Protestant.

Chief among Luther's works in terms of their contemporary effect are his prose writings, a few of which are among the finest and most powerful literary products of the century. These works breathe the very spirit of the age: they express not only thoughts but actions and conclusions with a rare conviction and determination. The most valuable of them is *Von der Freiheit eines Christenmenschen* (1520), an incomparable work consisting of thirty sections in which two contradictory propositions are investigated: that a Christian is master of all things and subject to no man; and that a Christian is subservient to all things and servant of all men. These writings – among which *Vom ehelichen Leben* (1524), a splendid hymn in praise of marriage and family life, should also be mentioned – may not exactly be called the first prose essays in the German language but they did make the essay-form the standard vehicle for the conduct of intellectual discourse.

Of virtually equal importance is Luther's translation of the Bible. It is not the first German translation, but it is the first to return to the original Hebrew and Greek texts – the former in Reuchlin's edition, the latter in Erasmus's. In contrast to his predecessors (e.g. the Zainer Bible) Luther did not plod through the text word for word but translated according to the ethos of the language that he heard among the people. The power of its language, its warmth, its sincerity, its fullness, its range, its imagery, its rhythm – these make it one of the great achievements in German literature, a fountain-head and a source of inspiration down to the present day. Even Luther's Catholic opponents had to base their own German versions of the Bible on his, and his *Sendbrief vom Dolmetschen* (1530), with its account of the way he set to work, is a splendid retort to the attacks they made on him while busily copying his translation. Thanks to the esteem and the wide circulation enjoyed by Luther's works, the language of the Saxon chancellery, on which they were based, soon spread over the whole German-speaking area and led to a unified German written language.

The third aspect of Luther's literary influence is that of lyric poetry in the form of his German hymns – religious songs for congregational use. Hymns were far from unknown before Luther's time but they did not form an integral part of the Catholic service, and their use on special occasions was only grudgingly conceded. Luther's new hymns are communal declarations of Christian faith, and he makes them part of the Protestant liturgy. As a collection they appear in his *Gesangbüchlein* of 1524, the best known being 'Ein feste Burg ist unser Gott' and 'Aus tiefer Not schrei ich zu Dir'. It is due to Luther and his successors in the sixteenth and seventeenth centuries that the religious lyric was for many years the most flourishing branch of lyric poetry.

Luther's connections with drama are slighter, though not insignificant.

By drawing attention, in his prefaces to the Book of Judith and the Book of Tobias, to the suitability of these subjects for dramatic treatment, he stimulated an interest which brought many writers, great and small, to the fore; in this way he helped to found Reformation drama.

Independent Religious Movements: The Anabaptists, Sebastian Franck, Paracelsus

The most powerful influence on German intellectual and literary life in the sixteenth century was that of Luther. But it would be a falsification and an over-simplification to regard the age as consisting merely of the struggle of the Lutheran Reformation against the Catholic Church on the one hand and against humanism on the other. The uncompromising strictness with which Luther divided the human from the divine was bound to stimulate other thinkers and to give rise to new, independent religious attitudes.

Zwingli, for example, to Luther's chagrin, evolved just such an independent theology by according humanist and Stoic philosophy an important role and allowing reason more influence in matters of faith (*Über die göttliche Vorsehung* (1530)). And though Christ still stands at the centre, Zwingli places Socrates, Plato, Scipio and other pagans alongside the Christian saints in the heavenly company (letter to Francis I of France (1531)). By making politics subservient to religion – an attitude which cost him his life in battle – he also revealed a sharp difference of opinion from Luther. But notwithstanding his vigorous *Kappelerlied* and the moving 'Prayer of the Man Stricken with the Plague', his poetic talent nowhere approaches that of Luther. He was greatly interested in drama and may well have had a not inconsiderable influence on the flourishing dramatic life of Zürich in the first decades of the sixteenth century.

In contrast to Luther and Zwingli the Anabaptists had only a slight influence; as a movement they were quickly suppressed by force and only able to survive in small, isolated groups. They therefore contributed little to the literature of the time (cf. the hymns of Manz and Blaurock, both of Zürich), but their influence was felt among the Spiritualists such as the Silesian nobleman Caspar Schwenckfeld, the Nürnberg schoolmaster Hans Denck and above all the gifted Sebastian Franck.

Born in Donauwörth, Franck first became a priest, then a Lutheran preacher and, successively, a soap-boiler, a printer and a writer; after an unsettled life in various towns in South Germany, where he was constantly attacked and persecuted, he died in Basle in 1542 at the age of forty-three. He was a theologian, a historian, a geographer, the compiler of a large collection of German proverbs and a master of the German language, whose richness of imagery, homely eloquence, power of description and warmth of personality make him fit to stand alongside Luther.

As a theologian Franck adopted a position of evangelical devotion from which he opposed all dogmatization of faith and all Churches. This attitude is strikingly expressed in a poem which opens with the refrain:

> Ich will und mag nicht Päpstisch sein,
> Ich will und mag nicht Luthrisch sein,
> Ich will und mag nicht Zwinglisch sein,
> Ich will und mag nicht Täufrisch sein.

(I do not want to be a Papist, and I never shall; I do not want to be a Lutheran, and I never shall; I do not want to be a Zwinglian, and I never shall; I do not want to be an Anabaptist, and I never shall.)

Ultimate power resided for him not, as for Luther, in the word revealed in the Scriptures but in the spirit which enables this revelation to be understood. His attitudes emerge in all his writings but his principal theological work is *Paradoxa* (1534), a collection of 280 'paradoxical' Latin statements about the nature of God and religious experience, with a learned commentary in German.

Franck found the revelation of God not only in the Scriptures, however, but also in the spirit of nature and of history. His *Geschichtsbibel* (1531), which has been called the first German history of the world in terms of a history of ideas, shows already in its title that he regarded historical development as a process of divine revelation. The most interesting section of the work is the 'Chronicle of Roman Heretics', where one finds Erasmus and other humanists, Luther, Zwingli, the Anabaptists, etc.: for Franck the world always sees true Christians as heretics. Erasmus was led by his inclusion in Franck's 'Chronicle' to complain to the civic authorities in Strasbourg, as a result of which Franck was forced to leave the city, but his influence on the religious literature of his own and the following century was considerable.

Franck himself was greatly stimulated by Theophrastus Bombastus von Hohenheim, who called himself Paracelsus (1493–1541) – physician, naturalist, religious thinker and powerful German writer, a man whose influence was stronger on later generations than on his contemporaries, who found his teachings and his manner alien and unsettling. He was neither Catholic nor Protestant, neither Spiritualist nor mystic, neither pantheist nor alchemist, yet partook of all of these. He has been called the first modern man by virtue of his belief that it is man's task to complete the creation of God's world. His powerful, highly individualistic attitudes showed themselves in his boundless self-confidence and energy, yet at the same time he was of a deeply pious nature wth a profound reverence for creation: this combination of qualities gives his writings both their intensity and their attractive sincerity.

Drama

Of the various literary genres it was drama that felt most powerfully and most immediately the impact of humanism and the Reformation. The Middle Ages had evolved two types of drama – the religious play and the Shrovetide Play. The former is not the expression of individual experience but the enactment of biblical scenes, from the Creation to the Day of Judgement, with the addition of legendary material that had collected around them; particular characters or episodes, such as those involving Mary Magdalene, or Christ's journey to Hell, might acquire a certain independence, but in general the poet's imagination was held in check – indeed, he was more a script-writer than a poet, and only in a very few cases, such as the play of the Ten Virgins and the plays on Theophilus and Jutta, does one find signs of personal originality. Similarly the Shrovetide Plays of the fourteenth and fifteenth centuries have no individualized content but are in part continuations of ancient pagan rites of spring, in part dramatizations of popular satirical material with characters who are types, not individuals. Thus the whole of medieval drama, with a very few exceptions, is virtually an impersonal collective product.

Humanist and Reformation drama, on the other hand, at least in its best moments, is something quite new and different: it is the individual presentation of personal experiences and a personal fate – a development only made possible by the birth of the individual in the age of humanism and the Reformation.

There were three main creative forces at work in the emergence of this new drama. The first and strongest is that of the Lutheran creed itself, which provided the dramatic tension almost completely absent from the medieval play. This tension produces the inner dramatic form, which is itself the prerequisite for the absorption of formal stimuli from without. Latin humanist drama also developed only after the Reformation, in the sense that the moral concerns of humanism only revealed their dramatic potentialities under religious influence. Thus all drama in this period rests on either the religious attitudes of Protestantism (Reformation drama proper), or on Christian morality (humanist and school drama, popular plays) or on the principles of bourgeois uprightness (Hans Sachs) – this last similarly dependent on Reformation attitudes. Important links between theological literature and drama are the dialogue and the polemical pamphlet as cultivated by Erasmus, Hutten and Luther.

The second force is that of the Renaissance, i.e. a sense of reality and a joy in life as it is, together with a realistic presentation of characters and situations. However, it is not the realism of the late Middle Ages, for whom reality meant nothing but crudity and coarse humour, but a reality informed by the new religious experience and by a feeling for fine detail of character and situation, and these qualities, linked with those drawn from Reformation sources, show themselves in the new dramas. Psychological interest and analysis, however, is rare (Gnaphaeus, Gart, Stricker). Classical authors provided sources for these writers to learn the art of realistic observation.

The third element is humanism, the awakening of a sense of dramatic form through the study of the classical drama – Terence, Plautus, Seneca, Sophocles, Euripides and Aristotle. Division into acts and scenes now becomes the custom, though how superficially the new principles of construction were sometimes understood can be seen from the fact that the *argumentum*, the summary of the action with which classical authors prefaced their dramas, was taken over as part of the play itself, whereas it had only been intended as an aid for the reader.

The new content and the new form also required new conditions for performance. The Shrovetide Plays of the fourteenth and fifteenth centuries were performed without a stage: the players went from house to house and performed in a room, surrounded by the spectators. Medieval religious plays were performed in public squares: the various scenes were set up in advance in full view of the audience, and the actors moved from one setting to the other according to the course of the action. With the Reformation came a change. Plays were no longer performed in the open but in a hall, with a raised platform behind which was a large board with a number of doors (the Terence stage). Alternatively the stage was divided into a front and a rear half separated by a curtain: the front could serve, for example, as a street, and the rear as the interior of a house. Another form was the Rederijker stage, consisting of two levels: the upper level might be occupied by the inhabitants of heaven, the lower level by the citizens of earth. But there was no enclosed stage or separate auditorium in the sixteenth century, and the audience sat around the stage as in Shakespeare's day.

Such developments are probably also to be traced to the change from drama as spectacle to drama as spoken word, for both Reformation and humanism, in their different ways, were servants of the word. It is highly significant that even in this field practical developments are to be explained in intellectual terms, i.e. in terms of Luther's new attitude towards language.

It is hardly possible to classify the great variety of dramatic works, Latin and German, written at this time, so heterogeneous are the elements from which they are compounded, but for convenience one may list a number of main types: polemic drama, serious religious play, serious secular play, Latin comedy, and German Shrovetide Play.

One of the earliest and liveliest of polemic dramas is Niklaus Manuel's *Vom Papst und seiner Priesterschaft*, sometimes also called *Die Totenfresser*, which was performed by a troupe of townsmen on Shrove Tuesday, 1523, in Berne. In an indirect satirical manner, similar to that of the *Epistolae obscurorum virorum*, representatives of the degenerate Catholic Church, from the Pope down to the monk and the verger, are made to display their cupidity, their avarice and their immorality, while Peter and Paul stand as heavenly observers in the background and give vent to their disgust of their successors. Then, with great dramatic effect, Manuel parades representatives of the common people whom the Church has been exploiting and who now point their own fingers in accusation. Yet despite the polemical tone one feels the author's own faith and earnestness, which come into the foreground at the end of the play when the Lutheran preacher Dr Lupolt Schüchnit prays God to help his people out of this immoral state and expresses his confidence in the goodness of the Almighty. Manuel's talent emerges especially in his plain and direct presentation of characters and situations, as well as in his pithy, yet vivid and colourful language, and this play is a most interesting document on the life of the times.

More progressive in technique than Manuel is Thomas Naogeorgus (Thomas Kirchmaier, born in Straubing on the Danube), the best satirist among the Lutherans, whose Latin play *Pammachius* (1538) shows the use of the new stage. Pammachius (=fighting everybody) is the name Naogeorgus gives the Pope, whom he regards as the Antichrist, the accomplice of Satan. The play is full of the conflict of the Reformation age, and its author portrays the events of the present against the backcloth of the Last Judgement. He sees these events as illustrative of the struggle between Christ and Satan: the Pope, who bends even the Emperor to his will, is the handmaid of the devil, while Christ finds a belligerent supporter in one Theophilus, who lives in a castle in Saxony (i.e. Luther). Naogeorgus left the fifth act unwritten, explaining that it could only be completed by Christ on the Day of Judgement. *Pammachius* is undoubtedly the most inspired and most accomplished drama of the age of the Reformation, and at the same time the first Protestant drama of ideas.

Apart from Murner's *Von dem großen Lutherischen Narren* the most outstanding Catholic satire is the Low German play *Ein gemeyne Bicht* (1534), the work of a writer who used the pseudonym Daniel von Soest. It is a satire on the moral and political confusion which, in Catholic eyes, had been caused by the introduction of the Reformation in the town of Soest, and, as the title indicates, the events of the play are meant to be taken as a 'confession' on the part of the Reformers. The author even makes bold to introduce into his play sixteen Protestant pastors and twenty well-known citizens of Soest by name, insulting and slandering them mercilessly. Leaving aside these distortions, however, one can still appreciate the rough, often obscene comedy and the tone of forthright enthusiasm which the work exudes; at times one is reminded of Wittenwiler's *Ring*, or of the crowd scenes in the paintings of Brueghel.

The experience of spiritual regeneration receives more genuine, more lasting expression in the religious plays of the time than in these polemical dramas, which rarely penetrate beyond external events and conditions. Religious dramatists found in Luther's Bible not only a mass of material suitable for dramatic treatment but also indications as to how this material was to be understood and interpreted. Two subjects in particular presented themselves: one was the parable of the Prodigal Son; the other was the Everyman story, which, though not of biblical origin, is closely related to the parable of Dives and Lazarus and is given a new meaning in the light of the new evangelical message.

Of the dramatizations of the story of the Prodigal Son (in Latin versions the hero is called Prodigus or Akolastus) the earliest, that by Burkard Waldis (the Low German *De Parabel vam verlorn Szohn*), performed in Riga in 1527, is the best. The source of its dramatic tension is the Lutheran antithesis of doing good works and being saved by faith alone: the returning prodigal declares his faith, while the son who had remained at home, unable to understand his father's act of forgiveness, makes it the startingpoint for the performance of harsh acts of penance through which to achieve his own salvation.

Alongside this dramatic tension and the clear presentation of rival ideas the play has moments of realistic description like those found in Manuel; one may mention in particular the events in the inn, where the rich young man squanders his money on women and gambling. The integrated construction of the play emerges even more clearly if, as has been done in modern productions, the author's theological interpolations put into the mouth of the actor are taken out. Waldis's play is the model for all subsequent Protestant religious drama; literature is made to serve the evangelical cause, the play has become an act of worship, and the stage has been turned into a holy place.

Another version of the same parable is *Acolastus* (1529), a Latin play written in the Netherlands by Gnaphaeus (Willem de Volder), a schoolman active in a number of North German cities. This is the first of the *comicotragoediae* written by schoolmen in the style of Terence. The humanists were more concerned with the principle of education than with problems of religious philosophy, and this play has not the dramatic tension found in Waldis, but it has an admirable clarity of construction and contains a number of attractive realistic love-scenes and tavern-scenes. In its whimsical treatment of the magic of love there is a trace of Renaissance – even of baroque. It was translated into German in 1530 by Georg Binder, a schoolman from Zürich, and this German version was performed by his pupils in 1535 in the Grossmünsterschule. Other versions of the same subject, some based on Gnaphaeus, others on Waldis, were written by Hans Salat of Lucerne (1537), Jörg Wickram of Strasbourg (1540), Hans Sachs (1556), etc.

Like the story of the Prodigal Son, that of Everyman, familiar to modern times through the version of Hugo von Hofmannsthal, was dramatized many times in the age of the Reformation. The original is an anonymous English play written at the end of the fifteenth century: when Death comes to take him, Everyman calls on Friendship, Strength, Beauty, Knowledge and other allegorical figures to accompany him on his journey to the judgement-seat, but the only figure to go with him and plead for him before God's throne is Good Works.

The Dutch humanist Macropedius (Georg van Langveldt) treated this subject in his Hecastus (1539), in which it is not Good Works but *Virtus* and *Fides* who help the dying Everyman, and in which a dry allegorical situation is turned into a realistic and lively play in the style of classical social comedy.

In his *Mercator* (1540), also in Latin, Naogeorgus launches a bitter polemic against the Catholic doctrine of redemption by works, whereas in the German *Homulus* (1539), written by a Catholic printer in Cologne called Jaspar von Gennep, Luther's *sola fide* is presented as a dangerous aberration. Towards the end of the century Johannes Stricker, a Protestant pastor from Holstein, wrote a Low German play *De düdesche Schlömer*, which depicts in a simple yet gripping style the dying sinner's desperate struggle for salvation; in its realistic portrayal of situations and customs and in the depth and subtlety of its characterization it is a forerunner of the psychological drama of the baroque era. An unusually lively treatment of a related biblical subject is the *Zürcher Lazarusspiel* of 1529, written by an anonymous follower of Zwingli, which is remarkable for the solemnity of its religious tone, its exploitation of the contrast between the lust for pleasure and the fear of death, and above all for the concept of compassion and concern for one's neighbour which meant so much to Zwingli.

Among the numerous adaptations of Old Testament subjects the *Susanna* (1532) of Sixt Birk, who was born in Augsburg but later settled in Basle, and the *Joseph* (1540) of Thiebold Gart from Schlettstadt, stand out by virtue of their realistic characterization and their freshness. The former shows us the virtuous Susanna, accused of adultery and threatened by the two old lechers, as an affectionate wife and mother whose fate is at first in danger of taking a tragic turn in the detailed courtroom scenes. Gart, with rather greater skill, produces a psychological interest by making Potiphar's wife Sophora a noble woman who fights against passion, and by making Joseph's brothers show their anxiety about the fate of Benjamin and their old father. These dramas are not concerned with questions of Christian faith but the influence of the Reformation is apparent in their evangelical ethos and also, in *Joseph*, in the appearance on the stage of Christ together with his disciples Peter and Paul, who stand on one side and comment on Joseph's fate from the point of view of the New Testament.

It is only a short step from these religious plays on Old Testament subjects to serious secular dramas, but these latter could naturally only develop in response to other than religious impulses. Such were to be found in Switzerland, for example, where alongside religious issues, and closely related to them, political matters came to be treated, whereas in Germany Hutten's clarion call, in so far as it was political in meaning, had little effect on dramatic literature.

In Switzerland it was above all the Milan campaigns and the Protestant wars which gave rise to serious warnings in dramatic form. Thus the oldest of such plays, the *Urner Tellenspiel* (after 1511), deals in blunt popular terms with events connected with the origin of the Confederation. In the anonymous *Von den alten und jungen Eidgenossen* (1513), in Pamphilus Gengenbach's *Alter Eidgnoß* (1514) and in *Etter Heini* (1542) by Jakob Ruf of Zürich figures of the past (Gengenbach calls among others on the great Bruder Klaus) are held up as examples to the present. Similar intentions may well have been in the mind of Heinrich Bullinger when in his *Lucrezia* (1526) he expounded the moral foundations of a free state in terms of the events that led up to the foundation of the republic of Rome.

The old German rhymed couplet was the appropriate form for these serious secular plays, but in the field of comedy and farce we find Latin and German side by side, irrespective of the subject-matter. Reuchlin, for example, took a late-medieval Shrovetide Play on the subject of Maître Pathelin and turned it into a Roman comedy with choruses in his *Henno* (1497); Hans Sachs then turned Reuchlin's play back into a German Shrovetide Play. Reuchlin and others based their dramas on Terence and Plautus; on the other hand the most considerable, and at the same time the most uninhibited writer of Latin comedies at the time, Nicodemus Frischlin, modelled himself on Aristophanes, whose works he also translated. In his most substantial play, *Julius Redivivus* (1585), Caesar and Cicero reappear in sixteenth-century Germany and engage in earnest discussions with the humanist Eobanus Hessus and Hermann, grandson of Arminius, on the conditions and problems of the time.

That the Shrovetide Play began in the sixteenth century to leave behind its crudities and obscenities and acquire a degree of refinement is due both to the formal influence of humanist comedy and to the spiritualizing effect of the Reformation. The man who exploited these influences and made himself the master of this simple genre was Hans Sachs (1494–1576). By trade he was a cobbler, and writing poetry was only a spare-time occupation, yet according to his own inventory he composed 4,275 poems, 1,492 rhymed proverbs and 208 dramas of various kinds (tragedies, comedies, Shrovetide Plays). His typically middle-class mentality and his view of literature as a craft rather than an art put success in the field of serious drama beyond his grasp, but in the restricted compass of the Shrovetide Play he found a vehicle ideally suited to his attitudes and his abilities, a form in which he could develop to the full his experience of life, his knowledge of human nature, his humour and his keen sense of theatrical effectiveness.

Everything in these plays is conceived in terms of theatre: every word, every gesture is related to the action, to the situation and to the nature of the individual character, and there is no empty speech-making. Indeed it is not simply by reading them that one should experience their real-life quality, their tautness of language and the irrepressible power of their human content, but by seeing them acted – or better, by acting in them oneself, for entertaining, if not undemanding works such as *Der fahrende Schüler im Paradies*, *Der Teufel mit dem alten Weib* and *Das Kälberbrüten* are still to be found in the repertoire of amateur theatrical societies.

The Lyric

It was in the nature of things that the intellectual tension generated in the age of the Reformation should be conducive to the development of drama. This is less true, however, of lyric poetry and narrative literature, which, with a few notable exceptions, did not greatly develop. As far as the lyric is concerned, the only genre to flourish was the congregational Protestant hymn founded by Luther, which was to rise to new heights in the seventeenth century. From the point of view of poetry, the German folksong, which had reached a climax in the late Middle Ages, stagnated in the sixteenth century, whereas in music it stimulated composers such as Heinrich Isaac, Ludwig Senfl, Heinrich Finck and Georg Forster. The continued popularity of folksong is attested not only by contemporary literary references, including many of a disapproving nature by Protestant reformers, but also by the existence of such collections as Georg Forster's *Frische teutsche Liedlein* (1539) and the songbook of Peter von Aelst, which latter has something of the spirit of the baroque. The Meistersang also continued to be cultivated but even Hans Sachs was unable to breathe new life into this moribund form.

The few gifted lyric poets of the time wrote in Latin and took their inspiration from Ovid, Horace, the elegiasts Catullus and Tibullus and other Roman models. Conrad Celtis (Konrad Bickel, from Franconia (1459–1508)), nicknamed 'the arch-humanist', wrote a four-volume work called *Amores*, in which he described his amorous experiences together with the circumstances in which his various lovers lived; in his passionate *Odes* he celebrates these lovers again, together with a number of his humanist friends. Similar in style are the lyrics, part love-poem, part landscape-poem, frequently set in France and Italy, of Petrus Lotichius (Peter Lotz, from Hesse (1529–60)), who has been compared with his contemporary Ronsard. He calls his poems elegies, and in contrast to the passionate, sensuous Celtis he displays a gentle, reflective nature akin to that of Hölty. The third of these lyric poets, Paulus Melissus (Paul Schede (1539–1602)) wrote both passionate love-songs and intense religious poems, in which, as in his versions of the Psalms, one senses the spirit rather of the baroque than of the Reformation.

Melissus's verse shows how fruitful the Latin lyric was for the development of the German lyric, which gained in intellectual content, linguistic facility and formal technique by contact with a more advanced literary tradition. To appreciate the historical significance of baroque lyric one has to go back to the Latin lyric poetry of the Reformation era.

Narrative Literature

The most important development in the field of narrative literature at this time is the change from the poem in rhyme to the story in prose. The late-medieval *Spruch* – a short verse narrative of didactic intent – received a new lease of life at the hands of Hans Sachs, who was most at home in this genre – as in that of the Shrovetide Play – and who used it to treat a great variety of subjects, such as historical and political events, farcical episodes, legends and anecdotes, often in allegorical form. Among the most attractive of these poems are *Die Wittenbergisch Nachtigall*, *Das Schlauraffenland*, *Der Baldanderst*, *St Peter mit den Landsknechten*, *Der wunderliche Traum von meiner abgeschieden lieben Gemahel* and *Künigundt Sächsin*. Goethe's poem *Hans Sachsens poetische Sendung* is a re-creation of this type of poem and at the same time a tribute to the Mastersinger of Nürnberg.

A special category of rhymed *Spruch* is the fable, cultivated in particular by Erasmus Alberus in his collection of 1534 and Burkard Waldis (in 1548), both of them Lutherans who used this form to convey the moral message of the Reformation. As in the drama, conventional and typical traits give way to a freer, more personal treatment of the subject: animals are given human characteristics and the action is located in specific parts of Germany; the life of the peasant (Alberus) or Hanseatic citizen (Waldis) is described, episodes from contemporary life or from the life of the writer himself are inserted, and unmistakably, though not obtrusively, the Protestant ethic shows through.

The remaining verse narrative poems of the time, such as Georg Rollenhagen's *Froschmeuseler* (1595), an adaptation of the pseudo-Homeric epic *Der Froschmäuserkrieg*, are unimportant. This is the age of the prose narrative, and it is in the anecdote, the chap-book and the romance that one finds the beginnings of new developments.

The stimulus for the prose anecdote comes from the humanists – specifically from the Florentine Poggio, inventor of the *facetia*. The *facetia*, a typical product of the Renaissance, is an expression of delight in life, of intellectual and erotic freedom, and of pleasure in the skill and subtlety of literary creation. Heinrich Bebel, a Swabian, is almost Poggio's equal in artistry, and his three books of *Facetiae* (1508 and 1512) contain charming anecdotes of Swabian life which are a kind of Latin counterpart to Hebel's *Schatzkästlein*.

These Latin collections were followed by a large number of similar works in German. *Schimpf und Ernst* (1522) by Johann Pauli, a Jew from Alsace, is such a collection, looser in form but less immoral than the sometimes indecent stories of Poggio and Bebel, and closer to the Middle Ages than to the Renaissance. Jörg Wickram's popular *Rollwagenbüchlein* (1555) is cruder, and later writers such as Jakob Frey, Martinus Montanus and Michael Lindener often reveal less poetic talent than attraction to immorality and obscenity. Hans Wilhelm Kirchhof, on the other hand, in his seven books called *Wendunmut* (1563 onwards), models himself on Bebel and sometimes anticipates Grimmelshausen in the freshness of his descriptions of common life.

A further form of German prose, one cultivated as early as the fifteenth century, is the chap-book (*Volksbuch*), the most popular of which were eagerly read by all classes of society. Some were prose versions of medieval French and German verse epics – Wilhelm Ziely's *Olivier und Artus* and *Valentin und Orso* (1511), the anonymous *Fortunat*, Veit Warbeck's *Die schöne Magelone* (1527) and Wilhelm Salzmann's *Kaiser Octavian* (a Christian legend). Others were original prose works, such as *Eulenspiegel*, the earliest extant version of which dates from 1515 but which as a story is far earlier; the *Lalebuch* (1597), the story of the dullards of the burgher class; and the most famous of all *Volksbücher*, the *Faustbuch*, first printed by Johann Spiess of Frankfurt in 1587. In this the life of Faust, a charlatan whose career aroused great excitement in the Germany of the time, is related from a strict Lutheran standpoint so as to hold him up as a terrifying example of the godless pursuit of knowledge, power and pleasure.

Pamphlet, anecdote and *Volksbuch* were the forms through which German prose acquired that flexibility and power of expression which laid the foundation for the novel as an art-form. The founder of the German novel was Jörg Wickram (1520–62), a native of Colmar. His tales *Galmy* (1539) and *Gabriotto* (1551) are in the style of the *Volksbuch* but in his *Knabenspiegel* (1554) he plunges into the everyday life of his time. The story tells of the fate of Wilibaldus, son of a Colmar patrician, whose mistaken upbringing has led him into evil ways and who is moved to record his experiences. Into this real-life situation Wickram introduces the figure of Fridbert, a hardworking, ambitious farmer's boy, who becomes a stepbrother to Wilibaldus; by juxtaposing the careers of these two characters, the one set on a downward path, the other in the ascendancy, the author produces a realistic description of various classes of society and achieves a considerable charm and attractiveness, as in the scene where the two boyhood companions meet again. The realistic, down-to-earth language is attractive too; the conventional middle-class morality of the work, on the other hand, makes for a certain poverty of characterization. *Der Goldfaden* (1557), a novel set in Portugal, is richer in poetic motifs and occasionally achieves real artistic power, particularly in the early sections; it was reprinted many times, and Clemens Brentano was sufficiently attracted to it to urge its republication.

The most powerful and independent personality among late-sixteenth-century German writers is Johann Fischart (1546–90) who, like Wickram, was a Protestant from Alsace. As a student in France and Italy he had outgrown the narrowness of his bourgeois German upbringing and become an adherent of Calvinism and an opponent of Catholicism and the Jesuits, a supporter of the Huguenots and an admirer of French intellectual life.

His works are of two kinds: polemical Protestant writings such as *Der Bienenkorb des heiligen römischen Immenschwarms* (1579) and *Das Jesuiter-hütlein* (1580); and satirical works, in which his patriotism leads him to expose, sometimes viciously, sometimes ironically, the shortcomings of the German character and of conditions in contemporary Germany. Thus, like Murner at the beginning of the century, Fischart sets himself up as preacher and judge, adopting the pose of mockery in order to proclaim the truth. His works include a rhymed version of *Eulenspiegel* (1572), in which he adds to the story from his own experience; an attack on soothsayers called *Aller Praktik Großmutter* (1572); a satire on human life called *Der Flöhhatz* (1573), in which men are chased like household pests; *Philosophisch Ehzuchtbüchlein* (1578), on the topical subject of marriage as seen through Protestant eyes; and *Das glückhafte Schiff* (1576), an imaginary journey along the Rhine from Zürich to Strasbourg by citizens of Zürich, in the course of which he digresses in a learned tone on all manner of moral subjects.

Fischart's idol as a fearless and independent critic of society was Rabelais, and the first impression made by Fischart's main work, his *Geschichtsklitterung* (*klittern* = scribble), the most bizarre and shapeless literary work of the period, is of a mere translation of Rabelais's *Gargantua*. Fischart indeed worked from the first book of *Gargantua* but eventually produced a work three times the length of his model, transferring the scene of the action to Germany and shifting the satirical emphasis from the realm of education to that of morality. There is no limit to Rabelais's mockery, even in religious matters, but Fischart, a Protestant with absolute faith in the Bible, preserves a certain dignity and religious respect in his satire.

As a man of the people, Fischart also addresses himself to the lower classes. Conditions in Germany, questions of education, food, clothing and marriage are discussed, and the vices of drunkenness and boorishness pilloried in the most grotesque and exaggerated manner. The climax is reached with 'Die trunkene Litanei', in which a feast of revelling is described solely by means of conversations, exclamations and songs, leaving the impression that one has experienced the whole scene, not with one's eyes but through one's ears, as a confused Babel of voices from which emerge shouts of joy, wild ejaculations and rowdy songs. The interminable digressions from the central action, itself of slender proportions; the changes from literal translation of Rabelais to episodes of Fischart's own invention; the often exaggerated use of puns, neologisms and other verbal tricks; the accumulation of qualifying epithets: these are some of the characteristics which, attractive as they were to Jean Paul, Wilhelm Raabe and others, make the work difficult for the modern reader to penetrate. One must see them as the results of a change of attitude towards life and art, as part of the transition to the age of the baroque.

Baroque

GÜNTHER WEYDT

The name 'baroque' is usually applied to seventeenth-century German literature, although there is general agreement that the European cultural movement that bears this name began before the year 1600 in a number of areas and continued to be a force down to the beginning of the age of Goethe. It had a lasting influence on the art, attitudes and conduct of almost all countries, yet its development was far from uniform.

Early nineteenth-century literary criticism was concerned with the identification of lingering Renaissance traits or of elements that anticipated classicism. Wilhelm Scherer (d. 1886), for instance, still distinguished between 'Reformation and Renaissance' (1517–1648) and 'The Beginnings of Modern Literature' (post 1648); the pre-eighteenth-century characteristics that did not fit this pattern were regarded, both by him and by like-minded critics as *Schwulst*, and all 'artificial' traits were seen as lapses of taste.

A change came with the art-historian Heinrich Wölfflin (*Kunstgeschichtliche Grundbegriffe* (1915)), who saw in 'baroque' not decadence but an original and independent style. Since Wölfflin Renaissance (with its qualities of line, breadth, self-contained form, clarity and variety) and baroque (characterized by decorativeness, depth, open form, obscurity and unity) have been regarded as independent styles of equal quality.

German literary criticism took Wölfflin's pattern to the point of oversimplification, seeking to define baroque by isolating its natural, dynamic, subjective and technically innovatory features; later research drew attention to those very features – strictness of form, self-containedness – which recall the Renaissance and humanist traditions. Ernst Robert Curtius suggested replacing the term 'baroque' by 'mannerism', which would emphasize the potential 'anti-classical element'. But despite these divergences it is not impossible to give a basic characterization of the period – although, as in all other periods, there is naturally an intermingling of the various trends and interests.

Throughout Europe the period from 1570 to 1750 is dominated by Renaissance, Reformation and Counter-Reformation. It is the second epoch of scientific discoveries and technical inventions. The Renaissance had increased man's awareness of life and discovered nature; the Reformation had reformulated the principles of the Christian faith and made man responsible to his own conscience at a time when humanism, Gutenberg's invention of the movable-type printing press and the discoveries of Copernicus, Columbus and others had introduced new perspectives which conditioned man's view of the world. As a result man felt both free and confronted with new challenges, and began to sense his individuality – on the one hand his insignificance in the universe, on the other his power to explore it. The organization of state and society assumed his power of action, yet the authoritative, class-dominated structure of that society restricted this power. The unity of Christianity had been destroyed, and the various confessions clamoured more and more urgently for the individual's attention. Man was living in an age in which emergent rationalist philosophy and experimental science were as important as the power of faith and the urge to mystic contemplation. It was a situation that encouraged the interaction of the most heterogeneous speculations and philosophies.

In literature writers turned to the vernacular languages, albeit taking their lead in poetry from antiquity and neo-Latinity, as well as admitting stimuli from neighbouring countries. Europe was flooded with translations, adaptations, paraphrases, parodies and imitations, and poets in Italy, Spain, France, the Netherlands, England and Germany saw themselves as their respective nations' Horace, Catullus, Sophocles and Seneca. When Fleming cried, believing that Opitz had just passed away, 'Du Pindar, du Homer, du Maro unsrer Zeiten!' – he was not just uttering a panegyric but couching his praise in a style which, though rhetorical to a degree, was based on precise knowledge of Opitz's own metres and stylistic traits. Poets were in fact expressly encouraged to compose 'Petrarchized' or 'Opitzized' verse.

The baroque period coincides with the age of the first full, free reproduction and distribution of books. The Renaissance and the Reformation had been able to make little use of this facility, since they had been concerned only with scholarly texts or with works of the most general interest, such as religious pamphlets and tracts, pro- and anti-Luther writings, political broadsheets, prophecies, songs, farces, chronicles and anecdotes for general consumption. Only after the Renaissance did printing serve a literature which was read, and re-read, for its own sake, such as the serious vernacular lyric.

The coincidence of new and old forces at this time produced a situation characterized as much by tension and conflict as by the desire for a reconciliation of opposites. Perhaps more violently than before or since, national and international, pagan and Christian, life-affirming and life-denying, conservative and progressive tendencies were in conflict, and one cannot typify the age by referring to conformity and rationalism more than to irrationalism and a trend to forthright individuality and mysticism. We must be prepared to meet a situation of paradoxes, sometimes circumstantial, sometimes implicit. Neither can baroque be seen as a movement dominated by the values of court civilization, Catholicism and Counter-Reformation or, on the other side, of North German Protestantism. Poets such as Spee, Opitz, Gryphius, Andreae, Vondel, Anton Ulrich, Silesius and Grimmelshausen may seem at times to be drawn to the one side or the other but they cannot be understood in terms of one side alone.

German baroque literature gives a generally true picture of the age. The religious schism brought about by Luther and Calvin had led to the confrontation of two warring parties well before the outbreak of the Thirty Years War. The conflict reached its climax during the war and lasted beyond the Peace of Westphalia but it also brought about a profitable intellectual debate and led men to clarify their attitudes. Herbert Schöffler (*Deutscher Osten im deutschen Geist* (1940)) has shown that the literary dominance of Silesia is due largely or even entirely to the complex religious situation in which a predominantly Protestant population with individual Catholic areas was ruled by both Catholic and Calvinist princes. Power changed hands several times in the course of the war, but under imperial Catholic rule the Protestants, though in the majority, were persistently denied the opportunity to have their own university. As a result Silesian scholars and writers went to study in Holland, particularly at the University of Leyden, where they learned about Calvinism and were brought into contact with the latest scientific and intellectual developments. Gryphius, for instance, obtained his knowledge of humanist and Jesuit drama in this way, while learning of Catholic and Protestant didactic literature in his native Silesia, further Protestant and Catholic dramas during his travels through much of Europe, and much else through reading works in foreign languages. A similar situation existed in the Protestant town of Nürnberg, where Catholic writings in Romance languages were studied, or in the valley of the upper Rhine, where Grimmelshausen's friends and patrons lived.

A further consequence of the bitter religious struggles in Germany was a delay in the arrival of the Renaissance proper. Opitz is virtually the first to have aligned German literature with the rules and practice of classical authors. The Renaissance thus only makes itself felt after German has already absorbed elements from various other national literatures. German literary baroque can be defined in part as a second Renaissance, modified by a modern, international humanism.

At the same time the German lead in printing since Gutenberg promoted the spread of other than literary works in the narrow sense. The rapidly increasing interest in printed matter of all kinds led to experiments, often involving other arts and sciences, as a result of which a literature arose which reached an audience far greater than that for *belles lettres*. Baroque literature in the wide sense is not simply a matter of dramas, novels and poems but also of innumerable writings of an encyclopedic, historical, religious, allegorical, political and lightly didactic nature which cut across the accustomed division into genres. Men of such contrasting talents as Andreas Gryphius and Christoph von Grimmelshausen derived the greater part of their knowledge from such publications, which dominated the book market with titles such as 'Memorial', 'Viridarium', 'Allgemeiner Schauplatz', 'Theatrum', 'Oeconomia', 'Historie', 'Gesprächsspiele' and 'Relationen'.

Foreign works from every conceivable source, many of which emphasized the unusual and the grotesque, had a similar effect. Until about 1693 there were more Latin works than German, and in the seventeenth and early eighteenth centuries the use of French greatly increased. There is also the appreciable influence on the courts of Italian opera and, for a time, of English drama, through the activities of the strolling players.

This excessive foreign influence was encouraged not only by the universal ideal of culture but also by the presence of foreign armies on German soil. Many writers complained of, and parodied, the resultant linguistic confusion, but they also acknowledged their debt to it by using it to increase their range of expression and give their work at least a veneer of scholarship.

Even 'pure' German literature often appears haphazard and occasionally absurd. Any effort towards common attitudes, tastes and procedures was thwarted by the absence of a single dominating court or of a metropolis like Paris. After 1648 the situation seemed to work against the development of the essay, the drama and literary criticism, whereas in the plastic arts and in music the late development of baroque proved of inestimable value.

What may be designated as 'modern' in post-medieval German literature starts with the baroque 'school' of Opitz. Born in 1597 in Silesia, Opitz acquired a wide learning at various Silesian schools and in the houses of various patrons, went to Heidelberg in 1619 and joined the circle of Zincgref and Lingelsheim. Avoiding the theatres of war, he visited Holland, Jutland and Transsylvania and spent most of his remaining years in Silesia and Danzig or on diplomatic and literary missions. He died in Danzig in 1639. Less a poet in the strict sense than a promoter of poetic activity, he was a figure of great influence; his numerous works demonstrated to the age the feasibility of composing classically inspired literary works in German, and his translations were long regarded as models.

His first significant publications, the *Teutsche Poemata* (published 1624, revised edition 1625) and the *Buch von der Deutschen Poeterey* (1624), achieved the all-important breakthrough: for in spite of his brevity, the poverty of many of his arguments and his almost total lack of originality, he brought about a revolution greater than that achieved by almost any other German writer before or since. His reforms had three main emphases: (1) the elevation and purification of the German poetic language; (2) the replacement of syllable-counting by the coincidence of verbal and metrical accent; (3) the advocation of certain specific metres and strophic forms for use in poetry.

On the first point Opitz refers to the significance and the age-old tradition of poetry, which he calls 'hidden theology'. He calls on Musaios, Orpheus, Homer, Plato and others as witnesses, and then on medieval court poetry, thereby dissociating himself from the less exalted tradition of the early seventeenth century. He warns against the use of dialect rhymes, as in the couplet:

> Der darff nicht sorgen für den spot,
> Der einen schaden krieget hot.

He issues further warnings against the use of any impure rhymes, anastrophe ('Das mündlein roht'), the excessive use of foreign words, the arbitrary use of the weak *e*, pleonasm, etc.

His rules on accentuation are still valid: accented and unaccented syllables come to correspond to the long and short vowels of classical prosody, as is natural to the German language. Before Opitz a strophe might run:

> Gott / welcher Geber ist vnsers und alles guts /
> Geb / daß die Teutschen auch / folgend jhren Vorfahren /
> Wie freygebig Sie seind jhrer Reichthumb vnd Bluts /
> Begihrig bleiben / Sein vnd Ihr Ehr zu bewahren.
>
> > (Weckherlin)

After Opitz's reforms, however, one finds:

> DEs schweren Krieges Last / den Deutschland jetzt empfindet /
> Vnd daß GOTT nicht vmbsonst so hefftig angezündet
> Den Eyfer seiner Macht / auch wo in solcher Pein
> Trost her zu holen ist / sol mein Getichte seyn.
>
> > (Opitz, *TrostGedichte*)

He only admits iambs and trochees, i.e. he insists, for printed lyric verse, on strict alternation, which was initially a beneficial innovation. Buchner (*c.* 1640) does on occasion reintroduce the dactyl, which Opitz had excluded, but not until Klopstock does one find the highest degree of discipline and freedom in the use of classical metres, and only in his odes does the use of hexameter and pentameter become possible.

As to metres and strophic forms Opitz prescribes, for the former, the alexandrine and the *vers commun*, for the latter, the four-line stanza, the sonnet and the ode, but his remarks on the various formal types, far from giving precise guidance, vacillate between mere description and attempts at classification, and instead of dwelling on the actual existing forms in Germany, such as prose narrative, folksong, *Schwank* and Meistersang, he writes on what, according to the classical canon, he thinks ought to exist.

Heroic poems, for instance, he describes as extensive works dealing with 'elevated subjects'; tragedy takes place among kings and great rulers and describes terrifying events; comedy deals with weddings, festivities, deceit, roguery, the irresponsibility of youth 'and similar matters typical of the lives of the common people'. Satire, epigram, elegy, ode, sylva and lyric are also mentioned. Equally uninformative are his comments on the eclogue, which treats of 'sheep, goats and agricultural matters' and, he goes on, 'pflegen alles worvon sie reden, als von Liebe, heyrathen, absterben, buhlschafften, festtagen vnnd sonsten auff jhre bäwrische vnd einfältige art vor zue bringen' ('deal in simple rustic style with love, marriage, death, courtship, celebrations and other such subjects').

Opitz's *Ars poetica* is neither original nor specific. Max Kommerell criticized Scaliger and the whole movement 'for disguising problems instead of facing them', and the same is true of Opitz. One must, however, remember that like all authors of treatises on prosody at this time, whether Latin or vernacular, Opitz was chiefly concerned with conveying information rather than with solving problems. He follows the line from Horace through Scaliger, Vida and Ronsard down to Heinsius, and at times even copies word for word from his predecessors – as, indeed, did many of these predecessors among themselves. Yet he did have a keen eye for essentials, and his activities proved of great benefit to German humanistic conceptions of poetry.

Opitz's *Buch von der Deutschen Poeterey* was frequently reprinted right up to the middle of the eighteenth century, and his example was quickly followed – Buchner's *Wegweiser* or *Anleitung* (circulated in manuscript form from 1638 onwards), Birken's *Teutsche Rede- Bind- und Dicht-kunst*, Zesen's *Deutscher Helicon* (1640), Harsdörffer's *Poetischer Trichter* (1647 onwards), works by Titz, Schottelius, Tscherning, Morhof, Christian Weise and, finally, Gottsched's *Critische Dichtkunst* (1730). Like Opitz's work, all these are prescriptive; at the same time they contain a far greater body of material for the use of both learned and budding poets than does Opitz's treatise. However, Opitz's reputation in the seventeenth century can be judged from a remark of Weise's in 1691 that the 'old manner' is pre-Opitz and the 'new manner' post-Opitz. Goethe, too, acknowledged these rules in his youth (*Dichtung und Wahrheit*, Book V), and in the *Theatralische Sendung* Wilhelm Meister studies poetry in the same spirit: Wilhelm's first great poetic achievement was a tragedy in alexandrines, composed according to theoretical principles of *imitatio*.

The attempt to lay down a norm naturally produced reactions, for dogmatism prevents creative experiment. Even Opitz indirectly modified his theory: there is nothing in his *Poetery* about romances or operas, yet in 1626 he translated Barclay's Latin romance *Argenis* (1621) into German, in 1627 he produced the first German operatic libretto (*Dafne*) from that of Rinuccini, and in 1638 he made a version of Sidney's *Arcadia*, which had appeared in translation shortly before and which hardly met the criteria of Opitz's own definition of pastoral poetry. In his *Schäfferey von der Nimfen Hercinie* (1630) he turns completely away from his own theories, for it is more a motley collection of learned and somewhat affected items than a unified poetic portrayal of pastoral life. And when we turn to his German rhymed versions of the complete Book of Psalms, translated from Latin, French and Hebrew recensions, we see Opitz, the founder of the early baroque school, both in his conservative and in his progressive roles.

Like Opitz, the so-called 'Linguistic Societies' (*Sprachgesellschaften*), groups of poets and men interested in literature, called for the elevation and purification of the German language. The demand was for symmetry, clarity, and conformity, though actual literary practice was very different.

The most influential of these Linguistic Societies was the 'Fruchtbringende Gesellschaft' of 1617, which counted princes, scholars, aristocrats, burghers, Protestants and Catholics from all parts of Germany among its members. Its object was the cultivation and refinement of the German language, and its methods followed those of similar linguistic societies in other countries, above all the 'Accademia della Crusca' in Florence. Other such societies were the 'Aufrichtige Tannengesellschaft' (Strasbourg, 1633); the 'Teutschgesinnte Genossenschaft' (Hamburg, founded in 1642 by Philipp von Zesen); the 'Löbliche Hirten- und Blumenorden' (Nürnberg, 1644), a group centred on the poets Harsdörffer, Claius and Sigmund von Birken; the 'Elbschwanenorden' (Lübeck, founded in 1656 by Rist); and the 'Kürbishütte' in Königsberg, attended by Simon Dach, Heinrich Albert, Robert Roberthin and other poets and musicians who were less concerned than other groups with making an impact on the outside world.

The 'Pegnitz-Schäfer' of Nürnberg are of particular interest. In poetry they went beyond Opitz in their search for onomatopoeic and neologistic extensions of the poetic vocabulary; at the same time they made translations and adaptations of many foreign works which came to have

EGL

considerable importance for Catharina von Greiffenberg, Anton Ulrich von Braunschweig, Grimmelshausen and others, and in spite of their strict Protestant attitudes and a tendency to rationalism they show themselves remarkably receptive to French and Italian Catholic writings. With the 'Pegnitz-Schäfer', as with all such reforming bodies, one observes many contradictions between theory and practice. On the one hand they demanded a 'pure' German, and on the other they tended towards a highly artificial use of language with many foreign elements; they wrote poetic dedications to each other in Latin and Greek rather than in German, and by affecting a desire for Arcadia behind the *persona* of pastoral poets, they revealed their activity as the literary game that it was.

The epigram, together with the couplet and the four-line strophe, is one of the most popular of baroque forms and is often regarded as the most characteristic lyric utterance of the age. One must not overlook, however, the great variety of subject-matter, which embraces classical motifs in the style of Martial at one extreme and mystic, pansophic material at the other. Opitz, for example, found himself confronted by such a rich, yet variegated epigrammatic tradition, and it is not surprising that in the survey of Middle High German poetry in his *Poeterey* he should have singled out Walther von der Vogelweide, Reinmar von Zweter and Marner. Marot in France, Owen in England and Euricius Cordus in Germany had revived the classical epigram in the Renaissance, but it was Opitz who brought the decisive influence to bear, in the form of rhymed epigrams of a classicistic type. According to his theory the epigram is a *satyra*, characterized by its brevity and its incisiveness, and in his own *Poemata* the epigram predominates. The type is extended by his translation of the *Dionysii Catonis Disticha* and the 'Quatrains of Herr von Pibrac', and subsequently by the numerous 'Sinnreden', 'Sinngedichte', 'Reimensprüche', 'Monodisticha', 'Beischriften', 'Grabschriften', 'Inschriften', etc., of later poets – Gryphius, Logau, Stieler, Hofmannswaldau, Abschatz, Wernicke and many others.

In kind these epigrams range from the homely, didactic rhymed *sententia* to the moralistic anecdote. In 1654 Friedrich von Logau, an adviser to various minor Silesian nobles, published under the pseudonym 'Salomon von Golau' a collection called *Deutscher Sinn-Getichte Drey Tausend*. Logau is the master of the direct, concentrated and penetrating *Spruch*; Lessing rescued him from oblivion and the nineteenth century esteemed him highly. One of his *Sinngedichte* has become well known through Keller's *Zürcher Novellen*:

> Wie wilstu weisse Lilien zu rothen Rosen machen?
> Küß eine weisse Galathe; sie wird erröthet lachen.

(How can you turn a white lily into a red rose? By kissing a white Galatea and making her blush.)

Kaspar Stieler – student, preacher, soldier, scribe, actor and writer of comedies – travelled all over Europe, fought first in the Thirty Years War, then in the Franco-Spanish and Polno-Spanish Wars. His *Geharnschte Venus* (1660) shows him as a German Catullus, Tibullus or Propertius, and to his lyric pieces he appends *Sinnreden* of a bold kind taken up again by later poets.

The epigrammatic style was also used to express the Christian message. Opitz had urged *carpe diem* in this transient world, and Gryphius gives this attitude a Christian slant:

> Mein sind die Jahre nicht / die mir die Zeit genommen
> Mein sind die Jahre nicht / die etwa möchten kommen
> Der Augenblick ist mein / und nehm ich den in acht
> So ist der mein / der Jahr und Ewigkeit gemacht.

(Mine are not the years that have passed or the years that are to come. Just the moment is mine: if I grasp it, I shall have grasped what time and eternity are made of.)

The strain of mysticism and bold religious speculation leads from Opitz, Böhme and Abraham a Santa Clara to Franckenberg, Czepko and Silesius. There are thousands of couplets which tell of man's craving for grace and desire for union with God. The *Sexcenta Monodisticha Sapientum* of Daniel Czepko provided Angelus Silesius (Johann Scheffler) with his starting-point. Silesius was a convert from Protestantism to Catholicism but at his most representative he is an almost pure mystic, and his *Cherubinischer Wandersmann* is a religious work free of any sectional attachment. These poems, like the work of Grimmelshausen, have a quality of timelessness which stands out in an age dominated by the thought of the transience of life:

> Nicht du bist in dem Orth, der Orth der ist in dir:
> Wirfstu jhn auß, so steht die Ewigkeit schon hier.

(You are not in a place; it is the place that is in you. If you throw it out, eternity is yours.)

or:

> Du selber machst die Zeit: daß Uhrwerk sind die Sinnen;
> Hemstu die Unruh nur, so ist die Zeit von hinnen.

(You yourself create time; your senses are what keep it going. If you curb your restlessness, time will vanish.)

The sonnet too shows the influence of the epigram, and has in this age a similar role to that of the *Spruch* in the Middle High German period. It treats of religious, political and didactic themes and also has erotic elements, usually of a meditative kind, as in poems in praise of woman. In construction these sonnets follow Romance convention: the two quartets are identical (abba abba), while the two terzets are independent. Attempts to break with these conventions are extremely rare, though critics have sometimes regarded such breaks with tradition as typical manifestations of the 'baroque' spirit. In the first instance it was a matter of learning these formal requirements. The important influences are Italian (Petrarch, Veronica Gambara), French (Du Bellay, Ronsard) and Dutch (the poets of the Bloemhof Collection); Weckherlin is the first real German poet to attempt to master the sonnet; Opitz experiments with its possibilities in his various translations and adaptations, but the first considerable poetic achievements in sonnet form are those of a later generation, above all Fleming and Gryphius.

To start with, Paul Fleming (1609–40) kept to Italian models, using hyperbole and other traditional figures of speech to intensify his lamentation:

> *Er redet der Liebsten Augen an, die er umfinge*
> Ihr seid es, die ihr mir die meinen machet blind,
> ihr lichten Spiegel ihr, da ich die ganzen Schmerzen
> leibhaftig kan besehn von mein und ihrem Herzen.
> Ihr Werkstat, da die Gunst die güldnen Fäden spinnt,
>   darüber Meister ist das kluge Venus-Kind,
> ihr, meine Sonn und Mon, ihr irdnen Himmelskerzen . . .

(*He Addresses the Eyes of his Beloved*. It is you who make my own eyes blind, you bright mirrors, in which I can see all the sufferings of my heart and hers. You are a place where Favour spins her golden threads, a place in which Amor reigns. My sun and moon, you heavenly candles burning on earth . . .)

But as Fleming's conditions of life were different from those of Opitz, who remained calculating and practical in everything, so we find that personal feelings and a greater intensity begin to show themselves, first in the strophic lyric, then in the sonnet. Fleming's sonnets are great achievements and carry conviction not only by their mastery of technique but also by their profound seriousness:

> Ich war an Kunst und Gut und Stande groß und reich,
> des Glückes lieber Sohn, von Eltern guter Ehren,
> frei, meine, kunte mich aus meinen Mittlen nähren,
> mein Schall floh über weit, kein Landsman sang mir gleich,

von Reisen hochgepreist, für keiner Mühe bleich,
jung, wachsam, unbesorgt. Man wird mich nennen hören,
bis daß die letzte Glut dies Alles wird verstören.
Diß, deutsche Klarien, diß Ganze dank ich euch.

(I was richly endowed with ability, property and rank, favoured by fortune, son of honourable parents, free and able to support myself, my poems were known far afield and no one was my equal; highly praised on my journeys, afraid of no hardship, young, watchful, carefree. My name will be heard until the day all the world is consumed by fire. And for all this it is you that I thank, O German Muses!)

Like Fleming, Andreas Gryphius, who was born in the year of Shakespeare's death and died 100 years after Shakespeare's birth, was far superior to Opitz as a writer of sonnets. As early as his small collection *Lissaer Sonnette* (1637) the few occasional poems are outweighed by the intensity and profundity of the religious motifs. These qualities grow ever more pronounced, until in the *Sonnette in vier Büchern* (including two books of *Sonn- und Feiertags-Sonnette* (1650 and 1657)), published in its final definitive form in 1663, we have the first really successful sonnet-cycle. A now familiar conversance with the Bible; an intimate knowledge of didactic Protestant writings; familiarity with symbolism; the work of Opitz: all these combined in an impressive *œuvre* whose unity rested on the allegorical modes of medieval thought and on the spiritual values of Christianity.

Both secular and religious sonnets continued to follow Romance models to a large extent. This is true, for example, of the mystical poetry of Catharina Regina von Greiffenberg (1633–94), an Austrian Protestant, behind whose religious exterior lies a spirit one could almost call adventurous. A member of the Nürnberg circle of Sigmund von Birken, she sought nothing less than to convert the Emperor to Protestantism and thereby solve the entire religious problem in Europe, and she directed her poetry to this end.

Of an even bolder temperament, and a man whose nature was far from what one conventionally understands by poetic, was Quirinus Kuhlmann (1651–89), a visionary who saw it as his vocation to found a new kingdom of peace. In company with many others he started as a scholar and virtuoso poet of the Silesian School; his *Grabschriften* show his skill as an epigrammist, his collection of aphorisms (1671) reveal his extensive learning and at the age of twenty-one he was made *poeta laureatus*. He then found his way into the company of various Dutch sects and was inspired by Böhme's *Mysterium magnum* to seek to found a new Christian state, about which he writes in his *Kühlpsalter* (1684–6). The spirit of rapture, of self-abandonment and of experimentation filled his life and his work, and in response to these urges he made journeys to

England, France, Rome, Amsterdam and Constantinople – where he even attempted to convert the Sultan. His final voyage was to Russia, where he was burned at the stake as an agitator and false prophet by order of the Patriarch. His religious sonnets, *Himmlische Liebes-Küsse* (1671), keep to the strict sonnet-form but contain a great number of paradoxes, antitheses, anaphoras and exaggerated images which have come to be regarded as a principal feature of baroque:

> *Über den Thränen-würdigen Tod des Sohnes Gottes | Jesus*
> Reiß Erde! reiß entzwei! der Printzen printz erblaßt!
> Der uns erschaffen hat | ist gantz zerritzt mit streichen!
> Gott | welcher ewig ist | wird nun zu einer Leichen!
> Es kleidet Purpur an des Leibes Alabast!
> Den nichts umschlüssen mag | den hat ein Holtz umfaßt!
> Der Berg und Hügel wigt | der wil am Kreutz erbleichen!
> Dem Erd und Himmel weicht | der wil dem Kreiß entweichen!
> Des Vaters Lust | GOtt selbst wird Salem eine Last.
> Di Sonne fleucht vor uns! . . .

(*On the Lamentable Death of Jesus, Son of God.* Rend thyself asunder, O earth! The Prince of Princes is dying! He who created us has been cut to pieces by whips! God, who is everlasting, is about to become a corpse! The alabaster of the body is clothed in a purple robe! The Incommensurable One is nailed to a plank of wood! He who moves hills and mountains is going to expire on the cross! He to whom earth and heaven bow is about to leave the world! The joy of the Father, God Himself, will be a charge on the conscience of Jerusalem. The sun is fleeing from us! . . .)

Alongside the sonnet we find the ode and the strophic lyric. The ode is principally a post-Reformation form, based on classical models put forward by the humanists and the poets of the Pléiade. Lyric poetry derives rather from the native tradition and, in spite of the artistic modifications to which it was submitted, it retained its closeness to popular tradition. The change from the communal poetry of the fifteenth and sixteenth century to the modern lyric came only gradually and in response to specific musical, linguistic, formal or intellectual stimuli.

The Italian *villanella* reached Germany in 1576 with the *Kurtzweilige Teutsche Lieder* of Jakob Regnart, a Dutchman living in Vienna. He was followed by Schallenberg, Denaisius, Hoeck and Schein, transitional figures in poetry and music, but even in High Baroque and later simplicity and directness retained an influence. The joys and sufferings of love are themes in the lyrics of Schede-Melissus, Opitz, Dach, Rist, Stieler, Abschatz, Birken and many others. Much apparently straightforward lyric verse, however, is not as uncomplicated as it looks, for besides having a ready intelligibility and accessibility, these poems are decked out with learned allusions and moralizing messages, and sometimes turn out to be religious allegories. Even the poems of the Königsberg circle – Albert, Dach, Roberthin and others – which have a simple, direct appeal felt even today, were generally given titles hardly remembered at the present time. Dach's well-known poem

> Der Mensch hat nichts so eigen,
> So wol steht jhm nichts an . . .

is not called 'Loyalty' but 'Perstet amicitiae semper venerabile Foedus'; and the poem

> Der Mey / des Jahres Hertz / beginnt . . . .

has the title 'Perpetui coelum tempora veris habet'. The well-known *Volkslied* 'Ännchen von Tharau', made famous by Herder, makes its effect by its expression of a true, unshakeable love, but it is not an individual utterance; rather it is a kind of wedding song which served a specific social function in the life of the time.

Simplicity, in fact, retains its appeal throughout the baroque period, and even a poet so deeply indebted to the Petrarchian sonnet as Paul Fleming expressed his feelings of love and suffering in a simple, sincere manner in his lyric verse:

> Ein getreues Herze wissen
> hat des höchsten Schatzes Preis.
> Der ist selig zu begrüssen,
> der ein treues Herze weiß.
> Mir ist wol bei höchstem Schmerze,
> denn ich weiß ein treues Herze.

(To know a true heart is as valuable as the richest treasure. It is a blissful man who knows a true heart. I am happy in my great suffering because I know a true heart.)

This matter-of-fact-ness is still present, albeit with a different subject-matter, in the *galant* lyric and in the hymn, which has changed little over the years. As in the sixteenth century the Protestant hymn now acquired great richness and variety; it had the status of true poetry and often opened collections of lyric verse. Though remaining a congregational form, as in Luther's time, it became personalized and began to interact with the personal lyric of both religious and secular content. The line of development from Philipp Nicolai's (1556–1608) 'Wie schön leuchtet der Morgenstern' to Grimmelshausen's 'Komm Trost der Nacht' provides much interesting material for study. The best of such hymns are found to be by poets otherwise remembered for their non-religious works (Fleming's 'In allen meinen Taten' and Rist's 'O Ewigkeit, du Donnerwort') or by preachers such as Nicolai, Johannes Heerman and the greatest of all, Paul Gerhardt (1607–76). Johann Matthäus Meyfart's best-known hymn is inserted in a sermon, thus showing that it was not intended to have its own independent existence:

1

Jubelgesang	JErusalem du hochgebawte Stadt
vnd dieses Orts	Wolt Gott / wer Ich in dir!
eingeführet	Mein sehnlich Hertz so groß Verlangen hat /
worden.	Vnd ist nicht mehr bey mir!
	Weit vber Berg vnd Thale
	Weit über flache Feld
	Schwingt es sich überale
	Vnd eylt aus diser Welt.

Also erseufften betrübte Christen / wenn sie den heutigen Zustandt / Elend vnd Jammer wo nicht ansehen doch erfahren. Sie wündschen:

2

O schöner Tag / vnd noch viel schönste Stund
Wenn wirstu kommen schier!
Da ich mit Lust / mit Freudenfreyen Mund
Die Seele geb von mir:
In Gottes trewe Hände . . .

(Jerusalem, thou noble city, would God that I were in thee! My heart has such great yearning and is no longer here: it is far away beyond the mountains and valleys and fields, hastening out of this world.

This is the manner in which disconsolate Christians react when they see for themselves, or learn from others, the cares and miseries of present life:

O beautiful day and most glorious hour, when wilt thou come? With joy and with praises on my lips I give my soul into the faithful hands of God . . .)

In the field of the Catholic lyric the combination of mystic piety and a pastoral style adapted to religious needs produces striking results, especially in Spee and Silesius. Friedrich Spee von Langenfeld (1591–1635), a Jesuit but an opponent of witch-hunts, whose collection *Trutz Nachtigall* was not published till well after his death (1649), achieves delicacy and sincerity in his lyrics, which owe something both to folksong and to art-song; the beauties of nature and the praise of God are depicted in a pastoral style both fashionable and naïve:

Eine Ecloga oder Hirtengesang

von Christo dem Herren im Garten, under der Person des Hirten Daphnis, welchen der himmlische Sternenhirt, das ist der Mon, allweil er seine Sternen hütet, kläglich betrauet.

Mon des Himmels treib zur Weiden
Deine Schaflein güldengelb,
Auf geründter blauen Heiden
Laß die Sternen walten selb.
Ich noch neulich so tät reden,
Da zur Nacht ein schwacher Hirt
Aller Wegen, Steg und Pfäden
Sucht ein Schäflein mit Begierd.
Gleich der Mon ihm liess gesagen,
Nahm ein lind gestimmtes Rohr:
Tat es blasend zärtlich nagen,
Spielet seinen Sternen vor.

(*An Eclogue or Shepherd's Song* of Christ the Lord in the garden, in the character of the shepherd Daphnis who is mourned by the shepherd of the stars, the moon, as he watches over the firmament. – O Moon, drive your golden sheep out to pasture and let the stars rule over the soft blue fields. This is how I spoke when a poor shepherd was anxiously searching the paths and tracks one night for a lost lamb. The moon spoke to him, took up a gentle pipe and played a delicate air to the stars.)

The 'classical' style of Opitz and his successors is offset by a 'non-classical' style, which is what one has in mind when talking of 'baroque' lyric or 'mannerism'. But rather than a direct contrast it is a kind of continuation and modification of existing forms which was already well advanced by the time of Lohenstein, Hofmannswaldau and other late-baroque poets. Seen in terms of the contemporary German situation, the inheritance of European humanism and the Renaissance had been successfully absorbed, and within the limits open to them poets like Fleming and Gryphius had shown their mastery of literary techniques. They depicted the lives both of individuals and of the community at large, graphically revealing the conflicts, the confusions and the religious trends of the time. But where the early Silesian School as a whole was energetically promoting the rational and moral development of the new German literature, Philipp von Zesen was already seeking to extend the potentialities of language and artistic expression. Going far beyond the followers of Opitz, he discovered new possibilities above all in metre and rhythm: he used the dactyl with remarkable skill, developed onomatopoeia and made all manner of verbal, syntactical and literary experiments:

O trautes härts! was härts? vihl härter noch als hart
o! stahl? mit nichten stahl; es lässt sich bässer zühen.
wi dan magneht? o nein; ihm ist vihl mehr verlihen.
ı̈st's dan ein deamant? auch nicht; dan diser ward
ım schäzzen nahch-gesäzt däs härzens wunder-ahrt. . . .

(O dear heart! A hard heart? Hard? Far harder than hard. Steel? No – it is easier to bend than steel. Like a magnet? O no – there is more in it than in a magnet. Like a diamond, then? No – for a diamond is inferior in value to the wonders of the heart. . . .)

(From the Klüng-getichte auf das Härz seiner Träuen)

The lyric poetry of the Nürnberg School of Harsdörffer and Claius shows the same tendencies, occasionally reaching a point where the border between poetry and music begins to disappear:

> Es drummeln die küpfernen Drummel und summen |
> Es paukken die heiseren Paukken und brummen |
> Es lüdeln und düdeln die schlirfenden Pfeifen |
> Schalmeien die Reihen und Spiele verschweifen |
> Trommeten | Clareten Taratantara singen |
> Es drönet und thönet der Waffen Erklingen |
> Es siegen und flügen die silbernen Fahnen |
> Die Truppen die klopfen | zur Freude aufmahnen.

(From Claius's Höllen- und Himmelfahrt Jesv Chrjstj)

Such attempts to reproduce physical situations are aimed above all at the idealization of reality:

> Ein ausgeputzter Reim und Kunstgebundne Schrifft
> Die sind des Todes Tod | des Gifftes Gegengifft.

(A pure rhyme and artistic writing are the death of death and the antidote to poison.)

(From Claius's Lobrede der Teutschen Poeterey)

Attitudes of this kind almost encouraged a view of poetry as a pastime with its own inner justification.

It is only, however, with the late-baroque Silesian poets, headed by Christian Hofmann von Hofmannswaldau (1617–79), that we meet a totally committed type of poetry within this 'anti-classical' tradition. As far as Hofmannswaldau himself is concerned, it is wiser to avoid terms such as 'un-classical' and 'manneristic', which are usefully applied only to his successors, those contributors to Neukirch's anthology (see below) who were in a position to absorb the developments of a hundred years and widen the field of poetry by parody and other means.

Hofmannswaldau and Lohenstein build on previous achievements, perfecting, refining and acquiring *facilitas*. One result is the loss of the passion and intensity of Gryphius's sonnets, the insistent sincerity of Fleming's poetry, the lyric qualities of the Königsberg poets and the visionary power of Silesius, for Hofmannswaldau and his followers, adapting themselves to changed historical circumstances, are concerned not only with matters of language and style but also with matters of content. Patrician Silesian society, linked to Italy via the Austrian courts, had regarded poetry as an intellectual entertainment; the younger generation now sought to adapt this division of emotion to the needs of a new kind of intellectual aspiration. Elegance of style, together with subtlety of treatment of form and subject-matter, becomes of prime importance.

Even the most highly developed technical accomplishment cannot conceal the reality of contemporary problems. Yet the main characteristic of this late-baroque poetry – a characteristic with an admirable as well as a questionable side – is an attempt to gloss over these problems by treating them as an intellectual game in which a detached, uncommitted attitude disguises the real conflicts. This poetry shows an elegant avoidance, not solution, of realities, and the triumph of intellectual sophistication. The range of subject-matter is wide, and anything capable of subtle and refined treatment is included. Particularly popular are erotic subjects:

> IHr bleichen buhler schwartzer zeit /
> Die ihr die nächte zieret /
> Und flammen voller lieblichkeit
> Durch trübe wolcken führet /
> Werfft einen strahl
> Von eurem saal /
> Und schaut / ob meine schmertzen
> Sich gleichen euren kertzen.

(You pale lovers who delight in darkness and send flames of passion through the dark clouds, cast a ray of light down from your abode and see whether my sufferings are the equal of your beams of light.)

Or:

> IHr hellen mörderin / ihr augen schliest euch zu /
> Jedoch die schönen brüste /
> Als zunder meiner lüste /
> Geniessen keine ruh /
> Ihr auffgeblehter schnee rafft alle krafft zusammen /
> Und bläst in meine flammen.

(O eyes, you bright slayers, be closed! Her beautiful breasts inflame my desires and leave me no rest; their snow-white form captures all my powers and kindles my ardour.)   (both by Hofmannswaldau)

Lohenstein's verse has far greater intellectual substance and treats in solemn tones the vital issues of the day:

> SO bricht der glantz der welt!
> Die zeit kan auch den purpur bleichen;

> Die reinste sonne muss zu bald den west erreichen:
> Die säule reich an ertzt wird zeitlich hingefällt.
> Des himmels spruch ist nicht zu widerstehen /
> Und wer ist groß genug demselben zu entgehen?

(Thus departs the glory of the world! Time can dull even purple hues, and the purest sun reaches the west all too soon; in time the strong bronze column will be toppled. The decrees of heaven are irresistible, and no one can escape them.)

At this time the theories of Boileau concerning what was 'natural' found their way to Germany and showed themselves in rococo and Enlightenment. The first volumes (1695–7) of Benjamin Neukirch's anthology *Herrn von Hoffmannswaldau und andrer Deutschen . . . Gedichte* bring together the last Silesian baroque poets, while the final volumes contain the first rationalistic, 'enlightened' poems of the so-called court poets. These former are the source of that term which has come to be applied to all the Silesian poets, early and late: *Schwulst*.

The baroque drama is easier to characterize than the lyric. On the one hand there is little by way of native tradition to take into account; on the other, the adaptation of classical and humanist models did not lead to a comparable florescence of original works of quality. Indeed, the only considerable form to evolve from the contact between the old, local theatre of limited social appeal and the forces of the international literary world was Silesian drama. Again the pioneer is Opitz; the principal figures are Gryphius and Lohenstein.

Developments in the world of the theatre can be traced back to 1600, when attempts had been made to move beyond the Shrovetide Play, the Meistersinger drama and the early word-centred school drama. Troupes of strolling players from England, France, Italy and Holland each brought their own ethos, while poets and patrons who took part in the *peregrinatio academica* were able to study for themselves this rapidly developing art. Theatres and opera-houses were built in towns and at courts, and professional actors and producers replaced amateurs to a large extent. In addition the use of stage-settings and décor, together with the recent introduction of wings, made possible the theatre of illusion.

Particularly stimulating was the advent of the so-called English Comedians, troupes which had arisen in England during the Renaissance, extended their art during Shakespeare's time and now found favourable conditions for their performances on the Continent. 'English comedies' were performed in Dresden in 1586–7, and in Cologne and Kassel in 1592. The actors, who were not only 'comedians' but also 'tragedians', had a repertoire of effective works, and considerable technical skill, although the works they performed were not of the best and their performances tended to degenerate as time went on, containing more and more melodrama and vulgarity. At first they performed in English, generally to uneducated audiences, and played extempore to an ever-increasing degree; as a result crudities and exaggerations multiplied, and the only thing that mattered was the action.

Nevertheless these troupes were of great importance for German drama: a new kind of acting appeared, and under its influence German troupes sprang up in all parts, while the dramas of men like Jacob Ayrer of Nürnberg and Heinrich Julius von Braunschweig (*c.* 1600) took their lead from these works.

At the same period the Jesuits opened up new possibilities for the theatre. From conventional school-drama they turned to the public stage and wrote many effective and attractive plays derived from the Latin comedies of Plautus and from morality plays and other popular sources – whose place, incidentally, they quickly usurped. These works were written in Latin, but they were also provided with summaries of the plot in German, and this, together with a lavish style of production, ensured a lively dramatic experience for the audience. By emphasizing the transience of earthly life and the eternal glory of God, Jesuit drama also served the interests of the Faith.

The climax of Jesuit drama is reached with Jacob Bidermann (1578–1639), a pupil of Jacob Gretser and Jacob Pontanus. Bidermann's first independent work, *Cenodoxus, der Doktor von Paris* (1602; translated into German rhyming couplets in 1635), treats of the already popular theme of Everyman, who gives way to the temptations of power, riches, lust, worldly honour and *hubris*. A number of very different sixteenth-century works had already shown how man could forfeit his salvation: such were the *Volksbuch* of Doktor Faust (1587), the man who fascinated his age by his life as magician, devil's accomplice and seeker after knowledge, and Rollenhagen's *Vom reichen Mann und armen Lazaro*, the tale of the ostentatious, pleasure-seeking citizen. In his *Cenodoxus* Bidermann makes a man from his own class into the villain: respected and to all appearances pious, he is led astray by Hipocrisis and Philautia and is punished by God. The play made a great impression, above all in the final scenes (reminiscent of Gretser's *Udo*), where the verdict is pronounced and Cenodoxus is consigned to Hell.

Bidermann's later plays anticipate the drama of High Baroque. In *Belisarius* (1607), for instance, it is not just one man but the whole of humanity that is exposed: the East Roman general experiences the whole gamut of fate, from supreme triumph to total misery; he has conquered the Emperor's enemies and brought peace to the Empire, but conspirators bring about his downfall, and he ends his days as a blind beggar, exemplifying the motto 'Vanitas Vanitatum Vanitas'. Further Jesuit plays also turn to historical subjects and the portrayal of Christian martyrs and develop into an art-form in which, like the operas performed at court, other arts join with literature to produce a kind of composite stage-work.

These Jesuit plays provided stimuli for the composition of secular German plays which only had their true effect some time later. The social situation, which prevented the emergence of a homogeneous public interested in such matters and capable of judgement on them, and the Thirty Years War, together with the particularism which it either caused or promoted, were the forces that delayed the working of these stimuli. Nevertheless the Silesian School did succeed in creating a literature that took account of all available influences, both classical and modern.

Following Scaliger, Opitz had prescribed for tragedy and comedy the unity of style, manner and *dramatis personae*: tragedy belonged to the upper classes, treated elevated subjects and used the *genus sublime dicendi*, while comedy belonged to the lower classes, treated simple, everyday matters and used the *genus humile dicendi*. In 1625, one year after his *Poeterey*, he published a translation of Seneca's *Trojan Women* and expounded in a preface his philosophy of 'grand tragedy'. In this he declares tragedy to be the concern of those of good fortune, i.e. mainly the rich and powerful of this earth; many of these had therefore turned their minds to tragedy, even as poets themselves, for as Aeschylus rightly said, noble deeds are imperfect as long as it is not demonstrated that both the enemy without and the enemy within, that is, the confusions of the mind, have been overcome. Man needs a sense of constancy with which to combat the troubles of life, and tragedy helps him to acquire this sense by bringing before him examples of a terrible, all-powerful fate; thus he could better bear the sufferings of his own country if he reflected on the sufferings of noble Troy, and more readily endure his own captivity if he considered that Hecuba, mother of such worthy heroes, had also been a prisoner.

Seneca's play on the suffering of the vanquished enjoyed a great reputation at this time, not least on account of its form. The most terrible events are portrayed with skill and in a highly rhetorical style, yet in his translation Opitz avoids giving further emphasis to these emotional moments. His classicistic manner emerges most clearly in the way he tones down the passionate outbursts and intellectualizes the dialogue. The speeches are cast in alexandrines and the chorus appears at the end of each act. His translation of *Antigone* (1636) shows the same features.

Gryphius, on the other hand, has an original mind. What distinguishes him from Opitz is not only his profounder poetic nature but his receptivity to highly varied stimuli, be they from great foreign literature or from his native tradition. In this ability to make use of the most heterogeneous material he is comparable only to Grimmelshausen.

His early years in Silesia were clouded by a number of unhappy events, yet at the same time he learned and wrote a great deal, and in 1637 he was crowned *poeta laureatus*. From 1638 to 1644 he studied and taught at the University of Leyden, probably the most advanced institution of the day. By any standards the range of his knowledge was remarkable: physics, geometry, astronomy, anatomy, trigonometry, logic, poetics, cabbalism were among the subjects he studied. He saw performances by visiting English, French and Italian theatrical troupes in the Hague and Amsterdam, and travelled for years through France, Italy and Germany. Towards the end of these travels he composed the first of his great tragedies: *Leo Armenius* was written in Strasbourg in 1646 and *Catharina von Georgien* in Stettin in 1647, and he spent much of the rest of his life translating and adapting plays.

Leo Arminius, the first historical tragedy in German, depicts the forces of intrigue which beset a powerful ruler. Its scene is Byzantium, a dictatorial Christian world set between antiquity and the East, a world with which the baroque age justifiably felt an affinity. The Emperor Leo has deposed the previous ruler; his victorious general, Michael Balbus, who has humbled the enemies of the Empire, is condemned to death, but the Emperor delays the execution in response to the Empress's supplication that Christmas is near, and Balbus escapes with the help of a group of conspirators; Leo is murdered before the altar and a new Emperor mounts the throne.

Leo is the victim of his own merciful act, and his death at the altar has a moral effect, but the Christian element is only part of the setting, and the play is not, like Gryphius's later works *Catharina von Georgien, Carolus Stuardus* and *Papinianus*, a drama of martyrdom transplanted into a secular historical situation. It is basically a drama of intrigue, and for dramatist and audience alike the main interest lies, not in moral questions or the struggle of an absolute ruler with the forces of the world but in the visual display of glory, danger, revolt, conspiracy and murder. Above all the sufferings of Balbus's widow, unable to take revenge or even to put an end to her pain through death, are, as in Seneca, dwelt upon at great length and made the object of pity.

The play is also a psychological dramatic study of a kind hardly found elsewhere at the time: by his hesitation the Emperor – like Hamlet – brings about his own destruction; the sinister atmosphere of murder and guilt, similar to that in *Macbeth*, grips the audience's attention. Much of this tension is absent from Gryphius's later plays, in which a spotless hero stands firm against the evils of the world in a manner more in accordance with Gryphius's own nature. Such are *Catharina von Georgien*

oder Bewährte Beständigkeit, Ermordete Majestät oder Carolus Stuardus and
Grossmütiger Rechts-Gelehrter oder Sterbender Aemilius Paulus Papinianus, the
titles of which alone show the nature of the hero's role. In *Catharina von
Georgien* we have the familiar drama of the oriental potentate, but this
time with a heroine firm in her Christian faith against temptation, suffering
and martyrdom.

In *Carolus Stuardus* that most contemporary of events, the Cromwellian
Revolution, together with the execution of Charles I, is portrayed on the
stage. Gryphius is a monarchist and hardly attempts to give a fair picture
of Charles's opponents, though he did study historical sources for both
the first and second versions of the play. On the other hand this one-
sidedness is offset, as so often, by an intensity derived from his sympathetic
insight into the character of the hero.

The climax of this series of plays is reached with *Papinianus*, which, though
set in the pagan Roman world, demonstrates the Christian virtue of
magnanimitas. Of all these plays this has the fewest faults and the most
virtues.

A few years earlier (*c.* 1650) Gryphius broke new ground with *Cardenio
und Celinde*, the first 'domestic tragedy', in which he not only frees himself
from the prejudices of poetic rules but also attempts a personal treatment
of the theme of love.

Gryphius's strengths and weaknesses both derive in large measure
from the fact that he drew on the most heterogeneous sources and sought
the most varied solutions to his problems. This is even clearer in his
comedies than in his tragedies. Taking English, Latin, French and Dutch
models, he translated, revised and adapted, since there was hardly a native
German tradition of comedy on which to build. *Herr Peter Squentz* (1657),
taken from *A Midsummer Night's Dream* and other sources, mocks in
particular the mannerisms of the Meistersinger tradition. In *Horribili-
cribrifax* (printed 1663) the old *miles gloriosus* or *capitano* is portrayed in
two separate characters and placed alongside various other lovers to
produce a plot of rich confusion. *Geliebte Dornrose* (1660) is a peasant
comedy in the manner of Jost van den Vondel, from whom Gryphius
also took motifs for his tragedies; starting from Vondel's *Leeuwendalers*,
a pastoral play in rhyme, Gryphius produced a comedy in Silesian dialect
which, performed together with another play, made up an evening's bill.

Daniel Casper von Lohenstein (1635–83) is Gryphius's legitimate
successor in the field of tragedy and the only baroque dramatist comparable to Gryphius. He was born at the time when Gryphius was
beginning to write, and his career belongs to the age that followed the
peace of 1648. Where Gryphius unmasks the deceitfulness of earthly life
and seeks consolation in metaphysical speculation, Lohenstein portrays
the world as a series of triumphs and defeats and hastens to glorify the

newly consolidated Empire in a new myth. His propensity to learning was promoted by his education at the Magdalenaeum in Breslau, and in 1650 he won a drama competition. His first tragedy, *Ibrahim Bassa*, was performed while he was still at school, and he subsequently had a successful career as lawyer, state official and politician.

Ibrahim Bassa, *Cleopatra*, *Agrippina*, *Epicharis*, *Sophonisbe* and *Ibrahim Sultan* are plays based on the careful study of source-material, but they show little effort to evolve an artistic form and a significant content such as we find in Gryphius. Lohenstein has been called 'the German Euripides' or 'the German Seneca', and Gryphius 'the German Aeschylus' or 'the German Sophocles', but such comparisons do not take one far. Lohenstein concentrates on one single type of play – the tragedy in which the urge for power and pleasure is portrayed with great intensity, with the emphasis laid on the strict exposition of the action, the elevated diction and the use of the chorus taken from his classical models. Gryphius, even where he is concerned with almost identical themes, is personally engaged in the events: *Carolus Stuardus* concerns the wickedness of the present day, *Cardenio* deals with the guilt of the common man, *Catharina von Georgien* puts the Christian faith to the test, and *Papinianus* treats of the conflict of loyalties in the mind of a public figure.

Lohenstein's plays are always remote in time and place, set in Turkey, Rome, Africa, etc., so that, despite ingenious allusions to the present, there is a gap between the audience and the setting. The visible impact is what counts: reason and passion reign, and faith, though not entirely absent, is no longer central. The characters strive, 'not for transcendence but for glory', and the plays point towards rationalism and the new empirical perception of the world.

Against the general view that the *Novelle* and short story in Germany only appear at the time of Wieland and Goethe one must observe that there are many such works in the seventeenth century – though the sources have as yet hardly been examined.

There are three main types. The first is a continuation of the sixteenth-century *Schwank* tradition, together with didactic pieces like *Predigt-Märlein*: old motifs are imitated, rhymed passages are inserted in the prose narrative, and individual pieces are collected into anthologies and calendars. The second type derives from the novellas of the Renaissance, which are translated, abridged, paraphrased, often supplemented with additional moralizing passages and with accounts of remarkable happenings in contemporary life. After the early works of Martin Zeiller (translations of the *Histoires tragiques* by Marguerite de Navarre) and Aegidius Albertinus we find the *Frauen-Zimmer-Gespräch-Spiele* (300 dialogues in eight volumes, interspersed with *Novellen* and anecdotes, published between 1641 and 1649) of Harsdörffer, a work of considerable importance for the development of German narrative prose. The form is that of the 'story-within-a-story' found in Boccaccio, and a group of men and women tell stories and hold conversations on a variety of subjects.

Harsdörffer's later collections of short stories and anecdotes – *Der Groß Schau-Platz Lust- und Lehrreicher Geschichte* (1650/1), *Der Schauplatz jämmerlicher Mordgeschichte* (1650 onwards), *Heraclitus und Democritus* (1652/3), *Geschichtspiegel* (1654) and *Nathan und Jotham* (1650) – also draw mainly on French (Jean-Pierre Camus de Bellay, Belleforrest), Spanish (Cervantes) and Italian sources (Bandello), together with contemporary reports and historical chronicles. There is a mass of material here but the style is formal and stiff: Harsdörffer is not concerned to look for personal characteristics but to display a mass of material set around with moral disquisitions and entreaties for the entertainment and edification of his readers. Indirectly he creates conditions which favour the development of significant German narrative literature after the middle of the seventeenth century.

This leads to the third group, which consists chiefly of large-scale works – novels or cycles of *Novellen* – into which these shorter works are absorbed. The novels of Zesen, Anton Ulrich, Beer and Grimmelshausen show this interspersion of short works: Grimmelshausen, for instance, introduces anecdotes and *Schwänke* into his *Simplicissimus*, and in his *Ratsübel Plutonis*, *Springinsfeld*, *Vogelnest I* and *Vogelnest II* he evolves hybrid works which are part novel, part *Novelle*-cycle and part dialogue.

Apart from the *Volksbücher*, which continued to be read, the only real sixteenth-century antecedents of the novel were the works of Jörg Wickram and Fischart. At the end of the century, however, the enormous work *Amadis of Gaul* reached Germany from France; the German version of this work amounted to twenty-four volumes and became one of the most popular, most often-quoted books of the seventeenth century, albeit to the considerable disapproval of moralists and theorists. Picaresque novels and other works translated from foreign languages appeared in large numbers between 1560 and 1660; among the most influential were *Der Landstörzer Gusman von Alfarache oder Picaro genannt*, freely translated by Aegidius Albertinus (1615), and Honoré d'Urfé's *Astrée* (translated in 1619), which helped to spread the taste for the new style of courtly formality. Opitz translated Barclay's *Argenis* in 1626 and Sidney's *Arcadia* in 1638; the novels of Mademoiselle de Scudéry and Monsieur de la Calprenède became current, and in 1662 there appeared a translation of Sorel's *Francion*. The only original German works – and those trivial and uninteresting – to exist alongside these importations were pastoral romances.

As a result of the charges of immorality and improbability laid against works such as *Amadis*, writers turned for subject-matter to historical subjects and personal experiences. The first work of this kind was Zesen's *Adriatische Rosemund* (1645). The translator of a number of French romances, Zesen explains in his preface that it is his aim to write a 'serious and graceful' love-story; the form is fanciful and the strange orthography makes the book hard to read, as does the affected style and the confused arrangement of the whole work. Yet it has a certain importance in that it is the first love-novel in German, and that the author is concerned to include in it something of his personal experience. It shows the characters in their social setting and attempts an artistic portrayal of their attitudes of mind and their spiritual conflicts. Markhold, the hero, is seen on his travels to Paris, Amsterdam and elsewhere, and the story tells of his unhappy love for the incomparable Rosemund, whom he can never marry because of the confessional difference between them. Zesen was greatly touched by the subject and treats it in a language that is often extremely skilful. If the book as a whole is less than a success, it is probably because the fictitious and autobiographical elements, like the epic qualities and the learned excursuses, are not satisfactorily blended; at one moment Zesen draws attention to the idealized picture, at the next to the real-life situation. The construction of the whole novel is in fact based on astrological principles, the decipherment of which may yet enable us to understand its true meaning.

Zesen's second independent novel, *Assenat* (1670), is derived from Grimmelshausen's *Keuscher Joseph* (1667), which it tries to outdo by adding historical and cultural material to the story. His last work is *Simson* (1679).

From about 1660 onwards novels were published in greater profusion. In 1659/60 there appeared *Herkules und Valiska*, a *roman à clef* by Johann Heinrich Buchholtz, a native of Brunswick, This work, of scant value, was intended as a national, Christian, historically authentic book which would drive out the 'shameful' *Amadis*, but this lay far beyond its power, as beyond that of its successor *Herkuliskus*.

In the realm of the pastoral romance, however, we now encounter the most delicate love-story of the time, *Damon und Lisille* (1663), by Johann Thomas (who used the pseudonym Matthias Johnson). Also to this time belong the greatest works in both the 'high' (i.e. historical and courtly) and the 'low' style. The summit of the former is reached with the multi-volume works of Duke Anton Ulrich. His huge stories such as the *Durchleuchtige Syrerinn Aramena* (1669–73) and *Römische Geschichte der Octavia* (1677–1707) differ from *Amadis* and other works of the age in the degree of their truth to history, their credibility, the quality of their subject-matter and the skill of their construction. Where the older chivalric romances had usually portrayed the love of a single faithful couple, Anton Ulrich portrays many such couples – there are twenty-seven in

Aramena – who become separated, reunited, separated again, and undergo all manner of hardships at the hands of fate until finally, having triumphantly withstood all their trials, they are joined together for ever. In a poem of homage to Anton Ulrich, Catharina von Greiffenberg wrote that his work was a mirror of all that the age could see and understand; from his single viewpoint he was able to give a unity to the manifold aspects of the work. Two further examples of the genre are Anshelm von Zigler's *Asiatische Banise* (1689) and Lohenstein's *Großmüthiger Feldherr Arminius* (after 1689), both of which – particularly the former – acquired lasting fame.

At the other end of the scale from the ideal world ruled by divine fate, dominated by courtly, historical values and exemplifying a morality in which virtue is rewarded and sin punished, is the picaresque novel. No longer does the great, virtuous hero undergo an endless series of symbolical adventures; instead a cunning, witty rogue looks back on his eventful life and, with a singlemindedness that bypasses the *Amadis* type of novel and recalls the directness of Renaissance narrative and popular storytelling, relates his biography in a highly personal and original manner.

Christoph von Grimmelshausen (post-1620–1676) has created in his *Abentheuerlicher Simplicissimus Teutsch* (1668) the greatest work of its kind, a work whose influence stretches far beyond the seventeenth century. Not only has Grimmelshausen incorporated his own biography in this work and employed a more graphic, more realistic style, but he has also included *Novellen*, anecdotes, descriptive matter and items of contemporary material in what is a highly integrated work. From the constructional point of view he has arranged his part-real, part-fictional biography as a progress through what the age regarded as the seven stages of the world, taking account of contemporary notions about the seven planets and their influence. From the lonely, mysterious, peaceful, simple sphere of Saturn, Simplicissimus is transported to the terrifying sphere of Mars, the brilliant sphere of the sun, the self-confidently autocratic sphere of Jupiter and the self-confidently hedonistic sphere of Venus, until finally, in the spheres of Mercury and the moon, he comes to experience and understand the fickleness of the world. A blend of art and nature, *Simplicissimus* contains in the highest degree that truth and attention to Christian morality which the age of the baroque sought in a work of art.

Among Grimmelshausen's successors mention must be made of the Austrian writer Johann Beer – whose works have only recently been discovered – who also wrote picaresque novels, among them the *Symplicianischer Welt-Kucker* (1677–9) and the *Jucundi Jucundissimi Wunderliche Lebens-Beschreibung* (1680). Far more superficial than Grimmelshausen's, and showing quite different artistic qualities, Beer's novels show a remarkable wealth of material but without any overall plan of construction, and appear to have been put together without effort or purpose. In his most interesting novels, *Teutsche Winternächte* (1682) and *Kurtzweilige Sommer-Tage* (1683), the picaresque hero only appears in the interpolated fragments of biography, while the virtual heroes are a group of young nobles who display a penchant for the picaresque life. Elements of the picaresque novel and the courtly romance thus combine to form a new type of story in which a greater realism of style is matched by a return to the middle-class values introduced by Wickram. The picaresque novel then turns in the direction of the 'political' novel of men such as Riemer and Weise, while the courtly romance evolves into the so-called 'gallant' novel.

The Age of Enlightenment

MAX WEHRLI

General

The word Enlightenment denotes in the first instance a development and an age in the realm of religion and philosophy. For literature it would be preferable to use a stylistic term, such as rococo, but this is too narrow and would exclude leading figures like Haller, Klopstock and Lessing. The chronological term 'eighteenth century', on the other hand, would include the emergence in the last third of the century of a new age of irrationalism. Indeed, it is doubtful whether one can find a stylistic term to describe the literature that lies between baroque and the age of Goethe, for this literature is concerned to a large extent with 'growing up' rather than with the rise and fall of a particular form, and artistic activity is often intellectually determined and purpose-controlled. We may most suitably talk, perhaps, of the 'literature of the age of Enlightenment', remembering that what is new has its roots in the baroque age, and that counter-movements appear from the 1750s onwards.

'Enlightenment is man's emergence from his self-inflicted state of minority', runs Kant's definition of 1784. The eighteenth century made man responsible for his own fate and brought him to an awareness of his reconciliation with God and the world. The attainment of the 'age of majority' showed itself above all in the acknowledgement of the power of natural reason and its free employment. But behind this lay a new experience of the glory of God, of transcendence, which is the true source of reason and whose presence has to be demonstrated. The word Enlightenment itself, and much of the vocabulary of the age, metaphorically alludes to the concept of brightness. The Christian faith which sustains most of the leading figures of the German Enlightenment is not a meaningless relic of a former epoch but a true conviction and commitment.

As to reason, the seventeenth century had sworn by it, but as a guiding principle, a defence against the transience of the world and the errors of the senses, a guarantee of permanent order, this *ratio* was a matter of form, not of substance. But since man and the world, both in nature and in history, are themselves rational, reason and nature become one and the same, and what exists is rational, i.e. true, good and beautiful, the best of all possible realities. Reason becomes a means of establishing relationships, whereas the decorative, allegorical methods of baroque had no causal purpose. The essence of things can be perceived by reason in the narrow sense, by sense-perception (the empirical tradition of Locke and Hume) or by emotional awareness (sensibility); what matters is that in contrast to baroque, with its dialectic and its fight for self-assertion, the Enlightenment assumes a universal pre-determined harmony.

This harmony is in the first place a harmony between the world and the Creator: the eighteenth century is both in theory (Leibniz, Haller, Lessing) and in practice the century of the theodicy, i.e. of the union of God and man, man and world. Individual freedom and eternal law are one and the same; reason is confirmed by experience. A powerful feeling of liberation and progress, a breadth of sympathy and a sense of ambition characterize the age – features most spectacularly present in Leibniz's philosophical mythology of monads, elements that reflect the divine universe which, each in its own way, they all serve. This is the youthful spirit of adventure which fills the age with confidence and a sense of happiness and makes it one of the greatest of all ages. Nor is this invalidated by the fact that its rationalism was spread in the popularized version of Wolff, which turned it into a facile utilitarianism, or that its optimism and idealism were superficial, or that in Germany as elsewhere a glittering façade of culture often concealed a reality of oppression, crudity and baseness.

The concepts of time and space underwent a radical change between the seventeenth and eighteenth centuries, chiefly by virtue of the discovery of temporal and spatial eternity in the train of Copernicus, Galileo, Bruno and Newton. The God-controlled, finite world burst open, and a terrifying cosmic infinity was revealed. The baroque poetry that took account of the new reality had stressed the feeling of helplessness in the face of this situation, and the new 'Enlightenment' needed to make a great leap forward to overcome the situation. Time is now given meaning within the context of eternity, and history becomes meaningful. From being the 'soulless mass' which Opitz contrasted with the sublime spirit of the Stoic philosopher, man becomes Nature, the 'most sublime image of God' and inseparable from the Deity. As the 'governor of fate' (Shaftesbury) man becomes sovereign, alpha and omega, a starting-point and a place of refuge. Consciously or unconsciously faith becomes pantheistic, except where extreme rationalism and scepticism destroy all mysteries. At the same time at a deeper level the infinity of time and space can be transcended in the name of God the Creator, and the infinite is to be distinguished from the eternal and the transcendental:

O Gott! Du bist allein des Alles Grund!
Du, Sonne, bist das Maß der unermeßnen Zeit.

(O God, Thou alone art the source of everything. Thou, O sun, art the measure of immeasurable time.)

The discovery of this new transcendence can be well followed in Haller and Brockes. The powerful movement of 'physico-theology', above all in the first half of the century, which tirelessly reveals 'with transfigured gaze' (Brockes) the glory and wisdom of God in creation ('Deus in minimis maximus'), is neither empiricist nor pantheistic but Christian, even orthodox.

In this realm of absolute time and space man then finds his place – man the master of his own fate, man in his 'majority'. To be sure, he is no longer the fixed centre of a finite world but he is a possible centre of the circle of infinity – in other words, the mystic formula of God as infinite space and universal centre is transferred to man, and the baroque dichotomy of time and eternity, animal and angel, appearance and reality is resolved. Man is given his proud place in creation and the direction in which he is to travel. This is the message of Leibniz and of Pope's *Essay on Man*; it is also what sustained Matthias Claudius, and when Lavater embarked on his physiognomical studies, his secret wish was to find the face of Christ in human features. Man has experienced salvation; nature speaks to him again, and the law of nature is again seen as the law of God. Admittedly Rousseau opened a gulf between nature and civilization by a demagogic confusion of an ideal and a historico-empirical concept of nature, but this in turn led to attempts to reconcile the two and examine cultures as autonomous, historical entities – a development associated above all with Herder.

This acquisition of a sense of history is another achievement of the age, though it was not until Herder and the Romantics that the achievement was consolidated. History as an autonomous force underlies the concept of individuality (Leibniz), the new pragmatic attitudes of Montesquieu, Voltaire and Bodmer, Lessing's *Erziehung des Menschengeschlechts* and Justus Möser's ideas on folk-culture. History is not simply 'revived' but becomes an essential element in human consciousness. Antiquity again becomes a model, chiefly by virtue of its 'natural', social and communal values – indeed the classical tradition is perhaps richer, more vital now than it became in the age of aesthetic classicism.

Alongside the forces of reason and natural law the pietistic movement – particularly strong in Germany – was influential in pointing to feelings as the basis of faith and knowledge. 'Living Christianity' was concerned with the image of God in man, with man's inner experience; it demanded 'good works' and produced, notably in Gottfried Arnold's *Kirchen- und*

Ketzergeschichte, a new view of history in which the true meaning of life was to be sought not in traditional, orthodox institutions but in individuals, even in 'outsiders'.

There are secular equivalents to these characteristics. Leibniz's monads, like the Platonic-cum-Renaissance concept of the virtuoso and the 'moral harmony of his powers' (Shaftesbury), can be explained on pietistic principles and reconciled with Christian attitudes. This counteracted the danger of a mechanistic rationalism of objective reason, such as Wolff's widely known philosophy contained. With an influence from England and from pietism, a feeling for the subjective spiritual life began to assert itself; truth and virtue became expressions of an inner spirituality, yet the primacy of reason remained unassailed. And if these attitudes were to degenerate into sentimentality, reason could always be invoked again and the call made for realistic action.

This discovery of the soul, the inner life, as a kind of 'third infinity', led to a new view of man, a view which is taken further by Hamann's protest against the narrowness of reason in the name of the totality of human existence, of the absoluteness of faith and of the new discovery that man's sensuous life is a form of revelation. This led in turn to the conquest of Enlightenment by *Sturm und Drang*, and to the diversion of interests and energies from the external to the internal, thus producing the man who shrank from the demands of life and took refuge in idyll, sentimentality, ideas and art. Nicolai describes him thus in his polemic novel *Sebaldus Nothanker*: 'He lived in the world of speculation, and a thought was more important to him than an action would be to most others.'

The eighteenth century is the century of man, especially after the moment when, under the influence of the English empiricists, man was studied not simply as a rational being but in the numerous forms in which he had appeared in the history and geography of the world. Moralizing journals such as the *Discourse der Mahlern* (1721 onwards), modelled on Addison's *Spectator*, deliberately treat of 'man in all his moral aspects', and *homo sapiens* is studied in customs and in art, in nature and in history, in physiognomy and in psychology. This is the spirit behind the anthropology of Lichtenberg, the psychology of Karl Philipp Moritz, the physiognomy of Lavater, the historical researches of Möser and the literary researches of Bodmer and Lessing. The climax is reached with Herder's historiography and concept of 'humanity'. The idea of man in his external, public nature is replaced by the idea of a harmony between the inner and the outer man, to be achieved by education, a feature prominent particularly since Rousseau's conception of 'natural' man and 'natural' society. This pedagogical notion is important in Bodmer and subsequently, in its comprehensive, practical form, in Pestalozzi; in later life Lessing concerned himself with it from the point of view of the philosophy of history. In the pioneering figure of Christian Thomasius, sustained by French rationalism and by Gracian, we have the somewhat conservative preacher of *bel esprit*, of good taste, of a philanthropic view of society. It is an age of social literature, and the new spirit is disseminated and discussed in satire, in elegant moral philosophy, in didactic poetry, in letters and in non-pedantic journals.

The new man portrayed in, and educating himself through, this literature is of the middle class. There was hardly any conscious opposition to the forces of feudalism and orthodox religion before the 1760s in Germany, but a middle-class ideology and a middle-class mode of feeling were certainly present. Where the ethos of the aristocracy had rested on objective standards of birth, power and dogma, middle-class values were based on the new spiritual vision of the rational, sympathetic, virtuous man. The vision first appears with Gellert, around 1740; its most powerful, practical manifestation comes with Lessing.

The importance of the aristocracy, of feudal officialdom and of the Catholic clergy declined; the Protestant pastor was in the ascendancy, and a world-centred, secularized theology informed the new values. This link with religion remained decisive in German literature until well into the nineteenth century. There also emerged spokesmen of a self-confident bourgeoisie in commercial centres such as Leipzig ('Little Paris'), Hamburg, Berne and Zürich. The freelance man of letters was still a rarity – and here again Lessing shows his independence.

'Middle class' is a European concept. The eighteenth century is the classical age of European communality, the age of open frontiers. In general Germany took its lead from other Western countries – discounting, that is, such powerful figures as Leibniz and such fashionable but short-lived successes as that of Gessner. France was the leader – names like Voltaire and Rousseau tell the tale. In Goethe's conversations with Eckermann one can still read how Voltaire, Frederick the Great's guest in Potsdam, dominated the 'whole moral world' – which included Goethe's own youth.

At the same times eyes were turned towards England, and it was Shakespeare and Milton, Pope, Young and Shaftesbury, Richardson and Sterne who enabled Germany to discover its own true nature, its own classicism, and thence to exert in turn its influence on the intellectual life of Europe.

This is the background to the role of art, above all of literature in the eighteenth century. Reason in the strict sense embraces only part of life; so too does religion, in so far as it was becoming more and more regarded as an aspect of temperament. The totality of human life, however, needed a focal point, a centre in which its various aspects combined in harmony and from which its development could proceed, absorbing all mankind, from the highest to the lowest. The age found such a centre in the faculty of taste, where Thomasius, Wolff and the early moral journals found a common cause. Art became increasingly the proper realm of this 'sixth sense', as Dubos called it, and the Enlightenment conception of harmony brought poetry and *homo aestheticus* to the fore. This is the only reason why the long and involved argument over poetics attracted so much interest, for what were in fact unproductive and unnecessary literary feuds between Zürich and Leipzig, between Berlin and Laublingen, between Frankfurt and Berlin only became important because all parties were convinced that education, of the individual as of the community, proceeded from art. However one may be inclined to regard German classicism as a spontaneous event outside the realm of deliberate aims and purposes, the historian cannot but observe that this marvel was consciously prepared and calculated by the teleological eighteenth century.

Because its task was a universal one, this new literature needed an objective, rational structure. Art retained its communicative, interpretative and unifying roles throughout the age. The new poetics certainly tended towards the autonomy of art, for art was to be released from the tyranny of rules and the imitation of nature and enabled to reach its own achievements of expression and creation, but it could not yet admit the arbitrariness and irrational subjectivity of the 'genius'.

Gottsched (*Versuch einer critischen Dichtkunst*, 1730) still sought to show literature the way to freedom by applying to it rationalistic rules derived from the French or from Wolff. On a broader basis Bodmer and Breitinger (*Einfluß und Gebrauch der Einbildungskraft*, 1727), with their gaze on England, attempted to evolve a 'logic of imagination'. In the manner of Horace they proceeded, by means of a comparison between painting and poetry, to determine the proper function of the irrational and, paradoxically, to interpret art as an educative *ars popularis* for the lower orders and at the same time as a vision of the future, but their *Critische Dichtkunst* (1740) did not amount to a systematic poetics. Yet they deserve praise for having seen the problems and reflected on their possible solution by building on the recently discovered great works of the past and present. Even their allusion (*Neue Critische Briefe*, 1749) to Shaftesbury's comparison of the poet with a Prometheus whose creative genius derives from a harmonious synthesis of his powers, had little effect.

The ensuing literary feuds, in which Bodmer and Breitinger found allies among the group of Leipzig contributors to the *Bremer Beiträge*, were overshadowed by the appearance of the greatest among the contributors to this journal – Klopstock, who built his poetic art on his religious experience. This great extension of the poetic realm is what gives his work its epoch-making importance – though in the next breath we must admit that this dangerous union of art and religion made the poetry sentimental and the religion aesthetic. The concept of the 'schöne Seele', originally a Platonic notion, still reflects this union.

It was left for Lessing, by his trenchant, perceptive critical writings, to direct attention to the real fundamentals of the poetic art, and in the field of drama he moved beyond Gottsched by taking issue with the French, by discussing the moral, national and practical problems of the theatre, and by advancing new models of a contemporary, middle-class drama which should absorb individual, political and ultimately religious questions. His *Laokoon* frees poetry from its uneasy alliance with the other arts and restores to it its own proper ethos.

Winckelmann, against whom Lessing pits himself, has his effect less through direct intervention in questions of the theory of art than through his whole personality. His longing for Greece was not just a theory but a mode of life, and his noble conception of antiquity released the hidden urges of the *homo aestheticus* of the time. His vision of classical humanity and his historical conception of classical art as a living organism lifted art right out of the field of theories and purposes and made it a form of pure existence – a development whose meaning was only grasped in the age of classicism. The persistence of the 'enlightened', educative aesthetic of 'good taste' is shown by J. G. Sulzer's compendious work, *Allgemeine Theorie der schönen Künste* (1771 onwards).

Within this development of aesthetics there was a conflict over the purpose of poetic existence itself, a dangerous conflict that derived from the universal role in which the poet was cast. In a small town-state like Zürich in the middle of the century it was possible for a kind of 'literature-state' to emerge: poetry, society and state formed a single unit, the urges of education and art, science and society, cosmopolitanism and local patriotism combined to form a miniature Athens. But when the first real poet appeared, the whole edifice shook, for the vision of such a cultural harmony could not be reconciled with the unconditional demands of the poetic spirit. On the other hand it soon emerged how independent and how unrealistic Klopstock's inspired and patriotic poetic vision was in the face of concrete situations. Switzerland in particular distrusted such high-flown claims; in his later years Haller repented the poetic sins of his youth, and even Bodmer came in later life to regard Klopstock and *Sturm und Drang* as traitors to the poetic vocation.

In the German-speaking world as a whole, despite the absence of political unity, there was a vigorous literary life sustained by groups of poets like the Bremer Beiträger, the Anacreontics and the Göttinger Hain, by literary periodicals and pamphlets, and by correspondence. It was Goethe who said that it was enthusiasm for Prussia and the victor of the Seven Years War that first brought real life into German literature.

But this enthusiasm was for an absolute ruler who took his lead from France, and the war itself, in the long view, was a questionable enterprise. Gleim's war-songs make a naïve impression, and the most rewarding figure, Tellheim, in Lessing's *Minna von Barnhelm*, is completely unpolitical. Wieland's hopes for 'enlightened' government from Joseph II were frustrated, and Klopstock's *Gelehrtenrepublik*, also addressed to the Viennese court, was utopian.

Yet Wieland perhaps represents most completely the Enlightenment conception of the poetic calling. No other German writer has so strong a sense of the social aspects of his art. He is a master of balance, a quick yet reflective writer who sees literature as pleasure for the intellect, material for civilized conversation and education, not there for its own sake but for the sake of the community. Where Brockes and Haller are pedantic and Klopstock emotional, Wieland is the entertaining sage of society. His limitation is that, because of his very comprehensiveness and his ironical detachment, he lacks penetration.

Lessing, on the other hand, is a quite different kind of Enlightenment figure – a merciless critic, a rational analyst who realized the necessity of deeper moral values and of a 'national' literature but knew at the same time that his own work lacked spontaneity and immediacy, and that he could offer, not truth but only the struggle for truth. His moral power is that of an utterly independent thinker, a fearless and free mind that scorned the achievement of self-satisfied virtue. To this extent he anticipates, in an intellectual form, the emphasis on the personality of the poet which held sway in *Sturm und Drang* and the age of Goethe; indeed, he will always be seen as the perfect example of the aggressive, unprejudiced, humane writer whose isolation is not a matter of sentiment but of necessity.

The cult of genius had been foreshadowed long before Lessing's and Wieland's maturity. Young's *Conjectures on Original Composition* were published in 1759, the same year as Hamann's *Sokratische Denkwürdigkeiten*, in which human creativity is again presented as deriving from the oneness of existence revealed in God.

Sturm und Drang vehemently reasserted the rights of pure poetry but surrendered the determination to achieve national self-assertion in a social or political sense. One should not judge the literary theories of the Enlightenment only by the extent to which they foreshadowed the concept of genius and personal experience, for there was good cause for caution in this respect. The cultural idealism of German classicism certainly became a triumph of *homo aestheticus*, but in so doing it took itself out of the context of national life, with certain fateful consequences. Even Herder's and the young Goethe's romantic notion of *Volk* could not alter this. It is both the strength and the limitation of the Enlightenment that it was not prepared to renounce the idea of service and rational obligation. And this is common to the didactic solemnity of Haller, the aggressiveness of Lessing, the emotional thought of Klopstock and the urbanity of Wieland.

Lyric and Didactic Verse

The stylistic originality of the age of Enlightenment is most clearly seen in lyric poetry, which has a richer, more continuous tradition than the other genres. The almost unconscious beginnings lie in a freer attitude to form, while preserving the religious or *galant* motifs of baroque. Certain poets of the Second Silesian School, such as the anthologizer Benjamin Neukirch, occasionally show a more rapid tempo, a less frequent use of nouns, lighter rhymes and a more natural enjambment; thoughts are no longer put out in dialectic form but work towards logical conclusions. The French classicistic manner outgrew the Marinistic style. But at the same time as the recondite manner of baroque receded, the language became flat and erotic motifs became lascivious. Freiherr von Canitz, a Berlin diplomat, represents the tendency towards the precise, French-inspired diction of the proud, superior man of the world, while the Saxon court poet Johann von Besser tends in the more ambiguous direction. This new style is supported by a satirical, anti-courtly 'German' movement, seen chiefly in the epigrammatic verse which persisted throughout the century, such as that of Christian Wernicke and Johann Grob.

More important than this secular verse is the religious answer to the problem, above all that given in the pietistic hymn. First in Gottfried Arnold, then in the pure, direct, edifying poetry of Gerhard Tersteegen (*Blumengärtlein inniger Seelen*, 1729 onwards) and finally in the bolder verse, also frequently didactic, of Count Zinzendorf, the strain of inwardness is touched which is never absent from the German lyric over the next hundred years.

The most striking breakthrough to personal lyric poetry in the modern sense, however, was achieved by Johann Christian Günther, 'the last Silesian'. The tragedy of his position lies not in any moral inadequacy, or in the cruelty of his father, who, the embodiment of orthodoxy, repeatedly rejected his son, but in the utter self-surrender of a modern personality to traditional forms and concepts which were anything but personal and confessional. Günther experienced the extreme baroque dualism of mind and body; the dualism crushed him, but he bequeathed to art a new directness of expression. The intense, despairing strophes of his greatest poem, *Geduld, Gelassenheit . . .* (1720) utter a curse on the baroque world and are the testament, both outspoken and humble, of a poet broken on the wheel of fate.

The Hamburg poet B. H. Brockes faces the position as a challenge less to life itself than to the separate realms of the senses and human reason. The nine volumes of his *Irdisches Vergnügen in Gott* (1721 onwards) are the product of his feeling of happiness and gratitude for the wonders of life in a wise and beautiful world, man's eternal home, in which the merciful hand of the Creator is everywhere in evidence. Brockes knows the spaciousness of Milton and the joy in nature of Thomson; nature, God's handiwork, has for the first time poetic meaning in its own right, small things (cf. Klopstock's 'Frühlingswürmchen') as well as big. In a flexible, effortless style he describes all the nuances of line, light and scent in the objects of nature, delighting in the perpetual movement. It would be impressionistic, if the outlines were not so firm, and the objects not so clearly positioned in a rationally ordered whole and made part of the reader's own experience, often with a homely didactic purpose. Poetic line and strophe are a loose framework which is covered by the cool, logical syntax of the sentences.

Albrecht von Haller learned a great deal from Brockes but had to acquire for himself, with greater seriousness and greater reservations, his new outlook on the world. His heavy alexandrines are not, as one might at first think, baroque rhetoric but his means of attaining this outlook, and he established his orthodox faith in the area between late-baroque melancholy and 'enlightened' doubt. He knew that he could only see the outer shell of nature; to him man had two sets of human rights – 'one in Heaven, the other in the void'. Yet he was engaged in a quest which he pursued to the limits of his power. His poetry is didactic in the truest sense – no longer, as in Opitz, a display of decorative knowledge but a passionate yet controlled struggle for understanding and thus a central human concern, the real stuff of poetry.

His longest poem deals with the basic problem in the optimism of the Enlightenment – the problem of the origin of evil. But perhaps his greatest work is his *Unvollkommenes Gedicht über die Ewigkeit,* in which he seeks with greater and greater efforts to grasp the thought of infinity, finally collapsing in exhaustion. The notion of natural creation as the ultimate criterion assumes a vital importance for him and does not become sentimental, as it does with Rousseau or Klopstock. In his *Die Alpen* (1729) he discovers the sublimity of nature and the purity of simple things – pastoral dreams of a baroque yearning to escape from the pressure of history but converted into a cultural and philosophical problem. Bodmer had extolled the primitive, i.e. natural customs of the mountain dwellers of Switzerland, and the Alps are for Haller a world-stage on which he portrays new scenes in a bold new style; even the making of cheese is considered worthy of elevated diction. Yet the image remains fixed in the concept, and Haller gave to an age threatened with the matter-of-fact and the comfortable the possibility of a heightened language and a deep moral seriousness.

It is difficult to understand today why Klopstock should have linked Hagedorn and Gleim with Haller in his poem *Der Zürcher See*. The popularity of Hagedorn and the whole of Anacreontic poetry (still respected, incidentally, by Lessing), with its acknowledged triviality, can only be explained by reference to the relaxation which its gospel of pleasure preached: people dared to be superficial and were happy to be so. This is rococo in the proper sense: wit, grace, merriment in the rhythm of poetry, contentment in a delicate Arcadian setting – in short, the hard-won victory over the emotional despair of late baroque. The themes of wine, love and natural life had been dignified by Horace, and in the background was the notion of a new ethic which would unite all men and make the upright, contented man happy and virtuous, sensitive and rational. 'Virtue and happiness are closely related,' proclaimed Gleim; a new world of middle-class values would overcome aristocratic rigidity and political dishonesty, though the prevailing tolerance would prevent any active opposition to the aristocracy. This poetry is not bound to a single confession but is common property, accessible – in Hagedorn, at least – to all of innocent mind. At the same time it can be used to proclaim the true philosophy and the true ethic.

Christian Fürchtegott Gellert was from the 1740s the preacher of such a rational, acceptable middle-class ethic. His sober *Geistliche Lieder* give a contemporary didactic form to the time-honoured Protestant hymn and make him by far the most popular didactic poet of the age.

Poetic fables, first by Hagedorn, then – for a broader public – by Gellert, and finally by Gleim, Lichtwer, Meyer von Knonau and others (Lessing's are in prose), unfurl a panorama of moral situations with a light accompanying commentary. The fable, indeed, as the most concise form in which the moral is combined with the 'miraculous', becomes something of a poetic paradigm and is discussed at length in the aesthetics of the day. Gellert turns Virtue from a strict goddess into an intimate personal friend; this feeling is at first objective, in that it concerns something communal and proper to society, but later, in the 1750s, it becomes tearful and sentimental, above all in Gellert himself.

In addition to these ethico-pedagogic elements one finds in the Anacreontic poetry of Uz, Goetz and to some extent Gleim, who formed a poetic circle in Halle, an intensification of sensuous elements. In a relaxed and melodious style Uz, above all, sings in his alexandrine poems of Anacreon's *joie de vivre* in a spirit of elegant Epicureanism. Immanuel Pyra and Samuel Gotthold Lange aim at higher goals and turn their poetic comradeship into an emotional ideal of friendship, giving greater weight – to the approval of the Bodmer school – to moral obligation.

The humanistic side of this Horace- and Anacreon-inspired poetry becomes more prominent and also influences matters of form. Unrhymed verse was the order of the day, and particular success was accorded to *Thyrsis und Damons freundschaftliche Lieder*. The absence of rhyme makes Gleim's *Scherzhafte Lieder* even weaker, and the classical spirit has not inspired them with new rhythm. The poetic treatment of nature and landscape, too, was a problem for the Anacreontics and their followers, for there was as yet no inner relationship between man and creation to offset the pastoral conventionalism.

Ewald von Kleist's *Frühling* (1749) represents a step forward by building up an idealized bucolic landscape and infusing it, in the spirit of Haller, with a new piety and reverence. The result is a hybrid work in which, although nature has been vivified and subjected to the poet's visionary imagination, the elevated diction falls short, leaving, as Lessing complained, an agglomeration of descriptions. In his hexameters also ('a mixture of hexameter and alexandrine', as Heusler called it) formal conviction is lacking. Nature, with her 'holy shades' and 'dark, slumbering delights', is an object of elegiac yearning which shall absorb all life; instead of the conquest of nature we have a 'longing for peace', even an escape from the pressures of life. Thus the optimistic determination of the Enlightenment finds itself broken by sentimentality even before the middle of the century.

The lyrical prose of Gessner's *Idyllen* is humbler but purer. The nature he describes has, as Goethe said, an excessive rococo sweetness, but Gessner did possess an all-consuming vision, whether it be of a classical seascape or of his native Sihlwald, and the classical serenity of this vision remains intact despite the inroads of sentimentality. Gessner's sonorous prose gives the purest sound in all rococo literature; it is an idyllic moment which, briefly, even had European significance.

Meanwhile the event had taken place which seemed to fulfil in a single word the secret desires of the age and has remained to this day the frontier post between historical and modern German verse: the publication of Klopstock's *Oden*. These works bring the solution to the problem of form, i.e. how to evolve a pattern of rhythmical movement which is not made to conform to prescribed limits yet does not become formless. The controlled variations of line and metre in Horace's odes provided the key to the problem but to the extent that these features became conventional, they soon came to be felt as restrictive. In 1758 Klopstock moved on to free rhythms as the basis of his poetry, and through his experience of classical rhythms, above all the Alcaic metre, he found a new power, a new dignity, a new range of possibilities. The ode is the language both of emotion and of elevated thought. By using the sublime language of the Psalms, Klopstock makes his odes different from those of

Horace, whose style was subsequently brought to formal perfection by Ramler, building on Anacreontic foundations.

Klopstock's religious emotion embraces both the intensity of his own experience and the power to speak like a priest in the name of humanity at large. He covers the whole gamut of experience, from the physical (the ode on skating) to the emotional (odes to his beloved) and the metaphysical (odes to the universe and on the meaning of life). His enthusiasm overcomes the complacent, elegiac passivity of the 1740s, but on the other hand the emotions he aroused tended all the more strongly towards the sentimental. As the work of Young and Elizabeth Singer shows, the new attitudes produce a solitary, abstract type of mind that luxuriates in thoughts of love and death. Poetry sheds its purely descriptive and didactic qualities; at the same time this pure dynamism showed its weaknesses – the abstract tension of emotion, the emptiness of the concept of virtue, and thought as an emotional experience that controls the use of language. This is part of Klopstock's debt to the Enlightenment, and it is responsible for making his later poetry arbitrary, stiff and artificial, and placing it outside the context of the age of Goethe.

Klopstock is also the spokesman for the German nation. Frederick II's Prussia had already inspired patriotic lyrics from Pyra and Lange, and Klopstock extolled Frederick in poems based on the English ballad – though he was later indignant at the King's French leanings. Gleim assumed the role of a Prussian grenadier and touched all hearts with his simple, folk-like patriotic lyrics, however lifeless they appear to us today. There was a latent desire for a patriotic life but in spite of J. G. Zimmermann's *Vom Nationalstolz*, Thomas Abbt's essay on dying for one's country, and the youthful Herder's glances towards the German past, it remained unfulfilled. It is highly significant that the patriotism of Klopstock should turn into a concern with the nebulous and only half-understood world of bardic poetry, of Macpherson's *Ossian* and Mallet's edition of the *Edda*. Neither Klopstock nor Gerstenberg nor their numerous followers could do anything to give reality to the situation and divert attention from this misleading mythology. Bodmer and Breitinger looked to the chivalric lyric of the Middle Ages, but this came too late for the Anacreontics and too early for the Romantics. The old ballads, however, exemplified by Percy's *Reliques*, proved more accessible; Gleim's work in this field in 1756 deserves mention. But the sentimental, 'literary' element still present here does not vanish completely until the renaissance of folk-poetry ushered in by Herder and Goethe.

Klopstock's collected *Oden* were not published till 1771. In the following decade the 'Göttinger Hainbund', inspired by a sentimental pietism, represent the continuation of the Klopstock line, and their influence continues into the nineteenth century. The more vital elements of the

Klopstock tradition, however, found their way into *Sturm und Drang*, while the sentimental elements became converted into a more genuine inwardness. The Horatian forms become suffused with a gentle melancholy or, as with Johann Heinrich Voss, are made to serve the needs of an idyllic domestic ideal. The grand scale of Klopstock's work becomes whittled down. The simple odes of Hölty, for example, denote a turning away from the world and an escape into loneliness, into the consolation of the imagination. Delicate in a similar manner are the poems of J. G. Salis, a follower of Kleist and an aristocratic officer whose thoughts were of his fatherland.

On friendly terms with the Göttingen circle, but not to be ranged with the members of any school, is Matthias Claudius, author of the *Wandsbecker Bote*. With his natural piety and common sense he kept apart both from the sentimentality and emotionalism of post-Klopstock poets and from the rationalism of the late Enlightenment; instead, in a manner new yet natural, he re-created the sixteenth- and seventeenth-century hymn, leaving poems which make him one of the most humane, most Christian figures in the history of introspective German culture.

Drama

Drama and the theatre are more closely linked to cultural and social conditions than is the lyric. In order to represent on the stage the Enlightenment's newly discovered sense of unity, not only dramatists but also organizers were needed. The literary baroque drama moved on an aristocratic level; popular drama had sunk to the level of mere spectacle, or, as in comedy, had been given over to the clowns; the didactic school-drama, such as those performed in Zittau under Christian Weise, was not strong enough to bear a tradition any more than were Christian Reuter's witty but crude, mocking satires of the Philistines, while opera concentrated on visual and musical effects and relegated the words to the background. The challenge was for the creation of a rational, middle-class world that could be presented on the stage, and then for the extension of this world to the nation as a whole. Strolling players had to be replaced by permanent theatres, and poet, actor and public had to agree over the composition of 'good taste'. But, as was to be seen, an 'enlightened' theatre of such a kind embraced the possibility neither of the heroic and the tragic nor of the genuinely comic, for its philosophy was optimistic, reasonable, philanthropic and didactic, and its plays undramatic and derivative; types of drama become confused, elements of tragedy and comedy intermingle, and the writing of plays, above all by the leading authors of the time, became largely a matter of theory and experiment.

The home of the new drama and theatre was Saxony, with Leipzig as its sophisticated centre; the areas where the non-literary 'popular' theatre had flourished, i.e. predominantly the Catholic areas of the German-speaking world, took no part in it. Theatrical reform is associated above all with the name of Gottsched, who used the troupe of Caroline Neuber to create a theatre with a real social function. His opposition to the clown (*Hanswurst*) and to operatic spectacle, together with his own plays and translations, made the theatre what Schiller later called an 'ethical institution'. He built on French classical tragedy, and his own great success was *Der sterbende Cato* (1732). This work, rationally constructed according to the principles of the three unities, was new and progressive in style, but the elevated tone of its diction made it unmodern, even though Gottsched sought to make its moral message generally accessible. Middle-class audiences continued to prefer comedies, and the content of the works performed by Caroline Neuber and her troupe, despite their occasional contemporary satirical character, had not enough content in them to hold the audiences of the day. The same is true of the skilful comedies written by J. E. Schlegel in the style of Holberg and the French playwrights (e.g. *Die stumme Schönheit*, 1747).

Nevertheless it was in the field of comedy that a temporary solution was found in the 1740s with the application of the semi-sentimental, semi-ethical world of the novels of Richardson to a domestic dramatic situation: such were the sentimental comedies of Gellert (e.g. *Die zärtlichen Schwestern* (1747)), again based on French models. Behind an inoffensive plot dealing with intrigues there are psychological studies of emotional conflicts (the hesitant lover, the girl torn between love and virtue, etc.), though in the last resort virtue and reason triumph and evil, i.e. human weakness, is its own punishment. In a welter of sentimentality all the qualities of an upright and honest middle-class society are displayed.

Existing alongside this type of comedy – and despite Gottsched's protests – was the *Singspiel*, a forerunner of the operetta, with prose dialogue and interposed songs. The master of this form was Christian Felix Weisse, also known as a translator and writer of tragedies and later also as a writer of books for children. Wieland's *Alceste* belongs here, as do some half-dozen works of Goethe.

More significant than the domestic comedy was the domestic tragedy, also of English inspiration. This is the moment when Lessing's leadership asserts itself. Through his great knowledge and his critical acumen, Lessing aggressively set the drama of the Enlightenment on a progressive course. His early plays are in the shadow of Gottsched (*Die Juden*; *Der junge Gelehrte*) but already have critical and intellectual features that bear the seeds of future development. *Miss Sara Sampson* (1755), still English in derivation, is a true tragedy in that it gives the common people real human dignity and thereby theatrical status. The conflicts in the play are, to be sure, psychological and derive from purely social contingencies, not from objectively tragic situations, while the virtue and villainy, together with the dialogue, are forced and exaggerated, yet it contains a broad human sympathy.

As J. E. Schlegel, with his *Hermann* (1740), had produced a national, as opposed to a classical, tragedy, so Lessing took a theme from contemporary history for his *Henzi*. Klopstock was also seeking to bring the dignity of religious and patriotic subjects into the realm of drama, although neither his Old Testament prose tragedies (*Der Tod Adams* (1757); *Salomo*; *David*) nor his 'Bardiete', i.e. dramatic poems on Germanic subject-matter (*Hermanns Schlacht* (1769); *Hermann und die Fürsten*; *Hermanns Tod*), were suited for stage production and remain literary curios.

The Seven Years War had a deeper influence on Lessing than on the lyric poets of the day. His *Philotas*, classical in form, is a passionate one-act play in which, recalling the death of Kleist, he praises the man who sacrifices himself for his country. *Minna von Barnhelm*, the first real German comedy, born of humour and love, combines domestic drama with the new social ethic. From being a heroic or sentimental theme, the question of honour is embodied in the new, real character of Tellheim and receives national meaning; at the same time it is set in charming contrast to the wise charm of Minna herself and thus given a real human context. *Minna von Barnhelm* has personal content yet uses all available literary traditions; it is patriotic yet humane, touching yet farcical, polished yet direct in dialogue – the summit, indeed, of Enlightenment drama.

This summit lies in comedy. Tragedy remained a national dream. Lessing's *Hamburgische Dramaturgie*, intended to bridge the gulf between dramatist and actor, critic and public, is the record of what was from the beginning doomed to failure. The relationship of German drama to French classicism and to Aristotle, as well as to the English models, was still uncertain. The famous seventeenth *Literaturbrief* conjures up Shakespeare and the German Faust-legend. Shakespeare had been quoted by Bodmer and Breitinger as a master of illusion, and Bodmer had pillaged his works for his own undramatic dramas; J. E. Schlegel praised his characterization in 1742, and in 1762, in Zürich, Wieland published his translations; it was only with Gerstenberg, however, that he became the centre of the cult of genius – a cult in which Wieland and Lessing did not share.

An interesting intermediate position between Shakespeare and the French is that occupied by Weisse, a friend of Lessing's in his young days. Weisse's tragedies, first in alexandrines, then in blank verse (*Die*

Befreiung Thebens (1764)), portray intense passion and unrestricted subjectivity, thus anticipating the drama of *Sturm und Drang*.

Lessing's critique of Aristotle in the *Dramaturgie* reveals the limitations
of his own dramas. His doctrine of the purification of the emotions by
fear and pity makes the purpose of drama its effect on the audience, so
that for him Shakespeare is a master of characterization whose scorn for
the 'rules' can evoke approval or disapproval. Thus Lessing's later
dramas also have little of the Shakespearian spirit. They are penetrating
and direct but have no atmosphere, and their characters are linked not
by material and spiritual realities but by abstract relationships. It is true
that *Emilia Galotti*, in a Shakespearian manner, portrays forces which have
moved beyond the conventional and the rational, leaving the agonized
characters uncertain of their decisions and provoking, far more strongly
than in *Miss Sara Sampson*, a protest against the absolutism of the social
structure. But the dialogue has an intellectual stiffness; there is a contradiction between sentimentality and rigid heroism; and the tragic outcome
has no inner motivation. Lessing's dramatic effect is therefore achieved
not on the stage but in a region beyond the art of emotional involvement
and theatrical technique.

His 'dramatic poem' *Nathan der Weise* is a didactic drama of ideas which
expresses in a calm tone the essence of his life and thought, a document
bequeathed by the great figure of the Enlightenment to the age of
humanity and classicism. Prevented by the censor from publishing his
views in the controversy over the question of revealed religion, he was
forced into the adoption of a dramatic fable, and in it he overcame his
disappointment and his bitterness. Nathan's message of tolerance would
be little more than a pallid exercise in appeasement, were it not for
Lessing's passion for truth, for the manifestation of a faith based on true
love and for the conversion of objective principles into moral acts.
Nathan points both backwards to the *Faust* fragment in Lessing's seventeenth *Literaturbrief* and forwards to the idealism of classicism. Together
with the essay *Die Erziehung des Menschengeschlechts*, written at the same
period, it shows a specifically German way forward from the Enlightenment.

Sturm und Drang had meantime cast off the shackles of a rational style
and a moral purpose and reopened the possibility, by virtue of a new
view of man, of true tragedy. Besides this Goethe's *Götz* introduced an
element of nationalism compared with which the undramatic, rhetorical
Hermann plays of Klopstock pale into insignificance. Schiller, for his
part, carried the domestic tragedy into the revolutionary political sphere
with *Die Räuber* and *Kabale und Liebe*, thereby creating the genre of the
idealistic tragedy.

Novel and Epic

The disintegration and realignment of baroque elements had taken place at an early stage in the realm of the novel. The novels of Weise had displayed a long-established realistic and satirical strain in the manner of the didactic Enlightenment; a kind of crude counterpart to this is Christian Reuter's *Schelmuffsky*, which satirizes the exaggerated adventures of the baroque romance in a vulgar, naturalistic style typical of a transitional period. The popular adventure story tended more and more to real-life situations which were present for their own sake, not as a framework for allegorical religious interpretation. Johann Beer's lengthy works (*c.* 1680) show how the motifs of baroque become light and trivial but at the same time how the characters settle into realistic, credible situations, while Grimmelshausen sought to give the novel a cultural significance, as seen, for example, in the sixth book of *Simplicissimus*, where the hero establishes a new bond between man and nature on his desert island. After Defoe's *Robinson Crusoe* (1719) a form emerged in which the adventure story was given a civilizational significance, i.e. the desert island becomes a place of refuge and a symbol of true cultural values, while the world of adventurous fate becomes the world of the common man.

In contrast there also emerges a form of the novel that is concerned with the biography of the inner life. Pietistic influence turns the novel into a spiritual story, and the world is portrayed as the reflection of the spirit. The narrator acquires an individuality, establishes a new relationship with the reader and makes the fluid form of the novel an important element in the emotional and intellectual life of the age. English influence is again dominant: Richardson's epistolary novels, with their new social content, lay bare the life of the virtuous soul; Fielding shows how to see the world with a humorous eye but a didactic intent; Sterne embodies the victory of a witty, sentimental, benevolent subjectivity that conquers everything. Like the other forms, the novel too has a new spiritual and social goal, and the new novel, leaving behind the timeless adventure-world of the rococo novel and the cumulative style of the picaresque novel, becomes based in a temporal and spatial reality.

Johann Gottfried Schnabel's *Wunderliche Fata einiger Seefahrer* (1731 onwards), on the pattern of *Robinson Crusoe*, is full of adventure stories of passion and intrigue representing a degeneration of the baroque world; the framework into which these stories are put, however, i.e. the island state of Felsenburg, depicts a contemporary, no longer utopian world in which men grow up in a single, virtuous community, and, as in Defoe, there is a somewhat pietistic emphasis on the cultivation of spiritual values.

Similarly Gellert's well-known *Schwedische Gräfin* (1747–8) caters for baroque taste by treating of passions, crimes, intrigues and catastrophes – the motif of the double marriage, later exploited in drama, is prominent – but it does so in order to draw attention to the newly discovered marvel of the spiritual life of man, which develops its feelings and its virtues through such conflicts. For all their sentimentality, however, the souls of which Gellert writes have a static virtue that recalls the representative lifelessness of baroque heroes. This is the first German imitation of the English family novel, above all Richardson's *Pamela* (1740), which was a decisive influence throughout the century. Gellert still retains the aristocratic setting, despite the middle-class attitudes of his characters, and does not use the fashionable revelatory form of the epistolatory novel.

By the canons of classicistic poetics the novel was not a legitimate form, since *qua* form it was too heavily dependent on its subject-matter and often had a tendentious and experimental character. It needs, and takes for granted, the existence of a world and a society which are rich in subjects, characters and problems, and it requires a flexible, accessible language in which to formulate this content. But Germany, which aspired to, rather than possessed, a national literature, scarcely produced an independent social novel.

Nevertheless one must not underestimate contributions from quite different quarters towards the formation of such a language, such as the prose satires of Gottlieb Wilhelm Rabener and Christian Ludwig Liscow. The intellectual and moral problems of the day were discussed in literary journals based on French and English models, and the educated middle-class public were concerned to learn, to cultivate their taste and to create an urbane, witty intellectual community. This popular satirical, polemical, philosophical literature proved of considerable value in the development of the novel, particularly for Wieland.

As for the epic, the seventeenth century had virtually accepted the heroic courtly romance, built on the principles of the epic and written in an elevated diction, as a substitute for the authentic epic, while the century of the Enlightenment and of rococo, following new directions and sustained by intellectual reflection or sentimentality, was certainly not the age to produce one. It was, however, conceivable that the feeling of having established an identity and of moving towards a Golden Age could lead to both an idyllic and an epic form – though worthy citizens do not make epic heroes, and in place of Odysseus we find the sentimental Robinson, a cultural pioneer whose world is that of the novel.

As the drama was revived from the direction of comedy, so the first essays in epic were undertaken in an ironical spirit. Thus J. F. W. Zachariä's *Renommist* (1744), on the model of Pope's *Rape of the Lock*, is a playful employment of a large-scale form for a small-scale purpose, the subject being student life in the squalid town of Jena and the elegant town of Leipzig, of which life the writer gives an ironic picture. The change in level can be seen from a comparison of this work with *Schelmuffsky*. Uz's *Sieg des Liebesgottes* (1753) represents the Anacreontic form of the Popean epic and also has ironical imitations of Klopstock's elevated style.

The possibility of 'noble' epic poetry had already been opened up by Bodmer and Breitinger, whose importance in this field corresponds to that of Gottsched in the field of drama. Their vision of a pictorial poetry dedicated to the forces of the miraculous had been realized in Milton's *Paradise Lost* (though Bodmer's translation of 1732 is in prose), and they also concerned themselves with other great epic poets, from Homer and Virgil to Dante, Tasso, Wolfram and the *Nibelungenlied*. J. E. Schlegel's epic *Heinrich der Löwe* remained a fragment; the first three cantos of Klopstock's *Messias*, however, published in 1748, made a tremendous impression. Klopstock's subject, the salvation of man, i.e. the reconciliation of time and eternity, is the product of a bold religious confidence which, pietistic in inspiration, is suffused with personal vitality. Klopstock's contemporaries argued over whether it was permissible to give such poetic treatment to the Gospel and whether the work did not have eighteenth-century man in mind rather than the Messiah. Yet Klopstock sees the poet as a prophet and his work as a religious affirmation; the profoundest Christian theme is clothed in the most classical of forms, and the hexameter becomes the vehicle of intense emotional expression. After almost a thousand years of biblical literature in German the 'divine poet', the 'seer', sought again the poetic synthesis of western Christendom.

But all the tears shed over the *Messias* could not disguise the fact that the new Zionist muse was a fragile creature. Klopstock's successors made this only too clear. Neither the biblical epics of Bodmer and Gessner, which looked backwards in time to a pristine idyllicism, nor the partly classicizing, partly sentimental-Christian hexameter works of the young Wieland were able to gain any popularity for the epic as a form, and the poetic formulation of a new, total vision of life remained the task of the novel. It was Wieland, after he had rid himself of Bodmer's oppressive influence, who showed himself at the end of the 1750s as the modern representative of this genre.

In reaction against the Klopstockian mood of rapture and ecstasy, Wieland characterized his *Agathon* (1766–7) as being part of the modern world, part of 'the nature of things'. Leaving aside fantastic, idyllic illusions, he makes his centre of attention human sensuality, which had hitherto been glossed over as 'feeling' or portrayed as a vice. Agathon, a Platonist, has his Platonism destroyed – to his own advantage – by the materialism of a Sophist and practical instruction on the part of a courtesan, but in order that sensuous pleasure should receive a higher meaning:

the physical and intellectual sides of man are reconciled in reason, good taste and moderation and in the realization of a higher harmony in life. Shaftesbury's ideal of the rule of goodness and beauty is thus transferred to the serene, rational world of rococo. As in *Emilia Galotti*, the hero of *Agathon* is made to overcome his virtuous simplicity and become a complete human being living in a world of tensions. In this moment an adventure becomes a means of education, and a novel becomes the chronicle of intellectual and spiritual development: the *Entwicklungsroman* becomes the most characteristic and most successful form for German novelists. Compared with Fénelon's *Télémaque*, which had replaced the mere adventure story with political and educative substance, *Agathon*, with its content of personal experience and self-knowledge, is virtually a true biography. The rationalism of the age shows its restrictive influence in that the hero's development is not so much intrinsic as a series of considered didactic opinions put into practice.

Agathon's problem of how to reconcile the sensuous with the supra-sensuous dominates the rest of Wieland's work. While working on *Agathon*, he wrote *Don Silvio von Rosalva*, a kind of satyric counterpart to it, in which he describes the light-hearted 'victory of nature over emotionalism' by an idealistic, sentimental Don Quixote. In other comic tales and equivocal anecdotes he toys with lasciviousness and portrays the victory of elegant wit, showing himself more on the side of French, Voltairean *esprit* than of the English novelists.

In the *Goldener Spiegel* (1772), written with the young Joseph II in mind, the new attitudes find their way into the political novel. It would be wrong to expect a logical plot, for this work, in its Chinese setting, is rather a discussion of the problem of nature and civilization which Rousseau had broached, and a demand for the well-being of state and society under the sovereignty of an 'enlightened', absolute ruler who would limit the activities of the men of economic power. His *Abderiten* deals in a free manner with the most heterogeneous moral and literary short-comings of the age; it is satirical in tone but takes a self-satisfied delight in the exercise of an elegant, ironical wit. This is the most poetic, most relaxed form – with a trace of Sterne's humour – attained by Enlightenment satire, which in the hands of Rabener and Liscow had been somewhat pedantic.

The main line of development from *Agathon*, however, leads to *Peregrinus Proteus*, *Agathodämon* and *Aristipp*, which are also set in the world of Greek moral philosophers and their schools. New in these works is the inclusion of the moral message of Christianity in the vision of Enlightenment man; initially it appears as only one of many ethical philosophies which have a pedagogical application but which can also lead to abuse and deception. In the last analysis there remains a pantheistic feeling of the existence of an ultimate power and the reality of human self-expression in goodness and happiness.

Wieland's general concept of man led him to set his novels in the Greek world, and his classical ideals derive from philosophy, not, as with Winckelmann, from art and beauty. In spite of the accuracy of historical detail Wieland's Greece is a modern land, and, as later in Thomas Mann, the ideal of humane values leads to a detached, ironical manner. Mind and matter, nature and civilization, antiquity and the modern world combine to form a new consciousness. Unlike later 'Romantic' irony, Wieland's intellectual irony does not derive from an inner conflict; the absolute demands of the mind are waived, while on the other hand man's baser aspects are ennobled. Poetic spontaneity vanishes and is replaced by deliberate artistry and calculation; the writer intervenes between work and reader and makes the novel a social conversation.

This also influences the construction of the work. Any thought of a self-contained 'poetic illusion' is banished, and by means of digressions, the destruction of illusion and a free disposition of the subject-matter the author appeals to his readers' superior intelligence. All in all, the value of these works lies not so much in their achievement of concrete results – for Wieland, as a declared sceptic, neither was, nor wished to be, an original or logical thinker – as in their free atmosphere, their interplay of taste and intelligence.

Wieland's poetical works, such as *Oberon* (1780) – perhaps a more genuine epic than Klopstock's *Messias* – live in the same non-didactic world. Not Homer but Ariosto is the model – for the form too – and the subjects come not from antiquity but from the romantic Middle Ages and the East. The citizen of the world has the literature of the world at his disposal. The chivalric world of the Middle Ages has the attractions needed to grip the attention and is at the same time sufficiently remote to allow free rein to the poet's imagination. *Oberon*, with its blend of dream and ever-present intelligence and its reflective yet animated poetic style, is a triumph of late rococo and at the same time a harbinger of the Romantics, who were to criticize Wieland so bitterly in the coming decades. Goethe gave him his due by sending him a laurel wreath.

On the long view, however, Wieland's road was a dead end. Intellect now dominated literature, and with it came a certain soullessness, a lack of commitment. Yet in the more light-hearted vein, and at a far lower level, Wieland did have his imitators: August von Thümmel (*Wilhelmine* (1764)), an immensely popular, somewhat sentimental writer; Arnold Kortum (*Jobsiade*), wittier and more popular in style and using the old *Knittelvers* metre; and Blumauer, a Viennese, the uninspired parodist of the *Aeniad*.

The serious German novel was too absorbed in intellectual and philosophical problems to engage in sustained competition with Voltairean wit, and in the 1760s and 1770s the older models regained their influence. At about the same time as the *Goldener Spiegel* appeared, Haller published three political novels which, devoid of elegance yet thoughtful and systematic, discuss the ideas of Montesquieu and Rousseau and investigate the advantages and disadvantages of the various political systems.

The question of religion was now raised directly for the first time. In 1771 Friedrich Nicolai, a friend of Lessing, wrote *Sebaldus Nothanker*, a protest against clerical dictatorship over individual conscience, which incorporated satirical attacks against aspects of contemporary life. The hero is fictitious but not an active fighter, and in the manner of Sterne he is infused with a measure of irrationality and folly.

Similarly indebted to Sterne is Thümmel's *Reise in die mittäglichen Provinzen von Frankreich* (1791), a far more elegant critical account of contemporary European culture, which, written in the free form of a diary, reflects both 'enlightened' intelligence and unspoiled emotion. The recently discovered *Gustav Aldermann* (1779) by Friedrich Traugott Hase is cast in the experimental form of a dialogue and reveals in a detached objective style something of the seamier side of the life of the time.

More substantial were attempts to use the novel to pierce the mystery of the human psyche and the freedom of the human will; from Gellert to Goethe the sentimental novel retained its influence. Johann Timotheus Hermes's epistolary novel *Sophiens Reise von Memel nach Sachsen* (1769), clumsy though it is, attempts for the first time to describe the cultural and spiritual state of the nation after the confusions of the Seven Years War, and in its portrait of the unhappy heroine it depicts a character whose pondered emotions lead to a kind of inner paralysis.

The first modern German woman novelist is Sophie von la Roche, whose Richardsonian heroine in *Das Fräulein von Sternheim* regains her self-assurance, after the catastrophe that befalls her, through social activity – a trait enthusiastically welcomed by the *Sturm und Drang*. The tragic analysis of the spiritual problem of the age, however, was left for *Werther* – yet for Goethe, too, it was only one single occasion. The unconditional demands of the genius, or the inner urges of the soul, always have to face the realities of existence and the insistent demands of morality, and this is the field in which the novel, conformist or revolutionary, comes into its own (Jacobi, Heine, Hippel).

Alongside the novel we find letters, diaries and autobiographies as the universal media for self-analysis and self-projection, above all in the tradition of pietism. The most considerable 'inner history of man' is that in Karl Philipp Moritz's autobiographical novel *Anton Reiser*, the German counterpart to Rousseau's *Confessions*. In it a lonely mind reared in a subjective idealism seeks desperately to find its place in the reality of life and to reconcile the ideal world with the facts of everyday existence. The pitiless diagnosis of this dilemma, which Goethe left behind in the worldliness of *Wilhelm Meister*, shows that as well as the Goethean path to classicism, there still remains the problem of sentimentality in a deeper sense. At one extreme this dilemma produces the idealism of the imagination; at the other it provokes the intellect to ironic self-destruction. From this vantage-point one can see the direct link between the Enlightenment and Romanticism, a link forged by Tieck's *William Lovell* and Jean Paul – the German Sterne – on the one hand and Kantian idealism on the other.

'Sturm und Drang'

WERNER KOHLSCHMIDT

Introductory

Whatever the differences, and indeed conflicts, between *Sturm und Drang*, classicism and Romanticism, they share certain important determining features. They are heirs to the Enlightenment and to pietism, both of which had a decisive influence on the German language around 1770. Rationalism made the language more precise and gave it a power of intellectual differentiation and abstraction that it had not had in the baroque age. The religious intensity of pietism, on the other hand, found a power of expressiveness which left far behind the mystic-subjective terminology of baroque and found a new range of subtleties through the act of self-observation. Both these linguistic developments underlie the position that German literature attains between 1770 and 1830. One may also apply to the situation Goethe's remark that his generation had rediscovered the language of Luther; but at the same time the urge to break new ground must surely have derived to a greater extent from Lessing's achievement in intellectual precision and flexibility and Klopstock's language of passionate insistence.

The condition for this linguistic development, which was inherited by *Stürmer und Dränger* and classicists alike, was the release of that subjectivity which produced in the secular sphere the philosophy of the Enlightenment, and in the religious sphere the sentimental introspection of pietism. The Bible-based world view of the baroque age, unshakeable and binding on both confessions, had completely disintegrated in the first half of the century – or at least had taken up its stance on completely different foundations. The new rationalist view was based on natural law and human justice, and the religious aspect was at best incidental. The changed role of the problem of a theodicy is significant, for God is now called before the judgement-seat of Reason, in contrast to Anselm's *fides quaerens intellectum*. And where, as in pietism, God is still at the centre, the theocentric concept no longer has absolute validity – and orthodoxy has even less. Orthodoxy could give rise to a Lessing but could no longer move men's minds. For its part pietism concentrated on the figure of

Christ, retained its cult-image only in restricted circles and introduced a liberalizing tendency through the idea of tolerance – an idea it shared with the Enlightenment. The power with which philosophy from Locke and Hume down to Kant made human subjectivity aware of its rights and the responsibilities of its maturity could no longer be held back. As the new science had replaced a geocentric universe with a heliocentric one, so the philosophical emphasis now became anthropological rather than theological.

Corresponding to this is the movement of the age, first found in England, towards empiricism, which in turn uncovered new human faculties and new areas of reality. Kant's *Critiques* had the effect of heightening man's sense of responsibility in his newly attained 'state of majority' (cf. its later destructive effect on Kleist) but served at the same time as a logical corrective to English empiricism, which also led to a new view of reality. Kant's thought thus offered legitimate support to Schiller's aesthetics, which aimed at a far subtler conception of aesthetic reality than the static conception held by the age of Gottsched.

This shift of values is already apparent in the way in which the Enlightenment treated the philosophy of Shaftesbury. The aesthetic assumes equal importance with the ethical, and from here it is only a step to Young's concept of Original Composition. The line of development leads from the release of aesthetic subjectivity in Shaftesbury to the release of aesthetic originality in Young; it was in fact already manifested by the great English novelists, Sterne, Richardson and Fielding. This development also contains within itself, however, the concept of education and self-development, for the notion of universal history and world-literature – the Middle Ages, folksong, Shakespeare, Milton, Greek and French classicism – was not a creation of Herder, Goethe and the Romantics but was already pursued by Gottsched, Bodmer and Breitinger, and the Bremer Beiträger. Classical antiquity is studied, not only with ever-growing critical acumen but from different starting-points: Winckelmann, Lessing, Voss, Heyne, F. A. Wolf give a new view of Homer and a revolutionary assessment of the values of classical art.

The exploitation of these two worlds – medieval/baroque and neo-classical – comes with *Sturm und Drang*, classicism and, in a more modern way, with the Romantics. Initially it was the universalism of Lessing, Winckelmann and Herder that showed the breadth of this world-literature, a universalism stimulated by the urge to educate and instruct which is so marked a characteristic of the age. Enlightenment attitudes and activities provide the basis of the age of Goethe in both its emotional and irrational, classical and didactic aspects. The changes that occur in the 1770s, therefore, are only partly revolutionary in nature; they also have their characteristics as entirely organic developments.

The Göttinger Hain

An organic development from the situation in the early 1770s comes with the 'Göttinger Hain', a group of poets, one of whom, Johann Heinrich Voss, turned the name into 'Hainbund' to convey the corporate nature of their activities. The group was founded on 12 September 1772 under the spiritual aegis of Klopstock, from whose ode *Der Hügel und der Hain* they took their name. This group of Göttingen students went out one night by full moon to an oak-lined glade where they pledged eternal friendship and moral uprightness, danced and crowned each other with wreaths. On the one side this is the sentimental aspect of the Enlightenment, on the other it is a youthful revolutionary outburst.

The important thing is not that such a group met formally, elected a leader, kept records of its meetings, celebrated anniversaries, etc. – the linguistic societies of the seventeenth century had already done such things – but that it should have produced the literary results it did. As well as Voss (1751–1826), the first leader, the members included Hölty (1748–76), the two Counts von Stolberg (Christian (1748–1821) and Friedrich Leopold (1750–1819)), Leisewitz (1752–1806) and Johann Christian Boie (1744–1806), publisher of the famous *Göttinger Musen-Almanach*. These are all North Germans – indeed, the Göttinger Hain can be seen as the North German counterpart to *Sturm und Drang*.

However, the revolutionary self-confidence of the *Stürmer und Dränger* was foreign to the Hain, whose links with *Sturm und Drang* in the narrow sense come with Leisewitz's drama *Julius von Tarent* (1776) and with the Stolbergs' meeting with Goethe in the course of the latter's first journey to Switzerland, as a result of which the Stolbergs acquired something of Goethe's mood of *épater le bourgeois*.

The most significant literary achievements of the Hain lie in the field of lyric poetry. The title of Friedrich Stolberg's little essay *Fülle des Herzens* (1777) – a title only possible in these changed times – fully conveys the attitudes and aims that link the Hain to *Sturm und Drang*. These young disciples of Klopstock turned the experience of time and place into a matter of pure rapture without entering the theoretical field of aesthetics. Much of their poetry is simply 'Fülle des Herzens', and it is not surprising that a great deal of it should have acquired such wide currency. 'Fülle des Herzens' also designates the odes of Hölty and the Stolbergs, even down to their metrical characteristics, such as the use of very short lines. There are idyllic overtones reminiscent of the Anacreontics but they are often infused with a new sincerity and subjectivity, so that imagination, love, nature, friendship and the fatherland become truer, more authentic than before, although as themes they are not new. There is a new intensity: lines like Hölty's, addressing the imagination –

> Reiß mich flügelgeschwind über die Wolkenbahn
> In den goldenen Sternensaal

(Gather me up like a bird through the banks of clouds into the company of the golden stars)

– have a dynamic power derived from Klopstock.

In the strophic idyll, too, we find verses which make Gleim, Ewald von Kleist and Gessner seem like formalists and which approach Goethe:

> Noch tönt der Busch von Nachtigallen
> Dem Jüngling süße Fühlung zu,
> Noch strömt, wenn ihre Lieder schallen,
> Selbst in zerrissenen Seelen Ruh.

(From out of the bush the call of nightingales rouses sweet feelings in the youth, and the sound of their songs brings peace even to tormented minds.)
(Hölty)

The subjectivization of the material world is only possible when there is an awareness of spiritual conflict. In the lyric poetry of the Enlightenment, based on optimism and a logical outlook, such an awareness was hardly possible, even in idyllic, Anacreontic verse. Most of the poets of the Hain share both the Anacreontic fervour and the inner conflict. Friedrich Stolberg's 'Süße heilige Natur', for instance, perhaps the most intense of their nature-poems, exists alongside the Alcaic strophes of the ode 'Genius', with its original vocabulary of words and phrases like *Urkraft, Sonnendurst, Durst nach Unsterblichkeit, Toben in der Brust, geistiger Flug* – words with a Promethean tendency (and almost contemporary with Goethe's *Prometheus*). Also of Klopstockian origin is the somewhat 'Germanic' mixture of poetic self-confidence and patriotism which, in the imagination, was to outstrip the national feelings of the 'Britons and the French'. In this respect too, and even including the theme of opposition to tyranny, the Hainbund made common cause with the more radical *Sturm und Drang*.

The second spiritual father to the Hainbund was Gottfried August Bürger (1747–94), who lived in Göttingen and whose career offered the young, enthusiastic poets, in a form far more intense than that presented by their own existence, a picture of the tormented life of the poetic genius. For Bürger was not simply the poet of the 'panting soul' – he *was* this soul, as much as Goethe at the time of *Werther* and as much as Lenz and Klinger. This makes Göttingen, home of the movement to establish the ballad as the prime form of folk art, the equal of Herder's Strasbourg in the folk movement: Bürger's *Lenore*, published in Boie's *Musenalmanach*, the literary journal of the Göttingen circle, is the paradigm of this success.

'Von deutscher Art und Kunst' as a Product of the Age

Whereas with the new subjectivism of the Göttingen poets the emphasis lay on poetic practice – apart, that is, from Bürger's essays on poetics, which, like Klopstock's, are in the nature of a self-justification – the pamphlet published by Herder (1744–1803) under the title *Blätter von deutscher Art und Kunst* (1773) is the manifesto of a revolutionary attitude towards poetry. The essays by Goethe and Herder in this publication represent the credo of a new generation, although the elderly Justus Möser's *Vorrede zur Osnabrückischen Geschichte* is also included with them. The most important items, Herder's rhapsodic essays on Ossian and on Shakespeare, were originally intended for the continuation of the *Schleswiger Literaturbriefe* of Gerstenberg (1737–1823), whose critical attitudes – with their disclosure of the *Edda*, Ossian, old English ballads, the Danish *Kaempeviser*, and their defence of *Don Quixote*, Klopstock, even Hamann, the 'Magus im Norden' – played a considerable part in the destruction of the Enlightenment. When Gerstenberg's journal did not materialize, Herder, who was at that time court chaplain at Bückeburg, decided to make his own plans and produced this manifesto by adding Goethe's and Möser's contributions to his own.

His *Auszug aus einem Briefwechsel über Ossian und die Lieder alter Völker* opens the work. It is only of secondary importance that Macpherson's 'Ossian' was a fraud which skilfully appealed to the prevailing mood of sentimentality. Far more important is that it became a symbol for the new generation of the absoluteness of the emotions and the senses. A Nordic counterpart to Homer, the quintessence of spontaneity, Herder's Ossian – the antithesis of all that Berlin Rationalism stood for – turns into Goethe's Werther. His concern is not with beauty but with authenticity – the authenticity of originality and genius.

In the realm of language too this shift of values goes far beyond Gerstenberg. Genius is originality, spontaneity, immediacy, and synonyms or near-synonyms like 'wild, sensuous, powerful, vital, immense, tangible, independent' acquire a new meaning, that of the force of nature in the human spirit.

The most spontaneous and most natural spirit, however, is also the most lyrical, represented above all by the 'bard' (Klopstock and the Hain poets were also primarily lyricists). This establishes a link with the old English, Scottish and Scandinavian ballads in which passion, sensuousness and fantasy triumph over logic. The folksong, too, remained uncouth and unpredictable, dark and mysterious, not subject to the pressures of conformity. Herder's German version of the *Edward* ballad from Percy's *Reliques of ancient English poetry* (1765) symbolize the ideal, and the folksong illustrates the new conception of genius. Originality thus becomes vested in the common people, and *Volk* assumes vital thematic importance from *Götz von Berlichingen* to Romanticism.

As Herder's Ossian essay was concerned with deep lyrical forces, with the primeval depths of folk-culture, so his essay on Shakespeare seeks to illumine the vision of the supreme artist who draws on both the outer and the inner world. Right from the opening picture of the gigantic figure of the genius on the rocky pinnacle, towering above the world of common mortals, everything is aimed at conveying the impression of grandeur.

The concept of grandeur, indeed, dominates *Sturm und Drang*. Ossian, Homer, Shakespeare, Sophocles, the power of nature and the power of human creativity, the figure of Prometheus (the second creator, as Shaftesbury, following late classical and Renaissance interpretations of the myth, called him) – such are the dominant forces, culminating in Goethe's ode and dramatic fragment of *Prometheus*. Also symbolical of the age is the story that Lessing's Spinoza-inspired interpretation of Goethe's myth brought about the death of Moses Mendelssohn, Enlightment philosopher of moderation and reason.

In Herder's picture Shakespeare is just such a Promethean figure. But it was not a question of 'rescuing' Shakespeare, as Lessing, Johann Elias Schlegel and Gerstenberg had defended him against Gottsched. It was a totally new view, based on empathy – *Einfühlung* (Herder's coinage) – on spiritual kinship, on a new view of history. Indeed, a whole new view of history is involved, for Shakespeare could not be expected to share the single-mindedness of the Greeks. In Herder's eyes he was the genius of modern times, the voice, in Dilthey's phrase, of 'the poetry of fantasy' in the modern age: 'As genius is more than philosophy, and a creator is greater than a critic, so Shakespeare was a mortal with divine powers.' These creative powers enabled him 'to combine the most varied elements into a wonderful new whole', and the simplicity of Sophocles is offset by a greater breadth and wealth of material, a combination of new and more varied experiences, making Shakespeare a historically more highly developed figure.

Compared with this profusion of ideas and this exuberant, rhapsodical language, which expresses a new anti-rational aesthetic, Goethe's 'Rede zum Shakespearestag' (1771) is but a shadow. Goethe writes as Herder's disciple, Herder as Hamann's, whose concept of poetry as the mother tongue of the human race Herder conveyed to a whole generation that was looking for the language of the emotions wherever it could be found, from the Greeks to Rousseau. This generation saw in Shakespeare the perfect exemplification of the divine freedom of the creative genius, and saw themselves, in the same spirit, as free of the rules of Aristotle, Opitz, Boileau and Gottsched. The *Sturm und Drang* answer to the *Querelle des anciens et des modernes* lies in the image of Shakespeare presented by the young Herder and the young Goethe. Dream, passion, magic, the wisdom of the fool, madness, thoughts of darkness and death, with an awareness of the comic and the grotesque hovering overhead – these become the proper constituents of an independent modern art, and the *Stürmer und Dränger* lost no opportunity to employ them in their works, above all in drama and lyric poetry.

Goethe's contribution to *Von deutscher Art und Kunst* does not go further than Herder's but it does cover a different field – and that, if anything, in an even more subjective spirit. His panegyric on Strasbourg Cathedral and its legendary architect Erwin von Steinbach is simply called *Von deutscher Baukunst* – and 'German' here reflects an emphasis which corresponds to Gerstenberg's and Herder's 'Nordic'.

In a sense Goethe's essay is a synthesis of Herder's *Volk* ideas from Ossian and the subjective philosophy of genius in the Shakespeare essay. The latter, seen in a Faustian, Promethean spirit, dominates in that Steinbach's passionate vision is portrayed as a force that set him among the gods, an irresistible force that demanded expression. For Goethe's essay is not just a rehabilitation of Gothic architecture – something which Herder had already concerned himself with – but an assertion, more powerful than Herder's, of the *Sturm und Drang* philosophy of genius. Goethe's greater assertiveness derives from the *Deus sive natura* of Spinoza and from his own Prometheus concept. His study of mystico-natural forces at this time can be followed from the experiments in alchemy in which he indulged with the pietistically minded Susanne von Klettenberg and of which his diary contains a record. Spinoza is a logical conclusion to these interests, which, starting from man's affinity to God, led first to complete pantheism and then to the fashioning of human genius by God. Prometheus can mock Zeus and force the gods to restore his own direct link with fate; the 'enlightened', rational citizen can be reduced to the status of an insect because he has betrayed the potentiality of genius within himself. Human creativity, obligated to no principles and no schools, re-creates beauty in truth, and nature in both – an act of creation that draws forth the epithet 'godlike'; trust in the artistic genius is boundless, for he is *natura sive Deus ipse*.

The reinstatement of Gothic art – the art denigrated by the rationalists and Renaissance theorists but to the understanding observer a symbol of the majesty of the creative urge in art – is merely the application of the concept of genius to the plastic arts. A rhapsody in the passionate Herderian style, it testifies to the spirit of enthusiasm for everything of stature. Yet in all such works it is the main concern of *Sturm und Drang* writers to create an appropriate atmosphere for the launching of their own work, to become themselves part of the free nature which they set out to portray.

Despite the enthusiasm of the young Herder and Goethe, however, *Von deutscher Art und Kunst* was not utterly original, a pioneer work, but the expression of an anti-Enlightenment tendency which had been growing for more than a decade and which is to be seen in the first instance as springing from Johann Georg Hamann. At the same time it must be seen in the context of the whole of Herder's writings from 1760 to the mid-1770s.

It is virtually impossible to dissociate these writings from the most important aesthetic and theological works of Hamann (1730–88). The 'Magus im Norden', possessed of the learning of the rationalist and the religious conviction of the pietist (he was converted in London in 1757), was a man of strong passions and intense reactions. The works that had the most lasting effect on his age were his *Sokratische Denkwürdigkeiten* (1759), together with the sequel *Wolken* (1761) and, of interest to aestheticians, the *Kreuzzüge des Philologen* (1762); in addition there is the *Abälardi Virbii Chimärische Einfalle . . .* (1761), which is a polemic against the *Literaturbriefe* of Lessing and Mendelssohn and in favour of Rousseau's *Nouvelle Héloïse*. The *Sokratische Denkwürdigkeiten*, ultimately religious in intent, present in the figure of Socrates, opponent of the rationalistic Sophists, a picture of the genius as represented over ten years later by the *Stürmer und Dränger* – the genius whose 'ignorance', in the rationalistic sense, was interpreted as 'feeling', the opposite of dogma. In Homer genius makes unnecessary a knowledge of the rules which Aristotle subsequently thought out. The same is true of Shakespeare.

The connection with *Von deutscher Art und Kunst* is obvious. It is even more so in the *Aesthetica in nuce*, the core of Hamann's *Kreuzzüge des Philologen*, where the link is apparent in style as well as in substance; even its subtitle 'A Rhapsody in Cabbalistic Prose' shows where Herder derived his picture of himself as a 'rhapsodist'. The terse, anacoluthic style, with its emphasis on images and sense-impressions, is reproduced in Herder's essays on Ossian and Shakespeare, and from Hamann comes the principle of all *Sturm und Drang* aesthetics: 'Poetry is the mother tongue of the human race.' Similarly: 'The senses and feelings deal exclusively in images.' Such theories anticipate in its entirety Herder's concept of folk-poetry and at the same time justify the use of the rhapsodical style with its mysterious allusiveness yet directly sensuous appeal. And behind this aesthetic stands a view of history which sees the challenge of the present as the reattainment of the true, natural naïvety of the unspoiled past – a view that takes its place in the contemporary trend towards irrationality and anti-rationalism. We are urged to become children again – cf. this motif in *Sturm und Drang* drama and in the realm of *Volkslied*.

The anti-rationalist barb appears in Hamann's vicious attack on Mendelssohn in his *Aesthetica in nuce*: 'Your deceitful philosophy has destroyed nature. And why do you urge us to imitate nature? So that you can have the pleasure of destroying the disciples of nature as well.' Small wonder that Hamann takes Rousseau's side. In his *Leser und Kunstrichter nach perspektivischem Unebenmaße*, an attack on Ludwig von Hagedorn, he states the logical, anti-rationalist, aesthetic viewpoint: 'If a man tries to remove arbitrariness and imagination from the realm of art, he is a charlatan who knows his own rules even worse than he knows the nature of ailments. . . . If a man tries to remove arbitrariness and imagination from the realm of art, he is attempting an assault on the honour and the life of art itself.' This attitude justified the attitudes not only of *Sturm und Drang* but also, subsequently, of Jean Paul and the Romantics.

Herder's early work *Über die neuere Literatur, Fragmente* (1765), written in Riga, already reflects Hamann's principle of a detached, non-optimistic, anti-Enlightenment view of the present age, which Herder regards as poor in original works but far richer in diaries and the like. Any great work of literature, he maintains, presupposes a great language; hence Luther's writings proceed from his 'revivification of the language', which contrasts with the artificiality and affectation of eighteenth-century style. He also praises the sublimity of the Gothic spirit at the expense of the fashionable 'cultured' values of the time.

In his *Journal meiner Reise im Jahre 1769*, written on a journey from Riga to Nantes, he keeps even closer to Hamann, both in substance and in style. Building on Hamann's invective against the desiccated world of rationalism, he draws a picture of a fully developed human being towards which he seeks to educate himself in the spirit of modern ideas of what constitutes genius. Much in this *Journal* anticipates *Von deutscher Art und Kunst*, Goethe's *Prometheus*, *Urfaust* and *Götz*.

Herder's yardstick is that of sensuous reality, i.e. a concept of man as a blend of mind and body which the intellectual bias of rationalism had destroyed. The whole man, the whole of reality, the conception of genius, of the arts, of language, God's plan for the world as the philosophy of history based on the Bible – all these are just different aspects of the view, derived from Hamann, which Herder held up to the time when he went to Weimar (his stay in Bückeburg, if one looks on his career as a whole, is not really to be seen as a moment of pietistic self-alienation, though it has sometimes been so interpreted).

Vom Erkennen und Empfinden der menschlichen Seele (sketched in Bückeburg, finished in Weimar, 1778); *Die älteste Urkunde des Menschengeschlechtes* (1774/6); *Über den Ursprung der Sprache* (printed 1772); *Plastik*; *Auch eine Philosophie zur Geschichte der Bildung der Menschheit* (1774): these are the works which, together with *Von deutscher Art und Kunst*, had a decisive effect as a virtually complete cycle of works testifying to the *Sturm und Drang* conception of man, God, history, the arts and especially language. They are all informed, theologically, psychologically, aesthetically and historically, by the view that the manifestations of human life form an organic whole and are emanations of an original sentient being. The theological framework for this outlook is given in *Die älteste Urkunde des Menschengeschlechtes*, and on its deistic foundation is built the notion of a sensuous life which God has ordained for man to experience. Its beginnings in the Old Testament are the beginnings of the history of mankind itself, and this Eastern origin conditions the nature of the human imagination.

The conflict between *Die älteste Urkunde* and *Über den Ursprung der Sprache* is only apparent. In the latter Herder opposes the rationalistic theory by which language arose as a kind of arbitrary convention, but he also opposes the conception of language as a gift of God, a kind of ready-made bequest. God remains the Creator, but man's pre-ordained path of self-expression is made to start as close to the act of Creation as possible, and language is thus present at the very beginning of man's development – 'the sounds of the soul', as Herder put it. The sounds of language emerge to correspond to man's growing stock of emotions and sensations; like Hamann, he sees original language as the sounds of nature, as opposed to the 'later, refined language of metaphysical usage' which insists on logic and 'correctness'. Both Hamann and Herder see a process of refinement in the development of language as an expression of the rationalist view of progress, both on theological and aesthetic grounds, but this refinement means a loss of strength, and the *Stürmer und Dränger* saw it as the mark of decadence.

The praise of childlike qualities as reflections of a one-time unspoilt and undivided consciousness runs right through *Sturm und Drang*. It plays its part in the background to Herder's *Auch eine Philosophie*, for example, in which is expressed, as well as the belief in man's progress to reason, a penchant for the oneness with the world which characterizes the childhood of man, a state governed by 'wisdom rather than knowledge, fear of God rather than wisdom, love rather than convention'. The conflict between 'impulse' and 'reflectivity' is a product of later centuries of decay, which means the loss of simplicity, the destruction of unity, the exaggeration of reason – in short, the mechanization of the whole of life.

These are the elements behind the bold new judgements on art and history first pronounced in *Von deutscher Art und Kunst* and in the

Frankfurter Gelehrte Anzeigen for 1772, where Goethe and Herder were joined by the friend of their Strasbourg days, Johann Heinrich Merck, in the production of a literary journal which for a short while was to enable them to propagate their ideas in a vigorous, almost presumptuous manner.

Lyric

On such foundations, and in this changed atmosphere, there arose in the first instance a new lyric poetry. The trend is already observable in some of Goethe's Leipzig poems ('Die Nacht'; 'Hochzeitslied'; 'An den Mond'), which break through the Anacreontic tradition, and from these to his Sesenheim poems is only a short step, for the main characteristic, the directness of expression, was present before Goethe became a disciple of Herder and entered his Shakespearean, Promethean phase: the sincerity of 'Erwache Friederike' and 'Mayfest', with their short lines, and the insistent rhythm of 'Es schlug mein Herz, geschwind zu Pferd' are extensions of this directness. The same is true of the emotive vocabulary of these poems, including some of rococo type, such as 'Kleine Blumen, Kleine Blätter', or in traditional rondeau form, like 'Ob ich dich liebe, weiß ich nicht'. The new feelings and attitudes are, however, still simply expressed, partly because of Goethe's temperament and partly under the influence of the *Volkslied*, to which, at Herder's instigation, he had directed his attention, collecting them in the surrounding Alsatian countryside. 'Heidenröslein', which Herder quotes in his Ossian essay as a folksong – though it had in fact only just been composed – shows how close the Friederike lyrics are to *Volkslied*, while 'Ach wie sehn ich mich nach dir', addressed to Friederike, derives its personal tone from its folksong-like use of repetition.

The spirit of *Sturm und Drang* shows itself in a different form in the hymns and odes which Goethe wrote at this time. Their starting-points are Klopstock, Ossian, Pindar and a number of free-verse poems of Herder, in which Goethe found a concreteness and directness of expression in such subjects as the power of nature, the irresistibility of the artistic impulse, the impelling forces behind human life and the relationship of man to the gods and to fate. Subjects of such magnitude cannot be absorbed in a simple subjectivity but demand a certain detached tone of awe, of mystery, with an intense, dynamic vocabulary that reflects an unmistakable singlemindedness of purpose and style.

Such, for example, is 'Wandrers Sturmlied', a poem of loosely connected, unequal strophes in free rhythm which Goethe tells us he recited aloud as he walked through the countryside during a storm. The shadow of Pindar hangs over it, but the vocabulary, full of neologisms, reflects what

Gundolf called *'Sturm und Drang'* Titanism' – the mighty spirit lifts the poet above everyday life to the eminence of the gods. The personal passion of 'Wilkommen und Abschied' becomes in 'Wandrers Sturmlied' the consuming passion of the artistic vocation. The image of a headlong journey through life recurs in 'An Schwager Kronos' and is also close to the 'Prometheus' poem of 1773, in which the theme of the artist's equality with the gods returns. This was the poem that F. H. Jacobi showed to the ageing Lessing and which both interpreted as a poetic transmutation of Spinoza. It is dominated by the ego's expression of confidence in itself as a creature in which the divine power resides and which is therefore in no need of a mediator. This creative self-sufficiency also underlies 'Ganymed' and 'Mahomets Gesang'. Ganymed, like Prometheus, symbolizes the transformation of the myth of suffering into a myth of creation; the image of the river in 'Mahomets Gesang' also embodies the dynamic concept of relentless forward movement, ending in universal unity; likewise 'Elysium', 'Pilgers Morgenlied' and 'Fels-weihegesang', written in Darmstadt, are sustained by the dynamic concept of immediacy that transcends all restrictions. Particularly striking in all these hymns and odes, and to a far greater extent than in the love-poems, is the originality of language: logical, grammatical constructions are done away with, new, vivid compound verbs are coined, and hyperbole dominates the whole scene.

These qualities continue to characterize Goethe's lyrics in the succeeding period, such as the noble transcriptions from Pindar and Ossian (these latter merge into *Werther*) and the Lili poems, above all 'Neue Liebe, neues Leben' and 'An Belinde' (with its superb rhythm). In 'Seelied', written in 1775 on his first journey to Switzerland, with its blend of love and nature, there is an urgency, a passion and an identification with the forces of fate that cannot be compared with anything the eighteenth century had yet produced.

There is no lyric poet among the *Stürmer und Dränger* to match Goethe. Herder's strength lay not in his original lyrics but in his understanding of the poetry of others; his poetic gifts are perhaps best displayed in his epigrams – 'Amor und Psyche auf einem Grabmahl', for instance, is one of the most attractive poems of the time. Hölty occasionally strikes notes that anticipate Goethe; more striking, however, is Matthias Claudius (1740–1815), whose *Wandsbeker Bote* (1771–5) shares with *Von deutscher Art und Kunst* a conception of the *Volk* as the repository of the naïve and the spontaneous. The poems that Claudius published in *Der Wands-beker Bote* are personal variants of the *Volkslied* manner; 'Der Mond ist aufgegangen' is the most beautiful evening-song since Paul Gerhardt, while 'Der Tod und das Mädchen' – the theme of death strikes the deepest chords in him – is a moving blend of the objective and the subjective.

At the same time his reflections on life contain a genuine popular humour which, unlike the idyllic tone of Gleim or the sometimes childish efforts of the Hainbund poets, is both realistic and direct.

Another lyric poet of importance is the unhappy Lenz (1751–92), Goethe's shadow in Strasbourg and Weimar. Parts of his poems to Friederike Brion can hardly be distinguished from Goethe's, but in its total effect his poetry appears as a somewhat exaggerated copy of Goethe's. His life consisted of sharing the love-affairs of others, or even of falling in love with portraits, as in the case of Henriette von Waldner; and in the same way his poems, including those to Friederike, are interventions in Goethe's poetic world, however moving some of these interventions may be, such as 'Wo bist du jetzt, mein unvergeßlich Mädchen?' and 'Ach bist du fort? Aus welchen güldnen Träumen / Erwach ich jetzt zu meiner Qual?' In his 'Freundin aus der Wolke' he imitates Goethe's short lines, while 'Nachtschwärmerei' is an outright imitation of Goethe's hymns and their Rousseau/Spinoza-inspired language. The song 'Rösel aus Hennegau' from the play *Die Soldaten* serves the same function as 'Der König in Thule' in *Faust* and is similarly dominated by emotional values.

There was, however, another direction for *Sturm und Drang* lyric poetry to follow, with one root in the emotionalism of Klopstock but a more important one in a side of Goethe's poetry that emerges most clearly in 'An Schwager Kronos' and 'Künstlers Morgenlied' – the tendency to naturalism. This is the realm of Bürger, of Schubart and of Schiller. In his *Anthologie* poems Schiller echoes this dissonance of the *Sturm und Drang* lyric, which is concerned, not with the eternal verities but with naturalistic directness and sensuous immediacy, while with Bürger and Schubart it is an expression of their own tortured lives.

The Titanism of Goethe's hymns and the fervour of Herder's odes are in the first instance the forceful expression of emotion, not the expression of an inner conflict or of an irrepressible urge which leads to naturalistic results, such as are found in Gottfried August Bürger. This is true not only of the unrestrained, macabre features of his ballads, above all 'Lenore', with its extremes of emotional outburst and gruesome description, and 'Der Raubgraf', in which the count devours himself limb by limb – such motifs being, despite their unpleasantness, the perverted expression of the characteristic *Sturm und Drang* passion for the fully committed and the totally demanding – but also of his early love-poems, which sometimes show a naturalistic directness that would be unthinkable in Goethe's early lyrics. This directness is a kind of pre-Expressionist scorn of all restriction or discipline in life – as, indeed, was Bürger's own existence.

Bürger's other side is that of the 'calculating reasoner', which is logically connected with a personal sense of genius which, unruly by nature, despises convention, demands its own freedom and will not be led. This attitude is seen in his 'Elegie' ('Als Molly sich losreißen wollte').

There is no better description of the conflict in Bürger than that given by Schiller in his review of Bürger's poems, which was to usher in his friendship with Goethe. The language of these poems reflects the almost paradoxical tensions of his personality – his love of life and his ardent emotions, yet his wish to escape 'into the empty void'; and on the one side anti-middle-class attitudes, with a publicly declared hatred of oppression, and on the other side a thinly disguised hankering after the idyllic – reminiscent of his association with the Hainbund poets. Indeed, alongside his rapturous passion, his motifs of killing and punishing, and the corresponding naturalistic style of his ballads, in which, for example, a duel could be described through the image of butchery, he is a master of that most cultured of traditional forms – the sonnet. This is endemic both to his psychology and to the nature of his imagination: for a poet of his type it was an almost more reckless task to attempt a strict formal exercise than to follow where his abandoned 'genius' led, and this situation reappears when we remember Bürger's disciple August Wilhelm Schlegel and the delight which certain Romantics found in the sonnet form.

A similar figure to Bürger is Christian Friedrich Daniel Schubart (1739–91), whose life and work show the same dichotomy and inner contradiction. His poetic career starts with his *Todesgesänge* (1769) in the Klopstockian style and then divides into, on the one hand, political poetry, which led to his imprisonment by Karl Eugen of Württemberg on the Hoher Asperg and, on the other hand, pietistic lyric verse in the contrafacture style.

His significance in his own age lies in the radical nature of his polemical response to authoritarianism. Poems such as 'Die Fürstengruft' and 'Deutsche Freiheit' reflect the same strained relationship to Karl Eugen as that of the young Schiller. Today one tends to draw attention to the Duke's humane wisdom under the mollifying influence of Franziska von Hohenheim, but at the same time his actions provided the starting-point for the *Stürmer und Dränger* of Swabia in their concern for political liberty. Schubart's 'Fürstengruft', with its realistic descriptions of physical decay and the dance of death, is an expression of this desire for liberty in what was probably the only form that could escape the censor, the theme that the aristocracy, like the common man, had to go the way of all flesh. The twenty-six strophes of this poem become increasingly bitter in their anti-aristocratic tone, and the macabre side of death is employed as a means of destroying the pride, the glory, the lust, the intrigue and the un-Christian attitudes of the nobility. With overtones of this kind, in a manner that resembles the naturalistic side of Bürger's poetry, it is not surprising that even one of the more tolerant rulers like Karl Eugen should have taken exception to Schubart's verse and seen it as a threat to his rule. And when one recalls that Schubart's well-known 'Kap-Lied', which was aimed at stirring up feeling against foreign alliances, was sung throughout the state like a folksong, one can understand that conflicts between men like Schiller and Schubart and the ruling powers were inevitable. Again the posture struck by the *Sturm und Drang* anticipates that of the Expressionists.

In contrast to Schubart Schiller did not write any political poetry in the strict sense until 1785, and it is only in a few social poems from the *Anthologie* (1781), like 'Rousseau' and 'Die Kindesmörderin', that we find any trace of what might be called a revolutionary mood. This is partly due to Schiller's greater powers of generalization, which found expression in poems such as 'Hymne an den Unendlichen', 'Größe der Welt' and 'Resignation', in which one can already sense the philosophical poet that was to come. They are not all in free rhythms like Goethe's odes but in free strophic forms in which the combination of short and long lines is intended to convey a turbulence of spirit. It is perhaps in vocabulary that they are closer to Goethe, with words like 'Zackenfels', 'Adlergedanke', 'Gewittersturm', 'Sonnenwanderer', 'Riesenschatten', 'Götterschwur' conveying concentrated emotion; the verbs too have a dynamic quality, possibly with a stronger tendency towards the naturalistic, but it is above all in the nouns that the linguistic power lies.

In Schiller's love-poetry and poems on death, however, or in occasional poems like 'Die Schlacht' and 'Gruppe aus dem Tartarus', where the emphasis is not on concepts, it is the colourful verb, and to a lesser degree the adjective, that predominates, again, as in Bürger and Schubart, with a boldness that presages the lyric of Expressionism. Poems of death, such as 'Brutus und Cäsar', 'Eine Leichenphantasie' and 'Elegie auf den Tod eines Jünglings' have the same power of language. A key climactic word in Schiller's vocabulary at this time is 'dumpf' or 'dumpfig'; the elemental and the passionate is everywhere in control, even in his love-poems, e.g. 'Amalia', the 'Phantasie an Laura' and 'Der Kampf' (addressed to Charlotte von Kalb). Schiller's early love-poetry burns, glows, rages, rises and falls – in short, attempts to convey, directly and without regard to convention, the dynamic intensity of the elemental force of love. This intensity characterizes the whole of Schiller's *Anthologie* period, its Elysian as well as its Tartarean aspects, its Dionysian as well as its macabre moments. There is everywhere an urge towards the depiction of opposites, extremes and exaggerations – in a word, the mannerist aspect of *Sturm und Drang*. Yet all this does add up to a style, even if an extravagant one, and whatever similarities of detail there may be, it is a style that cannot be confused with that of any other *Sturm und Drang* poet.

Drama

It is no accident that Herder should have illustrated his views on literary genius by reference to Shakespeare as well as old folksongs, for in addition to lyric poetry it was logically drama that was the form which best expressed the impulses of *Sturm und Drang*. Here too certain key motifs were in the air: the Faust theme was treated not only by Goethe but also by Maler Müller and Klinger, while the motif of the child-murderess underlies not only the *Urfaust* but also Wagner's drama and Schiller's ballad. Italy, the land of passion, provided the setting for Gerstenberg's *Ugolino* (1768), Leisewitz's *Julius von Tarent* (1776), Klinger's *Zwillinge* (1776) and *Simsone Grisaldo* (1776) and Schiller's *Fiesko* (1783).

Farce, literary satire and political satire become vehicles for views on contemporary events: attacks on tyranny are contained in Schiller's *Räuber* (1781), *Fiesko* (1783) and *Kabale und Liebe* (1784) as well as in Leisewitz's short drama *Der Besuch um Mitternacht* (1775) and, with a bigger element of social criticism, Lenz's so-called comedies *Der Hofmeister* (1774) and *Die Soldaten* (1776). Outspoken literary satire is found in Lenz's farce *Pandaemonium Germanicum* (not printed until 1819) and in Goethe's *Götter, Helden und Wieland* (1774) and *Satyros* (1773). Voltaire also comes in for criticism, e.g. Wagner's *Voltaire am Abend seiner Apotheose* (1778). Goethe's *Götz*, on the other hand, takes the great conflicts of the moment – justice *versus* injustice, loyalty *versus* intrigue, the courtier *versus* the common man, freedom *versus* oppression – and treats them not satirically but with a Herder-like passion and sense of history. Finally there is that subjective dramatic outburst which gave its name to the whole movement, Klinger's unperformable *Wirrwarr* (1776), which the Swiss *Stürmer und Dränger* Kaufmann rechristened *Sturm und Drang*.

The *Urfaust*, only discovered in 1885, and that by chance, combines virtually all the important elements in *Sturm und Drang* drama: scenes loosely assembled without regard to the unities; *Knittelvers* metre derived from old German sources via Herder; and interpolated scenes in prose, imitative of Shakespeare and also naturalistic in the manner of Bürger.

The motivation derives from two sources. The theme of infanticide is used to criticize social convention and justify the killing; the Faust theme, as yet without its universal application, is pregnant with potential power. Faust is the product of Goethe's alchemical studies after his return from Leipzig. He is not yet the restless, questing traveller through life but he already shows a dissatisfaction with the dead world of book-learning and a determination to penetrate the secret of the world of which his imagination has already given him an inkling. The only way to do this is by magic. Behind these parts of the opening monologue – from the spirits in Old Norse ballads to the celebration of the infinite and the universal – stands the figure of Herder. The confident, self-assertive Faust is mockingly called a 'superman' by the Erdgeist, but the superman is not created in the image of God, for in the next moment he discusses professional scholarly matters with Wagner like a man of earth and is ironically parodied by Mephisto when he makes his unmotivated appearance in the scene with the student.

The link between these elements and the motif of infanticide in the Gretchen scenes is forced, for whereas in the study scenes Faust is the powerful, unique personality in the *Sturm und Drang* sense, in the Gretchen scenes he appears only as the conventional seducer, his originality, stimulated by Mephisto, declining into an exaggerated sophistication. The two aspects are not really compatible. Thus he is finally defeated by Gretchen's innocence. This too makes the *Urfaust* a mere torso – but as such it is the epitome of *Sturm und Drang*. Nature; mystery; the world of spirits and fantasy; the vitality of youth (Auerbachs Keller); the quality of childlike innocence in its union with the world and in the moment of its betrayal (Gretchen), expressed in folksong ('Der König in Thule'); middle-class degeneration (Frau Marthe); the motif of the dead letter (Wagner, scene with the student); the undogmatic, mystical, emotion-dominated interpretation of religious faith: all this is the purest *Sturm und Drang* in its conscious originality – so too is the philosophy of love, which is that also found in Goethe's lyrics of the period.

As mentioned above, the defence of moral protest against conventional ideas of right and wrong is one of the main concerns of *Sturm und Drang*. This is what links Schiller's *Räuber*, for instance, with the motif of infanticide in Goethe and Leopold Wagner. At the same time this is only one of the forms taken by social criticism at the time. There would have been no need for the *Stürmer und Dränger* to be followers of Rousseau or to have their own cult of genius and nature if they had not questioned the whole social structure. Everything in this field – the power of the aristocracy, whether despotic or 'enlightened' (in the latter case they saw it as a mechanistic, intellectual curbing of the ego); the prescribed rigidity of the class structure; religious and bourgeois prejudices – appeared to them as an attack on liberty.

Thus to the ethical critique in the motif of infanticide Lenz, in *Der Hofmeister* and *Die Soldaten*, adds a specific critique of social conditions. These are comedies with a strong satirical flavour, attacking contemporary conventions and making seduction the point of crisis. In *Die Soldaten* it is the usual seduction of an innocent middle-class girl by an immoral officer – the situation in *Emilia Galotti* but with the seducer one degree lower on the social scale, and also resembling Lessing's play in its dramatic exposure of the utter defencelessness of the middle class and the infamy of the officers' cadres. In *Der Hofmeister* it is the hero, with the sinister name of Läuffer ('fleer'), who seduces his employer's daughter; thus the guilt of the classes is virtually the reverse of that in *Die Soldaten*, or at least is more fairly apportioned. This appears illogical, but one must remember that the uprightness and geniality that characterize the aristocracy in *Der Hofmeister* are not intended to be conservative but rather that an unsatisfactory kind of middle condition should be uncovered through the motif of fashionable education at the hands of *Hofmeister* (private tutors). The guilt of the upper class lies in its frivolity and in matters of education. The comedy has become the medium for an attack on conventionality in the spirit of Rousseau's ideal of education.

The element of social criticism is also integrated, though in a very different way, into Schiller's first three plays, written during the unsettled period between leaving Swabia for Mannheim and then for Jena. It is most prominent in *Fiesko*, whose historical theme is least connected with it; in *Die Räuber* and *Kabale und Liebe* it is subsidiary to the problems of the main characters. The basic concept in *Die Räuber* (like that of infanticide in the *Urfaust*) is that of the Prodigal Son in the context of a family intrigue: this intrigue destroys Karl Moor's relationship with his father and his fiancée and also, as a consequence of his passionate self-assertiveness, with society as such. Robbery becomes the extreme expression of freedom, a symbol of the refusal to compromise in matters of honesty. The agonizing price he has to pay for this consists not only of his own banishment but also of a break with those dearest to him, and he becomes both a victim and a seeker after vengeance, a tragic figure in both aspects.

His is the tragedy of the 'man of genius' who, driven by the demonic power within him, opposes the limitations and the treacheries of the world by fighting convention from an emotional rather than an intellectual standpoint. Schiller invests him with greatness not only in his final moment of renunciation and self-sacrifice but at an earlier stage, even when he acts unlawfully; yet the deepest suffering and the most agonizing decisions spring from the nobility of his character and his self-dependence – this is what remains of the theme of the Prodigal Son. The end is never happiness – but it is destiny and thus greatness, and it is here, far more than in the somewhat obtrusive moralizing of the end of the play, that the remarkable effect of the work lies.

Kabale und Liebe, in contrast to Lenz's comedies, is a 'domestic tragedy' like *Emilia Galotti*, and as such its social criticism is sharper than that of *Die Räuber* – which, incidentally, received its motto 'In Tyrannos' from the publisher, not from Schiller. Yet the conflict of depraved court and noble citizen is not political like that of oligarchy and republic in *Fiesko*. Lady Milford, for instance, outwardly the most dubious representative of court society, has human sympathy, humanity and social conscience. while Ferdinand, Luise's real lover, who kills both her and himself in his delusion that she does not love him, is the son of the President, who is the great rogue at court: class distinctions are not the simple reflection of ethical distinctions, as critics used to think. Wurm, too, the President's intriguer, is portrayed as a middle-class citizen. The tragic irony lies in that, from the social point of view, Wurm is Luise's legitimate suitor, whereas Ferdinand, the nobleman, is excluded from her company both by her father and by his own. The object of attack here is class barriers themselves: nobility of character brings the nobleman and the middle-class girl together, while Wurm, the degenerate middle-class citizen, is as unworthy a partner for Luise as Franz Moor is for Amalie.

Even more important than such facts is the argument behind them: the aristocracy is largely degenerate, but so too is the middle-class world, witness Wurm and Miller's eagerness for Ferdinand's money. This is not a question of black *versus* white, and Schiller is not taking up a class-position; rather he is portraying the tragedy of human qualities which are made to bow before the callousness of inhumanity, and this is independent of matters of class.

In contrast to *Die Räuber* and *Kabale und Liebe*, human tragedies with only peripheral political elements, Schiller's one historical play of his *Sturm und Drang* period, *Fiesko*, is basically political. The venerable Doge Andrea Doria rules the Genoese oligarchy, but his regime is threatened by the Pretender Gianettino, his nephew, a violent autocrat, who is described in the *dramatis personae* as 'of stunted education'. It is against him that the conspiracy is directed, led by Fiesko, a nobleman whose conscience is represented by Verrina, who seeks to lead the opposition to the establishment of a real republic. After seemingly overcoming the Dorias, however, Verrina comes into conflict with Fiesko's selfish ambition to acquire the fruits of the rebellion for himself; Verrina kills Fiesko, and the old Doge regains his former position which, in the final scene, the Republican Verrina also pledges himself to support. This is not a contradiction, for the drama is concerned with the temptations of power: Fiesko fails as a conspirator and as a man because he covets the title of Duke, and the most dramatic scenes are his conflicts with Verrina on this issue. Verrina sees that a change of roles will achieve nothing and that therefore Doria is the more rightful ruler, though he detests his regime; and Fiesko's trial at Verrina's hands is the expression of a deep disillusionment with the man who had betrayed the republic.

The fundamental human motif in the drama is the conflict between egoism and service in Fiesko's soul, and the notion of power as something inherently evil besets his inconsistencies and inconstancies, taunting him and ultimately destroying his far from despicable personality. If one is to set the interests of the community above one's own – as does Verrina alone – one needs an unconditional moral altruism, and until such an altruism conquers the world, the world will naturally remain an object which the forces of tradition will seek to dominate. *Sturm und Drang* thus represents here not only the republican view in politics but the absoluteness of the moral imperative.

Perhaps the summit of *Sturm und Drang* drama is the language of these early plays of Schiller. It has not the forced casualness or affected *naïveté* of Klinger and Lenz, and its richness of imagery and vocabulary is the expression of a youthful dynamic passion not found in the *Anthologie* poems of the same period. It is the language both of primitive emotion and of spirituality, accessible to all ranks of society, sensuous, the vehicle of men of passion who yet reflect upon life; the passionate outbursts of Schiller's heroes have thus far more conviction than those of the other *Stürmer und Dränger*: examples are Franz Moor's cynical confession at the end of the first scene of *Die Räuber*; Lady Milford and Miller in *Kabale und Liebe*; Verrina the Republican and Gianettino the villain in *Fiesko*. Karl Moor's self-characterization in Act I, Scene 2 is like a list of all the *Sturm und Drang* motifs, while at the same time glowing with all manner of imagery and rhetorical devices.

A comparison with the historical dramas of the earlier *Stürmer und Dränger* reveals the same. Gerstenberg's *Ugolino*, for instance, has the macabre motif, taken from Dante, of the father together with his three sons thrown into the tower by his mortal enemy, the father being forced to watch his sons starve to death one by one, his agony made all the more poignant by the arousing of false hopes of their survival and by hopeless attempts to console himself over their fate. No depiction of suffering in Schiller's works is so cruel as this. It is the tragedy of greatness which is rendered powerless and made to witness its own defeat and the suffering of others – a hyperbolic presentation typical of *Sturm und Drang*. There are linguistic anticipations of Schiller, but a sense of effective, gripping theatre, with a growing climax and a final catastrophe, is missing.

From this latter angle J. A. Leisewitz's *Julius von Tarent* and F. M. Klinger's (1752–1831) *Die Zwillinge*, both treatments of the same subject – the jealousy of two brothers and its tragic outcome – are closer to Schiller than is Gerstenberg. In both plays it is the selfish, hot-blooded, yet more interesting brother who loses his self-control and kills his gentler, more congenial, yet duller twin, and in both plays the father takes the law of retribution into his own hands. This is clearly the same attitude towards fate as is found in classical drama, where a whole family can be cursed, and as a type it recurs in Schiller's *Braut von Messina*. Yet at the same time the *Sturm und Drang* concept of genius contradicts this. In both these plays the murderers are portrayed in a naturalistic and quite un-classical manner and their self-centredness is utterly modern, while the climax of the works takes the form of fury at the world and against the laws that restrict the expression of the individual ego. The gentleness and goodness of the other brothers, on the other hand, achieves no dramatic effect.

In the last analysis, and quite logically, this kind of *Sturm und Drang* drama is a monodrama, for even though the five-act form, the climax and the final catastrophe are preserved, they have lost their traditional power to convince, and give way to the concept of genius as the unifying force. The hero cannot tolerate a rival but at the most a partner of his own breed who can add to the singleminded power of the action. Klinger's *Der Wirrwarr*, virtually the last product of the South German 'genius'-worshippers before they broke up after Goethe's departure for Weimar, also shows this. Such colourful language as that used by Guelfo in *Die Zwillinge* shows the typical tendency to excess and exaggeration, and these features appear all the more prominent because there is no Schillerian thought to sustain them. Such language, found also in *Der Wirrwarr*, abounds in words of violence and extremes, in hyperbole and in onomato-poeia; it is consciously ungrammatical and elliptic in syntax, and goes to lengths never attempted by Schiller or Goethe, or even Lenz. In fact this is *Sturm und Drang* at its superficial level, not in its profoundest meaning, such as one finds in the young Goethe and the young Schiller, and even occasionally in Bürger.

The action of the play too, which is set in America, is a veritable 'Wirrwarr' (confusion), based on the vagaries of chance, the glorification of instinct and primitive urge, and a delight in the repellent, with the merest coincidence as *deus ex machina*. Three typical abandoned *Sturm und Drang* rapscallions give vent to their confused emotions; a tribal feud, in whose name the most horrible deeds of hatred are committed and in which lords talk and behave like privateers, ends improbably with a partly sincere, partly reluctant reconciliation brought about through the stilted device of a marriage between the youngest children of the warring families. There is no psychological motivation, and there could have been other endings equally logical. It is not surprising that even in Weimar under Karl August, Klinger could not get himself accepted with such a play. It is eloquent in destruction but leaves nothing in its place, and even its crude naturalism is a form of arbitrary realism barely more authentic than the middle-class world it was attacking. This is *Sturm und Drang* existing merely for itself, without a goal.

More substantial was the literary farce, which the *Stürmer und Dränger* developed into an original genre. In this they portrayed the contrast between their own conception of literature and that of the Enlightenment, attacking above all Wieland, also Nicolai, Voltaire and even Herder (in Goethe's *Satyros*). The form used is either *Knittelvers* (doggerel) or prose satire. Goethe later added, in Weimar, a stylistically authentic parody of a baroque drama in alexandrines to his *Jahrmarktsfest zu Plundersweilern*, mocking the emotionalism of the courts and the orderly baroque world. There is also much parody of contemporary conditions in this work, but today it is only possible to identify a small part of it – most obviously, perhaps, in the mockery of the prim and proper middle-class onlookers.

The position is different with the 'perverted' antiquity of *Götter, Helden und Wieland*, in which Wieland, in a nightcap, cuts the worst possible figure in his satirical confrontation with true antiquity, like a little man confronted by giants. The narrow-minded, tiny man of the Enlightenment, respectable and conceited, a petty moralizer who does not even worry himself about the dream in which he is destroyed, cannot grasp the standards of an Alcestis or a Hercules. It is interesting to note that when Wieland visited Weimar shortly afterwards, he made no effort to take his revenge on the author of this piece.

Related to this exuberant and direct satire of the young Goethe are works such as Wagner's farce directed against Voltaire and Klinger's *Prometheus, Deukalion und seine Recensenten*, aimed at Nicolai. In his *Pater Brey*, an attack on Leuchsenring, and his *Prolog zu den neusten Offenbarungen Gottes*, directed against Bahrdt, Goethe himself satirized pietists and religious hypocrites in his *Knittelvers* style. All these works reflect the *Sturm und Drang* demand for openness and honesty, qualities which lead to the choice of *Knittelvers* as a form and of the market place as the scene of the *Jahrmarktsfest zu Plundersweilern*, both of which are true reflections of the *Volk*. There is also a clear connection with *Götz*. In his *Satyros oder der vergötterte Waldteufel* Goethe even satirizes Herder, the idol of *Sturm und Drang*, but in a more refined, more subtle, allusive style than his attacks against Wieland and Bahrdt. Satyros's proclamation is a perfect parody of *Sturm und Drang* effusiveness and the fascination that it exerted. All these works, written between 1773 and 1775, have the bold, irreverent spirit of *Sturm und Drang*, with a playful quality about them. The last works in this style, however, starting with *Der Triumph der Empfindsamkeit* (1777), belong to Goethe's early classical period.

Lenz's literary farces remained unpublished: one of them, now lost (*Wolken*), followed the line of Goethe's Wieland polemic, while the other, *Pandaemonium Germanicum*, is an outspoken literary review in which Lenz attempts to parody whole classes, such as 'the Imitators', 'the Philistines', 'the Journalists'. They all tumble around at the foot of a mountain – the symbol of genius – at whose summit sit Goethe and Lenz himself. (This is the image at the opening of Herder's essay on Shakespeare and also influences Goethe's Aristophanic *Die Vögel*.) The symbol of the mountain is characteristic of *Sturm und Drang*, though in the second act of *Pandaemonium Germanicum* it gives way to the allegorical Temple of Fame, where

French and German men of letters (among them Wieland again) converse – whereby the Germans emerge in an unfavourable light; otherwise the work is concerned with the passing of literary judgements. The image of the mountain is also very Goethean and serves to symbolize the *Sturm und Drang* conception of genius, pre-eminent among whose representatives were Lessing, Herder, Shakespeare, Klopstock, Goethe and (in Lenz's eyes) Lenz himself. Certainly much of the work preaches to the converted, and it is quite unperformable and often ridiculous, but it does state a firm position, and as such is a highly revealing utterance of the movement.

In Goethe's *Götz* – both the first version, *Die Geschichte Gottfriedens von Berlichingen mit der eisernen Hand dramatisiert* (1771), and the final play, *Götz von Berlichingen mit der eisernen Hand* (1773) – the individual, human, historical, revolutionary, Herderian-Rousseauesque elements of *Sturm und Drang* all come together. Both versions are Shakespearian in their freedom from the unities, and their prose has the same spontaneity as the prose scenes in the *Urfaust* – a greater freedom from stylization, moreover, than the prose version of *Iphigenie* or *Egmont*, both of which have concealed four- and five-stress iambic lines in them. *Götz* is the pure expression of *Sturm und Drang* naturalism, without, however, the unbridled exaggerations found in the language of Klinger and, to some extent, Lenz. Underlying this naturalism is Herder's concept of the unity of the *Volk* within itself and with the world, and the unity of the hero or man of genius within himself. This concept shows itself in the language of knights and peasants alike, as in that of the hero, his wife, his sister and his son, in contrast to the affected court speech of the opposing party – Weislingen, Adelheid and the Bishop. Linking this contrast is Goethe's striving after a Lutheran style of simplicity and directness, with elision, apocope, inversions and archaisms, giving a primitive richness of vocabulary which is nevertheless far from being an exercise in historical imitation. Unlike the *naïveté* deliberately affected by Klinger and Lenz, Goethe's language serves a basic unity of time and character.

The same is true of the subject-matter. Götz and Elisabeth, together with their followers, represent an ideal picture of *Sturm und Drang* man, as their treacherous opponents represent the side of Wieland and Voltaire in the literary farces. Part of Götz's tragedy is that he, the man of action, sees in his hesitant, simple-minded son a kind of punishment, an embodiment of feelingless degeneration, and in true *Sturm und Drang* style he is allowed to perish as a heroic, ideal figure. Particularly significant in this respect is the scene from Act II of the original version (later omitted) in which the boy's parents decide, because of his weakness and effeminacy, to send him to a monastery: his mother sees him as a knight of doubtful quality, and when her sentimental sister suggests that he might have a noble role to play in life, she claims that that could not happen in an age of 'real men' but only in a hundred years' time, when human beings will have sunk to some inconceivable low level – a thought that obviously springs from Herder's view of the decadence of men and cultures as expressed in *Auch eine Philosophie*. Götz knows that he marks the end of an epoch in which simplicity of mind, sensuous awareness and the morality of chivalric loyalty could still be combined, and all the subsidiary plots – Georg, Bruder Martin, Weislingen and Adelheid – serve only to underline this. No other drama of the *Sturm und Drang* era is so thoroughly and richly typical of the driving forces of that era, or so original and satisfying in its Shakespeare-inspired form.

Novel

The formal influence of pietism is seen at its most fruitful in the realm of the novel. Apart from Church hymns, such as those of Susanne von Klettenberg, the elderly friend of Goethe's youth, and her spiritual consort Lavater, together with some of those of Klopstock, it is above all in lyric poetry that the feeling of confidence in one's aesthetic message, or in the passion of one's love, or in the sincerity of one's self-absorption into nature is at its most powerful. The drama tends to reveal rather than to conceal, even in the religious sphere, and is furthest removed from didactic tendencies, above all where the career of the active 'hero' is concerned.

The novel, on the other hand, had already become in the whole of Europe a repository both of sentimentality and self-analysis by about 1770. From Gellert's *Schwedische Gräfin* to Sophie von la Roche's *Fräulein von Sternheim* (1771) – praised in Lenz's *Pandaemonium Germanicum* – the moral sentimentality of the Enlightenment and the moral self-investigation stimulated by pietism united in order to uncover, to confuse and then to reconcile the destinies of human beings. Alongside the traditional narrative form pietism contributed the letter and the diary as familiar media for the expression of guilt, ecstasy and violent emotion.

All this is present in Goethe's *Werther* (1774), as it is, in a different form, in *Götz*. At the same time the ego reveals itself here, not in a less direct manner than in the lyric, but in a less typical form than in the drama. For all his individuality, Götz is the representative of true manhood, and is supported as such by Sickingen, Georg and Lerse; Werther, on the other hand, is a unique, untypical man of passion, notwithstanding the fact that his famous attire became fashionable among young people. For he was not a product of this fashion but created it himself. And when Goethe warned his readers against following Werther, it was not only an expression of shock at the effects of his autobiographical novel but a legitimate interpretation of it.

Who, then, is this individual called Werther? Certainly not the pitiful young Jerusalem, whose suicide gave Goethe the outer framework; certainly not the Goethe of Wetzlar days, who vied with Kestner for the favour of Charlotte Buff. This is clear, and was so long before Thomas Mann's *Lotte in Weimar*. But Goethe has breathed into these two historical characters a highly personal *Sturm und Drang* yearning and produced a character who has to perish through his emotional imbalance and his excess of passion. The second sentence of the first letter could stand as a motto for the whole work: 'Bester Freund, was ist das Herz des Menschen!'

It is significant that Werther does not just live out his life but consciously and consistently poses this question. The epistolary form is in itself reflective rather than active, and the inner form of the book rests on the tension between what Werther knows himself to be and what he would wish to become, i.e. a man who lived by his emotions and lived life to the full. Again the epistolary form encourages this intimacy of expression, as a comparison with the epic narrative style of *Wilhelm Meister* reveals.

This symbolizing of Werther's conflict both in the inner and the outer form underlies the well-known letter of 10 May and similar passages. It is the letter which recalls *Ganymed*, with its self-immersion in the universality of nature – though while *Ganymed* is pure lyricism, *Werther* is the confession of a man who knows, and is reflecting on, his own nature, so that his descriptions of his violent emotional experiences are fundamentally epic, however lyrical the means he employs. From the psychological standpoint the latter form meant to the *Stürmer und Dränger* complete frankness and, at the same time, self-exposure to the limits of human endurance, even to the possibility of self-annihilation. Thus the epistolary form of the novel itself foreshadows Werther's ultimate tragedy; or, put the other way round, the force of Goethe's emotions compelled him to use this particular form. From all angles, therefore, and not only that which makes his suicide the natural outcome of his passion, Werther is a logical character.

Of *Sturm und Drang* inspiration is Werther's Herder-like longing for the peace of childhood, such as in the scene after the introduction of Wahlheim and the scene through which he finds his way to Lotte. This is the happy presence of nature in man, the nature that symbolizes man's yearning. Werther's views on art, too, stimulated by his own drawings, are *Sturm und Drang* realism, for his first sketch of children was made, as he said, without adding anything of his own, which strengthened him in his determination to allow nature to dictate to him as she had to all great artists. The meditation that follows, on the 'rules' which can produce Philistines and mediocrities but not even remarkable villains, let alone geniuses, recalls Goethe's *Von deutscher Baukunst* and *Rede zum Shake-*

spearestag – indeed, the whole of Herder's influence. Genius must burn itself out, independent of common canons of judgement: this is Werther's concept of his own life, and it is the concept by which he perishes.

As in other genres, Lenz copied Goethe in the novel also. His fragmentary *Der Waldbruder*, largely written during his unhappy visit to Weimar in 1776, is a personal *roman à clef* and also an epistolary novel in the wake of *Werther*. Where Goethe is to the point, Lenz is exaggerated. The hero is a thinly disguised self-portrait depicting his passion for Henriette von Waldner, whom he knew only from a picture and who was already betrothed to another man (cf. *Werther*); the picture is stolen from the hero, which causes his utter collapse – again, a typical *Sturm und Drang* exaggeration, turning an almost ridiculous illusion into an all-consuming passion. The hero bears the symbolic name Herz ('Heart'), modelled on the symbolism of Wild ('Savage') and Feu ('Fire') in Klinger's *Wirrwarr*. The hero's renunciation of the world to become a hermit – significantly called a 'romantic' decision in the book– is a crude derivative of *Werther*, though Werther's loneliness remains spiritual. In form too it shows its obvious descent from *Werther*, except that it has no epic, descriptive sections but relies entirely upon letters, and there are no fewer than eight different writers from whose correspondence the inner and outer biography of the hero's unhappy love emerges.

1776 also saw the publication of the sentimental novel *Siegwart*, set in a monastery and not unrelated in theme to *Der Waldbruder*, by Martin Miller (1750–1814), a pietist pastor from Ulm. Here the hero already dreams in his youth of renouncing the world. His love-story, like the pietistic religious content, is sentimental, not in the passionate style of *Sturm und Drang* but rather in the general mode of sensibility, with many motifs of little more than contemporary sociological interest. Nevertheless it shows far more direcctly than *Werther* the employment of pietistic emotions and values in a prose narrative genre.

This process can, however, be traced in terms of more significant works, genuine autobiographical novels of pietistic inspiration which, unlike *Werther*, whose centre of gravity lies in the aesthetic sphere, are the true representative works of *Sturm und Drang* in the realm of prose narrative. They are both autobiographies and confessions, for religious principles require strict honesty; they are also both descriptions of spiritual development and accounts of the divine educative forces which press upon the personality. There is also a link with Herder at this point.

This range of aspects is particularly apparent in J. H. Jung-Stilling (1740–1817), whose *Heinrich Stillings Jugend*, published by Goethe in 1777 and later expanded into a full-length autobiography, combines the educative, the philosophical and the physical. From the dawning of consciousness in the child, his conflicts with the world of parents and grandparents, of the village and all its practical concerns, we pass to the question of his education, of nature and of God, whom the author is concerned to present as a living force. There is a certain inner similarity to the affectionate realism of the world of Matthias Claudius, who did not, however, employ the novel as a form.

Theodor Hippel's *Lebensläufe nach aufsteigender Linie* (1776 onwards) started as a family chronicle but turned into a four-volume autobiography. In a realistic manner, like Jung-Stilling, Hippel (1741–96) treats his own youth as a series of events of virtually equal importance.

The psychology of human development, however, is far more deeply treated, also in terms of a sensitive childhood, in *Anton Reiser* by Karl Philipp Moritz (1757–93), a friend of Goethe's with whom he discussed aesthetic questions in Rome in 1786. Hippel and Jung-Stilling saw experience, meditation, instruction and sermon as means of education, as did Moritz, but there is in Moritz's work a psychological depth, shown, for example, in Reiser's meeting with the quietist sect of Madame de Guyon, which even anticipates Dostoevsky and the French, German and Scandinavian naturalists, while the amphibolic effect of this confessional Christianity, free, as it is, of all trace of religious dogma, on a young, impressionable mind gives Moritz's work a greater realism than that of either Stilling or Hippel.

Thus the *Sturm und Drang* novel not only shows the sublimation of passion, the conquest of aesthetic isolationism, worldliness and the realities of a childlike world, as in Werther and its successors, but demonstrates how, as in drama, self-observation develops from a starting-point in pietism, an objective self-analysis beyond the reach of Gellert's or Nicolai's sentimentality or even the emotional-cum-rationalistic moralizing of Sophie von la Roche's *Fräulein von Sternheim*.

The Swiss educational reformer Johann Heinrich Pestalozzi (1746–1827) also needs to be mentioned here, a man who, influenced by Kant and deeply imbued with the *Humanitätsidee* of the eighteenth century, had his roots in the Enlightenment. Goethe, however, was not receptive to his ideas. In the free odes of Pestalozzi's *Abendstunden eines Einsiedlers* there are reminiscences of Klopstock and the Stolbergs, while the first part of his educative novel *Lienhard und Gertrud* (1781–5) is far more than one of the first 'village novels'. In a manner recalling that of Matthias Claudius, he displays a simple emotional directness which has given him an importance that outlasted his age and the reputations of many of his literary and pedagogical contemporaries and successors.

Classicism

WERNER KOHLSCHMIDT

Goethe's Rejection of 'Sturm und Drang'

The *Sturm und Drang* cult of genius, with its exaggerations of style, especially as evidenced by Klinger and Lenz, was destined to be as short-lived as the *Werther* fever. Such phenomena were the products of youth, shot through with passion, intolerance and immaturity, and as these young writers grew older there came an inevitable change in their attitudes and their style. For the whole movement was derived not from experience but, even at its height, from the ideas and hopes of its supporters, and it is hard to realize that when Goethe and Herder went to Weimar they were both still young men.

The choice facing the less talented members of the movement was between turning away from their youthful impetuosity – because they could not go on indefinitely saying the same things – or making their peace with the middle-class world they had been attacking. Leisewitz follows this latter course; so also, eventually and not without irony, does Klinger, who became an instructor in the Russian army and was elevated to the aristocracy. The Stolbergs, who in 1775 had joined Goethe in his youthful protests against the middle-class morality of Bodmer and Breitinger, became officials, and Friedrich Leopold also joined the ranks of the Christian moralists. Jung-Stilling, also a permanent government servant, lived more and more for himself with each new instalment of his autobiography, while Hippel, a successful lawyer in Königsberg, became one of the landed gentry. Hölty, the most sensitive and gifted of the Göttinger Hain poets, died of consumption at the age of twenty-eight, while from 1777 Lenz was completely mad and later died a miserable death in Russia. The passion-torn Bürger retained his sanity but had less and less of value to communicate. The only one who managed to retain contact with Herder and Goethe was Karl Philipp Moritz, who shared with them the movement to early classicism, while Schiller, whose *Sturm und Drang* experience came later, when the movement as such had passed, followed his own path to classicism.

The year 1776, when Goethe secured Herder's appointment in Weimar, was a traumatic moment for the *Sturm und Drang* movement. Klinger and Lenz suddenly appeared as uninvited guests and set about trying to influence the young and still impressionable Duke Karl August to set up a kind of academy of the muses in Weimar. Goethe, however, without exactly turning them away, allowed them to compromise themselves to such an extent that they had to leave. His action, sometimes mistakenly regarded as a betrayal of trust, was prompted not by such considerations as jealousy of Klinger's remarkable personal presence but by a long-term view of his own interests: Klinger and Lenz represented to him his own immediate reckless past, from which he now shrank. This is perhaps the first, albeit largely unconscious decision of the emerging 'classical' Goethe.

What lay behind this change? Compared with England, France and Italy, all of whom had already experienced a 'classical' literature, the little court at Weimar had neither economic wealth, historical and cultural tradition, nor even a prosperous aristocracy. Yet one need only recall the petty, miserable circumstances from which Winckelmann emerged almost by his own efforts to become the most important theorist and historian of classical art in Europe. It is a feature of the German cultural tradition that literary movements arose from modest circumstances and not from centres established under wealthy patrons; a modest degree of patronage and the presence of a few important figures sufficed to produce an intellectual and literary centre of attraction which in other countries would only have been possible under far more lavish circumstances. Yet it is remarkable that in this century of subjectivity, and perhaps in its most sensitive decade, the movement should have been away from the purely personal and towards the committed, the ideals of service and objective form, not stopping at the mere rejection of unbridled, emancipated 'genius'.

As it was, understandably, a princely court in which this spirit flourished, so it could equally well have been, in Germany, a university town: the Hainbund poets were in Göttingen, South German *Sturm und Drang* was in Strasbourg, pietists and rationalists assembled in Leipzig and Halle, and the Romantics were later to find their way to Jena, Heidelberg, Halle and Berlin. But a university is a restless community, and literary groups tend either to be short-lived or to petrify, as in Leipzig, so that for a literature that was tending towards classicism a small court offered more favourable, because more permanent, conditions as a cultural centre. Moreover, as one can see in Goethe's own case, discipline and the ideal of service are closely linked with this, whilst at university the individual spirit is still in process of discovering itself (though after it has, it often becomes pedantically academic).

The simplicity of the Weimar court is personified in the Dowager

Duchess Anna Amalie of Brunswick; widowed before she was twenty-one and before the birth of her son Karl August in 1758, she brought him up with dignity and acted as a wise, understanding regent. She summoned Wieland to be the young duke's tutor, and when, on Goethe's arrival in Weimar, Karl August reached mature age and married Princess Luise of Darmstadt, Anna Amalie collected round herself, independent of her son, an intimate circle to which Wieland, Goethe and Herder belonged. This was the company in which Goethe met Charlotte von Stein and many educated aristocrats like the Knebels and the Einsiedels, who were capable of holding their own in any conversation, including matters of classical antiquity. Making translations and paraphrases, composing music, writing poetry, acting, discussing – such was the atmosphere which Goethe and Herder found, the atmosphere in which copies of works like the *Urfaust* could be made and preserved as valuable documents, an intimate, provincial circle yet intellectually lively and with pretensions to originality.

Perhaps even more decisive was the personality of the Duke himself – youthful, impetuous, with a tendency to recklessness. Yet in face of the need to consolidate the dukedom – a task not within the power of his benevolent tutor Wieland – he found himself looking to Goethe, who had himself only just left behind the impetuosity of his own *Sturm und Drang* and now suddenly found himself facing responsibilities on which the fate of the little state depended.

Wieland's presence in Weimar was undoubtedly of great psychological value to Goethe. His early career vacillated between religious and erotic sentimentality on the one hand and an occasionally scabrous wit on the other, but by the time of the *Komische Erzählungen* (1765), *Musarion* (1764–88) and above all *Agathon* (begun 1766) he had found the manner best suited to his versatility. These works made him famous throughout Germany. In them he finally threw off his seraphic Christian *persona* and adopted a more appropriate air of elegant wit, modelled on Lucian.

Unlike the entirely earnest manner of Winckelmann and Schiller, Wieland's pursuit of classical values follows the freedom which antiquity allows to nature, a form of naturalism close to that of the French enlightenment and closer to the manner of the *Stürmer und Dränger* than the latter realized. Wieland, in his rococo, man-of-the world style, sought a blend of antiquity and the modern world. He allows Paris to regard the three goddesses as fairies – an exoteric, homely attitude very different from the *Sturm und Drang* cult of Homer as a powerful 'genius of nature'. In his *Musarion* he opposes religious bigotry, like the *Stürmer und Dränger*, with a sensuous, sometimes hedonistic vision of antiquity which is part of early German classicism and which Goethe pursued in the period of his Italian journey.

Wieland shared the influence of Shaftesbury with Herder, Goethe and Schiller, and it is this side of his nature that led him to justify himself to Lessing as 'a mind of classical bent', in proof of which he wrote his *Agathon*, a stylized, Platonic psychological novel in which, with the spirit of Shaftesbury ever present, the irreconcilablility of virtue and sensuality is demonstrated *ad absurdum*. Shortly before going to Weimar, Wieland reasserted this belief in the novel *Sokrates Mainomenos*, and it was as a man who sought to mediate between antiquity and the present that he was installed by Anna Amalie at her court.

He did not disappoint his patron. As tutor to the young Duke, and as the author of texts of *Singspiele*, dramatic cantatas, etc., he raised the intellectual level at court to a point from which Goethe could carry the process further. Works like *Alcest, Die Wahl des Herkules* and *Pandora* are drawn from classical mythology and, though somewhat stylized, retain an atmosphere remarkably close to that of the original subjects. His satire on the eighteenth-century idyll, *Die Geschichte der Abderiten* (1774–80), is also cast in classical mould and, second in popularity only to *Agathon*, has an anti-provincial tone which reaches its climax in the age of German classicism.

The qualities which Goethe needed but did not find in Wieland – direct and unhesitating criticism, personal and intellectual stimuli – were brought to Weimar when Goethe had Herder appointed court chaplain. For Herder it was a choice between this and a chair at Göttingen, where he would have had certain unwelcome academic commitments; he had virtually come to the end of his pietistic Bückeburg period, and he brought to the Weimar court his qualities of brilliant conversationalist, stimulator of new ideas and gripping preacher. Goethe, until after his return from Italy, shared with Herder both the common aesthetic interests of their earlier time together – interests which they had both since learned, in similar ways, to control – and a new concern with the philosophy of Spinoza. Goethe read Spinoza's *Ethics* with Charlotte von Stein and discussed it with Herder, whose book on Spinoza, *Gott* (1787), is the climax of this interest. After this, however, Herder and Goethe went their separate ways, especially with the growth of Schiller's influence.

Both externally – for there was resentment at the special favours he received – and psychologically it was hard for Goethe to adjust himself to this milieu. The eighteen-year-old Duke began by seeing Goethe as the youthful *Stürmer und Dränger*, and this made him all the more aware of the dangers and absurdities of that mode of life which he had just left behind; the antics of Lenz and Klinger only aggravated this feeling. Wieland, however, was moderation itself, and Herder, a man of responsibility and firm convictions, was very different from the friend of Strasbourg days. Anna Amalie was the unchallenged ruler of the court, while the weak Countess Luise suffered in silence at her husband's eccentricities, which were held in check only by his good nature. The problems of this marriage brought fresh responsibilities for Goethe. Charlotte von Stein, for whom his passion lasted until he left for Italy, was for a long while his intellectual equal, and this too drove him towards the restriction of his own ego and the acceptance of personal responsibility. Thus in three fields – the problem of Karl August, the problem of his responsibilities as a court official, and the problem of his own emotions – Goethe felt the meaning of self-restraint.

In his efforts to arouse in Karl August a sense of responsibility, Goethe had to avoid appearing to spoil the young Duke's pleasures. To start with, therefore, and much to the distaste of the elder courtiers, May dances, student festivities and the like continued to take place. But within ten years Goethe had succeeded in directing Karl August's mind away from selfish pleasures and towards the interests of his country, setting him a personal example by taking over such tasks as road construction, forestry, mining and even recruitment for the militia. No sacrifice was too great for Goethe – but all this was at the expense of his own literary activity. Neither *Iphigenie*, *Egmont* nor *Tasso* was completed during these first ten years in Weimar, and *Wilhelm Meisters theatralische Sendung* was put on one side; only in the lyric did his emotions mature. Yet, as revealed in 'Ilmenau', the poem written for Karl August's birthday in 1783, he could review with satisfaction the effects of his educative influence on the Duke, while the journey to Switzerland which the two men made in 1779 also helped to achieve this goal – a goal which Wieland could never have reached.

Goethe's development can most clearly be traced in his lyrics. 'Seefahrt', for instance (1776), shows how at the very beginning of his Weimar period he turned from the vision of the titanic Prometheus to a conception of humanity which contained a very different interpretation of the classical relationship of man to the gods, and the poems written between 1776 and the early 1780s ('Grenzen der Menschheit', 'Das Göttliche') reflect ever more clearly the values of moderation and self-restraint. The development can be followed from his rejection of the gods in 'Prometheus' to their acceptance in 'Seefahrt' and their veneration in 'Grenzen der Menschheit' and 'Das Göttliche'.

With this development came a strengthening of humanitarian sentiment, a feature that is also mirrored in the rhythm of the poems, for 'Grenzen der Menschheit' and 'Das Göttliche' are not in free rhythm, like the *Sturm und Drang* poems, but in classical metres. The number of neologisms and compound words is also reduced. 'An den Mond' (first version 1777) shows the same pattern of development: the first version describes the guilt that attaches to the thought that the shadow of Werther can drive a girl to suicide – in other words we see Goethe rejecting the philosophy of his own Wertherian days.

'Die Geheimnisse' (1784–5), an uncompleted allegorical poem in *ottave rime,* shows the emergence of a Spinoza-inspired humanitarianism and is at the same time a testimony to his friendship with Herder, whose own parallel path of development was from Ossian and Shakespeare to the *Ideen zur Philosophie der Geschichte der Menschheit* (1784–91) and the *Humanitätsbriefe* (1793–7). These fragments Goethe adapted into 'Zueignung', the work which he later used as a preface to his collected poems.

The growing formal strictness of Goethe's poems corresponds to the rise of his interest in the natural sciences. This interest was stimulated by his duties in the realms of forestry and mining and was matched by an urge to understand nature, not merely through the emotions but through knowledge. The influence of Spinoza is important here as imposing new obligations to learning. Starting with the alchemy of the *Urfaust* period, Goethe proceeded to Lavater's analytical physiognomy and thence to an enthusiastic objectivity forced upon him by his official duties in Weimar and encouraged by his relationship to the University of Jena. Botany, zoology, mineralogy and anatomy became for him means of objectifying his existence, and the seeds of his later concepts of the *Urpflanze*, of metamorphosis, morphology and optics were sown at this time.

Here too, as befits Goethe's nature, the development is organic. He became obsessed with the notion of law and causality, and in many contexts, like that of the journey to Switzerland in 1779, we find statements about the underlying laws of physical, inanimate and animal nature. The fragment *Über die Natur* (1781), inspired by Goethe and formulated by Tobler, together with Goethe's own essay *Über den Granit* (1784) are early examples of this development towards scientific objectivity, i.e. the attempt to blend Spinozan nature-philosophy with controlled observation of nature, expressing itself in the Tobler–Goethe essay in the idea of circularity, as opposed to the rationalistic idea of progress; the form of the idea is expressed as a dialectical antithesis which is resolved as *deus sive natura*. *Über den Granit* also is both dithyrambic and objective, religious and neutral, reflective and emotional. The existence of natural laws is seen as a stimulus, not, as in Goethe's mature classical period, as a call to resignation. One month after writing *Über den Granit* Goethe discovered the *os intermaxillare*, and this silenced any further charges of amateurism.

The Italian Journey and its Consequences

There were various motives behind Goethe's remarkable 'flight' from Karlsbad to Rome in the autumn of 1786 – an action only possible with the Duke's consent. In the first place his official duties had become excessive, resulting in the fragmentation of his first decade in Weimar. His relationship to the Duke, too, had suffered a number of reverses, and when Karl August followed his adventurous nature by joining the Prussian army in 1786, Goethe's prime commitment in Weimar ceased, and it became possible to replace him. Finally his platonic relationship with Frau von Stein had reached a pitch of tension which threatened to destroy his peace of mind. Thus his escape to Rome was an attempt to overcome his stifled passion, to preserve his personality as a poet and to stimulate his poetic faculty by new experiences. After the masculine-dominated world of Weimar he needed new stimuli, new surroundings, new acquaintanceships, and his *Iphigenie* pointed to antiquity as the ideal synthesis of personal freedom and communal law.

Goethe's own *Italienische Reise*, written many years later, gives a some-what remote and stylized picture of his experiences, and it is from diaries and letters – above all the correspondence with Frau von Stein, Herder and Karl August – that one derives the truest and most realistic impressions. The first signs of emotional relaxation appeared when he was in South Germany; in Upper Italy, where he made his first contact with the classical world, he revelled in the new sense-impressions, after which he pressed on almost desperately to Rome, paying scant attention to such places as Florence on the way. The notion of spiritual rebirth dominated the journey from the beginning, a rebirth not only in the sense of classical studies but as affecting his entire existence. A poem like 'Kennst du das Land' shows how his yearning for Italy became one with his love for Charlotte von Stein. His first sight of classical columns moved him to tears; this private, subjective reaction was then followed by an objective search for the classical elements in Palladio's buildings at Vicenza and Venice – a kind of classical self-discipline in which his desires and his needs were one, creating a unity of experience whose acquisition his stay in Rome made him see as a duty. A diary entry for October 1786 notes his intention to take up practical studies, above all in chemistry and mechanics, after his return, for it was here, rather than in the aesthetic realm of beauty, that he saw the needs of the future – yet another example of his disciplined progress towards the ideals of classicism, in whose light the activities of the artist, the scientist and the statesman are united.

Shortly after his return from Naples and Sicily Goethe wrote to Frau von Stein that he was on the verge of discovering the principle of the *Urpflanze*, that ideal phenomenon which, whether it had existed or not, was no illusion but, as he put it, 'had an inner veracity and necessity . . . demonstrable in all living things'. The *Urpflanze* embraced nature in Spinoza's sense and nature as it appeared to the scientist – and both visions were vouchsafed by Italy in all its glory, sustained by a common ideal of service to truth, to beauty and to the community. This extension of the classical ideal beyond the realm of the aesthetic, the realm to which Winckelmann – whose works, particularly his history of art, Goethe studied seriously for the first time in Rome – had restricted his gaze, gives German classicism a new foundation, and it is in this spirit that Goethe shared the company of artists in Rome – Tischbein, Hackert, Angelica Kauffmann, and also Karl Philipp Moritz, who had likewise sought refuge in Rome and with whom Goethe conversed at length on matters of art.

Following Winckelmann, Goethe studied the Laocoon, the Niobe, the Apollo Belvedere, the Ludovisi Venus, and the Otricoli Zeus – works of late antiquity which, however, like Winckelmann, he took to be classical. He also cultivated his sketching, concentrating on strict perspective and anatomical studies, and discovered standards by which to distinguish great from inferior art. In addition he took up again the study of Greek, especially in Sicily: in Palermo he bought a copy of Homer in the original.

In this rich but confused atmosphere it was hardly possible for new literary works to be conceived. An attempted 'Homeric' drama *Nausikaa*, for example, did not get beyond a few impressive opening scenes: Goethe was not yet able to absorb his Mediterranean experiences into a large literary work, although he converted his prose version of *Iphigenie* into verse and wrote some important scenes of *Faust* in which some of these experiences reveal themselves.

The first version of *Iphigenie* was written between official journeys in 1779 in the space of a few weeks and breathes a strongly pre-classical atmosphere; classical influence begins to show itself in the ethical demands made of Iphigenie, Orest and Thoas. From the beginning Goethe had 'humanized' the Euripidian barbarian Thoas, while 'sentimentalizing' the relationship between Iphigenie, Orest and Pylades. Both these features show how he introduced Winckelmann's precept of 'noble simplicity and serene greatness', for by ennobling Thoas's character to the limit of credibility, he gives Iphigenie a magnanimity which provokes the Christian conflict of conscience through which she displays, in Winckelmann's sense, her humanitarian integrity. This is both an unwitting departure from classical models and a rejection of the *Sturm und Drang* view of Greece, which stemmed from the concept of the gigantic in the affairs both of the gods and of man. Goethe was far more concerned at this moment with the ethical content than with any concept of the titanic. Yet in form his original *Iphigenie* of 1779 is a mixture of semi-naturalistic prose and semi-idealistic verse; the revisions of 1780 and 1781 revert at the end to prose, but in Italy all is turned into regular verse, and this is the first, most positive proof of the regenerative power that accrued from these early months in Italy.

Goethe also resumed work on *Faust* in Italy, namely on the 'Hexenküche' scene, which mirrors the rejuvenation of his own sensuous life. In the *Urfaust* there had been no transition from Faust the scholar and alchemist to Faust the seducer, but Goethe now felt this discrepancy, and through the image of the mirror in which he sees the beauty of the female form, but only at a distance, Faust acquires a new aesthetic dimension, anticipating the later Helena episode. The rejuvenation scene is Faust's first step towards becoming a complete human being, a move symbolized by the supersession of the traditional *Knittelvers* by blank verse, which also occurs in the scene 'Wald und Höhle', likewise written in Italy. This scene presents the conflict of conscience involved in Faust's sensuous experience and makes the Gretchen plot worthy of Goethe's conception of the figure of Faust.

Tasso, the first two acts of which, in prose, had been written in 1780, was another work to which Goethe returned – specifically, in Sicily, after his first stay in Rome, although he had passed through Ferrara, the town in which the play is set, with no sign of interest. Shortly before leaving Rome for the last time, he had read a recent book on Tasso, and this, together with his awareness of the responsibility attaching to his new-found classicism, led to the central conflict between Antonio, Tasso's moral counterpart and symbol of his conscience, and the egocentric Tasso himself. Goethe worked on the drama during his journey back to Weimar and completed it there in the spring of 1789. Significantly, it was above all the final scenes that occupied Goethe in Italy, for there is an inner relationship between these scenes and Goethe's own plans for the future, about which he had already written to the Duke. The core of the work is the reconciliation of the individual and society, and this gives its classicism a steely topicality which *Iphigenie* does not have, for Tasso stands as a proof of Goethe's belief that without pattern and discipline in his life man is doomed to destruction, and the stylized form of the work, the small number of characters, the strictness of the prosody and the controlled nature of the language, all reflect this emphasis on equanimity and restraint.

With *Egmont*, on the other hand, the situation is different. Started before Goethe had gone to Weimar, it had been continued but not completed there; now, however, during his second stay in Rome, he composed a second version. The echoes of his love for Lili and for *Sturm und Drang* realism were too strong to be erased: the hero's 'casualness' deeply disturbed Schiller, for instance. But Egmont, as Goethe conceived him, could not be turned into a national hero and protagonist of political liberty like Marquis Posa: the qualities of national leadership and responsibility belong, not to Egmont but to the cold, calculating Oranien. Goethe wisely refused to try to turn a drama of character into a drama of ideas.

Egmont is a man of stature, generous, frank, even reckless, with a free-and-easy arrogance, but he is no patriot; for that he lacks the faculty of complete sympathy. At the same time he is a great lover and a warm-blooded human being, a man who lives his own nature to the full. Goethe, with his new classical slant, could only channel this *Sturm und Drang* energy into classical humanitarianism, converting the *Sturm und Drang* realism into the classical realism which later was to characterize *Wallensteins Lager*. Conceived as it was in a Shakespearean spirit, *Egmont* could also be brought closer to classical tragedy through the idea of fate: the gods strike with blindness the man whose destruction they have decreed. Following his *daimon*, Egmont goes voluntarily to his doom, a young hero responsible only to himself – unlike the historical Egmont, who was middle-aged and the father of many children. The great individual must find in the nobility of his own personality the strength to overcome all fear, even the fear of death.

It was in many ways a different Goethe who returned from Rome to Weimar. The values of antiquity were no longer matters of theory and objects of yearning: they had become matters of experience and knowledge. But the feeling he had had in Rome of being at one with himself and with the world could not survive in the small world of Weimar, and his attempt to import his new attitudes, including that of so-called classical paganism, inevitably led to conflicts in the dukedom. Even so liberal-minded a friend as Herder was unable to accept either this 'paganism' or Goethe's new cult of the senses, any more than Frau von Stein could excuse the manifestations of these two attitudes – the most scandalous being when he took Christiane Vulpius, a young domestic servant, into his house as his mistress. What, as a stranger, he could afford to do in Rome without attracting attention was bound to be seen in Weimar as a deliberate flouting of all social convention on the part of the Duke's chief minister and confidant. Apart from being the talk of the town, it cost him the friendship of both Frau von Stein and Herder, but he made no move to legitimize the relationship – or the status of his and Christiane's young son – until 1806, when Christiane risked her life to rescue him from a dangerous situation during the Napoleonic Wars.

When he took her into his house in 1788, Christiane was energetic, attractive and sensual but also crude and uneducated, and in every way his intellectual inferior. Goethe was fully aware of this but acted out of defiance. The same resentment showed itself when, shortly after his son's birth, he was sent officially to Venice to await the arrival there of Anna Amalie, who was returning from a trip to Italy in the company of Herder. This social obligation, especially as it separated him from his young son, irritated him, and the *Venezianische Epigramme*, written at this time, show this clearly. The *Römische Elegien*, written shortly before, also reveal the social conflicts of his new life in Weimar and a hankering after the life he had led in Italy, conveying in the figure of Faustine both the spirit of his Roman sojourn and his feelings for Christiane. It is not by chance that the original title was *Erotica Romana* or that, when they were published some years later in Schiller's classically inspired *Horen* (1795), the new title should have transferred the emphasis from the content to the form. The *Elegien* have something of the cosmopolitan superiority found in the *Kophtische Lieder*, also written in Rome; furthermore both groups of poems share a satirical scorn of philistinism, conventionality, narrowmindedness and the stupidity of fashion.

The essential classicism of the *Elegien* lies, however, in their philosophy of *humani nihil a me alienum puto*, and their full beauty only emerges when their purely biographical aspect, i.e. that associated with Christiane, is left on one side; without this degree of detachment the mythical apologia for free love in the third and fourth elegies becomes trivial, and the parody of Herder's *Plastik* in the fifth elegy becomes almost obscene. In reality this is the influence of the *vis superba formae* of the late humanist Johannes Secundus but in a new stylized strictness. The poetic expression of the Italian ethos, which Goethe had been unable to achieve at the time of the *Nausikaa* fragment, now characterized the most beautiful parts of the *Römische Elegien*. The thirteenth elegy, above all, embodies this moment in the evolution of Goethe's classicism, a stage beyond that of the metrical version of *Iphigenie* and a moment in which true understanding of antiquity and personal sensuous experience of the world flow into a single channel.

The *Venezianische Epigramme*, on the other hand, leave a more negative and less convincing impression; the very fact that he had been ordered to go to Venice clouded the purity of his experience and gave the *Epigramme* a harsher, more incisive tone. Few of them, indeed, are stylistically the equal of the *Elegien*, and they contain a good deal of bad-tempered polemic, even journalistic gesturing, in the manner of the *Xenien*. Even his classical 'paganism', to him a positive quality, is given a bitter, aggressive slant, and the infamous 66th epigram, in which Christ is put alongside tobacco smoke, bugs and garlic as a most undesirable phenomenon, represents an extreme beyond which no one can go. His spiritual equilibrium had been destroyed, and his classically inspired confidence had turned to pride. The harmony of past and present was shattered.

Schiller's Progress to Classicism

It was in June 1787, while Goethe was in Italy, that Schiller first went to Weimar. Ten years younger than Goethe, he came of a very upright family which was far less well-to-do than Goethe's. Where Goethe's career seemed to be a matter of course, Schiller had to struggle to make his way, and the toll on his health caused his early death. He had broken away from the life of a *Karlsschüler* and army doctor and placed his revolutionary dramatic talents at the service of Dalberg in Mannheim, but for years he was driven from place to place, away from his family and his native Swabia, and only found security when he met Körner in Saxony and was taken into the Körner household.

But here too he was restless to go to Weimar. His *Sturm und Drang* period was behind him and he was putting the finishing touches to *Don Carlos*, the work that stands on the edge of his classical maturity. This work, which, like *Iphigenie* and *Tasso*, was first conceived in prose and then converted into iambic pentameter, started as a chronicle of a noble family but became Schiller's first real drama of ideas. The dominant principle is freedom of thought and its political application, exemplified by the character of Posa. As Schiller's conception of Posa developed, so did that of the tragic situation of the king. The fates of these two men, both in human and political terms, are inextricably linked, and the result is a study in humanitarianism in Winckelmann's classical sense. As a drama of ideas, *Don Carlos* is closer to Lessing's *Nathan der Weise* than to Goethe's early classical plays and lacks Goethe's real-life quality; this was to come in *Wallenstein*. But the sensationalism of his *Sturm und Drang* years was behind him, and although he had not Goethe's immediacy of response to the real world, he was Goethe's equal in the presentations of ideals and in formal organization. Moreover he was seeking the motives and underlying laws of the human spirit, and this side of his nature emerges not in the dramas but in the narrative works which he wrote before going to Weimar. These works show him as far more of a realist than he was in his plays. *Der Verbrecher aus verlorener Ehre* and *Der Geisterseher* reveal this, as does also his interest in Pitaval's *Causes célèbres* and various collections of memoirs which he undertook to edit. It is no accident that, before he met Goethe, Schiller had already, in his *Geisterseher,* lighted on the subject of Cagliostro; the realistic interest of Schiller, the idealist, in this figure is not unrelated to Goethe's scientific realism.

Like his dramas, Schiller's lyric poetry of the 1780s shows only his idealistic side, in contrast to his earlier *Sturm und Drang* naturalism, and poems such as the 'Lied an die Freude' (1785), 'Die Götter Griechenlands' (first version 1788) and 'Die Künstler' (1789) reveal the extent of his development from the time of the *Anthologie*. The dithyrambic 'An die Freude', still hyperbolic in tone but free from extremes of exaggeration, is a product of the convivial atmosphere which prevailed in the Körner household and still has traces of the Anacreontic emotionalism of Hagedorn and Uz, together with a prophetic quality derived from Klopstock. Its spirit of enthusiasm was even more marked in the first version, with its choral form; later this was converted into a refrain. It also marks the beginning of Schiller's 'enlightened' classicism.

'Die Künstler', on the other hand, shows this change already accomplished, and the poem's longwindedness is part of the change. In it the proud cosmopolitanism of the eighteenth-century man of the Enlightenment is blended with praise of the one-time golden age of human unity – a blend of Winckelmann and Rousseau. There is no logical reason why this perfect golden age should be superseded by the age of reason and progress, but this is an early expression of the problem facing 'classical' man – the conflict between nature and reason, consciousness and subconsciousness, duty and desire.

In 'Die Götter Griechenlands', however, all concern with the inevitable advance of reason is left behind in a flood of enthusiasm for antiquity itself. In the first version, though less so in the later, the world of the Greek gods is set against the world of Christianity, to the detriment of the latter, in a manner reminiscent of Winckelmann, but the conflict lies in the realm of the aesthetic, whereby the symbolic beauties of antiquity, accessible to our senses, are portrayed as free of any dogmatic associations.

As a theorist and critic too Schiller had much of the classicist about him when he arrived in Weimar. In Mannheim he had proclaimed humanitarianism as the goal of the theatre in *Die Schaubühne als eine moralische Anstalt betrachet* (1784), in which the spirit of 'being a man' recalls that of *Don Carlos*. The *Brief eines reisenden Dänen* (1785), subtitled 'The Classical Gallery in Mannheim', is also a kind of study for 'Die Götter Griechenlands'. The Mannheim collection of reproductions of famous classical works, which Goethe describes in Book XI of *Dichtung und Wahrheit*, was a valuable source of knowledge to, among others, Goethe and Lessing, for originals were rare in Germany. Schiller, who worked with concepts and ideas, was not worried by the fact that these were merely reproductions, any more than he was – contrary to Goethe – about approaching Homer through Voss's German translation. In fact he even argued that one could the more purely appreciate the Mannheim reproductions because they were free of the disturbing conditions of poverty and hardship which surrounded the originals in their Greek situation, conditions which disturbed the aesthetic content. He was thus able to invest these plaster casts with ideal qualities and enthuse over them as objects of a personal experience.

His choice of examples (Laocoon, Apollo Belvedere, Belvedere Torso, Niobe, Antinous), following Winckelmann, is governed by his educative purpose, and what does not serve this purpose is excluded; he thus queries the presence of a bust of Voltaire in the Classical Gallery, for, despite his greatness, Voltaire is out of place in this company.

Schiller's philosophical development in his pre-Weimar period can be seen in his *Philosophische Briefe* (1786 and 1789), written in collaboration with Körner. This work examines the conflicts which human reason has to overcome in its progress towards a state of wisdom. In it the extremes of naïve, spontaneous response and rational understanding are portrayed, with ultimate truth residing in their reconciliation. The goal is the ideal of humanitarian harmony.

On Goethe's recommendation Schiller was appointed Professor of History at Jena in the summer of 1789, a post he held until his illness in 1791. The position offered a new but not uncongenial challenge, for as Goethe used his official court duties and his scientific researches to help him acquire a sense of universality, so Schiller used his study of philosophy and history. Both men were working towards a sense of full, mature humanitarianism.

This emerges in Schiller's inaugural lecture *Was heißt und zu welchem Ende studiert man Universalgeschichte?* in which history is seen as a formative power working on 'the whole moral world'. This vision is a mixture of the ideal of education through the classics and a rationalistic confidence in individual self-development, and Schiller's concept of history is one dominated by the principle of causality. Similar in character are *Etwas über die erste Menschengesellschaft nach dem Leitfaden der mosaischen Urkunde* and *Die Sendung Moses*, both of which portray Moses as the man leading the people out of the primitive golden age of instinct into the age of reason. As in the *Philosophische Briefe* man attains the spiritual maturity also represented in Goethe's early classical works.

It was, however, not these works but Schiller's three literary essays – on *Egmont* (1788), on *Iphigenie* (1789) and on Bürger's poetry (1791) – that first made Goethe sense the similarity between his and Schiller's ideals. The first two essays contain a whole aesthetic of drama and lyric. Schiller maintains, for example, that *Egmont* belongs to the lineage of Shakespeare and not to that of the Greeks, whose tragedy was built on 'situations and passions'; the unity in *Egmont* he sees as derived from the hero himself, with his ideal qualities, but at the same time he takes exception to Egmont's human failings, which detract from his ideal qualities. *Iphigenie* he depicts as a classical work in that universal sense which Goethe gave to the word, and one feels Schiller's greater sympathy for the work *vis-à-vis Egmont*; he also demonstrates from *Iphigenie* that contemporary classicism could not consist in the imitation of the external features of Greek tragedy. Lacking Goethe's personal experience of Italy, Lessing's philological knowledge and Herder's scholarship, Schiller found his own way to the problem of how to establish a modern classicism in the Greek mould. Goethe now realized that here was a man working on an intellectual level the equal of his own.

Schiller's essay on Bürger – which Goethe said he wished he had written himself – made the situation doubly clear. Goethe found a discrepancy between Bürger's poetic genius and his life, a discrepancy which Schiller's essay resolved by viewing Bürger as a creature of the contemporary aesthetic mood: in an age dominated by thought, said Schiller, poetry was virtually the only force that could restore the wholeness of man, and the poet had to be both original, i.e. true to himself, and part of his age. Bürger did not measure up to this classical ideal, thinking himself, as a 'poet of the people', to be above it, but Schiller, using the language of Winckelmann and Goethe, asserts the aesthetic and moral virtues through which alone the ideals of classicism can be attained.

Even in the year after Goethe had obtained for Schiller his professorship in Jena the feeling between them, as seen in Schiller's letters to Körner, was in Schiller's words, 'a strange mixture of love and hate', the result of Schiller's injured pride over Goethe's rejection of a close attachment. Schiller disliked Goethe's egoism, while Goethe sensed the contrast between them through what he saw as Schiller's scorn of nature, a contrast confirmed by Schiller's *Über Anmut und Würde* (1793). Appropriately, it was the very question of nature – their famous discussion in July 1794 about the *Urpflanze* – that first polarized their viewpoints and then led to a fruitful exchange of views.

From their first discussion on Kant in 1790, when Schiller observed that Goethe drew from sense-impressions what he, Schiller, drew from his soul, Schiller had been decisively influenced in his philosophical and aesthetic attitudes by Kant, whereas Goethe had been drawn more and more to nature. In 1794 Schiller enlisted Goethe's help for his journal *Die Horen*. Then came the meeting that produced Schiller's famous statement apropos Goethe's explanation of the *Urpflanze*: 'Das ist keine Erfahrung, das ist eine Idee.' ('That is not an experience, it is an idea.') To Goethe it *was* an experience, and his initial reaction was again unfavourable, but the conversation turned to Kant and the problem of realism, and both men began to realize how much they had to give to each other. This is the moment that marks the beginning of the friendship which dominates Weimar classicism.

Goethe and the French Revolution

Goethe's return from Italy almost coincided with the outbreak of the French Revolution, and it soon became clear that this event produced a confrontation between modern, political pressures and the vision of classical antiquity propounded by Winckelmann in an excessively idealized form.

Tasso and *Egmont* are both fundamentally anti-revolutionary and humanistic in that they depict the reconciliation of extremes. Similarly conservative in attitude is the *Unterhaltungen Deutscher Ausgewanderten* (1794), which is deliberately anti-revolutionary in tone and a natural continuation from the point which had marked Tasso's defeat: Goethe's classical humanitarianism leads to the rejection of intolerance and of the destruction of formal values. In so doing he is applying to the contemporary situation the principles he had learned in Italy. In the name of universality, of which his scientific researches are as much a part as his ethical, historical and aesthetic views, he opposes the Revolution, just as in the argument between the Vulcanists and the Neptunists he opposes the revolutionism of the latter in favour of the organic conceptions of the former.

The challenge is to the applicability of the classical image of man, the acknowledgement of the proprieties that lead to the establishment of a humanistic morality. For it is primarily a matter of the individual, not of the state, since the individual embodies classical virtues which derive not from revolution but from continuity. Goethe's later admiration for Napoleon is not a matter of political preference but precisely the expression of a classical predilection for the forces of law and order.

The flirtation with chaos in which the Jena Romantics were indulging could only repel Goethe and Schiller, for the classicist needs tradition – a point made by Goethe in the 1790s with an insistence almost amounting to passion. And, as he later wrote in his essay 'Bedeutende Fördernis durch ein einziges geistreiches Wort' in the *Beiträge zur Morphologie*, it was above all the French Revolution – 'this most terrible of events' – that he had to overcome as a poet. The results can be seen in works ranging from the *Venezianische Epigramme* through the *Unterhaltungen Deutscher Ausgewanderten*, the comedies *Der Großkophta* and *Der Bürgergeneral* and various fragments (*Das Mädchen von Oberkirch* and *Die Reise der Söhne Megaprazons*) to the classical epics *Hermann und Dorothea* and *Reineke Fuchs*. Its final appearance is in the intended trilogy of revolutionary dramas, of which only *Die natürliche Tochter* was completed.

At the same time the whole construction of *Wilhelm Meister* is guided by the spirit of order and obedience that characterized Goethe's attitude to the Revolution. The comedy *Der Großkophta* (1791), based on an interesting psychological subject he had brought from Italy, is given symbolic contemporary meaning; it is a subject allied to that behind the figure of Benvenuto Cellini, whose biography Goethe also adapted in the 1790s. He also came to see the figure of Cagliostro as a factor in history, a symptom, like the famous necklace affair of which he tells in the *Annalen*, of the corrupt social conditions that made the Revolution possible. He thus established a historical explanation for the necessity of the Revolution, but he saw no reason why this should lead him to be enthusiastic about the chaos that it produced.

In *Die natürliche Tochter* (1799–1803) Goethe, through the character of the Gerichtsrat, almost accepts the legitimacy of the Revolution but finally allows it to perish through human weakness, and his own faith in continuous, organic development is what comes to predominate. To achieve this, however, one must display patience and resignation – a resignation that preserves one from chaos.

This is also conveyed by the involved symbolism of the *Märchen* in the *Unterhaltungen Deutscher Ausgewanderten*, with its allegory of the ages and its metamorphosis of the snake into the symbol of the bridge. But the destructive tyranny of the masses remains a potential source of chaos for Goethe. His conviction of this makes *Der Großkophta* heavy and deprives it of its character as a comedy: only the servants have names; the principal characters just have symbolic titles, such as the Domherr and the Ritter. And because the power of the rising new class is ignored, the play cannot become a political play of any substance – in fact, it is little more than a satire on the class-structure.

In *Der Bürgergeneral* (1793), on the other hand, the masses have the decisive role. The success of this one-act comedy – a success not shared by *Der Großkophta* – lies in its quality as a village *Schwank*: a legal squabble at the centre of the action, with narrowminded, cunning, boasting 'revolutionary' villagers in the kingdom of a paternal and benevolent nobleman. By ridiculing the 'revolutionaries' Goethe, more emphatically but in a narrower context than his *Großkophta*, asserts his belief in the restoration of conservative government. In the same year he planned a political drama, *Die Aufgeregten*, based on Holberg's *Politischer Kannengießer*, which he adapted to the more extreme political passions of the revolutionary period, showing a reluctant admission that the revolutionaries had a moral right to certain things that had been denied them but still condemning violence as a means of redressing the wrong.

After his meeting with Schiller Goethe turned from comedy and political drama to tragedy for treating the subject of the Revolution, with the uncompleted *Mädchen von Oberkirch* (1795–6) and *Die natürliche Tochter*. Both these are set in France. The justifiable aspects of the Revolution he finds already present in the representatives of law and order, above all in Napoleon, who stood for the values that he himself held. Goethe was certainly not, as Stefan George and his followers maintained, a visionary who stood above party in this respect.

The theme of the Revolution runs through the *Unterhaltungen Deutscher Ausgewanderten*, is present in the fragmentary allegorical novel *Die Reise der Söhne Megaprazons*, drawn from Rabelais and Thomas More, which depicts the catastrophic effects of the Revolution in France, and also appears in the verse epics of Goethe's classical period. In the *Campagne in Frankreich*, dealing with the events of the year 1793, Goethe describes the links between the Revolution and *Reineke Fuchs*, the manuscript of which he had with him in France. Here he deals, through the beast allegory, with the human failings revealed by the Revolution, failings, however, which, far from leading to a nihilistic attitude, can be redeemed through an awareness of human qualities and potentialities. This is most strikingly revealed in *Hermann und Dorothea*, where human shortcomings are absorbed in the ideal of classical humanism.

An important expression of this is the classical forms used by Goethe in *Reineke Fuchs, Hermann und Dorothea* and the elegies, forms which are not simply expressive of his anti-revolutionary attitudes or are in the nature of experiments but symbolize the universality which overcomes the naturalism associated with the revolutionary attitude and makes classical self-knowledge the power by which to decide the great intellectual and political issues of the day. It is in this that the modernity of the classical works of Goethe and Schiller lies.

As the allegory of *Reineke Fuchs* reflects the unchanging, and thus always contemporary, virtues and vices of man, so *Hermann und Dorothea* (1798), unlike the idylls of Gleim and Bürger, emerges from the real historical background of the French Revolution. Nowhere does one find so idealistic a portrayal of a revolutionary as in Dorothea's first betrothed as he emerges from her own account of his fate. The essence of the work lies in the fusion of personal fate with the pattern of world events, and it is this alone that gives the idyllic situation a quality of fate and involves the little town in the events of history. This classical universality, composed of enthusiasm and restraint, agitation and serenity, passion and objectivity, breadth and intimacy, owes much to the influence of Schiller.

Hermann und Dorothea was followed by the unfinished epic *Achilleis* (1799), the elegies and the epistles. The use of elegiac metres and hexameters represents in part a consolidation of classical form, a subject treated in Goethe and Schiller's *Über epische und dramatische Dichtung*, and the formal power of Homer makes itself felt under the particular influence of F. A. Wolf's *Prolegomena ad Homerum*. Compared with *Hermann und Dorothea*, however, *Achilleis* lacks genuine classical quality, perhaps because it has no historical framework. The elegies 'Alexis und Dora' (1796) and 'Euphrosyne' (1797–8) are purer, if more stylized, and their humanistic qualities are given historical significance, while retaining a more-than-historical application.

The final work of Goethe's Weimar classicism is his essay *Winckelmann und sein Jahrhundert* (1805), in which Winckelmann is praised as a man who lived life to the full and whose Platonism, aesthetic outlook, relationship to Christianity and classical vision of man represented all that Goethe, as man and artist, stood for. Like Winckelmann Goethe accepted life as it was, seeing in the life-giving forces of nature the basis for optimism and for the retention of the *status quo*. It is this self-sufficiency, as he found it in Winckelmann, that Goethe expresses in his works of this period.

Kant and Classicism

It is a long way from the *Philosophische Briefe* of the mid-1780s to Schiller's almost hectic activity in the field of aesthetics at the time of his friendship with Goethe. These letters are an attempt to reconcile Rousseau's view of nature with the rationalism and optimism of the Enlightenment, while the aesthetic writings of the 1790s assume a detailed knowledge of Kant and represent an attempt to use Kant's philosophy to arrive at a typology of aesthetics, above all that of literature. His intention was to enable classicism to better understand itself by giving it a poise and lucidity appropriate to its nature, and at the same time to resolve the dichotomy between himself and Goethe by establishing a balance in aesthetic terms; for this purpose he found stimulus in Kant's firm ethical system and plan of aesthetic autonomy.

Initially Goethe disapproved of what Schiller was doing, for in Goethe's eyes Schiller was abusing nature, the nature that he, Goethe, contemplated and revered. Such was his reaction to *Über Anmut und Würde*, written in spring 1793. Yet the concept of the 'schöne Seele' in this work represents a departure from Kant's dogmatism in favour of Goethe's freer attitudes. The 'schöne Seele', embodiment of a grace produced by the marriage of duty and desire, is only conceivable if one removes the logical possibility of evil. Freedom, for Kant, was only present when an act was the product of a feeling of duty, but the concept of the 'schöne Seele' in Schiller's sense required a distinction between freedom and duty, while perfect grace only occurs as a gift bestowed by the goddess of love. Both Kant, who deals with *Anmut und Würde* in the second edition of his *Religion innerhalb der reinen Vernunft*, and Schiller, who called Kant's dogmatism 'slavish', underplayed the extent of their differences. Schiller's aristocratic conception of freedom was broader than Kant's and closer to Goethe's, and the influence of Shaftesbury, seen particularly in the concept of genius, is still evident.

At the same time Schiller's concept of dignity is closer to the Kantian world. Indeed, as Goethe may well have perceived, the 'schöne Seele' and dignity are not really rival concepts but exist on different levels, for while the latter is an attainable part of the classical ideal of man, the former is a gift from above. The antithesis is not systematic but psychological. Grace is the dynamic element, dignity a serene spiritual and intellectual force to set against it; while the former brings Schiller closer to Goethe, the latter is more in keeping with his own idealistic moral leanings. The conflict persists in other works of this and the subsequent period – *Über das Erhabene*, *Über das Pathetische*, *Gedanken über den Gebrauch des Gemeinen und Niedrigen in der Kunst*. If grace is morality become nature, dignity is controlled sensuousness, displayed in specific 'real' moments.

Thus in his shorter essays Schiller approaches closer to Winckelmann's position, while in the debate over Laocoon he sought to reconcile Lessing's emphasis on sensuous reality with Winckelmann's emphasis on classical spirit; in other words, he tried, on the basis of the *Humanität* of Herder and Goethe, to conquer the Stoicism characteristic of baroque and French classicism, and to bring the sensuous values of *Humanität* to bear on his interpretation of emotion.

On the other hand he also needed to distinguish between his own classical aesthetic and the sentimentalities of *Sturm und Drang* and the age of sensibility. Classical emphasis on manly courage and discipline entailed, for example, the banishment of music in so far as it serves to arouse disruptive passions. In his search for the golden mean Schiller approaches Goethe in the latter's dislike, after his Italian journey, for paintings of the Passion and of Christian martyrs, and at the same time adopts Winckelmann's distinction, derived from the Dutch painters, between what is common and what is noble. Schiller's search for greatness is part of his aristocratic classical ideal with its aesthetic bias, as opposed to the eighteenth-century moralists' approach to art. The same universalist tendency emerges in his distinction between the moral and the aesthetic effect of a historical event (*Über das Pathetische*); in his example of Leonidas both the moral and the aesthetic senses are satisfied, and the event thereby acquires added validity. The long-current nationalistic interpretations of *Tell* and, in part, *Die Jungfrau von Orleans* are seen to be false – if one accepts Schiller's attack on the use of national subjects – because they rest only on one limited consideration; such subjects may have incidental value but should not be used as starting-points, precisely because of their limited validity. The aesthetic of the motif of death, on the other hand, is an eminently classical concern (*Über das Erhabene*): man can rise above death, and both Goethe and Schiller's concept of resignation forms part of this anti-Christian complex.

The fullest statement of Schiller's aesthetic is given in his letters *Über die ästhetische Erziehung des Menschen* addressed to the Duke of Augustenburg, who for three years acted as Schiller's generous patron. Being written for a prince, they had to treat of man both as an individual and as a ruler responsive to education. They were composed in 1793–4 and published in a revised form the following year in *Die Horen*, just after the original manuscript had been destroyed. Starting with an acknowledgement of Kant as the highest exponent of the universal human gift of reason, they proceed not in the manner of a philosophical treatise but rather of a general essay on man and the possibilities of his perfectibility in aesthetic terms. To a large extent the work thus deals with the contemporary situation and is given contemporary relevance. But the spirit of the times was not conducive to aesthetic values, and for this very reason Schiller dwells on beauty rather than on freedom, although the latter word was on everyone's lips at this time. Schiller portrays aesthetic education as the means by which the purely physical and the purely ethical sides of man can be linked; man will be lifted beyond his temporal existence and shown the ideal of his humanity, thereby acquiescing in the ideal towards which the State is striving, and the classical golden mean will be achieved by respecting human differences yet not allowing them to dissolve into anarchy.

The fifth letter shows the contrast between the ideal and contemporary reality, and Schiller makes this the starting-point for his depiction of the ideal situation as it existed among the Greeks and as it has been lost in modern times: only art can restore the lost unity, and the ninth letter, the core of the work, shows Schiller's vision in terms not of linear progress in the Enlightenment sense but of cyclical movement. The aesthetic also usurps the realm of the religious, and the aesthetic educator becomes a religious prophet.

On this basis Schiller then erects his well-known division of human impulses into the sense impulse, the form impulse and the play impulse, the last-named being the mean between the extremes of pure sensuousness and pure morality, between necessity and law. Classical antiquity is the highest manifestation of this impulse, and thus embodies the universality of man. The play impulse alone releases the individual from his subservience to nature, and art becomes the means by which man achieves spiritual freedom and harmony. Similarly the play impulse is the means by which the State preserves personal freedom between the pressures of, on the one hand, the dynamic State (based on the sense impulse and resting on power) and, on the other, the ethical State (based on the form impulse and resting on the rule of law). The aesthetic guarantees harmony between the individual and society and makes all classes equal in terms of aesthetic education – though Schiller was well aware that his ideal was an aristocratic one, reserved for a select few, like all the educative ideals of classicism.

Schiller's last aesthetic essay, *Über naive und sentimentalische Dichtung* (1795), penetrates deep into the essence of literature. His distinction between the 'naïve' and 'sentimental' is that between mind and nature: he sees himself as representative of the former, Goethe of the latter, in their attitudes towards the world. In conversation and correspondence the two men had come closer together: Goethe had profited from Schiller's discipline and superior intellectual power, while Schiller had become more concrete in thought and more tolerant, and in this work the problems of aesthetics broached in the *Ästhetische Briefe* are given a historical and psychological dimension. The classical ideal is presented as something within reach, yet Schiller is reluctant to give up the principle of reason, and as in the *Ästhetische Briefe* he had proposed a synthesis by which a cyclical view of history (a return to the Greeks) could incorporate a linear view (eighteenth-century rationalism), so here he transfers this idea to poetry.

The 'naïve' is the product of our origin (the past) and our task (the future), and, as with Rousseau, our progress through civilization has to be followed by a return not simply to our origin – which would be an abdication of our historical role – but to a position from which our lost unity can be imagined to be restored. A 'naïve' modern poet has to forget the accumulated rationality and morality of history if he is to move beyond the 'sentimental', which is the product of the history of human consciousness, whereas the 'naïve' is a theoretically attainable condition in all ages. The 'naïve' for the present day has to be given a greater moral content than in antiquity, since human development has brought with it an ever-increasing number of discrepancies between man and nature which have to be overcome. The typological and historical aspects of the 'naïve' can thus be reconciled: Goethe is presented as the modern 'naïve' poet, while Schiller is of the 'sentimental' type and has both the easier and the more difficult task in transcending his own age.

The concepts 'naïve' and 'sentimental' rest on the contrast between nature and art. The 'naïve' involves an ideal and moral state, it is a necessary quality of genius, and whereas antiquity has this quality 'by nature', the modern age is trying in its 'sentimental' way to regain this lost oneness with nature. The great genius, however, interrupts this development: Shakespeare, for example, whom Schiller portrays, by virtue of his '*naïveté*', as opposed to the spirit of his age, is a lone figure. The 'sentimental' poet, on the other hand, takes as his moral task the regaining of this lost unity, for he can never shake off the 'sentimental' weight of his historical position. Elegy and satire are seen as typical 'sentimental' forms. From this point in his argument onwards Schiller's work becomes a kind of history of literature, above all in terms of 'sentimental' poets (Haller, Klopstock, etc.). *Werther* is adduced as an example of a 'sentimental' subject treated by a 'naïve' poet. The idyll partakes of both categories: *Hermann und Dorothea* and Voss's *Luise* are both classed as 'naïve'; the danger here is that the 'naïve' poet – here Schiller recalls Winckelmann's warning – may lapse into the realm of 'common nature'.

Schiller's conclusion is that mankind needs both the 'naïve' and the 'sentimental' in order to achieve its ideal: the one complements the other; neither the realist nor the idealist can exist alone.

Schiller's lyric poetry after 1795 corresponds to his theoretical demands.

Realism and idealism are combined in the distychs of 'Spaziergang', which takes its lead from Goethe, and 'Das Glück' (1798) praises the gods for possessing both virtue and grace. 'Die Glocke' (1799), too, blends the human and the ideal, while in 'An die Freunde' (1802) he restates his philosophical position, starting from the reality of the world around us and moving towards the classical ideal of antiquity.

The Ballad Year

It is not an accident that Goethe and Schiller, who from this time onwards did not embark on any substantial work without discussing it verbally or by letter, should have entered into competition with each other in the particular field of the ballad. Goethe, in the train of Herder, Bürger and the folk-ballad, had already been active in this field, and the ballads of his *Sturm und Drang* period breathe the atmosphere of ghostliness ('Erlkönig', 'Der Fischer') and Nordic, Ossian-like heroism ('Der König in Thule'). By contrast, the classical poems of the 'ballad year' of 1797 sprang from his discussions with Schiller on epic and drama, i.e. from the classical urge towards the delineation of literary genres. This new type of ballad poetry emerges in 'Der Schatzgräber', stimulated by reminiscences of *Faust* and an illustration to a work of Petrarch's. Unlike all Goethe's earlier ballads, it is allegorical-didactic in intent: the demonic element has moved from the sphere of the elemental and the mysterious into the classical world with its emphasis on moral self-justification, and become a poem of ideas with an allegorical conclusion. His next ballad, 'Die erste Walpurgisnacht', has a similar intellectual tone; indeed, the manner in which the old witchcraft legend is explained, with an imagery derived from freemasonry, is virtually rationalistic.

Schiller's intellectual poetry is the dominant influence on Goethe's ballads at this time, although, as in 'Das Blümlein wunderschön', he also instinctively retains his links with his old tradition. Not for nothing did he place this ballad next to 'Der König in Thule' in his collected poems. 'Hochzeitslied', a delicate, dream-like ballad using a new epic strophe, is in the same category; it is also an onomatopoeic *tour de force*, and the 'classical' element is confined to the concentrated exposition of the subject-matter.

The four dialogue-ballads about the miller's daughter (a subject derived from an opera by Paesiello), written on and after his third journey to Switzerland, are from the formal point of view, with their overtones of *Singspiel* and aria, in the style of the modern ballad which Goethe and Schiller discussed in letters; at the same time the dialogue-form (*Wechsel*) recalls 'Das Blümlein wunderschön'. Their diction is extremely charming and cultivated, and they contain nothing sinister, mysterious or even mythical; the atmosphere is direct and idyllic, the action straightforward but more refined than in 'Ritter Kurts Brautfahrt', written somewhat earlier.

The three central works of the 'ballad year' all have trochaic metre – 'Der Zauberlehrling', 'Die Braut von Korinth' and 'Gott und die Bajadere'. 'Der Zauberlehrling', experimental in that the narrative element is completely absent, is based on a story from Lucian but is treated in a medieval Faustian manner. 'Die Braut von Korinth' – Goethe's 'vampire poem' – is a philosophical ballad in Schiller's style, an accusation against Christianity of opposition to the forces of life, while 'Gott und die Bajadere', based on an Indian legend, is a tale of purification and a justification of hetaerism. Both these poems are classical philosophical ballads, representative of worldly humanitarian values, and concede a great deal to Schiller's influence, but even here we still find the demonic element inherited from Herder and Goethe's own earlier years. In fact Goethe returns here to his own inner nature, while 'Der Schatzgräber' and 'Die erste Walpurgisnacht' represent tentative steps towards an allegorical, rationalistic treatment of ideas; the culmination of his ballad poetry is reached in a synthesis of the two tendencies.

As Goethe's ballads show a move towards philosophical idealism, so Schiller's reveal Goethe's influence in the restriction of intellectual content and an increase in the sensuous element. Eight of Schiller's twelve great ballads – 'Der Taucher', 'Der Handschuh', 'Der Ring des Polykrates', 'Ritter Toggenburg', 'Die Kraniche des Ibykus', 'Der Gang nach dem Eisenhammer', 'Der Kampf mit dem Drachen', 'Die Bürgschaft' – were written between the summer of 1797 and that of 1798, while the remaining four – 'Hero und Leander', 'Kassandra', 'Der Graf von Habsburg', 'Der Alpenjäger' – were composed, one in each year, between 1801 and 1803, after the main impetus had passed.

Schiller's ballads, in accordance with his nature, are more markedly philosophical than Goethe's, and however powerful their dramatic or pragmatic qualities, they leave no unresolved doubt or ambiguity in the ethical world-picture they present. They are, indeed, despite their narrative tension, on the way to becoming parables. The first is 'Der Taucher', based on a subject given him by Goethe (the subject of Nicola Pesce, also treated in a ballad by Conrad Ferdinand Meyer), in which he turns a little tale into the breathtaking story of the venture that leads the gods into temptation and thus inevitably ends in tragedy. The thought is classical; the cause of the *hubris* – *Minne* – is medieval. The dual nature of the story has a modern psychological motivation, while in the realm of style the onomatopoeia has become justifiably famous.

'Der Handschuh' and 'Der Ring des Polykrates', both written, like 'Der

Taucher', in June 1797, also deal with the temptation of the gods. In 'Der Handschuh' he found his moral conclusion already present in the story itself, to the chivalric substance of which he gave added depth in the shape of the subjective element – only conceivable after the eighteenth century – which provokes the knight to an unchivalric act after coolly and chivalrously taking the glove from the wild beast's cage; by throwing the glove into the face of the noblewoman who is tempting the gods, he displays the anger of a modern personality which finds its dignity wantonly called in question. Here the gods seek their revenge on the source of the temptation itself, not on the man who has provoked them. In 'Der Ring des Polykrates' the tyrant, as in Herodotus, from whom the story is taken, challenges the gods, for by congratulating himself on his good fortune, he interferes in the workings of fate; Goethe felt the particular effectiveness of the end of the poem, where the inevitable catastrophe is left implicit.

In 'Die Kraniche des Ibykus' a flight of cranes causes the murderers involuntarily to confess their crime, but as well as vengeful fate the inevitable force of conscience, and hence of morality, is also at work. 'Ritter Toggenburg' and 'Der Gang nach dem Eisenhammer' are linked by the motif of loyalty; the hero of the former, which is in motif and style related to 'Der Handschuh', is a symbol of faithful love which inflicts mortal wounds; only in death is he relieved of the bliss or suffering he undergoes every day at the sight of his lost beloved, and the question is left open whether the highest bliss does not reside in suffering and renunciation. This is the very opposite of 'Der Ring des Polykrates'. 'Der Gang nach dem Eisenhammer' tells the story of the monk Fridolin in terms of the non-classical, modern-cum-medieval theme of loyalty – modern in the meting out of punishment and reward, and also Christian, as is 'Der Kampf mit dem Drachen', the story of the burning, fiery furnace, which does not, however, measure up to the best of Schiller's ballads. In the source of this poem, taken from the history of the Knights of St John, the knight is spared punishment by intercession, but in Schiller's ballad the catastrophe is averted by the moral excellence of the judge and the accused, so that Christian virtue only appears as a symbol of the classical virtue of self-conquest: divine order coincides with the moral law of reason.

The last of these ballads, 'Die Bürgschaft', is based on the late-classical fables of Hyginus, but Schiller has added his own element of moral provocation and made the culprit's friend a real hostage: the ideals of humanity and friendship are vindicated by the culprit's voluntary return, and the ethical values of eighteenth-century Enlightenment are transferred back into the world of antiquity – in which, in turn, Schiller can now find the elements of his ethical ideal.

Of Schiller's four remaining ballads, written in the first four years of the nineteenth century, two are based on classical themes, the other two on mythological subjects. In 'Hero und Leander', taken from Musaios, the jealousy and vengeance of the gods, which destroy the love-idyll, are classical, while the form, like the theme of real passion, is romantic: in short, an original attempt at a synthesis. Similar in its use of trochaic tetrameter is 'Kassandra', in which the fate-motif is more pronounced and in which it is not personal but communal fate that is at stake, since the prophetess is caught up in her own vision. The visionary elements, above all at the end, achieve an uncanny effectiveness; no Romantic could have romanticized antiquity better.

'Der Graf von Habsburg' and 'Der Alpenjäger' are by-products of Schiller's work on *Wilhelm Tell*: the latter, Schiller's last ballad, is a sentimental echo of the type of poem represented by Goethe's 'Schatzgräber'; the former is a moralizing version of Goethe's 'Sänger'.

One may summarize the ballad-writing of Goethe and Schiller as follows: Goethe, the poet with the personal experience of antiquity, did not attempt a ballad on a classical subject – apart from 'Die Braut von Korinth' and 'Gott und die Bajadere' all his ballads are taken from medieval sources; Schiller, on the other hand, based almost half his ballads on classical material, often casting them in the form of a romance. Only four of Goethe's ballads can be classed as ethico-philosophical in intent, while three-quarters are erotic-anecdotal in nature; Schiller has at best two love-ballads, and none of an anecdotal type. From Goethe's *Annalen* and other sources it is also known that Goethe conceived a number of ballad-subjects, some of them on classical material, and gave them to Schiller.

What conclusions can be drawn from this situation? In the first place, that neither poet relinquished his own individuality in this 'ballad contest', and that each interpreted the genre in his own way. While Goethe, with a few concessions to the philosophical ballad, keeps to the traditional strophic type, Schiller does not use the latter at all, and while dramatizing the epic element, makes no move towards the tradition that runs from Bürger through Herder to the young Goethe. All Schiller's ballads have an underlying *Weltanschauung*, though at the same time he seeks to acquire something of the sensuousness he so admired in Goethe; he adopted motifs which repelled Goethe and sought to mould them to his purposes. Goethe may be the gentler of the two – but this does not make him the inferior.

Schiller's Return to Drama

Between *Don Carlos* and *Wallenstein* lies Schiller's encounter with Kant, with antiquity, with Goethe. This makes it unthinkable that he could have returned to the style of his earlier dramas. *Wallenstein* was started at the time of his *Geschichte des dreißigjährigen Krieges* (1791), before his involvement with Kant, but the first completed parts in prose, written on his extensive Swabian journey of 1794, already show a new objectivity: formerly he had set to work on any subject that aroused his enthusiasm, but now he worked rationally and deliberately, using his aesthetic theories and his critical insight. He already recognized himself, indeed, as a 'sentimentalischer Dichter'.

His aesthetic judgement now diagnosed the weaknesses of his early dramas – their subjectivity and their remoteness from the world of antiquity. The new attitude, he explains in a letter to Körner in November 1797, is one of detachment from the subject-matter, of 'disinterested pleasure', and the practical consequence of this attitude is his resumption of work on *Wallenstein*. The figure of Wallenstein now repels rather than attracts him, but its tragic grandeur makes it sublime; it is no longer a matter of singleminded goodness or evil but of a boldly complex character. He studied source-material, read Shakespeare and Sophocles and wrote, with Goethe, the essay *Über epische und dramatische Dichtung*. The motif of tragic fate also came into his conception, and the opening part of the trilogy became detached, a bold, independent work which owes its verse form to his desire to compete with the *Knittelvers* of Goethe's *Faust*.

The remainder of the work was completed in verse over the following two years, and the completed trilogy, in the titulation of whose parts Goethe had a hand, was published in 1799 as a 'dramatic poem', faithfully reflecting Schiller's aesthetic development and the relationship between his theories and his newly found self-confidence.

Wallensteins Lager is more than a technical exposition of the entire trilogy for it avoids both the unhistorical manner of *Don Carlos* and the tabloid naturalism of *Die Räuber*. Its portrayal of the *Volk* – soldiers, citizens, peasants – is historically authentic and establishes a realistic background against which the passion and greatness of the hero are presented: from the 'naiv' world of the *Lager* we move to the 'sentimentalisch' action of *Die Piccolomini* and the catastrophe of *Wallensteins Tod* – in other words, we are confronted with the practical exposition of Schiller's *Über naive und sentimentalische Dichtung*. 'Sentimentalisch' is the love between Max and Thekla and the emotional friendship between Max and Wallenstein, and the further elements of dubious diplomacy (old Piccolomini, Questenberg) and cynicism (Illo, Terzky) add to the tragic triangle of Wallenstein, Max and Thekla. As Wallenstein preens himself with patriotic intentions and reveals cruel traits which bring into question the sincerity of his human relationships, even with those closest to him, so the ambiguity of his character becomes evident. Added to this is the enigmatic motif of fate, which paralyses and ultimately destroys the star-struck hero, while the situation which brings about Max's downfall has a similar ring of irony.

Everywhere one sees the products of Schiller's theoretical work. Apart from the contrast between 'naiv' and 'sentimentalisch', the 'schöne Seele' of *Anmut und Würde* is present in Thekla, and Max's self-analysis echoes the lament of Julius in the *Philosophische Briefe*. Above all Schiller's return to the drama reflects the conclusion of *Über naive und sentimentalische Dichtung*, which had proclaimed the complementary nature of the ideal and the real which is embodied in *Wallenstein*, the first drama of his classical period.

With *Maria Stuart* and *Die Jungfrau von Orleans*, dramas of purification, Schiller returns to his characteristic world of lofty emotions. For Wallenstein no purification was possible: he was not a man to change his nature, and he had to perish by the laws of the situation into which he had entered. In the heroines of his following two dramas Schiller portrays a moral perfectibility which, for all its lapses and conflicts, shows its greatness in death. It is the theme that he treats in the *Zerstreute Betrachtungen über ästhetische Gegenstände* and *Über das Erhabene* – the triumph of reason over physical nature. This is no longer 'naiv', in his sense, for 'grace' (*Anmut*) ceases at the point when one throws one's life away and when death redeems former and present guilt. Schiller's use of heroines rather than heroes may be seen as an attempt to soften the 'masculine' ethic of reason which would otherwise have to be presented as the antithesis of the 'schöne Seele'.

Maria Stuart goes back to plans that precede *Don Carlos*, i.e. it belongs, like *Wallenstein*, to Schiller's pre-Kantian period. He resumed work on it in 1799, eighteen years after its conception, and it was first performed the following year. As with Goethe's classical works, one now observes in Schiller a leaning towards French classical tragedy and also towards the stoicism of the German baroque, a tendency to which the Laocoon motif, starting with Winckelmann, also contributed. In both writers the noble retention of the inevitability of death is an intensification of the theme of martyrdom in baroque tragedy; the difference lies chiefly in the higher degree of realism achieved by Goethe and Schiller *vis-à-vis* the almost utopian power to transcend death which baroque heroes display. In classical tragedy it is a matter not only of guilt but also of awareness of guilt, and thus of the dignity of purging this guilt. Mary and Joan of Arc accept their cruel fate through the exercise of a superior moral reason which transcends the material facts of their situation.

Die Jungfrau von Orleans, despite the visionary 'voices' and the subtitle 'eine romantische Tragödie', is far from romantic in the problem it presents, in its construction, in its presentation of the Middle Ages and in the purity of its language. Where, partly in response to Goethe's suggestions, Schiller had rearranged much of the almost over-abundant material in his *Wallenstein,* both *Maria Stuart* and *Die Jungfrau von Orleans* are of a piece and were both completed within a year. On the one hand *Die Jungfrau von Orleans* represents a reaction against Voltaire's *Pucelle,* on the other the inspiration of Shakespeare's *Henry the Sixth.* Where Voltaire had treated Joan in a naturalistic fashion, Schiller, as his nature would have led us to believe, treated her idealistically and, like Mary Stuart, in a classical spirit. Like Mary again, Joan is the embodiment – albeit with the addition of certain naïve, romantic traits – of ethical, humane values, seen in her maintenance of an unshakeable dignity even in the moment of death. In April 1801, shortly before finishing the work, Schiller himself expounded these thoughts to Goethe.

There is a direct spiritual link between these classical dramas and *Die Braut von Messina* and *Wilhelm Tell,* on which Schiller worked simultaneously, the latter being his last completed drama. *Tell* continues the theme of individual greatness in times of national crisis: here the theme is made absolute and treated in terms of a tragic conflict of character but there is no final destruction. In *Die Braut von Messina,* which was finished before *Tell,* Schiller fuses the classical motif of fate with a romantic subject and produces what is virtually a late-classical return to the Wallenstein problem, though with less complicated characters (Don Manuel, Don Cesar). The notion of purification is even more inappropriate here than in *Wallenstein,* since the limits of personal action are held within the terms of an Oedipus situation, yet despite this classical limitation it is revealing that there is no question of a blind determinism, leading to a restriction of individual freedom. The theme of jealous fratricide, taken from *Sturm und Drang* (Leisewitz, Klinger), is supplemented by the theme of incest and turned by Schiller in *Die Braut von Messina* into the theme of the individual's struggle, hopeless yet not pointless, to salvage something of his freedom, even of his freedom to incur the guilt that is in part responsible for his fate. The later Romantics, who saw the fate-tragedy as resting not on action but on suffering, and who built on a simplified view of *Wallenstein* and *Die Braut von Messina,* interpreted the latter merely as a depiction of the workings of fate, whereas to Schiller the action depended on the historical situation and relationship of Beatrice and her two brothers.

As in *Die Braut von Messina* man is shown as a victim of the fate which he himself has in part brought down upon himself, so in *Wilhelm Tell* (1804) we find the hero whose conflict lies in his individual transcendence of his historical position. If Schiller has anywhere succeeded in identifying man's historical situation with the categorical imperative, it is here. For *Tell* is not a national drama, as it is so often misunderstood to be: Schiller considered popular national dramas, like Körner's *Zriny* or Heyse's *Kolberg,* to be beneath him, and said as much in such statements as that to Körner, that patriotic concerns 'were only fit for immature nations'. The same view is found in *Über das Pathetische*, where he attacks the overestimation of national subject-matter and identifies its essentially non-aesthetic nature. Thus for Schiller the Swiss content of *Tell* is not the starting-point, not a cause, but a consequence, a part of the outcome; Tell, the great moral individualist, struggles with himself and with the patriotic enthusiasm of his people to discover both his own true self and, by acknowledging the priority of duty over desire, his own people. Historical fate can be overcome by the supreme act of the individual; at the same time this fate reaches an almost paradoxical conclusion in the tyrant's murder which Tell himself found repulsive. (The Parricida scene, indeed, to which Schiller's contemporaries also objected, represents a somewhat crude intervention in what is a ruthlessly logical action on the personal level.) Nowhere is the theme of personal freedom, in Schiller's and Kant's sense, treated with a more powerful inner compulsion than here.

The emphatic quality of *Wilhelm Tell* may be the reason why the drama *Demetrius*, on which Schiller worked from 1800, remained a fragment, albeit an impressive one. Even during the period after completing *Tell* he allowed his attention to be drawn to other projects, and at his death only sketches of the first two acts had been written. As in *Tell*, the concept of justice was to have been the central issue, but not in the direct, 'naïve' form appropriate to Tell and his people; Demetrius, enemy of justice, fully conscious of his deceitfulness, was destined to perish, firstly as an ironical means of restoring the true, objective status of history as the repository of justice, and secondly as the tragic representative of modern man with his knowledge and his premonitions. Had it been completed, *Demetrius* would have shown in a modern sense the conflict between the forces within the hero and the forces above him.

Goethe's Return to 'Faust' and 'Wilhelm Meister'

Goethe's resumption of work on his large, unfinished projects was in response to Schiller's continual pressure. The *Urfaust* was reworked, supplemented by material from his Italian journey and published in 1790 as *Faust. Ein Fragment*, while Schiller's stimulus during the early years of their contact had also led to the completion of *Wilhelm Meisters Lehrjahre*, a source of great inspiration to the Romantics. Work on *Faust* from 1797 culminated in the completion of Part One in 1808: working with a new verve, Goethe put the dungeon scene (one of the earliest prose sections) into verse, clarified the opening of the whole work and fashioned its conclusion. As the beginning of the play creates the cosmic setting, so the conclusion seals the universality of the work by ironically linking it with the present.

The three introductory sections written in 1799 – 'Zueignung', 'Vor-spiel auf dem Theater' and 'Prolog im Himmel' – are linked to world literature through the Book of Job and the Indian drama *Sakuntala*, and the classical additions to 'Walpurgisnacht' and 'Walpurgisnachtstraum' which are incorporated at the end give the work its range from the domestic to the universal and from primeval times to the present. With the 'Zueig-nung' comes a marked break with the earlier Ossianic stage of the work; the 'Vorspiel', in parodistic tone, reasserts both the poet's complaint and his new self-confidence, demonstrates the conflict between ideal and reality in terms of the theatre, and hints at the remarkable events that are to follow. The conflict between the extreme realist (the theatre director) and the extreme idealist (the poet), like the apologia in the 'Zueignung', contains the new classical point of departure, while the formal stanzas present the poet as the glorifier of the harmony of the world, and the poetic vocation as the demonstration of man's highest power. One recalls *Wilhelm Meister* at this point, though at the same time one must see it as Goethe's own interpretation of Schiller's aesthetics, just as the mediating character of the 'lustige Person' – less sceptically realistic than the director but more realistic than the poet – corresponds to Schiller's synthesis of the realist and the idealist.

The metaphysical background and framework of the Faust story proper is introduced in the 'Prolog im Himmel', which recalls the medieval mysteries; subsequently the conclusion to Part Two was added as a formal counterpart, a correspondence which Goethe had originally planned for the conclusion of Part One. The characters of Faust and Mephistopheles now emerge: Faust, the man who demands the extremes of physical and spiritual experience; Mephistopheles, the spirit of negation. Faust him-self, moreover, embodies the polarity of human existence. From the poetically dualistic world of the *Urfaust* the drama has entered the world of classical Neoplatonism.

The addition of 'Walpurgisnacht' and 'Walpurgisnachtstraum' to *Faust I* gives a deeper meaning to the Faust–Gretchen theme which is both ironically parodistic and tragic. The world of Mephisto is presented as the counterbalance to Faust's inevitable progress: as Faust experiences the lowest forms of physical pleasure under the spell of the demonic, so the Gretchen motif is indirectly made 'noble', in Schiller's sense; the simultaneity of the two moments, like Faust's vision of Gretchen in the midst of his decadence, creates a tragic irony and emphasizes the con-ception of Faust's 'two souls'. It also motivates Faust's attempt to save Gretchen, while the spatial and temporal scope of the action is expressed through the world of dream and magic.

In the body of the drama Goethe added the conclusion of the scene 'Nacht' and the two scenes 'Vor dem Tor' and 'Studierzimmer I', together with a further forty lines of 'Studierzimmer II'. Faust's great monologue after the scene with Wagner and the Erdgeist, in which he experiences his own insignificance, now introduces the element of classical resignation in the face of reality, the element which also contains, as in *Wilhelm Meister*, the concept of an inherited curse. This resignation culminates in his attempted suicide, which is not only the denial of Christianity but an expression of the individual's freedom to do with his life what he wishes – a thought that recurs in modern existentialism. The agent of salvation is not faith, which the choruses, in the manner of *Wilhelm Meister*, reduce to activity and brotherly love, but the sentimental memories of childhood.

In this way Goethe elaborates and makes explicit the character of Faust as defined by God in the 'Prolog im Himmel'. Faust's relationship to the common people, as realistically portrayed in the scene 'Vor dem Tor', serves the same purpose; the 'two souls' scene shows Faust torn between aesthetic sensuousness and conscience. It is not a question of the Schillerian alternative of material happiness or peace of mind, but of attaining a synthesis in which humane values are preserved. Faust expresses this symbolically as he sits translating the Bible, and his sequence of renderings of *logos* – word, meaning, power, act – shows, under Herder's influence, the essentially sensuous nature of Goethe's new conception of his hero; it is no accident that immediately after this episode Faust finds the ironical, lifelong company of Mephisto, and with it the experience of the dialectic of life itself. Faust can no longer be an enthusiast for one thing at the expense of all others: he becomes a resigned universalist, as Goethe, moving from metaphysical speculation to the study of science on his return from Italy, himself did. The pact, product of Faust's universal nature, becomes the symbolic expression of a classical disposition which finds its vitality in pure form, a form compounded of resignation and insatiability.

As *Die Braut von Messina*, both in form and by virtue of the motif of fate, is Schiller's most obvious 'classical' experiment, so the 'Helena' fragment of 1800 – which follows the 'Hexenküche' scene written in Italy but was only later incorporated in its finished state into *Faust II* – is Goethe's experiment with classical form. On the one hand lies his use of iambic trimeter and choric strophes; more vitally, the Gothic figure of Faust gains experience of classical beauty and achieves a truly classical universality. The Gretchen motif was openly Christian; now, in the person of Helena, the innocence of pure sensuousness, ambiguous to the Christian ethic, enters Faust's life – 'his endless longing for what he has recognized as supreme beauty', as Goethe puts it in *Dichtung und Wahrheit*, strives to be fulfilled.

Goethe's reshaping of *Wilhelm Meister*, undertaken somewhat earlier, leads to similar results. The novel belongs in its origins to Goethe's pre-classical days; the Zürich version of *Wilhelm Meisters theatralische Sendung*, preserved by Bäbe Schulthess, shows the transition from *Sturm und Drang* to the demand for aesthetic education, to be achieved in this case through the theatre; and as the context is that of troupes of wandering players, with all their vices, Wilhelm's education becomes based on the idea of a reform of the theatre.

This educational process derives to a large extent from interpretations of Shakespeare, by means of which – above all in *Hamlet* – Wilhelm is to pass from mere enthusiasm to an adult understanding of what constitutes world drama. The theatre thus also becomes a medium through which to understand the world and in which the realities of the hero's character can be developed to the full. If one compares even the earliest version of *Wilhelm Meister* with *Werther*, one observes the growing realism of por-trayal, part of which is due to the more relaxed style; and whereas in *Werther* subjectivity is carried to its utmost limits, in the *Theatralische Sendung* it is tempered by experience and by the force of circumstances.

The six completed books of the *Theatralische Sendung* were written between 1777 and 1785. When in Italy, Goethe told Karl August in Weimar that it was impossible for him to work on the book. The new title *Wilhelm Meisters Lehrjahre* dates from 1793, but intensive work on the novel, ultimately finished in 1796, only began under Schiller's constant insistence; Goethe even sent successive instalments of the novel to Schiller for critical judgement.

Faust and *Wilhelm Meisters Lehrjahre* are the most faithful reflections of the classical Goethe's view of man. Whether the title of the earlier *Theatralische Sendung* is to be taken seriously or ironically, i.e. whether the theatre is really an educative force or merely a transitional phase, is open to discussion. If the latter, it ought to have been comparatively easy for Goethe, with Schiller's stimulus, to revise the work. Goethe himself maintains in his *Annalen* – though his mother and Tieck were of the oppo-site opinion – that he always held the view of the theatre as transition, but at the same time it is known that he tended in later life to rationalize such matters. The original story was cast as a straightforward historical narrative; the *Lehrjahre* is given a 'classical', objective character by being set in the form of a reminiscence, and the Romantics – Jean Paul de-veloped the form himself, while Friedrich Schlegel approved of its universal potentialities – accepted this epic form of retrospection.

Wieland and Herder, on the other hand, who knew the earliest version, regretted the loss of immediacy – a comparison of the theme of the puppet-theatre in the two versions hardly bears them out – but in any case they could not follow Goethe in his progress towards classical ideals. Like Schiller's plays from *Wallenstein* onwards, the indirect narrative of the

Lehrjahre points to an objectification, and from the point of view both of universal content and of objectivity, the novel is analogous to the classical stage of *Faust*. As Faust acquires a significance that goes beyond the personal, so the hero of the *Lehrjahre* also acquires representative qualities. The atmosphere of the *Theatralische Sendung* may be more intense, but the *Lehrjahre* has a deeper, wider human content with a broader educative function based not just on the theatre but on life itself.

This added breadth enchanted Friedrich Schlegel, but Schiller, in a in a letter of 2 July 1796, found it beyond his grasp, admiring the 'consistency' of the novel but unable to see its 'unity'. What started as the story of an artist has in fact become the story of a man, a man who has sacrificed the artistic leaning of his youth to the rigid demands of reality; Schiller finds that the work has grown beyond that state of aesthetic serenity to which he himself was prepared to devote so much study. In the *Lehrjahre* Wilhelm's subjectivity is restrained by the demands of experience, and these demands constitute his education. In this sense it is a didactic work, corresponding to Goethe's own statement in his *Annalen* that man reaches human maturity only by coming to terms with his mistaken tendencies through the events of his experience. It is the essence of classicism to meet life head on.

Thus Wilhelm progresses from the crisis of everyday life to the classical crisis of genius, subjectivity and the problem of harmonious development, and thence to the recognition of the objective forces of education represented by his responsibility towards Mignon, the Harper and Felix, forces which prepare him for reception into the Society of the Tower. Only through these forms of resignation, of self-abnegation, does he achieve the maturity of personality which makes him worthy of Natalie's love.

In essence the *Lehrjahre* is a work close to Schiller's heart, but the *Bekenntnisse einer schönen Seele* (Part II, Book 6) – a title which disturbed him – was something of a bone of contention between him and Goethe (though not as psychologically divisive a force as Wagner's *Parsifal* was for Nietzsche). This Book 6 portrays one of Schiller's central aesthetic concepts, but he regretted that the notion of the 'schöne Seele' should have been introduced here and not left for the character of Natalie. Goethe's interpretation of Shaftesbury's 'moral grace' is in fact somewhat different from Schiller's, who thought Goethe had misunderstood him. Goethe's 'schöne Seele' is ultimately a pietistic child of God, a reflection of his earlier relationship with Susanne von Klettenberg; indeed, he was accused of merely having adapted her posthumous papers to his purpose. And Schiller, in his *Ästhetische Vorlesungen* of 1792–3, had originally treated the subject – though not the specific concept – as analogous to religion. In *Anmut und Würde*, however, this is no longer the context; Natalie, indeed, is the true poetic analogy to this essay. Schiller could not but be confused by finding in the *Lehrjahre* his own aesthetic formulations from *Anmut und Würde* applied to so extreme a form of Christian pietism and childlike devotion. The 'schöne Seele' – to Kant a contingency demonstrable in religion, for Schiller a classical, aristocratic manifestation of human potentiality – is in *Wilhelm Meister* a profound psychological problem central to the human meaning of the work.

Romanticism

WERNER KOHLSCHMIDT

The Early Romantics

Romanticism is not the historical successor of classicism, for its beginnings and its principal achievements coincide with classicism: Wackenroder's *Herzensergießungen* was conceived in Schiller and Goethe's 'ballad year', while Goethe's *Pandora* and *Wahlverwandtschaften* appeared after *Des Knaben Wunderhorn* and only shortly before Uhland's first volume of verse. Romanticism and classicism are linked in a series of attractions and repulsions. The Jena Romantics of the mid-1790s saw Herder as their model, Schiller as their godfather and Goethe as their idol. Where Herder and Schiller were repelled by the lack of morality and the wayward playfulness of these young poets, Goethe, whose *Wilhelm Meister* they saw as the epitome of universalism in literature and which continued to fascinate German novelists down to Mörike (*Maler Nolten*) and Keller (*Der grüne Heinrich*), showed himself on occasion so receptive to Romantic ideas, forms and discoveries that one can hardly talk in terms of a division between classical and Romantic elements. Arnim and Brentano appropriately dedicated *Des Knaben Wunderhorn* to him, and in the period of the *Westöstlicher Divan* he still appreciated the medieval paintings in Boisserée's collection. Herder's spiritual influence on Romanticism is immense, and the mutual stimulation of classicism and Romanticism is hardly less evident than their contrariety. The real anti-Romantic force is that of the Enlightenment.

The origins of Romanticism are equally complex. Many writers came from eastern areas such as Silesia, East Prussia and Berlin (Wackenroder, Tieck, Arnim, Eichendorff, E. T. A. Hoffmann, Kleist), but the Schlegels were Hanoverians and Novalis was Middle German, while Steffens was a Norwegian with Dutch ancestors; against the Silesians Schleiermacher and Fichte one can place the Swabians Schelling and Hegel, and the Romantic circles in Berlin and Jena are offset by those in Heidelberg and Swabia. Hamann and Herder were East Prussians, nor must one overlook the English influence from Young's *Night Thoughts* and the sentimental novel: sentimentality, together with the achievement of form in a context of freedom, derive both from East Prussian pietism and from the English Enlightenment and Age of Sensibility.

The word 'romantisch' itself is also influenced by English usage. The original meaning is 'what pertains to the romance', i.e. the tradition of strange, fantastic stories from popular romances and ballads to the baroque novel (*Roman*) and above all the novels of Richardson, Fielding and Sterne. But besides this the early Romantics found *Wilhelm Meister* supremely 'Romantic', and this is a long way from the popular use of the term to describe external superficial characteristics: the Romantics themselves saw their activity in the context of idealist philosophy, which gives the word a very different value from that applied to descriptions of forests, streams, ruins and supernatural beings. Indeed, the applications of the term have become so various and imprecise that its usefulness in the context of literary criticism has been called in question.

The beginnings of Romanticism lie in groups of young poets, critics and philosophers formed in the mid-1790s, rather in the style of the Göttinger Hainbund of an earlier generation. The attitudes of the Romantics to their friendships, however, were freer, fuller, more committed, and despite personal nuances one may speak of a common basic outlook. The philosophical reflections of Novalis, Schleiermacher and Friedrich Schlegel on the nature of friendship are attempts, based on an idealistic vision of man, to discover one's individuality within the shared emotional context, and this leads beyond the sentimental Anacreontic friendships affected in the time of Klopstock, Gleim and the Göttinger Hain.

The opening moves in the Romantic campaign were made in Berlin, the capital of German rationalism, by Wilhelm Heinrich Wackenroder (1773–98) and Ludwig Tieck (1773–1853), both native Berliners. Tieck, talented son of a tradesman, felt an urge to literature at an early age and embarked in his youth on a number of highly accomplished stories of suspense and horror; had it not been for Wackenroder's influence he might well have stayed in this position, but Wackenroder, a clearer-sighted, more sensitive mind, enabled him to overcome his crisis of melancholy and self-doubt. In fact, however, Tieck was the stronger of the two, for he only felt the onset of nihilism, whereas Wackenroder went to an early grave, consumed by a yearning for an artistic career which his father, a Prussian civil servant of puritanical, pietistic leanings, had always forbidden him. His brief but happy period as a student in Göttingen and Erlangen culminated in his friendship with Tieck and his tour of Middle Germany and Franconia; he died at twenty-five. Tieck lived to a ripe old age as *Geheimrat,* enjoying an esteem not unlike Goethe's.

Wackenroder bequeathed his only two works – the *Herzensergießungen eines kunstliebenden Klosterbruders* (1797) and the *Phantasien über die Kunst für Freunde der Kunst* (1799) – to Tieck, who added his own contributions to each, including, in the *Herzensergießungen*, the motif of the Klosterbruder, which was suggested by the composer Reichardt. Tieck was vague about his own contributions, and in many sections it remains unclear how far his own hand is present and how far Wackenroder is responding to his friend's more highly strung sentimentality.

The *Herzensergießungen* stands as one of the most representative manifestations of the Romantic 'religion' of art. Goethe rejected it as expressive of an anti-classical aesthetic, but it is less so than its style and content would lead one to suppose. His enthusiastic account, in the much-quoted 'Ehrengedächtnis unsers ehrwürdigen Ahnherrn Albrecht Dürers', of the medieval town of Nürnberg, which he also describes in letters and journals, recalls the young Goethe's account of Strasbourg Cathedral; the essays 'Von zwei wunderbaren Sprachen und deren geheimnisvoller Kraft' and 'Einige Worte über Allgemeinheit, Toleranz und Menschenliebe in der Kunst' are testimonies to Herder's emotional aesthetics, employing words such as 'Wunder', 'Geheimnis', 'Ahnung' and 'Sehnsucht' at the expense of the terminology of logic and reason; and 'Das merkwürdige musikalische Leben des Tonkünstlers Joseph Berglinger' is the first tragic Romantic story of an artist, in the style later developed by Hoffmann. But detectable beyond the Tieck-influenced sphere of the religion of art there lies, in the essays on the Italian Renaissance (Raphael, Leonardo, Francesco Francia, Piero di Cosimo, Michelangelo), the stylization of this art in the classical, Winckelmannian sense of balance and order. This is no delight in chaos, such as Friedrich Schlegel has: like Winckelmann and Schiller, Wackenroder wishes to see the sun reflected in calm, not in troubled waters, and the other side of Leonardo and Michelangelo disturbs him. Characteristic is his Graecophile interpretation of a madonna he saw in Pommersfelden which he took to be by Raphael.

In this mood Wackenroder is no anti-classical revolutionary, and the religious foundation of his aesthetic ideal of balance and order is deceptive, for we are here confronted, as in Friedrich Schlegel's early works, with a highly personal interpretation of classical aesthetics in the spirit of 'noble simplicity and serene grandeur', an ideal that retains its character despite the Catholicizing language of Wackenroder's Klosterbruder. It is not here that the anti-classical Wackenroder is to be found but in the Berglinger stories, in which music is a disturbing, destructive demonic force which sets life and art in opposition to each other.

Both aspects of Wackenroder are portrayed in Tieck's novel *Franz Sternbalds Wanderungen* (1798), which ranges from the purity and serenity of the Winckelmann ideal of the Renaissance to Bacchanals in the spirit of Heinse's *Ardinghello* (1787), from which latter aspect one can pass to Schlegel's *Lucinde*. This world is basically closer to Tieck's personality than are the Romantic descriptiveness of his *Sternbald* and his *Märchen* of the 1790s, which copy and exaggerate genuine characteristics of Wacken-roder's manner. His cult of 'folky' elements and his use of synaesthesia have a ready-made quality about them and lack the sincerity that Eichen-dorff later reveals, while in *Märchen* such as *Der Runenberg* and *Der blonde Eckbert* (1797) he builds on a mood of despair created by an excessive use of titillating effects of widely varying kinds. This inner nature of Tieck is seen most clearly in *Die Geschichte des Herrn William Lovell* (1795–6), a novel in which the hero is an aesthetic nihilist and solipsist, the quality of whose life sinks lower and lower as the work proceeds.

Tieck's discoveries in the realm of *Volksbücher* and medieval poetry – as the works later collected in his *Phantasus* confirm – are a kind of romantic substitute for the lack of direct purpose in his own life. On the other hand his quickness of perception and breadth of sympathy made him a great dramaturge and a fascinating reciter of poetry. With an instinct for the needs of the public, yet full of irony at the expense of middle-class values, he was the first to arrive at the fate-tragedy (*Karl von Berneck*, 1793–5), while in *Der gestiefelte Kater* (1797), his most successful play, he anticipated certain features of the modern drama, such as audience participation and multi-level satire, giving his comedy a Romantic breadth and a new freedom to combine heterogeneous elements. In his historical drama *Kaiser Octavianus*, on the other hand, the Romantic concern with the past shows itself in a wordy, rhetorical use of classical metre.

In his lyrics Tieck leaves behind the cynicism of *William Lovell* and seeks the self-abandonment of the subjective poet, an authentic expression of melancholy at the transience of earthly things, and new ways of surrender-ing to the world in a harmony of colours and sounds:

> Wie schnell verschwindet
> So Licht als Glanz,
> Der Morgen findet
> Verwelkt den Kranz,
>
> Der gestern glühte
> In aller Pracht,
> Denn er verblühte
> In dunkler Nacht.
>
> Es schwimmt die Welle
> Des Lebens hin
> Und färbt sich helle,
> Hat's nicht Gewinn.

(How quickly all brightness and glory vanishes; the morning finds the withered garland which yesterday blossomed in splendour but died in the darkness of the night. Life sweeps onwards and grows pale if it brings no reward.)

With his ever-widening experience, from antiquity and the Minnesinger to Don Quixote, Grimmelshausen and above all Shakespeare, he became ever more like Goethe as time went on, as is seen in his later short stories, written in a cool, calculated style reminiscent of the Italians (*Der Aufruhr in den Cevennen* (1826); *Der junge Tischlermeister* (1836); *Vittoria Accorombona* (1840)) – but these lie outside the period of Romanticism.

At the same time as Tieck and Wackenroder were active in Berlin, a circle of Romantics was formed in Jena in close association with the egocentric philosophy of Fichte and the *Naturphilosophie* of the young Schelling, developing a philosophical theory of Romantic emotion and Romantic art. It was due to Goethe and Schiller that the brothers Schlegel (August Wilhelm (1767–1845); Friedrich (1772–1829)), members of a family of theologians already important in literary history, went to Jena, where Fichte and Schelling were teaching at the university, and to which Schleiermacher (1768–1834) and Novalis (1772–1801), both from a background of Zinzendorfean pietism, also came. In addition there were the women: Friedrich Schlegel's wife Dorothea, daughter of Moses Mendelssohn, shrewd, lively, inventive, and with the gift of penetrating to the root of things; Caroline, wife first of August Wilhelm Schlegel, then of Schelling, daughter of the Göttingen scholar Michaelis, an intense, almost demonic woman of powerful emotion and intellect christened 'Dame Lucifer' by Schiller and his wife.

At the start Schiller encouraged both Schlegels, particularly Wilhelm, who had earlier found the patronage of Bürger, and as literary critics they supported his activities. But soon Schiller, who was a keener and therefore less tolerant thinker than Goethe, broke with them, and they in their turn began to look to Goethe. Herder, with whose attitudes and ideas, from the objective point of view, they had most in common, also turned away from them in his old age, leaving only Goethe, of the Weimar classicists, still in touch with them. Goethe behaved in a diplomatic, conciliatory manner, and also owed a large part of his reputation among the public to their enthusiastic reception of his works, paramount among them being *Wilhelm Meister*, which Friedrich Schlegel and, initially at least, Novalis received with an exuberance which served to re-establish the long-severed link between Goethe and the public. Thus in Jena the formal aesthetic programmes of the Romantics were worked out, to the bitter disapproval of Herder and Schiller but to the intense interest of Goethe.

The most gifted poetic talent among the Jena Romantics is Novalis (Friedrich von Hardenberg). From being a student of law in Jena, Leipzig and Wittenberg he turned, under the influence of his interest in the philosophy of natural science, to the study of mining and spent the few years of his professional life in this field. His teacher at the academy in Freiberg was Werner, with whom Goethe discussed questions of geology and mineralogy and who served as the model for the master in Novalis's fragment *Die Lehrlinge zu Sais*. The name Novalis is a symbolical interpretation of Neurode (='newly cleared land'), the name of one of the Hardenberg family estates. By nature delicate and sensitive, like Hölty and Wackenroder, but far more creative, even revolutionary, than they, he exhausted himself at an early age under the weight of his thoughts and plans and the death of his young fiancée Sophie von Kühn.

His *Geistliche Lieder* and *Hymnen an die Nacht* (1798) are, with some of the poems of Tieck, the only early Romantic lyrics to have outlived their age. They express two basic Romantic themes: that of pietistic mysticism, with a strong tendency to Catholicism; and that of an anti-rationalistic, anti-classical aversion to light and day and a predilection for the dark and the mysterious. The *Hymnen an die Nacht* are a denial of the world of Schiller's *Götter Griechenlands*.

The fragmentary novel *Heinrich von Ofterdingen*, of which only the first part was finished, is the story of an artist, like Tieck's *Sternbald*, but its poetic and philosophical substance is incomparably greater, dealing with the spiritual development of the legendary Minnesinger of the title in a series of ever-widening circles, in the manner of *Wilhelm Meister*. The theme is sustained by a pattern of transcendental figures, physical and spiritual, seeking the 'blue flower'. Fichte's 'ego' and Schelling's 'nature' combine in a counterpoint of will and fate, of demonic powers within and without.

The figure of Schelling also hovers above the transcendental 'nature philosophy' of *Die Lehrlinge zu Sais*, while in the essay *Die Christenheit oder Europa* (1799), with its poetic overtones but its basically philosophical intent, Novalis passionately seeks, as in *Heinrich von Ofterdingen*, the restoration of the pristine unity of the universe which was destroyed by the age of reason but still experienced by the Middle Ages. This theme of the lost golden age finds its most perfect expression in Novalis; by comparison the vision of the Middle Ages depicted by Tieck and Wackenroder is a shallow one.

Novalis's posthumous writings highlight a feature peculiar to the Romantics: the frequency of the fragmentary. Where the rationalist and the classicist work towards a logically constructed and completed whole, *Sturm und Drang* and Romanticism, in accordance with their artistic theories, are bound to break through conventional forms. And since behind the Romantic aesthetic lies the concept of the inexpressible, much Romantic writing remains fragmentary, whether as parts of an uncompleted whole, like *Heinrich von Ofterdingen* or *Die Lehrlinge zu Sais*, or simply as loosely constructed works like Friedrich Schlegel's *Lucinde* and, later, Brentano's deliberately 'unplanned' *Godwi*.

But as well as such works – all based, incidentally, on principles of free composition which they claimed to have discovered in *Wilhelm Meister* – the Romantics also developed a theory of the fragment as a characteristic form in which extreme brevity was linked with extreme concentration of thought. About half of Novalis's posthumous writings take the form of allusive, provocative, imaginative aphorisms with a highly concentrated intellectual content – linguistic experiments in which religious, aesthetic, analytical and speculative truths point challengingly to the mysteries of the universe. Friedrich Schlegel was also a master of the aphoristic fragment, and Wilhelm Schlegel and Schleiermacher made their own contributions to the form.

Many of these fragments were first published in the main Romantic journal *Athenaeum* (1798–1800), which first appeared in Berlin, then in Jena, where its chief contributors settled and where, besides Fichte and Schelling, the physicist Johann Wilhelm Ritter was also active in the pursuit of an idealist philosophy of nature.

The theologian Schleiermacher sought to hold the balance between the speculative and the analytical sides of the early Romantic movement in his *Reden über die Religion* (1799), an apologia for religion as a concern of the emotions, a medium 'for the understanding of the eternal' which comes from 'the contemplation of the universe'; church dogma is replaced by subjectivity, which is related to the aesthetic mode of perception. Schleiermacher's defence of subjectivity later led him to defend so solipsist a work as Friedrich Schlegel's *Lucinde,* and in his *Vertraute Briefe über 'Lucinde'* the breadth of his emotional sympathy virtually takes him beyond the realm of the theologian.

As Schleiermacher's Romantic theology seeks to reconcile the outer and the inner world, so Schelling's and Ritter's philosophy of nature seeks to reconcile nature and mind. Where Kant and Fichte had seen spirit in terms of moral freedom, new discoveries such as those of galvanism and magnetism led to the belief that mind and nature were not opposites but aspects of one and the same force. Schelling's *Ideen zu einer Philosophie der Natur* (1797), *Von der Weltseele* (1798) and *Erster Entwurf eines Systems der Naturphilosophie* (1799) all aim at the resolution of this dualism. Poets and scientists alike sought to break down the barriers between philosophy, science and religion; in the realm of art this attitude took the form *inter alia* of obliterating the distinctions between words, sounds and colours.

Behind all such activities lies the desire to penetrate the mysteries of nature and mind, the separation of which was blamed upon the Enlightenment: the world was originally at one with itself, and man's subconscious still knows this pristine unity, the unity symbolized by the 'blue flower' which Novalis's Ofterdingen seeks. Furthermore it is a unity which is in no way threatened by the often purely intellectual and fanciful exercises in which Friedrich Schlegel, and also Novalis, indulged.

The Schlegels' careers were launched in the shadow of Schiller and the classical view of Greece, and among Friedrich's critical works between 1794 and 1798 were *Von den Schulen der griechischen Poesie, Vom ästhetischen Werte der griechischen Komödie* and *Über die Diotima*. He studied the elegy, the idyll and the epics of Homer, and found himself facing the ever more pressing problem, as posed by Lessing, of the true relationship between the classical and the modern. After his conversion to Catholicism in 1807 he gave various sets of lectures in which, as in those of his brother, the problem is treated as one proper to world literature *in toto* – a logical consequence of the aesthetic principles they had both laid down in the *Athenaeum*.

All the most important innovations of the early Romantics are found combined in the *Athenaeum*: A. W. Schlegel's satire on the Enlightenment, *Der literarische Reichsanzeiger*, in which wit is carried to almost ridiculous lengths, is there, as are Friedrich's most important early writings, including his interpretation of *Wilhelm Meister* and the *Rede über die Mythologie*, which latter takes up Schelling's demand for a new, modern mythology and states the premiss, 'It is in the Orient that we must seek the highest Romantic values'. Later he was to take this interest further in *Über die Sprache und Weisheit der Inder* (1808). It is hardly possible to imagine Goethe's *Westöstlicher Divan* as independent from such activities on the part of the Romantics.

The *Athenaeum* also contained Novalis's *Hymnen an die Nacht* and a mass of important fragments by Schleiermacher, the Schlegels and Novalis. Friedrich Schlegel and Novalis, the two most challenging and inventive minds, developed a theory of the fertility of chaos, in which one is continually making new beginnings, and a theory of wit and irony as means to the achievement of this chaos and as the foundations of a Romantic communality. Above all the sixteenth fragment in Novalis's cycle *Blütenstaub* and Friedrich Schlegel's Fragment No. 116 from the *Athenaeum* – the former proclaiming the subjective path to knowledge and the conquest of temporality, the latter defining Romantic poetry as 'progressive universal poetry', i.e. virtually as the essence of poetry itself – contain the core of the early Romantic view of art and life.

All this inevitably led, for all the Romantics' veneration of Goethe, to attitudes that became more and more at odds with those of classicism. But except for Novalis and Tieck's lyric poetry, no great literature resulted. Wilhelm Schlegel composed skilfully wrought romances and ballads in the manner of Schiller and evolved a form of descriptive sonnet; his drama *Ion* (1803), like his brother's *Alarkos*, is classicistic in form and metre, and Romantic elements are virtually limited to onomatopoeia and the occasional interpolation into the classical verses of *terze rime* and sonnets. Friedrich's novel *Lucinde* (1799), on the other hand, is a deliberate exercise in formlessness and lack of discipline, in which are assembled all the individual thoughts and moments which find expression in collections of fragments; at the same time it continues the tradition of Romantic solipsism which starts with Tieck's *William Lovell* and moves on to the nihilistic irony of the anonymous *Nachtwachen des Bonaventura*. *Lucinde* is a storehouse of information on early Romanticism – on friendship, love, marriage, the attraction to a state of chaos, the ever-questioning intelligence (*Allegorie von der Frechheit*), idleness (*Idylle über den Müssiggang*), Romantic psychology and the Romantic ideal of a 'free community' – but it never becomes a work of art.

The early Romantic circle in Jena dissolved in 1801, after the *Athenaeum* had stopped publication and as a result of numerous personal quarrels. Wilhelm Schlegel's epoch-making Berlin lectures of 1801–4 contain a résumé both of Romantic aesthetic theories and of world literature as seen through Romantic eyes. Wilhelm himself divorced Caroline and joined Madame de Staël; Friedrich went first to Dresden, then to Paris, where he finally married Dorothea, with whom he had been living for many years; Novalis died in the spring of 1801. One of the most impressive accounts of these early years of German Romanticism is that given by Henrik Steffens (1773–1845), the Norwegian friend and supporter of the movement, in his memoirs *Was ich erlebte* (1840–4).

The Younger Generation

A new generation of Romantics had already appeared on the scene by the time of Schiller's death. But they were not Romantics who felt they had to justify themselves by continual reference to antiquity, to Dante, to Shakespeare or to Goethe. The emphasis shifted from aesthetic speculation to nature, the Romantic way of life and poetic activity itself – a new atmosphere and a new set of sociological assumptions described in Eichendorff's memoirs *Halle und Heidelberg*.

The move from Middle Germany to Heidelberg was itself a symbolic experience, and Eichendorff, for one, gave an account of the specific Romantic values of folklore and medieval life which this old city embodied. His interpretation is a Romantic one but it is based on experience, not speculation. The magic and the merriment of youth could thus develop more freely, as in Eichendorff, than among the philosophically inclined older Romantics, and the intellectual precocity of the Schlegels, the literary efficiency of Tieck and the delicate, ethereal quality of Wackenroder and Novalis give way to youthful enthusiasm.

Clemens Brentano (1778–1842) was the son of a Frankfurt merchant family of Italian origin; his mother was Maximiliane von La Roche, a friend of Goethe's youth. In 1798 he went to Jena and made contact there with the Schlegel circle, but soon parted company from them. His free, Bohemian style of life matched that of the early Romantics, with whom he shared a predilection for the uncontrolled and the chaotic, as did his sister Bettina (1785–1859), who married his friend Achim von Arnim.

His first extended work, the novel *Godwi, ein verwilderter Roman* (1800), is in the formless tradition of *Lucinde* but its content has no philosophical basis; rather it depicts a character whose life is so confused that it ends in destruction – a pattern that derives from Brentano's relationship with, and brief marriage to, Sophie Mereau, an older woman his equal in emotional faculty but his superior in the conduct of life. She died in 1806, and it was many years before Brentano recovered from the shock of her loss. This was the time when *Godwi* was written; he expresses from personal experience the mood – seen in his 'Musikantenlied' and in the 'Lorelei' ballad, in which he meets Schelling's demand for a new mythology – which in *Lucinde* has only a manufactured quality. Loeben, Eichendorff and Heine later took up the Lorelei motif again, but it is to Brentano's greater powers of concreteness that we owe its formulation.

Wackenroder's influence on Brentano is seen in the element of a religious attitude towards art in *Godwi* and also in Brentano's early passion for anything that appears to come from the mysterious depths of the *Volk*. The two are combined in the subject-matter and archaic language of the original sketch (1802) of the novel *Chronika eines fahrenden Schülers*, the archetype of those innumerable chronicle-stories of the Romantic and *Biedermeier* periods, down to Meinhold's *Bernsteinhexe*. This side of Brentano's activity finds expression above all in his activity as a collector of folksongs, folk-tales and old chronicles, an activity that is most perfectly summed up in the folksong collection *Des Knaben Wunderhorn*, in which Arnim collaborated.

Achim von Arnim (1781–1831), from an aristocratic Brandenburg family, came to literature from the sciences, and in Göttingen, where he took up literary studies, he wrote his first novel, *Hollins Liebesleben*, in the style of *Werther*; this was followed by *Ariels Offenbarungen*, written in Switzerland while he was on the Grand Tour of Europe. It was in Göttingen that he met the Brentanos, on whose restless, unsteady temperaments his cooler northern nature had a beneficial influence.

The climax of Arnim's relationship with Brentano came with *Des Knaben Wunderhorn* (1805–8), in substance and extent the first really significant collection of German folksongs, dedicated – to his no little pleasure – to Goethe. Herder's *Stimmen der Völker* had given very little space to German songs and had not distinguished so strictly between folksong and art-song. At the same time Brentano and Arnim were not concerned, like Uhland later, to produce philologically accurate texts but to capture the spirit of the songs, and they did not hesitate to alter the texts to make them conform to their Romantic convictions. This stylization was to prove an influential force in literature.

It was highly appropriate that *Des Knaben Wunderhorn* should be published by Zimmer in Heidelberg, for here, in the period of the Napoleonic Wars, were to be found not only Brentano and Arnim but Otto von Loeben – the epitome of Romantic decadence – Eichendorff, Görres, discoverer of the *Volksbücher*, and Creuzer, Romantic interpreter of mythology.

Joseph Görres (1776–1848), a Rhinelander, wrote his *Die teutschen Volksbücher* (1807) in enthusiastic response to his reading in Brentano's collection of early pamphlets and *incunabula*. Dedicated to Brentano, it is devoted to the spirit of German regeneration (like the second part of the *Wunderhorn*) and perpetuates Novalis's vision of the unity of the Middle Ages; its opening and concluding sections, like the essay that Arnim added to the *Wunderhorn*, convey a mythological interpretation of popular poetry and the Middle Ages, and not without reference to the unhappy conditions of the early nineteenth century.

The friends of the Heidelberg circle were scattered by the events of war but were reunited after the Peace of Tilsit and now joined by the lawyer Friedrich von Savigny – also a brother-in-law of Brentano's – and the brothers Grimm, who left their native Hessen for Heidelberg. Together the group published Creuzer's *Heidelbergische Jahrbücher* and the *Zeitung für Einsiedler*, edited by Arnim in 1808. Among the contributors to the latter were, besides Brentano and Görres, the Grimms, Uhland and Justinus Kerner, the painter Philipp Otto Runge and Zacharias Werner, the semi-mystical, semi-coldly-calculating dramatist who made the fate-tragedy, taken from Tieck, a fashionable form of literature. Among the works published in this journal were Wilhelm Grimm's translations of Old Danish heroic lays, Runge's 'Märchen vom Machandelboom', Brentano's 'Das Uhrmachers BOGS wunderbare Geschichte', and 'Bärenhäuter', which owes its presence to the rediscovery of Grimmelshausen.

The basic question for the Heidelberg Romantics was the relationship of legend to literature and history. The members of the circle were highly dependent on each other, and Caroline von Günderode's suicide over her unrequited love for Creuzer is only the most tragic example of this dependence. But by the end of 1808 the group had dissolved, and not even the attacks on the *Jahrbücher* and the *Zeitung für Einsiedler* by old Johann Heinrich Voss had the effect of uniting them.

If one measures the achievements of the Jena and the Heidelberg Romantics in the spheres beyond creative literature, one finds that, like Lessing and above all Herder, they stimulated many kinds of scholarly activity. The early Romantics in Jena, Berlin and Halle made important contributions to idealist philosophy; they also stimulated the writing of literary history, involving, particularly in the various series of lectures by the Schlegels, world literature and the history of individual genres. The Schlegels, among others, also launched Indo-European and Oriental studies, and their names are inseparable from the early development of Romance philology and the propagation of Spanish, Portuguese and Italian literature. Above all the great translation of Shakespeare by Wilhelm Schlegel, Dorothea Tieck and Count Baudissin, under Tieck's supervision, turned the greatest of English poets into a German classic.

The principal achievements of the Heidelberg Romantics, on the other hand, lie in the field of pioneering studies in Germanic philology and folklore: *Des Knaben Wunderhorn*, Görres's work on chap-books and Meistergesang, Creuzer's studies in the symbolism of mythology, the works of the brothers Grimm (*Kinder- und Hausmärchen* (1812–23)) and Uhland (*Alte hoch- und niederdeutsche Volkslieder* (1844–5)). The early historical writings of Ernst Moritz Arndt (1769–1860), the farmer's son from Rügen, are worthy representatives of Herder's tradition, while in Savigny, Adam Müller and the younger Haller the Romantic influence penetrates to the realms of law and politics. No student of history or literature can afford to underestimate the Romantic contribution to these disciplines, a contribution in terms both of inspired suggestion and of practical methodology.

The Romantics' concern for national values, present already in Wackenroder's pieces on Dürer and Hans Sachs and enhanced by practical knowledge and the first-hand study of sources, led them to take an active part in the Wars of Liberation. This activity came, on the one hand, with the patriotic lyrics of Arndt, Körner and Max von Schenkendorff, and on the other with the diplomatic work of Wilhelm Schlegel and Friedrich Gentz, with the formation of patriotic societies like Arnim's 'Christlich-deutsche Tischgesellschaft' in Berlin and with publications like Arndt's *Geist der Zeit* and *Der Wächter*, Adam Müller's and Kleist's *Berliner Abendblätter* and Görres's *Rheinischer Merkur*. Thus although at first glance so much Romantic activity may seem to be directed away from the present, in fact it is often very relevant to specific contemporary problems, even to the point of having a significance as propaganda.

The original poetic achievements of the Heidelberg Romantics, especially in lyric poetry, are fuller and more varied than those of the earlier Romantics, except Novalis, whose profundity they cannot attain. Almost all of them tried their hand at the novel and succeeded in writing effective *Novellen* and *Märchen*. Their dramas are less successful, though an occasional comedy makes its mark.

With the exception of a few items like *Fürst Ganzgott und Sänger Halbgott* and *Der tolle Invalide auf dem Fort Ratonneau* (1818), Arnim's tales are somewhat stiff and cramped. Brentano's, on the other hand, drawn from

Italian, Spanish and German sources, are full of sparkling wit and satire: the *Rheinmärchen* (1811) and *Die Geschichte vom braven Kasperl und dem schönen Annerl* (1818) are typical products of the later Romantics. His satires, however, directed against Voss and the Enlightenment, as well as against contemporary literature in the style of Kotzebue, are less effective, though his comedy *Ponce de Leon* (1801–4) and his Singspiel *Die lustigen Musikanten* (1802–3) – set to music by E. T. A. Hoffmann – left their mark on Büchner's *Leonce und Lena* and on Hofmannsthal. The value of *Die Romanzen vom Rosenkranz* (1803–11) lies more in its lyrical qualities than in the highly Romantic story of how a family curse is ended by an appeal to Catholicism (cf. Hoffmann's *Elixiere des Teufels*). He has also left a number of charming lyric poems – ballads, cradle-songs, night-songs – in which words, sounds and colours intermingle in magical fashion; the same feature characterizes his confessional poems from the period of his conversion to Catholicism.

Brentano's Protestant friend Arnim returned again and again, in dramas and novels, to the theme of guilt and repentance. This is the substance of *Ariels Offenbarungen* (1803), *Armut, Reichtum, Schuld und Sühne der Gräfin Dolores* (completed 1810) and the drama *Halle und Jerusalem* (1811), and in these works the psychology of the 'dark side of nature', also treated by Kleist and Hoffmann and instigatory of Brentano's and Kerner's concern with the mysterious world of visions and supernatural manifestations, is developed, a psychology which can be traced from Schelling to G. H. Schubert. Similar mystical tendencies underlie Arnim's long historical novel *Die Kronenwächter*, set in the popular Romantic age of the Reformation and full of extravagant mystical symbolism (only the first volume was completed, 1817), in which the influence of Novalis's *Heinrich von Ofterdingen* can also be detected. At the same time Arnim is occasionally capable of a remarkable realism.

An interesting work that marks the transition from the 'nature philosophy' of Schelling and Ritter to the study of extreme psychological conditions by G. H. Schubert, and subsequently by Kleist and Hoffmann, is *Die Nachtwachen des Bonaventura* (1804), an anonymous work of which Schelling – who had used the pseudonym of Bonaventura – was at one time believed to have been the author. Existing on many levels, and full of suggestive satire, the sixteen 'vigils' describe the life and thoughts of a vagrant figure of mysterious origins who ends in a state of utter nihilism; by virtue of its atmosphere, its philosophy, its concern with the psychology of the artist, with madness and with the mysterious side of nature, it is a work that epitomizes the art of the later Romantics.

Die Nachtwachen des Bonaventura leads naturally to the writer in whom these tendencies are most powerfully combined – E. T. A. Hoffmann (1776–1822). In professional life he was a judge – and a highly efficient one; in spirit, however, he saw himself as a writer and a musician, and this is the dichotomy which he makes the theme of his work. For a while he did succeed in making his living as a Kapellmeister in Bamberg, Dresden and Leipzig, and when he settled in Berlin as a Prussian civil servant he drew on this experience for his tales.

Der goldene Topf (1814) shows his characteristic position in the context of Romanticism, namely his portrayal of everyday reality as possessing a mystical hidden meaning which, as depicted in the *Märchen*, reveals the true significance of that reality. It is basically the same attitude as that of the 'nature philosophy' conveyed by the motif of the Classical Walpurgisnacht and Homunculus in *Faust II*, though there is less allegorical matter in Hoffmann than in Goethe.

In *Der goldene Topf* Archivarius Lindhorst, ordinary citizen yet magician in disguise and, like Rosabelverde in *Klein-Zaches*, a symbol of human dualism and the world of the spirits, struggles to win the soul of the student Anselmus, who does not yet know where his true place is. The conflict between internal and external fate fills Hoffmann's works: in *Die Elixiere des Teufels* (1815–16) it takes the form of the Romantic motif of the accursed family and its release from the curse. A host of further stories deal with subjects such as hypnotism, robots and dual personality, and in his stories of the artist, of the closeness of the artist's life to madness, and of its incompatibility with everyday life – embodied in the character of Kapellmeister Kreisler in the items of *Kreisleriana* and in the novel *Kater Murr* (1820), in the character of the singer in the story *Don Juan* and in the unbalanced hero of the story *Ritter Gluck* – he takes the theme of the artist and his art far beyond the point reached by Tieck.

Heinrich von Kleist (1777–1811), despite his independence and isolation, must also be considered among these Berlin Romantics. Of aristocratic Brandenburg descent, like Arnim, but without the latter's security of position, he fought the outward circumstances of his life and finally, in a state of desperation, committed suicide. The greatest experience in his life was his encounter with the works of Kant, from which he derived, not a confirmation of the power of rational optimism, like Schiller, but a conviction of its refutation.

Not by accident does Kleist's greatness lie in the field of drama, a field in which he outstrips all the Romantics, although during his lifetime he met with no success. Goethe, for one, withheld his approval, and it is easy to see the conflict between Kleist and classical drama. This conflict does not arise so much from his choice of Romantic subject-matter, such as *Die Familie Schroffenstein* (1803) and *Das Käthchen von Heilbronn* (1808–10) or even *Die Hermannsschlacht* – a subject already used in the eighteenth century; moreover his *Penthesilea* (1808) and his adaptation of Molière's *Amphitryon* (1807) draw on classical material. His anti-classicism is the result of a highly un-Goethean interpretation of nature and history, and thus of human nature and human existence. The family tragedy of *Die Familie Schroffenstein* rests on the Romantic concept of the fate-drama and the accumulation of guilt. In *Das Käthchen von Heilbronn, Die Hermannsschlacht* and *Penthesilea* fate is also irrevocable, driving men to extremes of cruelty and destruction which are far removed from the ideal of classical restraint. *Penthesilea* represents, however, a highly personal view of antiquity, the orgiastic fury and self-mutilation of the antiquity not of Apollo but of Dionysos. In Penthesilea's savaging of the body of her lover Achilles, and in her own suicide, lies Kleist's profoundest problem – the transcendence of consciousness at the decisive moment of action or experience. And in *Penthesilea* it is a problem intensified by the rationalist's sufferings over his own position, by the critical system of Kant and by the Romantic preoccupation with extreme psychological conditions. Käthchen's fate is foretold in a vision; Prince Friedrich von Homburg's conflict is provoked – and resolved – by a dream; Penthesilea awakes from the horrors of her unconscious deeds; Thusnelda is driven to murder by an uncontrollable and insane patriotism.

Trances and dreams are equally important in Kleist's *Novellen*, which are sustained by a remarkable objectivity and impenetrability of style. Both *Die Marquise von O. . .* and *Michael Kohlhaas* derive from the mystery of the unconscious, a mystery described in the essay *Über das Marionettentheater*, in which the instinct of the animal is contrasted with man broken on the wheel of rational consciousness, and where the infinite consciousness of the manipulator (God) unites with the unconscious gravitational actions of the puppet – a union in utter grace and beauty.

Kleist, for whom the notion of justice was as fascinatingly problematical as was the relationship between emotion and will, provided, in *Der zerbrochene Krug* (first performed 1808), one of the most successful Romantic comedies, taking as his subject the self-demonstration of justice and treating it with an inexorable logic; Goethe's division of the play into acts could not but destroy it, and Kleist inevitably felt that no one understood him. His life, his outlook and his works are parts of a great, indivisible whole.

Also connected with the Berlin Romantics were two writers of French descent, Friedrich de la Motte Fouqué (1777–1843) and Adalbert von Chamisso (1781–1831). Fouqué, with his historical and mysterious tales, was a victim of his own fecundity and outlived his reputation; the only work by which he is now remembered is the delicate *Märchen, Undine* (1811). Chamisso, however, was equally successful as poet and as storyteller. *Peter Schlemihls wunderbare Geschichte* (1817) treats the Romantic subject of the double – in this case the story of the man who sells his shadow to the devil and becomes a homeless wanderer over the face of the earth. Chamisso's lyric poetry, sustained by feelings of melancholy for the experiences – real, not imagined – of the past, speaks of the mystery of nature and history and, though stylistically not so adventurous as the poetry of Brentano, has its own directness and sincerity.

From Chamisso the line of lyrical poetry leads to the Silesian aristocrat Joseph Freiherr von Eichendorff (1788–1857), in whom Chamisso's conflicts were resolved, and his loneliness overcome, by an impregnable Catholicism. The many converts to Catholicism which Romanticism produced could never attain such a naturalness and inevitability of religious conviction: to be sure, Eichendorff's world knew the challenges of chaos and nihilism, but these were always held in check by a sense of divine order which was never in doubt. It is a world in which, like guilt and innocence, there were two apprentices (most of Eichendorff's heroes are young): one loses his way in the confusions of the world, the other exchanges the great wide world for a modest portion of human happiness; one perishes because he seeks the ultimate and is lost in the depths of the infinite, the other remains within more restricted bounds, becomes part of society and accepts the fate of humanity. Both are subject to the law: it allows the one to make his compulsive aesthetic venture but makes him pay for it with his life; it allows the other to enjoy love and family happiness but makes him pay for it with the loss of the absolute. Eichendorff's own heart is perhaps with the former, the Romantic; but it is the latter who is justified in terms of divine order.

This is the fundamental problem in the *Novelle, Das Marmorbild* (1819). In his novels *Ahnung und Gegenwart* (1815) and *Dichter und ihre Gesellen* (1834) his sympathies are with his unsettled young heroes, but his mind turns rather to resignation. This is also true in the last analysis of his story *Aus dem Leben eines Taugenichts* (1826). The young wanderer sees all reality as a miracle, but in the end everything that had seemed miraculous becomes attractively rational. Here is no inner conflict, for the child of God has eyes both for the charm of idyllic, middle-class life and for the mysterious nocturnal landscape and the excitement of Italy. Like no other Romantic poet, Eichendorff manifests both the profound dichotomy of the divine and the diabolical, and the young man's artless joy in the physical world. This is apparent also in his comedies such as *Die Freier* (1833), and it lies behind every line of *Halle und Heidelberg*; taken together with his faith in a divine order of things, it also entitles him to be one of the earliest to write a historical account of Romantic poetry (1846). With Eichendorff Romanticism enters a quieter phase – the musical quality of his lyrics contributes to this. At the same time the symbolic nature of his language leads one to suspect that he marks an end of Romanticism and a beginning of the middle-class realism of the Restoration, represented by Mörike and Stifter.

This leads to what was formerly known as the Swabian School – in reality a group of friends of very different natures: Ludwig Uhland (1787–1862), a Tübingen Germanist; Justinus Kerner (1786–1869), a public health official in Weinsberg; the German-Hungarian aristocrat Nikolaus Lenau (1802–50); and the Stuttgart schoolteacher Gustav Schwab (1792–1850). The social centre of the group was Kerner's house in Weinsberg, in which a warm atmosphere of conviviality prevailed. Kerner himself was fascinated by hypnotism, somnambulism and other phenomena connected with Romantic 'nature philosophy' and possibly drawn in part from the Swabian mysticism of an earlier age, and even believed in spirits and demons. Uhland, on the other hand, was of a sober, more realistic disposition which showed itself in his researches into legends and folksongs as well as in his literary scholarship, represented by his biography of Walther von der Vogelweide. By 1815, and in spite of his fame as a ballad poet, he had outgrown the Romanticism of his early poetry, though it still appears in his later dramas such as *Herzog Ernst von Schwaben* (1816–17), *Ludwig der Bayer* (1818) and the unfinished *Konradin*.

Gustav Schwab's works also have a flavour of the soil, though with an admixture of pedanticism. If one compares his best-known ballad, *Der Reiter auf dem Bodensee*, with the ballads in the grand style by Herder and even the young Uhland, one sees the common man portrayed as one who cannot bear the thought even of a danger that has already passed. This too is a form of resignation, albeit unconscious.

As Uhland and Schwab avoid profundities and give Romanticism a homely aspect, so Kerner presents a strange, characteristically Swabian mixture of melancholy and quaint humour, not without macabre overtones, in his *Kleksographie* (1859). His *Reiseschatten* (1811) is a synthesis of Eichendorff's *Wanderlust*, melancholy musing on the past, the mysteriousness of the *Nachtwachen des Bonaventura*, the frivolity of Jean Paul, travelogue, lyric, the musicality of Brentano, the symbolism of Hoffmann and the 'nature philosophy' of Schubert. In real life he affected a rough, realistic, humorous manner and lived to a ripe old age.

The generosity of the Swabian circle led to their taking into their midst Nikolaus Niembusch von Strehlenau, who adopted the name Nikolaus Lenau. He had led a vagrant existence, partly in America, and torn between the ties of home and the lure of travel, between passionate emotion and cool reason, between desire and self-denial, he could not make his peace with life. His treatment of women, who both attracted and repelled him, was impulsive and unpredictable. In America he was fascinated as much by the exoticism he found and by the idyllic existence of the settlers as by the possibilities of making money – a trait which recalls Stifter rather than the Romantics to whom he was otherwise deeply indebted. In religion and philosophy too he was a vacillating character, moving from his childhood faith to Stoicism, to Spinoza and Schelling, and to an eventual denial of Christianity; he then sought refuge in Kerner's mysticism and at times came near to total nihilism. The hero of his *Faust* (1835) commits suicide; in *Savonarola* (1837) he gropes his way back to Christian revelation; and in *Die Albigenser* (1842) he uses Hegel to ward off nihilistic doubts. His Faust is an autobiographical figure whose tragic end reflects the confusion and hopelessness of the man who has experienced all the facets of his Romantic heritage. Lenau is at his best in his lyrics, where, alongside sophisticated forms like the Persian ghazal, he has left many pieces on the theme of the gipsy, treating it with a melancholy which eventually turns to madness.

The late-Romantic form of the drama is the fate-tragedy of Zacharias Werner (1768–1823) and his followers. This too is a genre that draws nihilistic consequences from Romanticism but it does so in order to set a fashion, not to reflect, like Lenau, the life of the artist. Its roots lie not, as the writers of these dramas themselves thought, in Schiller's *Wallenstein* and *Die Braut von Messina*, but in Tieck's *Karl von Berneck* (1793–5), which contains the elements both of the *dies fatalis* and of the *instrumentum fatale* essential to the form. Other precursors of note are Arnim's *Halle und Jerusalem* and Kleist's *Käthchen von Heilbronn*.

But there is a mechanical quality about these fate-tragedies of Werner and his successors; their characters are puppets at the mercy of a pitiless fate. Werner himself, a native of Königsberg, was an ambivalent character born into an excessively pietistic family; after marrying three times he became a Catholic, and was even ordained a priest. His play on Luther, *Die Weihe der Kraft* (1807), he retracted after his conversion to Catholicism. Goethe allowed himself to be drawn into rivalry with him in the field of sonnet-writing, and, with the intention of instilling some classical discipline into him, stimulated him to write his first fate-drama, *Der 24. Februar* (1809). The hectic, horrific result – an attempt to dramatize the 'dark side' of life – is hardly to be laid at Goethe's door, but it is a model of what terrifying effects can be achieved in a one-act play with only three scenes and only three characters. The classical unities are observed, and within this framework the merciless exactment of atonement is exhibited, each moment in the action precisely calculated yet presented as proceeding from the unconscious, with fate itself being assigned an almost treacherous significance. This is no place for freedom and humanitarianism. The dispensable classical element in the whole genre is the motif of the family on which a curse has been laid; the late-Romantic element in it is its sentimentality. The mysterious link, in the subconscious or unconscious sphere, between human action and an unknown avenging power brings about the fusion of the Oedipus theme and the dark side of nature. Werner marks only the beginning of the success of this genre: it is carried to even more grotesque lengths by Ernst von Houwald and Adolf Müllner, and even Heine and Grillparzer start their careers in its shadow. It is perhaps the *locus classicus* of the decadence of Romanticism to the level of popular sensationalism, a parallel to the reduction of the art of narrative to the level of almanachs and novelettes.

The Power of Originality

There are certain figures in the literature of this period for whom the terms classic and Romantic are manifestly inadequate. Neither Hölderlin nor Jean Paul nor the late Goethe can be classified in this way, although all three are closely linked with these two styles and philosophies.

Historically these three figures span a wide period. Jean Paul, Herder's friend in the latter's old age, has his roots in eighteenth-century sentimentality, before Weimar classicism and before the appearance of the early Romantics; like Schiller, he underwent the experience of Kant. Hölderlin's progress started with Klopstock and Schiller, and his most important works coincide with the period of 'high' Romanticism, but they constitute a blend of Romantic and classical elements which is utterly original. Goethe was no longer the unmistakable classicist after the death of Schiller and Herder: *Pandora*, *Die Wahlverwandtschaften*, *Wilhelm Meisters Wanderjahre*, the *Westöstlicher Divan* and *Faust II* are unique combinations of classic and Romantic and defy categorization. Such is the justification for treating these three figures separately.

Jean Paul Friedrich Richter (1763–1825) hardly left his native Franconia throughout his life. Born of a poor country family, he started life as a teacher but eventually achieved such literary fame that he was given the title of *Rat* and granted a modest pension which enabled him to live out his lonely independence as a writer in Bayreuth.

There is a remarkable contrast between, on the one hand, the restricted nature of his material life and, on the other, the richness of his poetic imagination and breadth of his education and interests. He made his experience of the ludicrous, affected, deceitful and sometimes corrupt figures in petty German courts and towns as much the objects of his fantasy as his visions of Italy and the inner world which his highly personal interpretations of world literature opened up to him. His *Vorschule der Ästhetik* (1804) shows him as a clear-sighted thinker of profound insight, and his *Levana* (1807) as a humane teacher.

Stylistically Jean Paul made great demands on his readers, and his involved syntax and often exaggerated imagery placed his language completely beyond the range of the public in the age of realism, though his fascination continued to be felt down to the time of Keller and Raabe. It is not by accident that his imaginative virtues were 'rediscovered' in the age of symbolism by Stefan George and his circle.

His career opened with satirical works reminiscent, though not in style, of Lichtenberg – *Grönländische Prozesse* (1783); *Auswahl aus des Teufels Papieren* (1789). His first two novels were *Die unsichtbare Loge* (1793) and *Hesperus oder die 45 Hundsposttage* (1795), works of strained originality. There is a pietistic element in both of them, and this softens the satire, producing that particular whimsical humour of which he was to become a master. This is the typical Jean Paul dualism. The cynical, mocking intrigues of Mathieu in *Hesperus* are matched by the sentimentality of Emanuel's death-scene, in which the pious blind man dies in a welter of blossoms and melodies. In his three masterpieces – *Blumen-, Frucht- und Dornenstücke oder Ehestand, Tod und Hochzeit des Armenadvokaten Siebenkäs* (1796), *Titan* (1800–3), and *Die Flegeljahre* (1804) – the two extremes of cynicism and sentimentality are united by humour, which mitigates the conflict and creates an atmosphere of gentle charm. In *Siebenkäs* and *Flegeljahre* the dualism takes the form, characteristic of Jean Paul, of the theme of the double, later developed in particular by Hoffmann and Chamisso. Siebenkäs and his double, Leibgeber, ensure the union of what Jean Paul thought should by nature be united – Siebenkäs's intolerably dull Lenette and the school-inspector Stiefel, and Siebenkäs in his broad humanitarianism and his intellectual equal, Natalie. In the *Flegeljahre* Walt, 'the guileless fool', could not become happy, as Herr van der Kabel's heir would remain an inept, unworldly figure, unless his long-lost twin brother Vult, who had all the qualities lacking in Walt, offered himself as his guardian angel.

In *Hesperus* and in *Flegeljahre* the individual is portrayed as imperfect, fulfilling himself only in communion with others, and in *Titan* a similar situation is presented with the hidden similarity between Liane and Idoine, Albano's two lovers. Albano needs these two pietistic 'schöne Seelen' to balance his passionate nature, rather than the titanic Linda, whom Jean Paul significantly makes the victim of Roquairol (a character who resembles Tieck's Lovell), the friend who embodies the distorted side of Albano's nature. But Roquairol too is far superior to Tieck's Lovell as a tragic mirror-image of Albano. These novels, and above all *Titan*, show Jean Paul's ability to create for his lovers, men and women alike, circumstances appropriate to their inner natures. The opening of *Titan*, the description of the sun-drenched Isola Bella, is one of the great examples of imaginative objectivity in German literature, worthy to be compared with Goethe's pre-Italian Mignon-poem and the landscape of Hölderlin's *Hyperion*. Of equal splendour are the idealized descriptions of idyllic landscapes in *Siebenkäs* and *Titan* so admired by Stefan George.

A further formal characteristic of Jean Paul's novels is the art of the preamble, the interpolation, the independent postscript, which he learned from the English novelists of the eighteenth century. In 'Das Leben des vergnügten Schulmeisterlein Maria Wuz', from *Die Unsichtbare Loge*, and 'Des Luftschiffers Giannozzo Seebuch', from *Titan*, it takes the form of an independent idyll, the symbol of a pervasive humour. In the additions to *Quintus Fixlein* (1796), an idyllic story of a pastor's life, it appears as a naïve, dream-like vision. Such visions sometimes touch on the most profound subjects, as in 'Die Rede des toten Christus vom Weltgebäude herab, daß kein Gott sei', from *Siebenkäs*, and 'Die Vernichtung', from *Dr. Katzenbergers Badereise* (1809). Where, as in these two last cases, the humorous element predominates, these visions of ultimate truth restore the significance of the metaphysical side of life.

This tendency of Jean Paul's towards an episodic style of construction is not a reflection of deficient formal sense but rather of an urge to universality through the dialectical juxtaposition of opposites. The quiet, assured, idyllic quality of characters like Wuz, Rector Fälbel, Quintus Fixlein and Schmelzle is offset by the mysterious superiority of figures like Leibgeber in *Siebenkäs*, Schoppe in *Titan* and Vult in *Flegeljahre*, whose quaintness acquires a broad significance which does not involve the supernatural world of Hoffmann. This is the realm of fantasy in which are absorbed all the oppositions and paradoxes mentioned above, the realm to which Albano and Liane, Natalie, Viktor and Klotilde, Don Gaspard and Roquairol belong. The dualism is also present in the theme of the journey (Rektor Fälbel, Doktor Katzenberger), which throws light on the home that they leave as well as on the distant parts that they seek (Giannozzo, dream motifs). A stylistic equivalent to this approach is the syntactical innovation which Jean Paul called the *Streckvers* – a long-drawn-out sentence which rises to a climax and then ends abruptly in a short, direct utterance.

Like Jean Paul, Friedrich Hölderlin (1770–1843) also developed his own expansive style which, in spite of its debts to Hölty, Klopstock and above all Schiller (in his middle period), soon establishes its originality. The themes of his early odes are love, freedom, friendship, fate, art, beauty and a vision of Greece that owes something to Schiller and Rousseau, and the tone of these poems – again not yet entirely his own – is one of youthful enthusiasm, symbolized most perfectly in the Platonic 'Gott der Jugend'.

At this time Hölderlin, who, like Schelling, Schiller and Hegel, was born in Swabia and a student at the Tübinger Stift, was a private teacher, among others to the household of Frau von Kalb, and one of Schiller's supporters in his *Thalia* in Jena – where he also met Fichte. In 1796 he became tutor to the family of the Frankfurt banker Gontard, whose sensitive, intellectual wife Susette he took as the model for the figure of

Diotima who appears in his novel *Hyperion* and in so many of his poems, which, still symmetrical in form and in rhyme, now acquire a new power and emotional strength, a kind of Apolline transfiguration leading to the proper fusion of the present with the unity of childhood. It was a love like Goethe's – physical as passion, Platonic as ideal. But Hölderlin could not overcome this love as Goethe overcame his attachment to Frau von Stein, who also meant for him the unity of past and present. Hölderlin's own grand poetic style grew from this overwhelming experience, which, after a bare decade of activity of unparalleled intensity, drove him to madness.

After Gontard's jealousy had driven him away from Frankfurt, he found refuge with his friend Sinclair in Homburg and continued work on *Hyperion* – an early part of which had been published in the *Thalia* in 1793. He now planned the drama *Empedokles*. But above all he evolved his own new poetic style in elegy and ode, testifying no less than the elegies of Goethe and Schiller to the possibility of a German classicism and achieving, by the identification of the child in mythology with the subjectivity of the present, a new kind of mythology such as that demanded by Schelling: the identity of the self with the gods and heroes of antiquity.

Hyperion oder der Eremit in Griechenland (1797–9), like *Werther*, to which it is also related in its attitude to nature, is an epistolary novel. Hölderlin's goal is that of Novalis: the oneness of the world as experienced by a child, and our insatiable yearning to return to it. He attains it, not by mysterious signs and symbols, like Novalis, but in moments of ecstasy, like Goethe in *Werther*. The mythology of youth as found in his poems finds its way into his novel in the form of narrative reality, with a philosophical import akin to that of Schiller's *Philosophische Briefe*. The work is written in rhythmic prose, a feature it retains throughout its various stages of composition; the letters all consist of confessions by the youth called Apollo to his friend Bellarmin, except for the exchange of missives between him and Diotima. As a form it is not classical, nor is it Romantic in the sense of *Godwi*. It strikes a balance between closeness and remoteness, a daring mode of expressing a fate which would have consumed the Romantics. The spirit of the work is the spirit of animate nature presented in the myth, nature conceived of as one's native land. Hyperion is the luckless pioneer fighting for the freedom of the new Greece, and has sacrificed his beloved in the name of fate; as she restores to his mind the power to overcome his suffering, so in the midst of a lament for the Germans to whom the lonely lover and freedom-fighter now turns, the last word to be heard is one of reconciliation addressed to youth and its perennial beauty.

The drama *Empedokles* is similarly sustained in all its stages by the motif of man's inner relationship to nature. The subject of the Greek philosopher who throws himself into the crater of Etna and thus returns to nature also occurs in *Hyperion* and in one of Hölderlin's mature odes. Like Hyperion,

Empedocles was a subject that Hölderlin conceived in philosophical terms, making him, already in the first Frankfurt plan, 'an enemy of onesided existence and thus dissatisfied with the beauty of his surroundings, a sufferer, a vagrant'. And as with Hyperion, it is a question of the urge towards the absolute and the universal: Empedokles parts from society and from every form of restricted existence, finding ultimate fulfilment in suicide and the consequent reunion with nature, which was also the goal after which Hyperion strove.

Hölderlin's greatest achievement, however, lies in his poems, the finest of which were written at the time of *Hyperion* and *Empedokles* and the five years or so that followed. Virtually unknown throughout the nineteenth century, Hölderlin was 'rediscovered', like Jean Paul, by Stefan George and his circle, and the significance of his later work, from his years of madness, was revealed by Norbert von Hellingrath.

The conception of *poeta vates* – the poet as visionary – now reasserts itself. In the odes and elegies of his maturity he repeatedly returns, as in *Hyperion*, to the theme of youth, combined with the themes of past and present, classical and German. To be sure, Klopstock had already done this, but not with that timeless relevance, that passionate blend of nature and a sense of historical need which characterizes Hölderlin's odes. To realize his originality one need only consider how far the mythical image of the Alps developed from Haller through Goethe's 'Gesang der Geister über den Wassern' to Hölderlin's elegy 'Heimkunft'; how the image of the great river developed from Goethe's 'Mahomet' to Hölderlin's poems on the Main, the Neckar, the Rhein and 'Der gefesselte Strom'; and how he celebrated, as in a myth, the glories of German cities such as Heidelberg and Stuttgart. His vision of poetic vocation, too, is to be compared with that of Klopstock. And all this is expressed in a verse-form based on Greek rhythms, on a stylized classical syntax and morphology, and on a remarkably intense yet wide-ranging vocabulary such as has only been possible since the time of Goethe, Schiller and the Romantics.

Above all his poetry represents a passionate effort to reconcile antiquity and Christianity ('Patmos'; 'Brot und Wein'; 'Der Einzige'; 'Friedensfeier'). In his late works ultimate maturity becomes the symbol of uncontrollable, ecstatic desire for self-expression which is no longer in control of its reason and lies beyond the frontier of consciousness. It is a frontier which Goethe never crossed – a frontier, indeed, which could only be crossed by a Graecophile to whom the Romantic philosophy of nature had become like nature itself.

In the first decade of the nineteenth century Goethe lost the three friends without whom his development would have been very different: Herder, Schiller, and finally Wieland. At sixty he was still eager for knowledge and experience, but his journeyings became more restricted and he did not travel again beyond the area bounded by Bohemia in the east and the Rhine and the Main in the west. Emotionally he was as susceptible as ever, and his affection for Minna Herzlieb, Marianne von Willemer and Ulrike von Levetzow (to whom he even proposed) shows how young at heart he still was. Even the death of Christiane and, finally, of Karl August, did not dampen his literary activity.

At the end of the historical period of Weimar classicism stands Goethe's essay on Winckelmann (1805), a reformulation of the classical aesthetic programme in which every word is pondered, but which also bears traces of Goethe's scientific methods. The Winckelmann he presents is both individual and type, and his formal, precise language is the counterpart of his subject; it is a work that would lead one to believe that the rest of Goethe's career would consist in the refinement of subjects and ideas already expressed.

But a few years later we encounter the drama *Pandora* (1808) and the novel *Die Wahlverwandtschaften* (1809), both works which testify to a continued receptivity to new stimuli.

In *Pandora*, based on a Greek mythological subject but using both classical and Romantic techniques, Prometheus, who had earlier been for Goethe the symbol of revolt and of the self-assertion of the genius, becomes the embodiment of classical masculinity and vigour. In opposition to him stands his brother Epimetheus, symbol of Romantic existence, with his mind on past loves rather than on present realities. Neither is completely right: the future rests on a synthesis of the two extremes, and civilization will emerge from the marriage of the passionate son of Prometheus to the gentle, self-sacrificing daughter of Epimetheus. Thus the 'masculinity' of Winckelmann, here embodied in Prometheus, is no longer *the* ideal but only one side of it, and the rich, progressive nature of the language, with its experimental rhythms and use of vocabulary, is the practical equivalent of the universality of the mythological subject-matter.

What separates *Die Wahlverwandtschaften* from Romanticism is almost solely its form, for its theme is that of passion which breaks through convention and ends in tragedy. As with the later Romantics, consciousness is superseded, but there is no attempt to impose a mythological framework, and the title itself, taken from the natural sciences, defines the law by which, in human affairs as in nature, relationships are controlled. All this is related in a detached, objective tone, with a logical progression of events and simple, direct syntax and vocabulary.

The loosening of form apparent in *Wilhelm Meisters Wanderjahre* is less a concession to the form of the Romantic novel than a manifestation of a kind of conglomerate style that becomes increasingly evident in Goethe's later life. It is seen in the *Italienische Reise*, in parts of *Dichtung und Wahrheit* and in his collected scientific works of the first two decades of the century.

As Goethe, during these years, saw himself increasingly in a historical context, so he began to assemble records of his earlier days. The *Wander-jahre* does not, strictly speaking, form part of this activity but it is related to it in its formal arrangement.

The subtitle of the *Wanderjahre* is *Die Entsagenden*, and this already shows its contrast to *Die Wahlverwandtschaften*; it also hints at the book's pedagogical nature, and with it the limitations of Goethe's narrative art in his old age. The letters, diaries and meditations in the novel, full of the wisdom of old age, serve this pedagogical end, and are not necessary to the narrative. As a novel it may convince by virtue of its abundant reflections and meditations on the problems of life but it has not the gripping power of *Die Wahlverwandtschaften*; its essence is perhaps to be found rather in its role as a repository of its author's mature attitudes than as a continuation of the *Lehrjahre*.

A similar synthesis of classical and Romantic to that in *Pandora* and *Die Wahlverwandtschaften* is found Goethe's lyric poetry from the *Westöstlicher Divan* to the *Trilogie der Leidenschaft* (in particular the 'Marienbader Elegie'). The coupling of East and West in the *Divan* reflects the late Goethe's polarity of self and world, subject and object in the form of the interplay of two civilizations. Traditional motifs such as that of the omniscient bird as the messenger of love mingle with the personal expression of his passion for Marianne von Willemer in the figure of Suleika; all is pregnant with meaning; the unique becomes the recurrent. The motif of 'Selige Sehnsucht' is Prometheus and Epimetheus in one – the moth is burned in the flame as a symbol of the destiny of all living creatures to sacrifice themselves to the inner process of life which gives human fate its transcendental quality. In its different way the lyrical exchange between Suleika and Hatem also reflects the removal of barriers, and the tone of Goethe's early poems joins with a bold new technique in vocabulary, rhyme and rhythm – a technique at its most striking in those moments when passion fills the ageing poet's heart.

A peculiarity of the style of Goethe's late lyrics is the use of a type of pluralization (e.g. '*an* Etna') which originates in science and philosophy and characterizes his philosophical poetry from about 1800 onwards. It is present, for example, in the poems written at the time of his Romantic interest in Schelling, such as 'Weltseele' and 'Dauer im Wechsel', while in the later 'Urworte, Orphisch' (1817) he pursues the 'dark side' of antiquity itself with which the early Romantics had concerned themselves. Goethe's style in such poems is both far more agitated and far less emotional than that of Schiller's philosophical poetry.

All these tendencies combine in one universal synthesis in *Faust II*, finished shortly before his death and published the year after. *Faust II*, notwithstanding the Helena motif, shows more Romantic than classical traits. Formally it shows the same love of experiment as *Pandora*: *Knittel-vers* and blank verse stand alongside the iambic trimeter of the Helena act, in which Phorkyas and the Chorus use *inter alia* trochaic octameter. Such combinations of rhythm are Romantic, as are the aria- and recitative-like parts and the baroque strophes and rhyme-schemes in Act V. Again this is far removed from Schiller's classical dramas, or even Goethe's own.

The action, too, moves restlessly through time and place, fusing antiquity, German Gothic and Renaissance. The classical sphere itself extends from the chthonian, Orphic world of the 'klassische Walpurgis-nacht' to the idyllic, and the lemurs who bear Faust's body to its grave take us into the Christian world of the Theban Desert. Faust's own path leads from the 'Mothers' to the realm of the blessed, as on earth he starts as a medieval sorcerer and becomes through his experience of the universe a philanthropist in the modern style. Not only is such an attitude to the drama – indeed, to reality itself – un-classical; it is virtually surrealistic, and the inner reality of dream and imagination is barely separable from the empirical reality of everyday life.

Of classical elements there remain the symbolic character of the action and the question of *Humanität* and its role in the world in the face of the individual's independence and loneliness. This emerges in the (formally very un-classical) chorus of angels with their famous words of salvation which both seal and generalize Faust's fate, and in the final *Chorus mysticus*. The wager and the pact thus find their logical and allegorical fulfilment. At the same time the *Faust* drama, using the world as its stage and inter-spersed with elements of opera, represents Goethe's progress through the experience of Romanticism. This, his last word, shows that by blending the human seriousness of classicism with the playfulness of Romantic irony he had transcended the limits of individual styles. It is this Goethean concept of freedom and universality that is represented, in their different ways, by Jean Paul's synthetic reality and Hölderlin's attempt to reconcile Dionysos and Christ. And this concept is not merely representative of Goethe's own maturity but embodies a profound principle of style which lies beyond classification in terms of classical and Romantic.

Realism
(1830 – 1885)

Introductory

The period with which we are here concerned is that between 1830 and 1885. Even if we admit certain overlaps, allow Romanticism to stretch forward to the mid-nineteenth century and deal with the precursors of the following epoch only *en passant*, we are not left with a body of literature that can by any stretch of the imagination be called uniform. There is no question of a common outlook or common religious assumptions, let alone any obvious uniformity of style. All one can observe is an underlying feeling throughout Europe at this time that a new age had come, or was about to come, which could not be dealt with in terms of traditional morality or hitherto accepted concepts of human society and political institutions.

Whereas in the past histories of literature have tended to isolate these individual tendencies, seeing Romanticism as merging into the Restoration, and the Restoration into *Biedermeier*, the first stage being basically political and the second being governed by considerations of social fashion and style of living, the present chapter seeks to see the period as a unit within which various contrasting and conflicting tendencies are contained. The mood of this new age is responsible for most of the new subjects and motifs, and also influences the nature, form and style of the genres taken over from earlier ages. The period of realism was in any case less rich in new poetic forms than the age of Romanticism, for interest lay in different directions from those pursued by a free-ranging poetic imagination.

Scientific progress had a considerable influence on the situation. The invention of the steam engine (1769) revolutionized first sea travel and then, through locomotives and the spread of railroads, land communications, encouraging a practical internationalism very different from the often mystical nationalism of the Romantics. At the same time the social structure began to crumble: the old feudal aristocracy was challenged by the entrepreneur from within its own ranks and from the middle class, and the machine was seen to be capable of doing more cheaply and often more efficiently the work of the individual craftsman. This, together with the growth in the population, flooded the market with cheap labour; wages were often kept at a bare subsistence level, and factory acts were only beginning to be talked about. The result of industrialization was not a general rise in living standards but a change in class-structure and an increase in class-tensions.

The eighteenth century had already uncovered the everyday realities of literature, but now, derived from Pestalozzi's view that education should be based on individual capacity and nature, not on a social norm, there arose a concern for the common man, for the physically and mentally handicapped and for the victims of social arbitrariness. Where the Romantic had put the miseries of common life out of his mind, the new generation turned to the problems of the common man and intervened on behalf of the poor, the sick and the criminal to a far greater extent than had the *Sturm und Drang*. The statements on human rights made in the eighteenth century and inscribed on the banner of the French Revolution were now the points of departure and determined willy-nilly the course followed by literature.

One result of technological progress was the spread of, and desire for, news. A mass of newspapers and journals catered for this need, expressing, in so far as they were not restricted, or even suppressed, by the police, the new political and social tensions. Many young talents used this means to make themselves heard; writing became a profession rather than a vocation, and a class of publicists and journalists arose who depended for their livelihood on the extent of their output. The greater the pressure to produce, the greater the threat to quality, and external compulsion took the place of inner drive. Many writers, like Gotthelf, were regarded by their editors and publishers as milch cows and had little time to devote themselves to their own plans or to develop their talents in their own time. And because, unlike today, newspapers, periodicals and books formed the only medium of mass communication, the need for them had an absolute, unqualified character about it. The supply of gifted writers was not equal to the demand, and the feeling that the few existing talents were rapidly vanishing was caught by Karl Immermann in the title of one of his most important novels – *Die Epigonen* (1836). In reality the situation was due simply to an inflated demand for works of literature. Added to this is the fact that the rise of science and engineering, mirrored *inter alia* in the establishment of numerous technical colleges, attracted many away from creative activity in other spheres.

The gulf which the Romantics had opened up by turning away from material reality was not bridged by the new generation; indeed, the urge to freedom and emancipation, felt at all levels of awareness and in all classes of society, wrenched men out of any feeling they had of security within the powerful Christian tradition and cast them into doubt and uncertainty, in so far as they had not, like Goethe, found fulfilment in solving practical problems or adopted some new ideology in place of religion. This uncertainty induced a vacillation between an almost blind confidence in progress and a despairing pessimism about human life, and even the best and boldest spirits of this age reveal the extent of the dichotomy.

After the fall of Napoleon came what Gottfried Keller called the *Papierblumenfrühling* ('paper-flower spring') of the Restoration period. Numerous petty princes strove to re-establish the old feudalistic autocracy, but in spite of censorship the social and political ferment continued. The revolutionary period had left only a few marks but a wave of influence now arrived from England, where the forces of liberal democracy had made great progress and where the first organized assemblies of the workers had taken place. Many, such as Heine and Georg Büchner, escaped from the police by fleeing the country; others, Gutzkow and Reuter among them, were given long terms of imprisonment and acquired the status of martyrs, which only increased the tension.

There was only one German-speaking state which had retained some of the rights gained in the revolution and was now moving forward on new democratic lines – Switzerland, where, following the stabilization of the constitutional relationship between rural and urban communities, and in the wake of the introduction of compulsory school education at the beginning of the 1830s, there arose the attitude that literature should provide not only entertainment and moral betterment but also instruction and culture. This was a philosophy stated by Pestalozzi and followed by Jeremias Gotthelf (1797–1854). The *Volksbuch* acquired a new meaning in this context, while certain of the political refugees who found refuge in Switzerland were also active in the fields of journalism and education, to the country's general benefit.

Young Germany

Those writers who stayed in Germany or, under the Metternich regime, in Austria, transferred their attention from politics to aesthetics. In Germany they gave themselves the name 'Young Germany', in opposition to the 'old' Germany of Romanticism. The name itself was coined by Ludolf Wienbarg (1802–72) in a set of lectures he gave in Kiel in 1834 under the title *Ästhetische Feldzüge*.

The Young Germans were less a new school with a definite programme than a group of malcontents who could not accept the fashionable cult of Romanticism and who reacted against an exaggerated Goethe-cult. They also attacked the prevailing mood of jingoism, but the movement lacked poetic ability and, partly as a result of the political pressure to which it was subjected, became lost in generalizations and abstractions. The political *engagement* they demanded was nipped in the bud, and even trivial offences against the rules of 'approved' literature were severely punished.

Apart from the *Ästhetische Feldzüge* Wienbarg did not contribute much to the movement. Karl Gutzkow (1811–78), born in Berlin, was one of the new breed of professional writers. In 1831 he edited a *Forum der Journalliteratur*, but four years later he achieved the status of a martyr when, as a result of his novel *Wally die Zweiflerin*, he was sentenced to three months' imprisonment in the state – Baden – in which it was published. In this work Gutzkow stands as a pioneer in the struggle for the emancipation of women, though today it seems a harmless book, and Menzel's criticism of it – the basis of the charge – remarkably petty.

Far more radical is *Der Hessische Landbote* by Georg Büchner (1813–37), son of a Darmstadt doctor. After studying medicine in Strasbourg, Büchner became involved in the students' movement and attacked the ruling classes with unparalleled fury under the slogan 'Peace to the cottages! War to the palaces!' Though not an actual member of Young Germany, he ranged himself alongside them. On the one hand he was, as a student of medicine, committed to the spirit of progress; on the other he was a deeply convinced Christian. In his short story *Lenz* he wrote: 'The poets who are said to express reality have no idea what reality is, but at least they are to be preferred to those who seek to transfigure reality . . . God made the world as He intended to, and we are hardly likely to manufacture anything better. All we should try to do is to imitate Him a little . . . let us immerse ourselves in the smallest of things and seek to convey its nature by allusions and by reactions.' Taking the story of the mad poet Lenz, Büchner describes how the poet's sufferings symbolize the suffering of the whole of humanity, and himself fulfils the demand he had made for a new objectivity.

Narrative Prose

Of the traditional literary genres that of prose fiction, at all levels, grew by far the fastest at this time. This is due partly to the growth of the reading public and partly to the general objectivization of literature. To cover a broader spectrum of human and social experience one simply needs more space, and multi-volume novels now became popular. Gutzkow's *Ritter vom Geiste*, for instance, ran to nine volumes.

The historical novel had flourished under the Romantics, but now it took on a new aspect by virtue of its closer adherence to historical facts. The history of the world, and above all the history of the German past, was converted into prose- and even verse-romances. Felix Dahn (1834–1912), a professor of law at various universities, achieved great success with his four-volume *Ein Kampf um Rom* (1876) and his novels on German history, and Gustav Freytag (1816–95) wrote a whole cycle of novels, *Die Ahnen*, in the wave of enthusiasm that followed the Franco-Prussian War.

Historiography too received a new impetus. This is the age of Leopold von Ranke (1795–1886), with his *Deutsche Geschichte im Zeitalter der Reformation*, and the powerful Theodor Mommsen, whose, *Römische Geschichte* (1857), though somewhat onesided in its concentration on the question of power politics, is written in a gripping style. Jacob Burck-hardt (1818–97) had a decisive influence on our view of the Renaissance with his *Die Kultur der Renaissance in Italien*; his *Griechische Kulturgeschichte* and *Die Zeit Konstantins des Großen* gave a new impetus to research into the history of civilizations, while his *Weltgeschichtliche Betrachtungen* sought to analyse and overcome a contemporary nationalistic tendency to think in terms of nothing but power politics. J. J. Bachofen (1815–87), also, like Burckhardt, from Basle, achieves a poetic beauty in parts of his *Mutter-recht und Urreligion* and other works on the history of civilization, and his *Griechische Reise*, the fruit of an adventurous journey through that new-born country, is one of the most attractive pieces of travel literature in German.

Whereas most historical novels, especially those written in the shadow of the events of 1871 and after, were short-lived – with a few exceptions discussed below – the social novel broke new ground, dealing not only with new social classes and new social situations but also with the spiritual life of its characters. This psychological interest, developed in the Age of Sensibility and refined by the Romantics, took the particular form in the Age of Realism of a concern with the fate of the individual and was fed by an increasing knowledge of the human personality, especially that of the physically and mentally sick and the criminal. It was appropriate that the new realism should turn to biography and give the life-story of one man from his birth to his death. Goethe's *Wilhelm Meister* novels had paved the way, while Mörike's *Maler Nolten* (1832), Romantic in original plan and still Romantic in style and atmosphere, contains many personal details which, like much of Mörike's later work, make for an air of pro-found realism in descriptions of emotions and psychological situations. This is even true of the Peregrina lyrics in the novel.

The year of Büchner's fragment *Lenz* (1836) marks the emergence as man of letters of the Swiss pastor Jeremias Gotthelf (pseudonym of Albert Bitzius, 1797–1854), who up to that time had been a contentious, politic-ally active cleric unconcerned with the new movements in literature. In *Der Bauernspiegel* he attacks the social evil of prejudice, drawing on his own experience of paupers' establishments, and shows, through the character of the boy Jeremias, how poverty leads to crime and how he is eventually saved from final degradation as a mercenary in a foreign army; yet on his return home, a changed man, he can find no job. It is Gotthelf's aim to open people's eyes to reality and to make the peasants in the canton of Berne, where his parish lay, aware of the running sores on the body of their own society. But unlike Büchner, Gotthelf, who had himself helped to establish the democratic principle of the equality of all citizens, could not make a backward government responsible for such prejudices: man himself is the enemy, with his indifference, his selfishness and his covetousness.

The tone of *Der Bauernspiegel* is provocative and aggressive, but it was followed by a series of works, such as *Uli der Knecht* (1841) and *Geld und Geist* (1842), in which Gotthelf gives his promised treatment of the 'sunny side' of peasant life. It would be wrong, however, to regard him as nothing but a writer of peasant stories, for these works, especially *Anne Bäbi Jowäger* and *Die Käserei in der Vehfreude*, have a universal human interest. Others of his novels, like *Jakobs Wanderungen* and *Der Herr Esau*, are set, in whole or in part, in urban or industrial milieux. His concern is with man and with human life, part of which involves God's self-revelation to, and presence in, the world, and when one talks of his realism, or even his naturalism, one must include this Christian dimension.

Gotthelf is also far removed from the humanitarian ideals of the classical age. In *Die schwarze Spinne*, as in the figure of the peasant of Dorngrüt in *Geld und Geist* and that of the hero of *Harzer Hans*, the demonic side of human nature breaks through in all its savagery; on the other hand characters like Änneli in *Geld und Geist* and Meyelis and Doctor Ruedi in *Anne Bäbi Jowäger* represent the Christian life as opposed to that of crude, carnal man. Only rarely, however, does Gotthelf fall into a black-and-white view of life: his characters represent a wide range of human personalities, strong and weak, courageous and cowardly, rich and poor, intelligent and stupid, good and evil; there are also those whose errors lead them to the truth, and those whose good intentions lead them into error, addiction and self-centredness.

Gotthelf restricted himself to narrative fiction: there are a few lyrical moments in his stories, but he wrote no poetry and scarcely considered writing a drama, though he was acquainted with the works of Schiller and Shakespeare. The stories of his maturity, particularly the shorter ones, show great technical skill in construction; their language is lively and full of vivid images, a blend of dialect forms and standard constructions, reflecting his desire to fuse the elevated world of the Bible with the real world of the canton of Berne, and to make the many Bernese dialects serve the purposes of art.

Like others of his age, he also felt the commercial pressures on the writer: *Anne Bäbi Jowäger*, the story of a quack, owes its existence to a publisher's commission, as do others of his twelve or so long novels and over fifty separate works written over a span of eighteen years, and in the last years of his life he was swamped with requests for novels, short stories and anecdotes for all manner of publications. In later life he also became increasingly concerned with politics, often to the detriment of the broad, flowing style of his novels. Where he had once been an enthusiastic supporter of the freedom movement, he now realized the dangers of anti-religious materialism, and thundered like a prophet against the radicalism which was becoming ever more dominant in the politics of his country. The novels *Herr Esau* and *Zeitgeist und Berner Geist* show this most clearly. Yet he was also still capable of works of great balance and beauty, such as the outspoken village story *Die Käserei in der Vehfreude* and the *Novellen Der Besenbinder von Rychiswil* and *Die Frau Pfarrerin*, in which the foibles of human conduct are presented with a delicate irony and a confident humour.

In his early days as a pastor, Gotthelf had railed against the current evils of poverty, neglect and official complacency, and his tract *Die Armennot* (1839) is the sole work to deal with the problem of the education of the poor. From struggles against injustices such as this there emerged the great writer who sought to understand man in his most fundamental aspects.

How greatly the problem of poverty and hardship among the working classes exercised the minds of the time – among them minds very different from Gotthelf's – is seen from the writings of Bettina von Arnim (1780–1859), sister of Clemens Brentano. Though born into Romantic circles and attracted above all to the classical Goethe, she allowed her emotional nature to involve her in the miseries of the lower classes after her husband's death in 1842, and in *Dies Buch gehört dem König* (1842), dedicated to the King of Prussia, in *Des Königsbuchs 2. Band* (1852) and above all in her large but unfinished *Armenbuch*, she sought to reveal the extent of this poverty. She used modern documentary methods, sending questionnaires to personalities all over Germany and building up a series of case-histories of poverty. In her haste, and with her not over-developed sense of modesty, she achieved little success, but her efforts show the extent to which the problems of the industrial age claimed attention. And four years after her unfinished *Armenbuch* appeared the work which was so profoundly to influence the political and intellectual life of Germany and the whole of Europe in the following generation – Marx and Engels's *Kommunistisches Manifest* (1848).

Literary history generally acknowledges not Gotthelf but Willibald Alexis (pseudonym for Georg Wilhelm Heinrich Häring (1798–1871)), born in Breslau, as the founder of the realistic manner. In 1822 he published translations of Scott, a writer who also influenced Gotthelf and an important force in the general impact of English literature on Germany in the nineteenth century. After these translations he wrote a drama on the theme of *Ännchen von Tharau*, and from the end of the 1820s until the onset of his insanity twenty-five years later a large number of stories and *Novellen* came from his pen, the best-known being *Der falsche Woldemar, Die Hosen des Herrn Bredow, Der Wärwolf* and *Ruhe ist die erste Bürgerpflicht*.

Like Gotthelf, Alexis strove for truth and directness of expression and, like Annette von Droste-Hülshoff, plays a role in the development of the modern thriller in that he portrayed criminal types equally successfully as aristocrats. He even founded a journal for such literature called *Der neue Pitaval*, which Hebbel read avidly in his youth. His scenic descriptions, in particular of the Mark Brandenburg, have a precise, realistic quality, and in his somewhat romantic historical tales, strongly influenced by Scott, he appears in the role of commentator on the history of Brandenburg; he was no revolutionary, but his liberal tendencies did on one occasion earn him a reprimand from the bigoted Friedrich Wilhelm. He lacks, however, the religious quality found in Gotthelf, and his activity as a speculative editor tended to divert his attention from the most serious concerns. Also part of the contemporary commercialization of literature were his travelogues, *Herbstreise durch Skandinavien* (1828) and *Winterbilder* (1833), in the line of Heine's *Reisebilder*.

Charles Sealsfield (as Karl Anton Postl called himself after fleeing from a monastery in Prague) was also a travel writer. His escape into the world – contrasted with the many escapes into the Catholic Church in the Romantic era – shows him as a man of his time. His flight took him first to Switzerland, then to the United States and Mexico; forced to give up the life of a farmer because of the bankruptcy of his employers, he finally took up writing, expressing the urge to travel that many felt in Europe at this time. After making his living as a reporter and editor, he finally retired in 1860 near Solothurn.

His books were prevented from becoming part of the romanticizing of distant lands – familiar since the baroque age – by his close personal knowledge of America, the keenness of his perception and his sense of ethnographical characteristics, and his novels which show the influence of Fenimore Cooper – the best-known is *Das Kajütenbuch* (1841) – were preceded by descriptive scientific studies such as *Die Vereinigten Staaten von Amerika nach ihren politischen, religiösen und gesellschaftlichen Verhältnissen betrachtet* (1828) and the *Transatlantische Reiseskizzen*, the former appearing under the further pseudonym C. Sidon. Such works encouraged many emigrants to make the journey westwards and decisively influenced the German image of America. A similar work on his native country, *Austria as it is*, published in London in 1828, was suppressed in Austria itself by

Metternich. A number of his works, indeed, were first published in English, and here and there he writes an attractive blend of English and German. He was one of the first to concern themselves with settlement problems in the United States and with the settlers' injustices to the Indians, and took as the motto of his novel *Tokeah or The White Rose* (German translation, Zürich, 1833) the words of Thomas Jefferson: 'I tremble for my people when I think of the injustices they have inflicted on the native inhabitants.' In his attitude to such matters, as in his descriptions of the American countryside and the life of the settlers, he is a true realist.

Apart from his political activity Karl Gutzkow (1811–78) became, both as a novelist and as a critic, one of the most influential, most successful and most feared writers in Germany at this time. He was a man of the intellect, quick of mind and with a remarkable memory but lacking any sense of poetry and emotional commitment. To disguise his lack of inner drive and his inability to conceive a work as an organic whole, he evolved for his novels – the nine-volume *Ritter von Geiste* (1850–2) and the anti-Catholic novel *Der Zauberer von Rom* (1858–61) – a 'technique of juxtaposition' in place of a logical unfurling of thoughts and actions. This intellectual structure was the only reason for the praise he received, partly out of fear of his power – for four years he was secretary of the Deutsche Schiller-stiftung – from people who ought to have known better.

Contemporary readers were attracted by the polemical tone and often vicious satire with which he attacked his real and imaginary enemies. All manner of public figures, thinly disguised, found their way into his works, and he was anxious to pander to the public taste for over-simplified and superficial presentation of such characters. Today his books leave an uninspired and boring impression, particularly as their style, partly from lack of skill, partly out of spite against what others considered good, became increasingly more careless. It is remarkable that this man, whose thirst for power, despite the liberal sentiments he professed, was almost pathological, could have reached a position of such importance in an age which had so firm a sense of values, for he lacked the intellectual substance and the power of reflectivity necessary for a true realistic style. Perpetually engaged in feuds, he was his own worst enemy, and the moods of depression which led him more than once in later life to attempt suicide reflect his awareness of the unresolved dichotomy within him. In short, he is a figure who embodies more completely than any other the weaknesses and the unhappy tendencies of his age, and were it not for his true, often powerful revelation of such weaknesses – as the novel *Die Söhne Pesta-lozzis* (1870) reveals the perversions of the Prussian educational system – he would have no place in literary history. The fact that his attraction to France – he particularly admired and emulated Eugène Sue – caused him to withdraw from, and feel embittered by, the post-1870 victory celebrations, shows him in a somewhat more sympathetic light. His passionate early supporter Heinrich Laube (1806–84), a native of Silesia, whose dramas were more successful and who, like Gutzkow, wrote numerous *Novellen* in the 1830s and 1840s, was politically more adaptable, but his nationalistic tendencies do not help to make him a sympathetic character.

The decree of the Frankfurt Bundestag forbidding publication of the works of the Young Germans threatened at once both their intellectual and their material life; it also aroused feelings of hatred and fear among many who had not in fact acted provocatively and led others to an attitude of fawning obeisance. Indeed, a situation arose which, whether the threat was real or imagined, created what became known in the Third Reich as 'inner' and 'outer' emigration, and those who lived in either of these emigrations felt their roots severed. It is no cause for surprise that Switzerland, where force and oppression were first done away with, should have produced in the persons of Gotthelf and Keller such significant independent minds.

Very little was changed by the events of 1848, and as the strength of Bismarck's Prussia grew, so there arose the confusion, present also in the minds of most men of letters, of freedom with aggressive nationalism. Prussian political success produced a literature dominated by the rhetorical cult of heroism, militarism, and patriotic, anti-French loyalty, which induced in the well-to-do middle classes a sense of complacency which retarded rather than encouraged their intellectual development. Moreover the creation of the Second Reich did not resolve social tensions but merely disguised them, and the same was true of the Catholic monarchy in Austria.

Fritz Reuter (1810–74), son of a Mecklenburg peasant family, almost became a victim of these circumstances. He had been a student in Jena at the time of the *Burschenschaften* movement, and when he returned in all innocence to the land of the 'most just' King Friedrich Wilhelm, he was arrested, tortured and condemned to death for plotting treason, a sentence subsequently commuted to thirty years' imprisonment; for seven years he was sent from one prison to another, and was only released to the Mecklenburg authorities after Friedrich Wilhelm's death. For almost fifteen years after his release he tried in vain to rehabilitate himself; he became a vagrant alcoholic and was saved from utter ruin by his native peasant humour and by his wife Luise Kuntze, whom he married in 1853.

It was almost by accident and without ambition, rather like Gotthelf, that Reuter began to write, in his native Mecklenburg dialect, his anecdotes and poems *Läuschen un Rimels* (1853), but their unexpected success spurred him to further activity. He wrote humorous memoirs and travel-stories and finally turned to the novel, using it to describe, through powerful characters and situations, the events of his own experience. Despite the coarseness of his work and its persistent use of dialect, it became widely read and admired for its power and its authenticity, as well as for the humour and the realism with which he combined historical and personal events in his novels. *Ut de Franzosentid* (1859) was followed by *Ut mine Festungstid* (1862), in which he writes of the injustice and suffering of his imprisonment, and finally by *Ut mine Stromtid* (1863–4), which is particularly rich in psychological studies of true folk-characters.

Fritz Reuter was big enough not to blame his suffering entirely on reactionary politics, for human characteristics, of whatever kind, were for him distributed without discrimination over the whole of humankind. His true power lies in the local idiom and dialect of his stories, and it is only the person brought up in this idiom who can understand him to the full. At the same time the works of Reuter and Gotthelf have considerably enriched the range and subtlety of the German language in general, and exemplify the interesting situation that peripheral linguistic areas do more for the cultivation of the language than the central areas in which the validity of the language is unchallenged. The preservation of the language becomes equated with the preservation of those who speak it.

This situation is particularly evident in Austria, whose leading author at this time was Adalbert Stifter (1806–68), from Oberplan in the Bohemian Forest.

Stifter is a difficult writer to classify. He was thirty-five before he started to write, and although classicism lay far in the past, his style is conditioned by classical values of balance, simplicity and clarity, the reflection of a man governed by ideals of order and sobriety. Nature and civilization, the world of things and the world of the spirit have their separate, dignified existences side by side. All overstatements, exaggerations, crude antitheses and sensational effects are avoided, and his works breathe a spirit of clarity and serenity. His early training in painting and drawing at school in Kremsmünster led him to paint a number of pictures in the impressionist style, and the qualities in these pictures are also found in his writing. At the University of Vienna he studied mathematics, law and science, giving himself, through a long and apparently aimless period of study, a comprehensive education which was the prelude to his career as a writer.

A biographical statement of this kind already points to his relationship to his age. People and nature are portrayed with such love and such precision in his works that one is entitled to speak of a profound, transcendental realism, informed by a pious Catholicism and a pure, unshakeable faith in creation and all forms of existence. This faith and love governs his entire literary work, and the objects and events of the material world are a collection of God-given images. The preface to *Bunte Steine* is Stifter's *credo*. His style is that of an objective realism dictated by the objects themselves, and this leads him to restrict himself to the forms of narrative fiction – short stories in his early career and the two great novels *Nachsommer* (1855) and *Witiko* (only made generally accessible in the twentieth century) in his maturity.

The serenity and clarity that flow from these works – conveyed in a language of perfect beauty – are not simple, naïve qualities but span a deep, mysterious depth. It is significant that the earlier versions of his stories are often more agitated than the final versions: the forces responsible for tension and agitation are neutralized, yet the inner tension remains, its directness conveyed with a limpidity reminiscent of Mannerism, above all in the historical novel *Witiko*. Nietzsche – one imagines with its epic power in mind – counted the *Nachsommer* as one of the three greatest German novels, and in the *Novellen*, all of which were written in the course of the 1840s, the violent, the powerful and the demonic are already present, albeit in a more muted form and made subject to the laws of beauty. Stifter is a writer whose importance has grown with time, and his works are among the imperishable treasures of the German language.

The third great German novel named by Nietzsche – alongside Goethe's *Wilhelm Meister* and Stifter's *Nachsommer* – is *Der grüne Heinrich* by Gottfried Keller (1819–90), son of a Zürich joiner. Whereas Stifter began with short stories, Keller started as a lyric poet and then found immediate success with this novel. Forced to leave school at fifteen for a minor disciplinary offence, he went to Munich to study painting, intending to make this his career, but the attempt came to naught and he returned home dispirited. Here he was caught up in the freedom movement which later found expression in the activities of the *Freischaren* and culminated in the foundation of the new Confederacy. With a grant from the authorities of Zürich he studied in Heidelberg and Berlin, and in *Der grüne Heinrich*, Romantic in theme, he gives what is virtually an autobiography of his spiritual life down to his early thirties.

Keller is the first writer in German literature to take realism not merely as a style and a mood but as a developed *Weltanschauung*. The visual faculty was particularly strongly developed in him, and the mysterious beauty of nature offered him a refuge in his loneliness. He was a deeply religious person but rejected all abstractions and transcendental tendencies at the time of the February revolution, and this, added to his feeling of personal deprivation, made him receptive to the philosophy of Feuerbach, whom he heard lecture at Heidelberg. From this point onwards his God was a secular figure, and he rejected Christian concepts of immortality as vain and self-indulgent. His concept of God, at least until his old age, stayed pantheistic.

The freedom movement which he passionately supported was for him the expression of a natural sense of human community. The hero of *Der grüne Heinrich* is destroyed because he has offended against the most natural of all human bonds – that with his mother, whom he left to waste away at home. In the second version he draws a more optimistic conclusion from his new materialistic philosophy and makes his hero enjoy a modest happiness in a post in which he can selflessly serve the community. It is a novel rich in conversations and reflections, and so full of vivid scenes that it is rightly counted among the most significant works of the nineteenth century.

Der grüne Heinrich marked Keller's liberation from the forces pressing upon him, and was followed by the series of cheerful *Novellen*, *Die Leute von Seldwyla* (Volume 1, 1856), and subsequently by two further cycles of *Novellen*, the *Zürcher Novellen* (1878) and *Das Sinngedicht* (1882). By this time he had realized the limitations to the application of democracy, and in *Verlorenes Lachen* (Volume II of *Die Leute von Seldwyla*) and above all in *Martin Salander* (1886), his last novel, he exposed the human weaknesses – selfishness, deceit and boastfulness – which followed in the train of the new freedoms.

Keller, as the great master of the realistic style, has an importance far beyond the then fashionable cult of realism. Like Gotthelf in *Die schwarze Spinne*, he put poetic freedom above the 'rules' of programmatic realism, adapting old material to his new outlook on life and spicing his stories with an attractive humour, particularly in the *Sieben Legenden* (1872) and *Das Sinngedicht* (1882). A predecessor of such stories is *Spiegel das Kätzchen* from *Die Leute von Seldwyla,* a kind of psychological fairy-tale for adults. The liveliness of his poetic imagination is as apparent in his letters as in his stories, and his language, with its elements of Zürich dialect, has, like that of other poets from the periphery of the German-speaking area, enriched the common stock of words and forms. As a citizen he felt himself to be Swiss; as a writer he saw himself as belonging to German literature in the widest sense.

Otto Ludwig (1813–65) made even more determined efforts than Keller to achieve a new 'realistic' *Weltanschauung*, particularly in his dramas. His *Novellen*, *Die Heiteretei, Aus dem Regen in die Traufe* and *Zwischen Himmel und Erde* (1857–8), are more straightforward. Though Ludwig came of a Thuringian patrician family, the characters in these stories are drawn from the dull, apathetic, instinctual proletariat and anticipate both naturalism and the dramatic, agitated mood of expressionism. Part of his true-to-life atmosphere derives from the Thuringian vocabulary and cadences of his language, which seems to coincide almost exactly with the events it describes. His qualities as a dramatist also emerge in these stories, and again as in naturalism an oppressive atmosphere prevails, unlightened by humour, such as befits the depiction of primitive emotion. Ludwig also concerned himself with the theory of literature, and the concept and programme of so-called 'poetic realism' stem from him.

Among the writers who expressed in its purest form the essence of realism is Theodor Storm (1817–88), a native of Holstein. In 1843, he published, together with the brothers Tycho and Theodor Mommsen, his first collection of lyrics, and four years later, after finishing his legal studies, he wrote the first of his many stories. As a man who came to occupy important administrative and legal positions in his native Husum, he was free of any economic pressure to write, and, realizing his limitations, he wisely restricted himself to the genres of *Novelle* and lyric, developing his art to a high level of subtlety.

Particularly appropriate to Storm's desire for a certain detachment and to his awareness of the patterns of middle-class society – the development of which, from his patrician but not hostile viewpoint, he depicted with that profound sense of the tragic which is rooted in human affairs – is his use of the story-within-a-story. His works are infused with the atmosphere of the lives of the peasants and townsmen among the fens and marshes, the character of the land they inhabit and their struggles to build dykes and win back a few precious acres from the invading sea. At the same time his works partake of the general contemporary dichotomy between the middle-class values of Church, State and community, to which, like Keller (with whom he became close friends in later years), he adhered, and the awareness of human transience. Devoted as he was to the middle-class values and customs of his North Sea homeland and to life in the family circle, his tales all derive in a sense from personal memories and experiences and thus possess, for all the subtlety of his narrative technique, a solid, earthy quality, even in a late work like *Der Schimmelreiter*, where irrational, supernatural elements merge with the most logical realism. His sensitivity enabled him to portray people of all ages, young and old alike, while the twin themes of renunciation and unredeemed debt recur with particular frequency. The close, observable relationships between small-town life and the life of the surrounding countryside are made a mirror of communal life and spiritual development in general.

Despite the general political oppression, there was a growing interest among the public in the 'simple people'. Village poetry became fashionable, and even aristocrats, especially aged princesses, were attracted to it. Gotthelf, for example, owed his success in Germany to the fact that his publisher, J. Springer, realized this at an early stage, and Keller's *Leute von Seldwyla* was drawn into the same area of popular taste. But the man who catered most completely for this taste was the Jewish writer Berthold Auerbach (Moyse Baruch; 1812–82), a native of the northern Black Forest. A schoolboy in Stuttgart and a student of law and philosophy at Tübingen, he was imprisoned for two months for participating in the *Burschenschaften* movement, then continued his studies in Heidelberg. His first publications were a biography of Frederick the Great and a novel on Spinoza which defended the Jews, after which came the long series, spread over more than forty years, of attractive and skilfully written *Schwarzwälder Dorfgeschichten*, items of which he constantly added to meet popular demand. Following J. P. Hebel he also compiled a popular calendar called *Der Gevattersmann*, later making a selection from it, also like Hebel, under the title *Das Schatzkästlein*. In 1846 he wrote on the theory of popular literature and later composed a number of large-scale novels which, like his other works, were cheerful, unproblematical and inoffensive. In 1871 his essay *Wieder unser* reflected the mood of the victory celebrations. Only in the last years of his successful life did he experience, in the midst of all the respect and praise, the first signs of anti-Semitism.

Another successful writer of the time was Joseph Viktor von Scheffel (1826–86), born in Karlsruhe. He originally intended to become a painter in Italy, and it was on Capri, encouraged by Paul Heyse, that he wrote his long verse-epic *Der Trompeter von Säckingen* (1853) (Scheffel had worked in Säckingen as a government inspector for some years), a work which was received with great enthusiasm in Romantic circles and brought him immediate fame; it went through more than a hundred editions during his lifetime. His novel *Ekkehard*, set on the Hohentwiel and in the Lake Constance area, had a similar success and still retains a certain value as a representation of the early Middle Ages, even though his themes and his language have an 'olde worlde', medievalizing air about them. These were the only two works Scheffel wrote, but his rich poetic imagination gave them an undeniable liveliness and colour.

The age of imperial Rome attracted a good number of writers in this period. So also did the achievements of Bismarck and the Hohenzollerns, above all after the victory of 1871, and such writers could naturally reckon on receiving official approval. Among them was Gustav Freytag (1816–95), who, instead of taking over the new materialistic outlook like Keller and Storm, followed the path of an earlier tradition and concerned himself, in a positivistic frame of mind, with the economic, social and cultural developments of his native Silesia and of Germany as a whole. As editor of the Leipzig journal *Der Grenzbote* from 1847 to 1870, he was also active as a political commentator of moderate views, while at the same time his interest in cultural history showed itself in his attractive collection of essays, *Bilder aus der deutschen Vergangenheit* (1859–67), in which he presents his impressive first-hand knowledge in a lively yet instructive form.

Freytag is one of the first to graduate to a literary career via a full academic study of German language and literature – in his case, in Breslau and Berlin – and, although his learning sometimes detracts from the freshness and spontaneity of his style, it also enables him to give his historical novels a remarkable degree of realism and historical veracity. He also tended, however, to look for – and to exaggerate – the qualities of German heroism, German uprightness and German conscientiousness: his heroes often appear as paragons of virtue and his heroines as sentimentally depicted faithful mothers whose sons will all become warriors. His lyric poetry is shot through with a similar patriotic sentimentality and moralizing. His one successful drama was the comedy *Die Journalisten* (1852), but in his prose fiction he achieved great popularity through the patriotic, moralizing tone of his books, which, together with his great learning, appealed to middle-class taste. *Soll und Haben* (1855), the story of a successful business-man, and *Die verlorene Handschrift* (1864), the story of a scholar who finds success both in scholarship and in love, were extraordinarily popular for decades, and after taking part in the German campaigns against France he made his contribution to nationalistic pride by writing a set of six novels under the title *Die Ahnen* (1872–80), in which, in an insistently didactic manner, the virtues of the present were shown to have always existed in German history.

So identified was Freytag's work with the Second Reich that when the latter collapsed, the former appeared to lose its validity. There is much in it, however, that deserves to survive, and many would see it as a source of regret that he allowed himself to be so caught up in the popular current of the time.

Paul Heyse (1830–1914), son of a Berlin professor, and of partly Jewish descent, was also in some degree the victim of his own success, though in another sense. He asserted no political or moral allegiance but devoted himself to aesthetic values and attached himself to the so-called 'Munich circle', not in any slavish, imitative sense but because the concept of the self-sufficiency of a work of art matched his own inner convictions. Everything came easy to him – and this, paradoxically, contributed to his problems. His admirers even regarded him as Goethe's successor as he moved from success to success. At nineteen he wrote a book of fairy-tales which was followed by a series of plays full of technical skills; but he found his true field in the *Novelle*, concentrating on the exploitation of a moment of tension and also offering valuable theories on the nature of this literary form. As time went on, he began to compose cycles of *Novellen* round a single theme and eventually turned, from about 1880 onwards, to the full-scale novel, for which, however, his talents were not suited. His plays are long forgotten, but his *Novellen*, individually rather than as whole cycles, are still to be admired for their virtuosity over a geographically and historically wide range of subjects. An age which comes to delight in the play of literary forms may well find new pleasure in Heyse, as in Wieland.

More ponderous, but also more substantial and more influential than Heyse's *Novellen* are the tales and novels of Wilhelm Raabe (1831–1910). Auerbach and Heyse spent their lives wandering freely from place to place, but Raabe's career, more solidly founded, was restricted to a few places. Born in the village of Eschershausen, near Wolfenbüttel, he embarked on his studies in Berlin after having worked in a bookstore in Magdeburg for five years; however, he had no academic ambitions, and as his desire to be a writer grew he gave up his studies altogether. His first work was the tale *Die Chronik der Sperlingsgasse* (1857), a small-town story owing a good deal to the Romantics, particularly Jean Paul, and similar in manner to the *Biedermeier* art of Raabe's contemporary Spitzweg. In time, the Romantic elements receded, although the motif of irony remained in the background; his characters, too, became fuller, more complete human beings. He nevertheless retained from the time of the *Chronik der Sperlingsgasse* a deep suspicion of everything successful, everything respected by the majority: the real heroes of his works are the stupid, the odd, the small, the neglected, the easy-going who are taken advantage of by the shrewd, those who meekly keep their place and make silent sacrifices which the world does not recognize. The growth of industry and technology, like the expansion of the power of the state, represented for him a force which could threaten and destroy men's minds and true values; he was devoted to his people and his native area but had no sympathy for large-scale politics, whose victims mattered more to him than the victories in whose name they were said to have died. He was thus accused of a lack of understanding and wilful pessimism, but his scepticism was to prove justified, for he saw man in his true social context – this was his realism – and abhorred all ostentatious gesturing. Where he drew on the past, it was not in order to bestow praise but in order to reveal timeless human realities, including the inescapable evils of treachery.

Particularly striking is his use of symbols as leitmotifs, such as the glass ball hanging from the cobbler's ceiling in *Der Hungerpastor*, and the title of the novel *Schüdderrump* ('bone-shaker', i.e. 'hearse'); he also shows great inventiveness in his choice of suggestive and ironical names. Though at times apparently given over to a casual, conversational manner, he can also make considerable aesthetic demands on himself, as, for instance, in the story *Horacker*, a kind of satire on the detective story, the events of which are compressed into half a day. Indeed, there is more to his stories than lies on the surface, for where other writers of the age present an agitated exterior, Raabe's unruffled manner conceals profound depths. His attachment to the weak, the strange and the under-privileged represents a reaction against the prevailing attitude of his day, according to which only great men could be significant and real; he felt no obligation towards his age, and the finest of his characters from the world of the deprived and the ill-fated have outlived it. The further Germany moved away from the emotional nationalism of the time, the more clearly the quality of Raabe's work emerged, and there is more of pure human value in his small-scale stories than in much that overshadowed them at the time.

Among the great figures who survived into a later age is also Theodor Fontane (1819–98), whose Huguenot ancestors had come from southern France and settled in Neu-Ruppin, in the Mark Brandenburg. Fontane developed late, and his best books were written after 1885; he began as a chemist in Leipzig, and it was here and in England that he felt his first stimuli as a writer. In Berlin he joined the group calling itself the 'Tunnel over the Spree' and met with some success with his ballads; for more than twenty years he lived as a journalist and editor, and in the course of this time paid many visits to England, getting to know the country and its literature well. His *Wanderungen durch die Mark Brandenburg* and similar travelogues, some of them in epistolary form, constitute, together with historical studies of the Franco-Prussian War, the preparatory stages of his real literary career, and contain a wealth of perceptive observations on people and things which he stored up and later used in more highly developed forms. Only in later life, after he had thrown off the burden of his journalistic activity, did his true career as a novelist start.

At no time, even in his old age, were his works overladen with didactic or theoretical disquisitions but remained firmly set in the middle-class and patrician worlds whose inhabitants reflect the conventions and prejudices of their social milieux, and which Fontane portrays with great skill, free of the triviality, the affected symbolism and the striving for effect which characterized much of the literature of his later years. His *œuvre*, represented by works such as *Unterm Birnbaum*, *Unwiederbringlich* (1891) and *Effi Briest* (1895), shows realism at its best.

A late developer like Fontane, but different from him in almost every other way, was Conrad Ferdinand Meyer (1825–98), a Zürich patrician. He was thirty-six before he published – anonymously – his first, ungainly, longwinded verses, *Zwanzig Balladen von einem Schweizer*. As a young man he was subject to fits of depression and spent some time in an asylum, where, cut off from the middle-class world into which he had been born, he was kept alive by his sister and by a group of friends; an inheritance relieved him of the need to earn a living – which his condition would in any case never have allowed – and miraculously he began to recover; with his recovery came the slow emergence of his literary gifts, which he cherished, as he said, like a 'holy flame'.

Huttens letzte Tage (1871), an epic poem in rhymed couplets set on the island of Ufenau in Lake Zürich, marks the beginning of his literary career, and was followed by *Engelberg,* a more gentle verse-epic set in the mountains Meyer loved so well. Then in 1887 began his sequence of historical *Novellen* and novels. The longest and finest, *Jürg Jenatsch*, set in the Grisons, treats of a divided personality at the time of Reformation and Counter-Reformation, a free adaptation of history which has been translated into many languages and become part of world literature. *Der Heilige* is based on the story of Thomas à Becket, and the list of his works continues through the Huguenot story *Das Amulett* (1873) to *Die Versuchung des Pescara* (1887) and *Angela Borgia* (1891). Meyer knew that his days of lucidity were short, and the tension and dramatic intensity of his works, their vivid contrasts and doom-laden atmosphere, reflect the terrible fear that overshadowed him. It is significant that his one humorous tale, *Der Schuß von der Kanzel*, comes approximately in the middle of his career (1877).

Both through personal relationships and intellectual leaning Meyer was drawn towards French Switzerland, and for a time he was uncertain as to whether to write in French or German; the Romance influence was further strengthened by his journeys to Italy, which helped to cure him of his sickness. But he remained a citizen of both worlds. Romance influence can be seen in his sense of form, in his syntax and in his vocabulary. He avoided the pitfall of mannerism by a close attention to detail and refinement of style and by the terse objectivity of his diction. While Fontane's work is still part of realism, Meyer already anticipates the new French influence of symbolism: the actions and conversations of the characters convey inner realities and inner dramas, and the steady narrative flow that characterizes the realistic manner gives way to a series of sketches and portraits, sometimes impressionistic, sometimes expressionistic, not dissimilar to the art of the film.

It would be hard to imagine a greater contrast in subject-matter than that between Keller's works and Meyer's. Keller was the son of an artisan, and was orphaned at an early age; Meyer was the son of a patrician *Regierungsrat* and an overly pious mother. As their social worlds were far apart, so too were their faiths; yet they both enjoyed their own kind of freedom, and what the one sought in his frank, open, natural way, the other strove to depict through portraits of psychological stress, stark contrasts and the adventures of Renaissance, baroque and medieval characters. Historical and geographical settings provide Meyer with a framework for the portrayal of intense passions and sufferings, including, as in *Die Leiden eines Knaben*, abnormal and pathological states: he seeks to protect and preserve his subjective visions by setting them in an objective framework.

Women Writers

The nineteenth century is the century of emancipations, and the emancipation of women, traceable from Friedrich Schlegel's *Lucinde* through Gutzkow's *Wally* to the end of the century, was among the most spectacular. This emancipation also shows itself in the field of artistic creativity, and the middle of the century sees the appearance of a number of women writers whose work is often characterized by an astringent, masculine beauty. Figures like Countess Ida Hahn-Hahn (1805–80), a Mecklenburg aristocrat who ended her adventurous life in a nunnery in Mainz which she founded herself, and Fanny Lewald (1811–89), a Jewish convert to Protestantism who led a no less adventurous life, gained a reputation as novelists.

Such figures become insignificant, however, in the presence of Annette von Droste-Hülshoff (1797–1848), lyric poetess and author of *Die Judenbuche*. Born on the family estate of Hülshoff, near Münster in Westphalia, she was deeply rooted in the mysterious, legend-filled world of her homeland, and her slender *œuvre* has its beginnings in Romanticism. The other early influence on her was that of Catholicism: at the age of twenty-three she published the first part of her *Christliches Jahr*, and the events of the Church calendar, its feasts and its meditations, dominated her life. But she soon left the vague, unworldly mysticism of Catholic legends behind, and we see a strong, almost masculine spirit wrestling with God, with itself and with the knowledge of man's dependence on grace. For all her terse, powerful language Annette von Droste-Hülshoff was a delicate, sensitive nature incapable of dealing with the injustices of life, short-sighted in observation but far-sighted in sympathy. Her love for Levin Schücking, which stimulated her most substantial works, ended in bitter resignation, and during her periods in Schloss Eppishausen with her brother-in-law Freiherr von Lassberg, the literary scholar, and later in Meersburg Castle, which Lassberg also acquired, she acted the role of the lonely spinster. Her last years, overshadowed by sickness, were spent in a vine-covered retreat overlooking Lake Constance.

Few lyric poems in the German language can equal the vividness and power of Annette's personal testament in 'Am Turme'. It is the power of an independent epic nature, neither sentimental nor romanticizing, and it reveals throughout her career a deep human understanding and a sympathy in particular for the dull, everyday character and the misfit. *Die Judenbuche* is a crime-story told with powerful directness and utter truth; the same truth and depth of meaning are found in *Der Spiritus familiaris des Roßtäuschers* (1842). Her powers of imagination recall Büchner, and as a poetess of the 'sweetness of terror', anticipating the expressionism of the twentieth century, she has no equal.

Annette von Droste-Hülshoff's most important successors were also aristocrats – a not surprising state of affairs, since women of the lower classes did not yet have access to that full education on which the development of literature depended. Her most important aristocratic successor, a writer who shows how extensive was the range of the upper-class milieu, is Louise von François (1817–93), descended from a Huguenot family from Normandy which became a member of the Saxon, and later Prussian, officer-class. She acquired her literary knowledge from reading aloud to her blind stepfather, and her social independence enabled her to view the people around her with remarkable objectivity. She started writing in order to support her mother after the family had lost its money, and to avoid accepting the charity which would have injured her pride. She began by subscribing pieces to light periodicals such as the *Cottasches Morgenblatt* and the *Dürrsche Novellenzeitung*, where they were published anonymously or pseudonymously. Her sole literary contacts were with Gustav Freytag, the only writer to publicize her qualities, Conrad Ferdinand Meyer and her fellow poetess Marie von Ebner-Eschenbach. She was too modest to recognize her linguistic subtlety and her almost unnatural self-assurance in moral and aesthetic matters. She sought the advice of Conrad Ferdinand Meyer, whose like-minded efforts she admired, but did not need it, since her own intuition and sensitivity were greater than his. Her best works are *Die letzte Reckenburgerin* (1871), the novel that established her modest reputation; *Frau Erdmuthens Zwillingssöhne* (1872), elegant in style, full of delightful irony, and revelatory of her dual Huguenot and Saxon descent; and *Stufenjahre eines Glücklichen* (1872). She was too remote from the spirit of her age to be appreciated by it, but her novels are a delightful blend of elements from earlier epochs such as rococo and the truth to reality characteristic of her own nineteenth century; even the patina of archaism on her works has its own authenticity.

The third of these women writers is Marie von Ebner-Eschenbach (1830–1916), descendent of the aristocratic Moravian family of Dubsky and wife at eighteen of Baron Ebner von Eschenbach, who later held a chair of science at the engineering college of Klosterbruck in Moravia. Of great influence on her literary career were her young married years in Vienna, where she was fascinated particularly by the performances at the Burgtheater. Her first literary efforts were in fact dramas, and her *Maria Stuart* was even performed in Karlsruhe. Otto Ludwig ridiculed her plays but she did not become discouraged, and the Burgtheater and other theatres performed a number of them.

Her real talent, however, lay in narrative fiction, from the fairy-tale *Die Prinzessin von Banalien* (1872), through the collected *Erzählungen* (1875 and 1881) and the *Dorf- und Schoßgeschichten* to the novels *Das Gemeindekind* (1887) and *Lotti die Uhrmacherin* (1889). These latter are also *Erzählungen* rather than full novels, for Marie von Ebner-Eschenbach's strength lies less in narrative construction than in her descriptions of social settings. These settings are only to a small degree those of her own aristocratic situation, for she had a deep insight into the world of the peasants and workers, and stories like *Das Gemeindekind* and *Krambambuli* already have something of the character of the naturalistic stories of the time.

She also had, as *Krambambuli* shows, an unusual sympathy with the animal world and appeared as the champion both of animals and of neglected, downtrodden human beings. In this she reflects the new spirit of the age more clearly than Louise von François. Her style has an Austrian charm mingled with occasional sentimentality, and she does not share the ironical humour of Louise von François. The directness, sincerity and wit of her style are best seen in her *Aphorismen* (1880), which, with their wit, their wisdom and the keenness of their observation, without prejudice or ill-will, of man and society, are not unworthy to be placed alongside the work of Lichtenberg and the *Xenien* of Goethe and Schiller. Her stories stand between the work of Stifter, with its clarity and purity of form, and that of Peter Rosegger, with its popular appeal; and what she has of this latter quality is, as with Gotthelf, of an authenticity far removed from any 'folksy' attachment to the soil.

Quite different is the Swiss writer Johanna Spyri (1827–1901), who has been called the classical writer of children's books. Probably no works other than Andersen's fairy-tales have been translated so often. Johanna Heusser, whose mother also had literary gifts, married Spyri, attorney and later town-clerk, in 1852, and at the age of forty-five published her first story. Her period of activity coincides more or less with that of Meyer, with whom she was on friendly terms. Her works – the best-known are *Heimatlos*, *Heidis Lehr- und Wanderjahre* and *Aus den Schweizerbergen* – were first published in Germany and still enjoy great popularity. Being set in Alpine parts, they catered for the growing cult of the simple shepherd life, spreading an atmosphere of goodness and simple humanity, and with a special concern for the trials of the young; urban and rural communities are shown in harmony and peace, and the scenes of nature are woven in a natural manner into the events of the fables. Johanna Spyri's language, moreover, is clear, fluent and free from all sentimentality and moralizing, and has a special appeal to youth.

Drama

Great efforts were made in the course of the nineteenth century in the field of drama. Few writers did not plan dramas of one kind or another, a situation for which Goethe and Schiller – especially the latter – were largely responsible. As its prosperity grew, middle-class society began to revel in the spectacular performances of famous actors and actresses in theatres both old and new.

But despite these efforts the quantity of material of lasting interest was pitifully small, and many would-be dramatists tried in vain to find a form of drama that would meet the acknowledged claims of the stage to be a place both of education and of free speech. Some simply indulged in wordiness; others – even men of the stature of Gottfried Keller and Conrad Ferdinand Meyer – dreamed of writing great plays, strove to evolve a satisfactory dramaturgy, then abandoned the attempt. One reason for this was the general aversion to theory and speculation at this time in favour of a commitment to the material world and human experience – something not easily reconciled with the technical requirements of the theatre.

More fundamental, however, was the fact that, the more firmly realism became established as a philosophy, involving a monistic materialism and an optimistic faith in scientific progress, the less justification there appeared to be for tragedy, the highest and noblest of theatrical forms. Historical drama, on the other hand, packed with heroic characters, flourished as it had in baroque times: the heroic stories of Old and Middle High German days were widely drawn upon, and well after the time of Kleist Hermann and Thusnelda were still the ideals of German loyalty and uprightness. But few of these plays have survived. The beginnings of tragic conflict appear in the first version of *Der grüne Heinrich*, where the profound needs of the community, embodied in Keller's mother, conflicted with the right of the individual to personal development, but there was no metaphysical basis from which human rights and duties could be derived. Equally, the commitment to social and political standpoints prevented the emergence of a free, creative irony which might have encouraged the development of comedy. By extending their range to include the provinces of history and the lower social orders, writers made the mistake of thinking that new subjects inevitably meant a new kind of drama. The art of dramatic production was, however, greatly advanced by the activities of first-rate theatres, above all in Vienna, Düsseldorf, Darmstadt, Berlin and Hamburg.

The career of Franz Grillparzer (1791–1872) stretches into the age of realism, but his greatest works were all written by the early 1840s, and after his enthusiastic reception in the Theater an der Wien and the Burgtheater in the 1820s, interest in his plays declined. *Des Meeres und der Liebe Wellen* met with no response, and although *Der Traum ein Leben* (1834) had a brief success, his comedy *Weh dem, der lügt* (1838) fell on deaf ears, owing to the rising popularity of Nestroy; for the remainder of his life he was almost completely absent from the world of literature. This is not a criticism of his dramatic talent but the proof that his plays belonged to an age that was past. And the cultured Viennese theatre-going public, however harshly it dealt with him, influenced him as much as he for his part contributed to its edification.

Grillparzer's poetic language is not that of the Romanticism in which he grew up but that of classicism, with a flowing rhythm and an incomparable formal beauty reminiscent of Goethe's *Iphigenie* and *Tasso* – as his characters too live by the classical ideal of *Humanität*. In the context of realist drama it stands like a rococo palace next to a rough log-cabin, and it is not surprising that Grillparzer should have felt repelled by the crudities of the new style. He avoided all extremes: his wit is subtle and refined, his emotional intensity – if one may speak of such – is directed towards beauty and euphony; in this respect his true successor is Hugo von Hofmannsthal, while one may also compare him with his compatriot Stifter, though the latter is more concerned with objective truth and the love of nature than was Grillparzer.

As in his comedies human goodness triumphs over coarseness, so in his tragedies, e.g. *Libussa* (1840), his last great play, nobility triumphs over baseness. Grillparzer stands in the tradition – to a certain extent he even represents its culmination – of drama which lives by the virtues of human morality and aesthetic beauty, and he is even prepared to sacrifice the credibility of his plot to these virtues. Both these aspects show the gulf between him and, on the one hand, the socially committed Young Germans, and, on the other, the practitioners of popular farce. Yet an awareness of modern times does emerge from the conclusion of *Libussa*, where the dying queen speaks of the arrival of a new age, an age, however, in which new spiritual values would only emerge in the distant future after the time of materialism had passed.

The work of Christian Friedrich Grabbe (1801–36), born of a working-class family in Detmold, also belongs to the period of transition from Romanticism to realism. A talented youth, he studied law in Leipzig and Berlin, where he became caught up in the *Burschenschaften*; he was something of an exhibitionist and felt attracted to the stage but became a dipsomaniac and died an early death.

Herzog Theodor von Gothland (1827), written while he was a student, attracted considerable attention; he wrote a further tragedy the same year, together with a comedy, *Scherz, Satire, Ironie und tiefere Bedeutung*, which has a place among the few good German comedies. However, he was more attracted by the pomp of historical tragedy, though his flamboyance prevented him from developing his true talents, and he left many works unfinished. As Gutzkow had worked off his feelings of inferiority and resentment by giving a distorted picture of Goethe, so Grabbe did the same with Shakespeare, from whom he had learnt all he knew, yet whom he portrayed in his essay *Über die Shakespeareomanie* as an ignorant bungler. From Shakespeare he took above all the use of crowd-scenes and comic scenes to release tragic tension and create local colour. His attraction to large-scale themes emerges from his choice of subjects: two dramas on the Hohenstaufen age, *Napoleon oder die hundert Tage*, a play on the Don Juan-Faust themes and *Die Hermannsschlacht* (published posthumously). His *Aschenbrödel, ein dramatisches Märchen* (1835), written for the Düsseldorf theatre, shows, like *Scherz, Satire, Ironie und tiefere Bedeutung*, the nature of his gifts. The realism in his plays lies principally in his use of local colour, while his penchant for extravagant historical subjects, like the course of his life, sets him rather among the late Romantics.

Georg Büchner shows a far profounder awareness of spiritual realities, as his story *Lenz* already showed. The heroes of *Dantons Tod* (1835) and *Woyzeck* are not loquacious extroverts but men torn between madness and confused feelings of guilt, living in a world in which reason and logic are but a thin veneer on a body of smouldering passions which obey only their own laws; Büchner sees men as puppets at the mercy of unknown and uncontrollable forces, and the language of his characters has an incomparable power. In technique his three dramas anticipate the epic theatre of Brecht, with their massive, rough-hewn style and their presentation of basic human situations through the accumulation and juxtaposition of human scenes. Büchner's life was too short – he died of typhus in Basle, where he was a professor of anatomy – for him to evolve his own theory of drama, but his plays are among the most powerful dramatic moments in the whole of German literature.

The Young Germans continued to write plays in large numbers. Gutzkow wrote twenty (see p. 262), most of which were performed in the best theatres, but only *Uriel Acosta*, a progeny of Lessing's *Nathan*, is now worth mentioning. Laube wrote fourteen, and was from 1849 to 1867 director of the Vienna Burgtheater; after a short spell at the Leipzig Stadttheater he returned to Vienna to found the Stadttheater there. These two Viennese theatres wielded great influence at this time, but it was only in part a progressive influence, and they were certainly also responsible, along with other theatres, for the prevailing mediocrity of standards.

Alongside these theatres, with their elaborate and often pretentious companies, there existed, above all in Berlin and Vienna, more modest popular theatres in which farces and parodies were performed, often with improvised interludes and interjections. This is the tradition of the theatre of entertainment, in which many important actors composed and adapted their parts or their plays, producing polished comedies and operettas from crude farces with stereotyped characters. The most famous of these actor-playwrights were Ferdinand Raimund (1790–1836), most of whose plays were performed in the Theater in der Josephstadt and the Theater in der

Leopoldstadt in Vienna, and Johann Nepomuk Nestroy (1802–62). Both were Viennese, and are inseparable from their birthplace. Nestroy became an actor and opera singer at twenty, and after a spell abroad he returned to Vienna and became a popular comic actor at the Theater an der Wien and the Theater in der Leopoldstadt, of which latter he was director for fifteen years and where he achieved his greatest successes with his farces, often based on French comedies. But all his best pieces, like *Lumpazivagabundus* (1833), *Der Talisman* (1840), *Einen Jux will er sich machen* (1842) and *Der Zerrissene*, breathe the spirit of the Viennese popular theatre and are largely written in Viennese dialect, and their appeal is still far greater in Vienna than elsewhere.

All is not triviality in these works, however, for Nestroy in particular portrays, albeit in a lighthearted form, the joys and sufferings, the wisdom and folly of mankind. Literary history has tended to pass them by, but they are more than just pieces of entertainment. Certain modern comedies, such as those of Dürrenmatt, have drawn attention to them again.

The most significant dramatist of the mid-nineteenth century is undoubtedly Friedrich Hebbel (1813–63), a figure who, in the wake of Goethe, Schiller and Kleist, seemed destined to bring to fruition what Büchner had sown. Struggling against his social situation – his father was a labourer in a rigid rural community in Holstein – he fought his way out of poverty and narrowmindedness, avoided becoming a bricklayer as his father wanted, and took a job as messenger and scribe in his native village of Wesselburen in Dithmarschen. Here he indulged his insatiable urge for reading, an urge which was also ministered to by various women. The first of these was Amalie Schoppe, editor of a fashion journal, who formed a group of friends to make books available to the young Hebbel, who had already written some verse, for him to pursue his education. After an abortive attempt at the age of twenty-two to attend school in Hamburg, he spent some years in Heidelberg and Munich, trying to live by his writing but also relying on the financial assistance of Elise Lensing, a seamstress who had also supported him in Hamburg.

In 1840 he wrote his first play, *Judith*, which was performed the same year at the Berlin Hoftheater. It was received with mixed approval and disapproval. The following year he wrote *Genoveva* and the comedy *Der Diamant*, as a result of which King Christian VIII of Denmark granted him a bursary with which he travelled to Paris, where he completed the family tragedy *Maria Magdalene* (1843). From Paris he went to Rome, then to Naples, finally settling in Vienna, the theatrical metropolis of Europe. Here he married an actress at the Burgtheater called Christine Enghaus, having broken with Elise Lensing, who had borne him two children, both of whom died young. Christine was a sensitive, gifted woman and even succeeded in gaining the friendship of Elise Lensing, but Hebbel himself transferred his hard upbringing to his personal relationships, making his artistic career the justification for his morality. Laube continually sought to keep his plays out of the Burgtheater but without success. In the last ten years of his life he wrote his most mature works, including the *Nibelungen* trilogy (1863), and he died shortly before finishing his *Demetrius*.

His life was full of violent movements, as much the product of his own nature as of his reception by the world, and was equally rich in genuine emotion and poetic vision as in ruthless and passionate outbursts; his mind was sharp, and his style never lost the power, the colour, the precision and the objectivity of the poor peasant community in which he had grown up. His art, like his life, was built on tension and conflict, and like that other self-taught genius of realism, Gottfried Keller, he was given to periods of moodiness and brooding, which shows itself in a style at once sharp and meditative, as seen particularly in the language used by the most completely satisfying characters in his plays.

The logical clarity of Hebbel's thought also emerges from his theoretical writings on drama, the most important since Lessing's *Hamburgische Dramaturgie*. The attacks on his works forced him to think out his position, and he had in any case concerned himself from his early days with philosophical problems. One detects a strong influence of classical drama, but he turned away from the drama of ideas as such and gave his works a historical cast – not historical in the Romantic sense, in the dialectic, positivistic sense or in the framework of German nationalism, but with a kind of historical pragmatism which bound together the phenomena of personal and corporate life. From this pragmatism he derived a new sense of authentic tragedy – the tragedy of man caught up in the treadmill of historical progress. This led him to set his plays at the great turning-points of history – from Germanic paganism to Christianity (*Nibelungen*), from Judaism to Christianity (*Herodes und Mariamne*), from the age of magic to the age of reason (*Gyges und sein Ring*).

Hebbel's passionate nature ensured that his principal characters did not remain mere types but became real human beings, and the moral and spiritual conflicts to which they found themselves exposed sprang from the conflicts which he himself had always known. The realism of his dreams comes, as he himself explains in *Mein Wort über das Drama*, from taking his personal experience as the ultimate criterion, and thus claiming the right to identify himself with the events of history. Even though he modified this claim in his later works, as the figure of Dietrich in the *Nibelungen* shows, his own temperament remains largely responsible for the individual natures of his characters, and his own psychology remains a vital part of his tragic power and of his conception of tragic guilt, a conception based not on the performance of guilty deeds but on a sense of inborn guilt in the human condition. The more 'individualized' the individual becomes, the deeper his involvement in this guilt, and the higher he rides above the common masses in the exercise of his individual responsibility, the greater his confusion and his awareness of sin. Guilt, like involvement in tragedy, is for Hebbel not metaphysical guilt but a consequence of life itself.

The sense of strain and violence that runs through Hebbel's life also fills his writings and manifests itself both in his style and in the psychology of his characters. In *Maria Magdalene* (1844) and *Agnes Bernauer* (1851), following the tradition of domestic tragedy that begins with Lessing's *Emilia Galotti*, he reveals a profound understanding of the lower levels of humanity and their attitudes, and the directness and plasticity of these works remain impressive even today.

The genuine tragic quality of *Agnes Bernauer*, felt as such even in the age of positivism, rests on the conflict between two equally valid principles of human society – the sacred, unchallengeable laws of the medieval feudal order, and the right of a woman to choose her own husband; in the end this right is sacrificed so that the social order shall be preserved.

His prose stories hardly demand attention, but his diaries, which he started at the age of twenty-one and in which he examines his own personality with great severity, are significant examples of this genre and contain the key to the meaning of much of his work and many aspects of his creative personality.

Otto Ludwig was also intent on achieving the greatest possible clarity in drama. In his posthumously published *Shakespeare-Studien*, which are among the best of nineteenth-century interpretations of Shakespeare, he also meditated self-critically on his own plays, seeking to elucidate by reference to Shakespeare the nature of the pure character-drama. His views contrast markedly with those of Schiller, whose works dominated the German theatres of the time, and also with those of the politically committed Young Germans. As his best play, *Der Erbförster*, shows, he was well equipped to write realistic drama, for here we find portrayed with remarkable realism the conflicts of a small, narrowminded community caught up in its own prejudices and dominated by a feudalistic outlook. Here Ludwig faithfully portrays the inhabitants of the Thuringia he knew and loved, and the tragic element present resides in the confusions and confinements which beset mankind. Chance and circumstance also play their part in *Der Erbförster*, but in many respects Ludwig anticipates the naturalistic drama of the young Gerhart Hauptmann. The other two plays that brought him fame were *Das Fräulein von Scudery* and *Die Makkabäer*, the latter his last dramatic work. An early illness made him paralysed; he was of a withdrawn, unpractical, poetic nature and also musically gifted, but his creative career suffered, like that of other

KGL

poets, under the conditions of the age and from the vagaries of fate.

Gustav Freytag's large-scale plays also had a considerable following at the time: his *Die Brautfahrt oder Kunz von Rosen* (1841) won a Berlin drama competition for the best comedy, and further plays followed, the most successful being *Die Journalisten* (1852), a comedy which pokes fun at the attitudes and behaviour of this new profession. It was still performed well into the twentieth century, whereas his serious dramas, like *Die Fabier*, hardly rose above an honesty of purpose and a historical correctness, mingled with homespun morality. His later stories reflect his gifts more truly than these dramas of his earlier career.

The Ballad

The ballad, introduced into German literature by Bürger under the stimulus of foreign, above all English, sources, retained its popularity throughout the Romantic age and down to the time of Uhland, but the advent of realism brought a setback. With its tendency towards the supernatural and its emphasis on extreme effectiveness of form and construction, it came to occupy a subsidiary position and, though often attempted, rarely achieved success: indeed, it is significant that the first ballad-poets in this period, Uhland – who stimulated Hebbel in this field – and Schwab, stood in the Romantic tradition, and most of their important ballads were written before 1830, as were those of Mörike ('Die traurige Krönung' and 'Das verlassene Mägdlein', both 1829) and Heine ('Belsazar', 'Die zwei Grenadiere', etc.).

Annette von Droste-Hülshoff's most important ballads were written in the 1830s, and, in contrast to the mechanical verses of contemporary poetasters like Freiligrath and Follen, have great poetic power and atmosphere together with a wealth of objective detail; they are often drawn from her native Westphalia and display, as in 'Das Fräulein von Rodenschild' and 'Der Knabe im Moor', a jagged forcefulness of style that is as original as that of her prose writings.

Hebbel's dramatic gifts also found expression in a handful of balladesque poems, in which he conjured up the moods of his native Dithmarschen and gave expression, most effectively in 'Der Heideknabe', to the fears that surrounded his youth.

The ballads of Friedrich Rückert (1788–1866) and August Kopisch (1799–1853) follow in the wake of Romanticism – the latter is one of the rare practitioners of the light-hearted ballad – as do those of Karl Simrock (1802–76). Keller is more original: his 'Jung gewohnt, alt getan' uses the same basic motif as that of *Der grüne Heinrich*; 'Der Taugenichts', derived from Eichendorff's story, is a tale of gipsies and beggars but without any magic elements, while 'Aroleid', composed somewhat later, is a colourful poem based on a Valais legend. Following Heine's example in the *Romanzero*, Keller also wrote parodistic romances, such as 'Der Apotheker von Chamonix' and 'Lebendig begraben', while his 'Feuer-Idylle' is a kind of realistic adaptation of the supernaturalism of Mörike's Romantic idylls.

The ballad was given a new impetus by the wave of nationalism later in the century, and a few dozen poems by Fontane and Conrad Ferdinand Meyer, both writers who concerned themselves with the ballad throughout their lives, show how highly developed the form had become.

Fontane's early ballads, published in his first collection of poems in 1850, show the influence of English and Scottish poems; more original are those written with the encouragement of the critics in the group 'Der Tunnel über der Spree', one of whom, Moritz Graf von Strachwitz (1822–47), had pointed to new paths of development. Fontane's style at this time recalls that of popular poetry but also has a certain gritty quality which, however, softens in his later translations and adaptations of English ballads. His range stretches from the historical world of the *Preußenlieder* to contemporary social and scientific problems, and he reveals a particular mastery of rhythm which helps to put his ballads – above all 'Archibald Douglas', 'John Maynard', 'Gorm Grymme', 'Der Herr von Ribbeck auf Ribbeck im Havelland' and 'Die Brück' am Tay' – amongst the best that German literature has to show.

The *Zwanzig Balladen von einem Schweizer*, published anonymously in 1862, was Conrad Ferdinand Meyer's first printed work. Quite different from Fontane's ballads, they are somewhat clumsy and longwinded, but they mark the beginning of an interesting development. They are based on Meyer's close personal knowledge of the careers of figures from the Italian Renaissance, the Huguenot tradition and the German Reformation and Counter-Reformation, and the quality of terse, dynamic characterization found in his stories is also manifest in these ballads, which, like his other poems, are the products of a process of continual refinement stretching over years. Among the best examples are 'Mit zwei Worten', 'Die Bettlerballade', 'Der Rappe des Komturs' and 'Die Füsse im Feuer' – the last-named, a Huguenot story, reaching the peak of dramatic brevity.

Mention must also be made in this context of Wilhelm Busch (1832–1908), the greatest humorous poet of the nineteenth century, who, after studying art in Düsseldorf, Antwerp and Munich, finally returned to settle in his native Hanover. The keenness of perception which found expression in his drawings for the Munich periodical *Fliegende Blätter* later issued in his witty poems on the foibles of human nature. His books, with his own illustrations – *Max und Moritz* (1870), *Der heilige Antonius von*

Padua (1870), *Die fromme Helene* (1872), *Balduin Bählamm* (1873) and *Maler Klecksel* (1884) – live by virtue of the good-natured quality of their humour, which never turns into viciousness or satire. He is both in, and above the human follies and weaknesses that he describes. He does not wish to give offence and he does not moralize or preach: he is simply concerned to hold up a mirror to common humanity so that we may all see our true nature.

Lyric Poetry

In an age so dominated by material concerns and so occupied with the problems of physical life, lyric poetry was inevitably at a discount, and even threatened with decay. Compared with both the preceding and the following fifty years, lyric poetry between 1830 and 1885 has little to show, yet it does have its own originality, an originality bound to the realist philosophy of the time, close to the physical facts of life and far from the speculative, free-ranging verse associated with Romanticism, although initially the Romantic influence was too strong to be drowned in the waves of Young German propaganda, or for the beauties of its form and language to be jettisoned without further ado. A poet like Eichendorff, indeed, who lived through much of this period, retained his Romanticism to the end, showing little difference between his early and his late poetry and remaining opposed to the new movement. A similar figure was the schizophrenic Lenau (see p. 244), whose first collection of verse, published in 1832, struck the note of resignation and *Weltschmerz* which made him famous (*Faust* (1836); *Savonarola* (1837); *Die Albigenser* (1842)) but which became an affectation from which he could never escape.

Eduard Mörike (1804–75), too, had his roots in Romanticism but his development outstripped all formal restriction. Under the stimulus of *Des Knaben Wunderhorn* and the Romantic poets in general, Mörike, a contemplative, sensitive, inward-looking poet, developed to become Germany's greatest lyric poet since Goethe. Like Goethe's verse, Mörike's is, in the deepest sense, occasional poetry, and, again like Goethe's, his verse has a symbolic significance as an *œuvre*. The magic of his language is to be found at one moment in the melody of the verse, at another in its rhythm, at one moment in a mystical image, at another in a serene, almost rococo playfulness, yet the entire personality of the poet himself is always present. Within his modest output he reveals complete mastery over the whole range from the simple *Volkslied* to the intense, sophisticated sonnet and the flowing hexameter, but there is not a single poem that is not internally and externally perfect. His originality, manifested in the freshness of his imagery and the directness of his language, is already apparent in his early poems, which are mainly love-poems. In the Peregrina poems, the sonnets 'An Louise' and 'An die Geliebte', and in 'An Wilhelm Hartlaub' human emotions – love, friendship, resignation – fill our hearts; in his nature-poems we find ourselves confronting scenes in which all the variations of the seasons are laid out before us, making him a kind of poetic forerunner of the French impressionists.

It is this authenticity of emotion and atmosphere that leads one to call Mörike realistic in the deepest sense – the lyrical description of an object or an event *per se*, without thought of symbolic meaning or of human relevance: the image is its own symbol and grips our attention as such. 'Auf eine Lampe' and 'Er ist's' are examples of this objective lyricism, while a poem such as 'Um Mitternacht' combines all the characteristic features of Mörike's verse. It is a natural corollary to his original poetry that, as a man who sought to uncover the inner mystery of things, he should have shown the power, in his translations and adaptations of classical poetry, to penetrate the essence of foreign literature also.

The 1850s saw the efflorescence in Munich, under the cultured patronage of King Maximilian II of Bavaria, of a group of poets calling itself 'Das Krokodil', after a poem by Hermann Lingg. The acknowledged leader of this group was Emanuel Geibel (1815–84), son of a Lübeck cleric and of Huguenot descent. As a student in Berlin he had come into contact with Eichendorff and Chamisso, and Bettina von Arnim arranged for him to take a post as tutor to the family of the Russian ambassador in Athens, where he stayed for two years with his compatriot Ernst Curtius. His first volume of poetry appeared in 1840; two years later Friedrich Wilhelm IV made him court poet, and after the death of his early patron Maximilian in 1864, King Wilhelm, later the Emperor Wilhelm II, anxious to retain his services, trebled his salary, whereupon Geibel became an enthusiastic supporter of the Second Reich. Such was his reputation that he was accorded a place on Olympus next to Goethe.

What brought him this reputation – a reputation derived solely from his lyrics, for apart from a single comedy, *Meister Andrea*, his plays were received with cold politeness? To a large extent it was his display of good taste; he had learnt his craft from the Romantics, from the Greeks, the Spaniards and from the French, whose works he had translated together with Paul Heyse, Ernst Curtius and Heinrich Leuthold, and possessed what the Greeks called τὸ πρέπον, 'what is fitting', the ability to compose rhythmical verses in accepted traditional forms. He wrote many poems in a popular vein which have become, with the melodies that inevitably came to be added to them, virtually folksongs. They naturally contain their moments of sentimentality and triviality but also a certain elegance, and Geibel skilfully blended figures from Greek and Germanic mythology into a gentle and peaceful landscape sketched in folksong style. This became the manner common to the whole Munich group, and its value lay primarily in the preservation of a formal sense in an age disposed to reject all formal restraints. Geibel's reputation was certainly exaggerated, and he was not particularly inventive, but it would be a mistake to forget him entirely.

Scheffel's sentimental student-songs, with their often rather homespun Romantic jollity, became equally popular, and 'Als die Römer frech geworden', 'Alt Heidelberg, du feine', 'Im schwarzen Walfisch zu Askalon' and 'Wohlauf, die Luft geht frisch und rein' are invariably found in student song-books. The splendours of the *Burschenschaften* and the hazy romanticism of the wandering scholars, seen against a background of romantic nationalism – such was the world imagined by the more prosperous classes, the classes which ignored the present and still lived in the past. Simple and undemanding, like Geibel's, Scheffel's songs enjoyed a greater popularity than their poetic quality deserved.

A temporary member of the Munich circle was the Swiss writer Heinrich Leuthold (1827–79), a native of the canton of Zürich. Of poor peasant stock, he came into contact with Meta Heusser, mother of Johanna Spyri, and subsequently studied a variety of subjects, above all law. But he neither completed his studies nor took up a permanent occupation, living mostly on the goodwill of well-to-do lonely women in Munich and elsewhere, until paralysis of the brain forced him to enter a mental asylum. The philologist J. Bächthold published a volume of his collected poems, some of which Geibel had rewritten in his own style, but Leuthold's poems were complete in their own way, and he particularly enjoyed the challenge of strict forms like the sonnet and foreign forms such as the *ghazal*. More serious than Geibel in his choice of themes, and rarely guilty of sentimentality, he shared with Lenau an elegiac mood to which he added his own presentiment of the coming destruction of the world. He was a philosophical rather than an emotional poet, keeping strictly within his limits but ranging from folksong and the joys of nature to a humorous, even mordant satirical style. Indeed, Leuthold epitomizes better than any other figure the dichotomy of the poet in the age of realism, and in this dichotomy, as in his sometimes morbid triviality, he reveals traits characteristic of the future expressionists.

Before the time when 'Das Krokodil' was founded, Gottfried Keller had come to Munich, only to return shortly after to his mother and to plunge himself in the study of literature – Goethe, the Romantics, Freiligrath and the freedom poets, and Anastasius Grün (1806–76), whose *Schutt* (1836) particularly impressed him. From this time onwards, as he himself said, he felt the rhythm of poetry in his veins, and in 1844–5, through the encouragement of C. A. Follen, who was staying in Zürich as a political refugee, his gifts as a lyric poet began to show themselves, partly in the form of unpleasant, aggressive political poems, partly in a macabre brand of love-poetry and partly in a remarkably strong and fresh nature-poetry. Before the time when, in Heidelberg, his intellectual development reached the stage of a firm materialistic philosophy, he covered in this poetry the entire range of natural phenomena, affirming his joyous faith in life and setting Mother Nature in the place of the Christian religion against whose dogmatic concepts he rebelled. No other poet of the period immersed himself so completely in nature, witness the poems 'Abendlied an die Natur', 'Waldlied I' and 'Unter Sternen'. He was, however, no blind optimist but gave himself over to the beauties of the world in full knowledge of their transience. Alongside these nature-poems we also find, as in Leuthold, poems on traditional themes, though Keller is not concerned with the display of poetic virtuosity for its own sake.

Keller counted the national life and development of his own country, and of all countries, among the phenomena of nature, and national festivals take the place of religious festivals: poems such as 'O mein Vaterland' reveal this patriotism.

In his late seventies Keller again produced a group of remarkably fresh lyric poems, among them 'Abendlied' and 'Abend auf Golgatha'. Also to this period belong ballads and romances in the manner of Heine, whose influence had already been evident in a number of satirical poems, starting with the very first poem of Keller's to be published, 'Jesuitenzug'. The whole of Keller's output is characterized by vividness of imagery, and his lyric poetry shows that his sense of melody and rhythm was equally powerful.

One of the last and greatest masters of realism, above all in lyric poetry, is Theodor Storm, whose style departed completely from the Romantic inclination to the timeless and spaceless metaphysical world of absolute emotion. As in his stories, so in his verse Storm restricts himself to themes depicting man in his social being – love and parting, reminiscence and hope – seeking to express in melodious, balanced, regular strophic forms the true nature of human relationships. A poem like 'Juli' embodies the spirit of this 'objective lyricism': personal feelings are objectivized in the relationships between the phenomena themselves, and these phenomena become symbols of existence. Among the scenes of nature in his poems it is the flat, marshy landscape of his native Holstein that dominates, most effectively in 'Die Stadt', 'Meeresstrand' and 'Über die Heide'. Like Keller, Storm turned his back on any semblance of transcendentalism and concentrated, with a singlemindedness rarely achieved either before or since, on the object itself.

An equal warmth and sincerity is displayed by Storm's compatriot Klaus Groth (1819–99), who, unlike Storm, attached himself, as did Fritz Reuter in Mecklenburg, to his native Holstein dialect and sought to give it literary currency. Groth's poetry captures the simplicity of folksong and expresses in simple forms an artless faith in life, above all in the life of the countryman.

Conrad Ferdinand Meyer was almost sixty when he published his first volume of verse – and indeed most of his early poetry is trivial and undistinguished. Ballads and historical poems predominate in this collection, as Meyer's nature would lead one to expect, and the true lyric poems are few; such as there are represent years of modifying and refining, the products of long reflection, yet in their final form they reveal little of these struggles. His themes and images are restricted – the passage of time, mountains, rambling, the nature of art – but each poem has its own melody and its own rhythm.

Meyer has been pejoratively called an 'instructive poet' but there have been few who have more successfully poured new wine into old bottles or more skilfully achieved an objectification of lyric poetry. In short poems like 'Zwei Segel', 'Nachtgeräusche' and 'Der römische Brunnen' his terse language produces a vivid image with a completeness and self-sufficiency that scorn support. Nor must one overlook the poems in which, in contrast to such 'objective' lyrics, he conveys states of agitation and tension – poems such as 'Noch einmal', 'Laß scharren deiner Rosse Huf', 'Hesperos', 'Alle' and 'Allerbarmen'.

Certain aspects of Meyer's poetry point to the French symbolists, others to the German expressionists. He worked between periods of madness, threatened, like Lenau and Leuthold, with total insanity – an insanity which symbolizes the spiritual conflicts and dichotomies of the age. Sometimes these latent tensions burst out, both in the social sphere, as a result of the spread of industrialization, and in the intellectual sphere, where the new attitudes derived from the advance of science clashed with the principles of religious faith; the deeper the religious convictions, the more intense the conflicts.

At the very end of this realist period stands the most conflict-torn figure of the whole nineteenth century – Friedrich Nietzsche (1844–1900). His significance far outstrips the field of lyric poetry but it is in his lyrics that his most personal thoughts and emotions find expression – and not only in his few actual lyrics as such but also in the lyrical moments of *Also sprach Zarathustra* (1883–5) and his aphoristic works. His dichotomy shows itself in the juxtaposition of solemn statement and savage judgement, of uncontrolled passion and destructive satire, of religious utterance and ruthless blasphemy. With Nietzsche the nineteenth-century tradition of faith in positivism and scientific progress, which Gottfried Keller still held, is at an end, and doubt, for all the growing material prosperity of the age, becomes the dominant mood. Nietzsche, professor of classics in Basle and colleague of Burckhardt and Bachofen, felt the conflicts in his own life, and in joyful destructiveness made the whole world listen to his tale of loneliness, abandonment and alienation from God. Gripped by the spirit of antiquity and the spirit of music, he uttered a series of dissonant sounds which finally became the ravings of a schizophrenic. These sounds heralded even greater intellectual revolts which were to follow in the twentieth century, above all that of expressionism, which was to succeed the brief interlude of naturalism.

Modern Literature
(1885 to the present)

ALBERT BETTEX

Conflicts in the Wilhelmine Age, 1885–1918

The foundation of the Second Reich in 1871 brought powerful secular influences to the fore which had been gathering strength during the 1860s, borne by a self-confident generation of men set on extending the frontiers of material life and filled with the knowledge, common to the whole Western world at that time, that they were participating in the irresistible progress of political, economic and technological forces. Introversion, like the plain and simple *Biedermeier* mode of conduct of the mid-nineteenth century, was at a discount; as Jacob Burckhardt complained, the world had become more vulgar since 1830. Germany changed from an agricultural to a predominantly industrial nation: in 1871 31 per cent of the population lived in towns; by 1895 it was 45·5 per cent, and by 1935 around 66 per cent.

This movement towards the towns is the most important force in the background of the literature of the time, creating an atmosphere of restlessness in which men sought new experiences, and providing a variety of new stimuli. German culture came into contact with other European cultures and with the cultures of America and Asia, and even those who feared an invasion of foreign values realized the European context of German intellectual life.

Under Prussian leadership the power and achievements of the Reich grew. Where the national-liberal novelist Hans Blum had written in 1860 of the present poverty but coming prosperity of Germany, Rudolf Stratz, a fashionable writer of the Wilhelmine age whose memoirs tell us a great deal about the time (*Reisen und Reifen*, 1926), wrote enthusiastically of the wealth that the Germans had in the meantime acquired. Life was seen as a ladder up which one had to climb as high and as fast as possible. As the population grew – in 1871 Germany had 41 million people, in 1914, 68 million; in 1871 the Austrian Empire had 36 million, in 1910, 48·5 million – so also did the tensions and conflicts, and during the Weimar Republic society became even more divided, with shocks and crises which, together with the runaway development of the economy, also left their mark on literary life.

Above all, however, the years after 1870 show the long-foreseen abandonment of the great idealist tradition of the century, and whether openly or in surreptitious ways men were increasingly freeing themselves from the demands and dogmas of all forms of transcendental belief.

There is a considerable body of writing, meagre in literary value but socially and intellectually revealing, and of great popularity in its day, which reflects the desire on the part of the upper and middle class between 1870 and 1914 to retain the *status quo*. These works were primarily intended as entertainment – works such as Felix Dahn's and Julius Wolff's novels of heroic Teutonic times, Marlitt's idyllic tales of the petit bourgeoisie and of countesses in disguise, the emotional iambic dramas of Adolf Wilbrandt, and the idealized Hohenzollern dramas of Ernst von Wildenbruch, which sought to blend the spirit of Potsdam with the spirit of classical Weimar. These works, like the novel of contemporary manners, with its successful men of affairs and captains of industry (Spielhagen, an 1848 liberal, had written similar works on a somewhat higher level), show the dubious values of the age and are written in a flat style full of commonplaces and external showiness; like the representatives of these values themselves, the writers of such novels cherished both idealistic and realistic principles, but neither set of ideas went deep enough. In order to be 'true to life' they crammed their stories with material: the most blatant example is the so-called archaeological novel, works with a mass of learned footnotes, compendia of knowledge not worth having, such as Georg Ebers's *Eine ägyptische Königstochter* (1864; 13th edition, 1889). Life was seen, in a crude simplification of Darwin's ideas, as a struggle for survival, and the earth, after Büchner and Moleschott, as part of a mechanical universe composed of mass and energy. This 'realism', however, led into idealism, for there was conceived to be some vague, pseudo-Christian 'higher being' which guaranteed the solidity of this 'realism' and exercised authority – 'like a police department', as Musil put it – over the affairs of Church, State and family. This is what the historian Karl Lamprecht called the Janus-like character of the age.

After 1890 we find, in the broader, more discriminating novels of men such as Rudolf Stratz and Walter Bloem, heroes who represent an epoch in which prosperity grew even faster, technical knowledge expanded and imperialistic confidence flourished. Every material and intellectual luxury was within reach and continued progress assured, and Germany, like other countries, seemed a land of boundless opportunities. The life of the lower classes, on the other hand, like the presence of new, revolutionary ideas, was barely heeded, and then only in a spirit of disapproval and ignorance of the new values that were at stake.

NATURALISM

Such was the background of German literature up to, and including, World War I. The new generation of writers felt itself to be the agent of a historical mission to oppose the spirit of Wilhelmine Germany, and 'modern' became at once the most popular and the most detested word in the language. The fashionable literature of the day was attacked in new journals, the first of which, *Kritische Waffengänge*, appeared in 1882, published by the brothers Heinrich and Julius Hart, and groups of writers, above all in Berlin and Munich, were formed to discuss critical principles. M. G. Conrad's journal *Die Gesellschaft*, founded in Munich in 1885, was a pioneer in publicizing the works of Nietzsche and Zola, while O. J. Bierbaum's Bohemian novel *Stilpe* (1897) gives a picture of the activities of these groups. All prevailing patterns of thought, philosophical, moral, social and political, were rejected, but the powers that be were not slow to defend themselves: a Junker in the Prussian parliament declared that the proper place for Gerhart Hauptmann was in jail, and the powers of censorship were called upon, as a result of which Karl Henckell's poems of social comment *Amselrufe* (1888) and Arno Holz's *Lieder eines Modernen* (1885) had to be published in Switzerland, while the earliest naturalist plays – Hauptmann's *Vor Sonnenaufgang* (1889) and Holz and Schlaf's *Die Familie Selicke* (1891) – had to be performed privately by the 'Freie Bühne' in order to escape the Berlin censor.

It took some time before the positive aspects of the new movement became apparent. The Munich group had its patriotic as well as its revolutionary moments, but in Berlin some, like Holz, carried the battle-cry of 'Truth' to extremes. Contemporary life supplied the subject-matter and the intellectual atmosphere, while it was the task of the poets to recognize and imitate the laws of nature which the work of Haeckel, Büchner, Forel and others had uncovered. The pioneer tract in this respect was Wilhelm Bölsche's *Die naturwissenschaftlichen Grundlagen der Poesie* (1887). The young naturalists saw man as part of a deterministic universe: nothing transcended matter. Their main concern was thus to depict characters who, in a world where innocence and guilt were meaningless, were the victims of a merciless fate invoked by immutable personal character and the conditions of an inescapable environment. Even the man who enjoyed a degree of inner freedom was made to bow to these sinister forces. They deliberately cultivated what the fashionable literature of the day ignored – the lower classes, workers' cottages, slums – while the other side of life was vested with all the marks of decadence. To the charge of betraying the cause of literature they retorted, in the words of Hermann Conradi: 'Please be so kind as to accustom yourselves to the inevitability of dirt, decay, sweat, slime and other perfumes.'

But for all their destructiveness and cynicism, the naturalists retained an unshakeable faith in the reform of human affairs and fought, as champions of the rights of man and apostles of human brotherhood, for such causes as the emancipation of the workers and the emancipation of women. In *Das Abenteuer meiner Jugend*, published in 1937, Hauptmann summarized the mood of these days: 'We were sustained by faith – faith in human progress, and faith in the victory of science and human knowledge. We believed that the victory of truth would destroy religious illusions and false gods, and that war would be seen as a passing chapter in history. We believed in the victory of human brotherhood.'

The most difficult task was the evolution of valid literary forms. The naturalistic lyric never progressed beyond rebellious verses in the style of Herwegh and melodramatic descriptions of misery and poverty. The winter of 1887–8 saw the appearance of the first work of what might be called thoroughgoing naturalism – Holz and Schlaf's prose sketch *Papa Hamlet*. This was a passionate attempt to bring German literature from its state of stagnation into the sphere of the social drama of Ibsen, the experimental novel of Zola and the disturbing, aggressive works of Tolstoy and Dostoevsky. A literature which sought absolute truth to nature could have but a single stylistic ideal: to obliterate the distinction between nature and art. 'Art tends to return to nature,' said Holz in *Die Kunst, ihr Wesen und ihre Gesetze* (1890) – hence the directness of the naturalist style, in which faithfulness to external reality is the only acceptable equivalent to the inner life of the spirit; hence also the use of milieu description and the so-called 'Sekundenstil' – the second-for-second narration of events – in naturalist prose, while in the drama elements such as poetic verse, monologues and strict construction were regarded as wilful aesthetic interference with reality, so that it was a rule to avoid all classical subjects and forms.

The work of Gerhart Hauptmann (1862–1946) stands out from the general run of naturalist literature, represented by works such as Max Kretzer's novels in the manner of Zola, the early plays of Max Halbe and Clara Viebig's tales of the Eifel. A Silesian by birth, his pulse beat with the pulse of the time, and already in Haeckel's lectures in Jena and Forel's in Zürich, as well as in the company of the leaders of the new literary movement in Berlin, he was well aware of the task before him. Right down to *Vor Sonnenuntergang* (1934), the last of his naturalist plays, he applied his remarkable gifts of critical observation and emotional understanding to produce a range of vivid, closely observed real-life characters unique in the literature of the modern German theatre.

Hauptmann's main concern was with man trapped in his own helplessness, at the mercy of a brutal environment and dominated by a desperate longing to escape. He created this character in the first instance by naturalistic means which went beyond the presentation of mere types: such are

Die Weber (1892), with its world of working-class misery, and the family tragedy *Einsame Menschen* (1891). In *Florian Geyer* (1896) he introduced the historical dimension into naturalism, which reached its climax in *Fuhrmann Henschel* (1899) and *Rose Bernd* (1903). In *Hanneles Himmelfahrt* (1894) and *Und Pippa tanzt* (1905) his naturalism is blended with a characteristically Silesian dreaminess and a premonition of mysterious forces at work in the world, a feature that anticipates the irrationalism of the twentieth century.

Following Nietzsche, Bachofen and others, the later Hauptmann – the travelogue *Griechischer Frühling* (1907) and the story *Der Ketzer von Soana* (1918) – saw human nature as having its roots in chthonian spiritual depths, while on the metaphysical plane his world was governed by the forces of destiny which the symbolically named philosopher Wann seeks in *Pippa* – forces present in Hindu philosophy, in Gnosticism and in the Silesian mysticism of Jakob Böhme. He is at his best when concerned with empirical reality, or when this reality is combined with his urge to transcendental speculation, as in *Der Narr in Christo Emanuel Quint* (1901); in purely meditative mood, contemplating ultimate reality (his epic in *terze rime, Der große Traum* (1942)), his intellectual powers show their limitations. The dramas of his old age, written in the style of Shakespeare or Aeschylus, rarely touch the heights. From the utopian ideal of his youth – a world free of poverty, fallacy and injustice – he moved to the utopian ideal of his old age – the vision of a religious saviour who will visit the earth (cf. his *Christophorus* fragment, written during the last months of the 1939–45 war, in which he developed further the figure of Wann).

The earliest literary works of naturalism were quickly overtaken by others which, in their concern with reforming the world, soon left naturalism in the narrow sense behind – the works of men such as Hermann Löns, Hermann Stehr and Paul Ernst. But the naturalist revolt had made its mark. Its attack on the spirit of Wilhelmine Germany had cleared the air, and the violence of its language had destroyed the validity of stock phrases; it had extended the range of 'reality', even if only in a downwards direction, and shown, albeit in an exaggerated form, the limitations of the concept of the 'free man'. Only by ignoring his conscience could the modern poet pretend not to see the controversial new spheres that the naturalists had uncovered, and their influence was still felt at the time of impressionism and the 'new objectivity'.

THE CULT OF POWER

The overthrow of traditional values had already been preached by Nietzsche and his followers in the name of an abandoned, Dionysian, life-affirming philosophy which accepts the whole of existence with its pantheistic joys and challenges, but also its destructive and sinister forces.

No modern philosopher has had such an influence on German literature as Nietzsche. In shattering the values of Christianity, patriotism, socialism and other creeds which stood in the way of his ruthless cult of the power, the glory and the beauty of life, he destroyed many of the humane elements of a great cultural tradition but at the same time assumed the mantle of a liberator, revealing how that tradition had become debased through human presumptuousness and sloth. Nietzsche's philosophy inflamed the minds of numerous writers, many of whom cultivated a virulent strain of enthusiastic hatred that fed on the nihilistic aspects of his thought.

Even more powerful than the nihilistic Nietzsche was the visionary Nietzsche of *Also sprach Zarathustra* (1883–5), the prophet of the elation of man in his awareness of his greatness and in his search for his destiny. This spirit gave many a sense of meaning to life and to art: Gottfried Benn and Ernst Jünger are only two of the many through whose works one can still hear Nietzsche's rolling cadences and see the grand, intoxicating images embedded in the precision – developed from Latin models – of his style and language.

By contrast the over-sensitive Nietzsche of the poem *Venedig*, the eulogizer of Wagner's *Tristan* and Schopenhauer's cult of suffering, retires into the background. And when he invoked not only Dionysos but also Jesus, he symbolized both his own personal dichotomy and that of the century that was to follow: the essence of life was not chaos but multiplicity, and a single mind cannot achieve that 'revaluation of all values' which he had demanded.

Allied in spirit to Nietzsche's philosophy was an individualistic movement in literature at the turn of the century. Richard Dehmel (1863–1920) sought, in his elegant, world-centred lyrics, to reconcile the vital forces of life with a joyful spirituality that embraced the whole of the universe, and pioneered, together with Wedekind, a new freedom in the presentation of sex as one of the most powerful forces in life (*Die Verwandlungen der Venus* (1907)).

While Dehmel's vision also encompassed the fate of the working class, Frank Wedekind (1864–1918) concentrated his gaze on eroticism and the individual. The power of pleasure and the pleasure of power were for him man's basic urges, and in his blunt, rugged dramas he contrasts the prostitute (*Erdgeist* (1895)), the speculator and adventurer (*Der Marquis von Keith* (1900)) and other amoral, 'unconditional' characters with those caught up in middle-class morality, whose vitality is sapped by protective conventions and who know nothing of the 'spirituality of the flesh'. This is Wedekind's subject from *Frühlings Erwachen* (1891), a tragedy of adolescence, right down to his last plays. Equally independent, forthright and caustic are the early social novels of Heinrich Mann (*Die Göttinnen* (1902–4); *Der Untertan* (1918)).

This literature, which had its points of contact with Strindberg, d'Annunzio and Oscar Wilde, mirrors two common phenomena in this age of European prosperity. One is the appearance of an increasing number of social rebels and adventurers, reacting against either the restraints of their aristocratic upbringing (cf. the stories by Countess Franziska von Reventlow, who became a courtesan in Schwabing) or their middle-class limitations; Wedekind's *Marquis von Keith*, interestingly and appropriately enough, was originally called *Münchner Szenen nach dem Leben aufgezeichnet*. The other is the growth of Bohemian artistic circles, a reaction against mass-development in society and an assertion of independence. In Montmartre, in Schwabing, in Friedrichshagen with the Hart brothers, in Monte veritá near Ascona and in other places lively colonies of artists grew up, among them political anarchists: two such were J. H. Mackay and Erich Mühsam, the former a follower of Stirner, the latter of Landauer, and together they wrote collections of aggressive verse (*Sturm* (2nd edition, 1892); *Wüste, Krater, Wolken* (1914)). One of the most authentic novels of the Bohemian life of the time is Hugo Ball's *Flametti oder vom Dandysmus der Armen* (1918). But few of these Bohemian radicals lived far into the century, and although they were to be found in plenty in the Weimar Republic, it was no longer dangerous to live such a life. One of the last of these Bohemians of 1900, the left-wing Erich Mühsam, was found in the Nazi concentration camp of Oranienburg in 1934, murdered by his guards.

Two further effects of the cult of individualism launched by Nietzsche remain to be mentioned: the appearance of a new art of parody and satire, often with grotesque overtones; and the stimulation to experiment. The satire was the product, partly of a proud self-confidence, partly of an undisguised pleasure in taunting the enemy. Such is the spirit behind the caricatures of the schoolmasters in Wedekind's *Frühlings Erwachen* and H. von Gumppenberg's parodies in *Der teutsche Dichterroß* (1901). A light-weight equivalent to such satires is the literary cabaret, founded by Bohemians following the French example: the 'Überbrettl' was founded by Ernst von Wolzogen in Berlin in 1900, and 'Die elf Scharfrichter' by Wedekind and others in Munich.

The poetic imagination ranged farther and farther afield. Wedekind moved away from the realistic drama and expounded his ideas in a series of free, independent, almost expressionistic scenes; others chose extreme, grotesque subjects, such as those found in the stories of Paul Scheerbart (1863–1915), with their space-travellers, their builders of glass cities, their moon-men and their inhabitants of paradise.

IMPRESSIONISM

The philosophy of extreme individualism and the emergence of life *à la bohème* by no means exhausted the possibilities open to progressively minded artists and writers. In the early 1890s the movement known as impressionism emerged, seeking fulfilment in the refinement of personal feeling, finding inspiration in nature-painting, and leaving behind the naturalists and the copiers of reality. Liliencron's unashamed sensuousness broke new ground, and Schlaf (in his sketches *In Dingsda*, 1892) and Holz (in his volumes of verse called *Phantasus* (1898 onwards)) also penetrated the world of refined experience. 'Our essence lies on the surface,' cried the rapturous Hugo von Hofmannsthal, expressing the poetic creed which was his aesthetic answer to the experience of the manifold glories of the world. Like Jacobsen, Proust and Anne de Noailles (whose sensitivity was so praised by the young Rilke), poets gave themselves over to the creative act of perception: characters in early works of Hesse abandon themselves to the joys of listening, seeing, breathing, feeling, and Spinell in Thomas Mann's story *Tristan* listens to the woman's playing with a nervous eagerness like that displayed by those with an insatiable hunger for the rich orchestral timbres of Wagner and Richard Strauss. This was the time of Ernst Mach's inflated claim: 'The only reality is sense-impressions.'

But impressionistic poets aimed higher than this. They were masters of atmosphere, whether of a landscape, an interior scene or a human relationship: the sensory and the spiritual are in the last analysis barely distinguishable. The unplumbed depths of the ego were an irresistible attraction, and they pursued the most arcane of emotions. They mistrusted the man who was self-assured, robust and active; their own characters were romantic yearners, seeking fulfilment in the sensuous and spiritual delights of the moment and identifying themselves with the mysterious transience of life as described by Georg Simmel in his early writings. In his *Brief des Lord Chandos* (1902) Hofmannsthal wrote: 'The essence of our age is ambiguity and uncertainty. Where older generations believed in stability, we know that our age is built on shifting sands.'

In contrast to the naturalists, the impressionists paid little attention to general conditions or to the public as such. Instead they turned their thoughts to those with whom they felt a special affinity: the refined, sensitive woman (Helene von Altenwyl in Hofmannsthal's comedy *Der Schwierige*); the child (Friedrich Huch's *Mao* (1907)); the artist (Carl Hauptmann's *Einhart der Lächler* (1907)); the Japanese man (Dauthendey's *Die acht Gesichter am Biwasee* (1911)); the aristocrat (Graf Bühl in *Der Schwierige*, and numerous characters in the stories of Eduard von Keyserling). While the aristocracy was losing more and more of its political power as the influence of the masses grew, so it attracted the minds of impressionist and, later, neo-idealist poets anxious to protect and preserve the best elements of a dying class, such as pleasure in the unusual and the daring, love of the beautiful things in the world, the law of elegance, the conviction of the human value of everything non-utilitarian.

Impressionist literature could not, and would not, present firmly delineated goals of human existence. Who could draw the border between good and evil, truth and falsehood? The concept of relativity was in the air. As for transcendence, the question was left open, and poets, confronted with the paradoxes of modern life, were often overcome with a new *Weltschmerz*. 'Happiness is but a moment', we read in Thomas Mann's *Buddenbrooks*. The suffering of the dissipated ego vanished when the ego experienced moments of timeless reality. Hence the intensity with which the impressionists portrayed the redeeming experiences of beauty and art, love – and death, the moment when the tortured Ixion's wheel, of which Schopenhauer spoke, was still for ever. Schopenhauer, indeed, was a clear influence on the impressionists, especially through the liberating doctrine of Nirvana which he preached.

Such a fear of everything fixed and rigid was bound to lead to a view of language as a profoundly inadequate vehicle of expression, and the impressionistic style is the reflection of a fear, both of a rigid, stifling use of language and of being mesmerized by the immeasurable wealth and complexity of the living word. These poets used a highly refined vocabulary and a remarkably flexible syntax. New forms emerged: Holz, for instance, strung together a loose collection of words and phrases in lines of uneven length arranged round a central axis in a pattern designed to appeal to the eye:

> Hinter blühenden Apfelbaumzweigen
> steigt
> der Mond auf . . .
> aus
> weichstem Dunkel
> traumsüß flötend, schluchzend, jubelnd,
> mein Herz schwillt über,
> die
> Nachtigall!
>
> (from 'Mondabend')

In the novel and the drama a resolute pursuit of purpose gave way to a pattern of loose, atmospheric scenes, and in the smaller forms miniature masterpieces were produced, like Thomas Mann's *Tristan*, Musil's and Mann's essays, Peter Altenberg's sketches *Wie ich es sehe* (1896), Hofmannsthal's one-act play *Der Tod des Tizian* (1901), and various collections of lyric poetry. Here the impressionists' use of a new, suggestive, partly precise and descriptive, partly allusive, colourful language, often showing a relatedness to music, had a lasting influence and laid the foundation for some of the greatest achievements in modern German lyric poetry. The impressionist world was not an unreal dream-world, nor can it be simply considered as the source of a new style, for it left profound marks on outlooks and attitudes even among those, like Thomas Mann, Musil and Hofmannsthal, who outgrew it. There is also a spiritual link between impressionism and those over-sensitive, inbred characters one meets in high society and Bohemian circles around 1900, and the names Katherine Mansfield, Chekhov, Jacobsen, Paul Bourget and Proust show how international impressionism had become, establishing a defence against the threat of domination by brute force and mass mediocrity.

In his early works Thomas Mann (1875–1955) uses the weapon of irony in the battle between artist and society. In the four generations depicted in *Buddenbrooks* (1901) it is sometimes the artist's sensitivity that is held up against the apathy of society, sometimes the practically minded citizen who is praised at the expense of the other-worldly artist. Yet although this ambivalence cannot produce firm judgements, one is given the clear impression that it is the artist, or the man who is both an artist and a willing member of society, who represents humanity at its highest. The most prominent of Mann's impressionistic traits is his creation of atmosphere – the influence of Fontane is apparent here – together with a tendency to dwell with relish on the ambivalent and uncertain aspect of things. At the same time he shows a growing determination to achieve a state of permanence and universal humanitarianism, such as that embodied in the fickle yet unbreakable bond between the lovers in *Königliche Hoheit* (1909).

Thomas Mann said that he was a historian of a decadence which he sought to overcome. If one reads 'ambivalence' for 'decadence', one has the clue to his later works, in which he turns his intense gaze upon what he saw as the basic conflicts and ambiguities in man and in the world. The subject of *Der Zauberberg* (1924) is 'the whole moral and political dialectic of the Western world', and the soul of Hans Castorp is a battleground between Western individualism and Eastern messianism. The tetralogy *Joseph und seine Brüder* (1933–44) expounds the dichotomy between hidden, mysterious spiritual forces and the manifest power of the conscious intellect, while *Doktor Faustus* (1947), written in America during World War II, treats, on the one hand, of the contradiction in the German character between the urge to destruction and the achievement of spiritual greatness, and, on the other hand, of the sinister depths of a creative, artistic nature. At almost every turn Mann is passionately involved with the problems of the modern age, from the exploration of middle-class ideals through depth psychology to the self-destruction of the Nazi state.

One must be cautious in one's use of the word 'decadent' in connection with these works. There is a barely visible line that separates an impressionism which, despite its sense of despair, welcomed the newly discovered riches of the world, and a weary art which, in a mood of triviality, cynicism or desperation, persisted in viewing man as an isolated creature. Only this latter – found in the destructive characters created by Leopold Andrian and Arthur Schnitzler, and characteristic also of most of the poetic work – but not the biographies – of the third of these Viennese writers, Stefan Zweig – is the equivalent of decadence. The value of Zweig's stories, such as those in the collection *Verwirrung der Gefühle* (1926), lies solely in their presentation of psychological case-histories and their lively interplay of instinct and intellect of the kind which the work of Freud had made familiar.

Vienna, with its frivolity, its wit, its easy-going atmosphere and its glitter, was a natural breeding ground for impressionism at the turn of the century, as is most strikingly seen in the three-volume social novel *Der Mann ohne Eigenschaften* (1930–43) by Robert Musil (1880–1942). This work, a challenge to all fixed forms of thought and life, posits a prototype of modern man in all his uncertainties, man searching for solutions to the problem of how he can retain his personal identity in a world full of confusions and conflicts without collapsing under the strain. The profusion of ambiguities, said Musil, was to his advantage, and in his *Skizze der Erkenntnis des Dichters* (1918) he stated the task as one of creating an image of man 'who had more to hope for from the unpredictable than from the certain'. It is a task beyond the power of man to achieve, because there is no fixed pattern of relationships, but Musil's own career as an officer, as a university teacher and as a scientist showed what could be done. He spent twenty years on his unfinished *magnum opus* as an impoverished writer and lived the last six years of his life in voluntary exile in Geneva. *Der Mann ohne Eigenschaften*, for all its essayistic rather than narrative style, is one of the richest, most subtle philosophical and psychological products of Viennese impressionism.

Musil did not achieve as great an independence of these forces as did Hugo von Hofmannsthal (1874–1929). Hofmannsthal's works show a progress from one kind of Austria to another – from the brooding, ironical, Viennese Austria of impressionism, bent on breaking with tradition – qualities that appear in his lyrics and in his early dramas – to the imperial Austria in which great European cultural traditions met and where Hofmannsthal experienced the meaning of a culture in which traditional religious values still flourished, a tradition of 'hieroglyphs of a secret, eternal wisdom whose presence I seemed to sense at times, as though behind a veil', as he put it. *Jedermann* (1911), the *Salzburger Großes Welttheater* (1923) and other similar plays are the expressions of this. 'Poetry contains the truth of things and the judgement on things', he wrote, with idealistic conviction. The most attractive product of his union of the urge towards the establishment of intellectual life on universally valid principles with the sensitive, over-refined concerns of his early career, is *Der Schwierige* (1921), the most successful of his plays.

Impressionism brought German literature a wealth of nuances of thought, feeling and language, and, together with the Nietzschean philosophy of the Dionysian life, was of all pre-1914 literary movements the one whose influence extended the farthest. Something of both these movements can be seen in the characters of Peter Hille and Robert Walser, as well as in the work of those – Morgenstern, Rilke, Schaeffer, Carossa – who sought more distant goals. This is the point at which, in 1900, a new generation of poets parted company with what had been regarded up to that time as modern.

NEO-IDEALISM

In *Bilanz der Moderne* (1904) the critic Samuel Lublinski observed that literary life at the turn of the century was dominated by the conflict between those who denied the forces of tradition – the naturalists, the followers of Nietzsche and the impressionists – and those who adopted a neo-conservative position. The latter mark the beginning of a movement, rich in creative talents, which can be traced down to the 1930s.

Its members regarded naturalism with disapproval as a movement held prisoner by a mechanistic philosophy and restricted to a concern with everyday affairs, above all with the seamy side of life. They were fascinated by the Nietzschean cult of grandeur and the impressionists' aesthetic subtlety but sought to reach beyond these to broader, more firmly based viewpoints. They were at one with those who strove to revive humane values but looked for a more comprehensive truth, for the ultimate sources of their rich, newly discovered, unassailable existence. 'Is it possible that, in spite of our inventions and our progress, in spite of civilization, religion and human wisdom, we are still only living on the surface of life?' – such is the question posed by Rilke in *Malte Laurids Brigge* (1909), a book which sounds a note of warning and reveals depths of despair but which also offers constructive insights into the problems it raises.

This 'conservative revolution' sought to renew life and art through the great timeless formative values in the manner described by Hans Carossa in his *Das Jahr der schönen Täuschungen* (1941): 'In the midst of massive technical progress and the spread of the craving for power, many poets watched man's true inner values decaying – his free and inspired soul, the nobility of moderation, reverence for the inexpressible, beauty, the creative power of mourning and of dreams. . . . For in all classes of society there were individuals who distrusted the extravagant claims of the age.'

This movement was called 'neo-idealism' by Hofstaetter and Peters in their *Sachwörterbuch der Deutschkunde* (1930); it has also been characterized as 'neo-classicism', 'neo-Romanticism' and 'symbolism', each of which, however, only concentrates on a particular aspect of the phenomenon as a whole. Most of these '-isms' were coined by their practitioners themselves and are not necessarily gross over-simplifications; they connote genuine unifying attitudes among contemporaries and have the power to convey something of the true historical quality of the age.

Neo-classicism

The epic *Prometheus und Epimetheus* by Carl Spitteler (1845–1924) lies like an erratic block in the desolate wastes of fashionable German literature in 1880. Here, three years before the first book of Nietzsche's *Zarathustra*, Spitteler defiantly proclaimed in a series of remarkable visions the message of man's unbroken strength and grandeur, at a moment when individualisms were being swallowed up in the development of mass attitudes among both the upper and lower classes. Spitteler links the realism of Keller and his Swiss contemporaries with the neo-classical urge for grand themes in grand forms. The former element predominates in his short stories, such as the experimental impressionist tale *Gustav* (1892) and the naturalistic *Konrad der Leutnant* (1898), the latter in his three great epics. Almost every one of his works, however, springs from a deep-seated suffering and rage – suffering, because of the pain endured by the innocent masses at the hands of a blind fate, and rage, because of the rule of inferiority in the world. All his works praise those spiritual forces which conquer the miseries of the world, and he gave his favourite characters a Herculean strength to achieve great things, almost in the manner of Nietzsche's *Zarathustra* but without the urge to nihilism. Only large-scale forms could contain such themes, and in his epics, above all in *Der olympische Frühling* (1900 onwards), he created his own classical world of gods and imaginary characters who lived out their adventurous lives on a realistically depicted earth.

By contrast Stefan George (1868–1933) devoted his poetic energies from the very beginning to the service of a single idea: the praise of heroic life through beauty. His *Teppich des Lebens* (1900) gives his definitive statement of what was to be pursued and what was to be avoided: the knights and ascetic monks, the classical shepherds and heroes of his earlier works all reflect his historical principle of distinguishing solely in terms of high and low, beautiful and ugly. *Das Jahr der Seele* (1897) had presented nature as the reflection of the moods of the beautiful soul, and *Der siebente Ring* (1907) embodies the cult of Maximin, the presence of the divine in a beautiful human being, through which George boldly attempted to give metaphysical validity to a purely aesthetic *Weltbild*.

George's apparently egocentric poetry, was, however, not cut off from the age, for it was meant as a warning against the dangers of neglecting the large-scale view of life, and as such it has links with other European movements. He was greatly influenced by the aesthetic gospel of the masters of *art nouveau*, who sought to protect man by surrounding him with beauty, including the beauty of everyday objects on which the artist had lovingly dwelt. From England came the influence of the pre-Raphaelites, from Paris that of Mallarmé and his circle; Nietzsche and Böcklin stood in the background, but it was above all the masters of antiquity to whom George was drawn.

He quickly gathered a circle of disciples round him, and the *Blätter für die Kunst* became its organ. Each year he was solemnly received by his assembled acolytes and preached to them, members of an intellectual élite, the strict message of the new life. From this circle came important critical works such as Gundolf's *Goethe* and Bertram's *Nietzsche*, which took the art of biography out of the narrow limits of positivism; at the same time there were not a few who assumed an intolerable intellectual arrogance and expressed themselves in empty, bombastic phrases. In *Der Stern des Bundes* (1913) and his other latter works George, sensing the threat to his work from contemporary events, addressed himself directly to his disciples and to the world at large, reviving the old form of the epigram with its directness and clarity of utterance.

Certain poems of George's, images of the beautiful life couched in a language of conciseness and precision, have become part of the German literary tradition, and his call for the purity of language and the worship of grandeur and beauty has been heard in many quarters. Yet this renewal of the aesthetic sense was based on the dubious premiss of art, not as servant but as master. George's aesthetic ephebes loved only part of reality, and their precepts had both a positive and negative aspect. Indeed, George's over-insistence on the values of beauty left its mark on his own poems, many of which ring hollow because their noble form is not matched by their nobility of content.

George's cult of antiquity stimulated many of his contemporaries, attracted by the timelessness of classical form. Isolde Kurz wrote poems and novels in the spirit of Burckhardt's presentation of noble Renaissance man, and Rudolf Binding, a master of the short story (*Der Opfergang* (1912)), relates in his *Erlebtes Leben* (1928) how he was captured both by the ideal of classical grandeur and simplicity and by the ideals of English chivalry. Many set to writing neo-classical dramas but none succeeded in producing a convincing work. These attempts did, however, lead to Paul Ernst's *Der Weg zur Form* (1906), an influential aesthetic treatise, while in his autobiographical novel *Der schmale Weg zum Glück* (1904), a work of great interest for an understanding of the age, Ernst shows his development from radical social criticism through idealist philosophy to the doctrine of Christian redemption.

In 1944 the Swiss poet Siegfried Lang published a selection of his verse called *Vom andern Ufer*, a series of strict verse-forms of great subtlety and refinement, treating of the strange, beautiful subjects which attracted George, the Paris Parnassiens among whom Lang lived, and, later, René Guénon, with his oriental mysticism. Similarly the Austrian poet Josef Weinheber (1892–1945) escaped from the fear, loneliness and suffering of his narrow, lower-middle-class upbringing into 'the inner nature of language', composing neo-classical lyrics in strict formal patterns which seemed to preclude triviality. Devoted to heroic ideals of sacrifice, discipline and the creative power of suffering, and opposed to the decline of values brought about by the 'new objectivity' and by expressionism, Weinheber served his ideals of grandeur and perfection by composing extended odes and hymns. At the same time he acknowledged his Viennese origins in his dialect verses in *Wien wörtlich* (1935). The summit of his at times somewhat forced achievement was reached with *Adel und Untergang* (1934), a level maintained in *Zwischen Göttern und Dämonen* (1938), and he rounded off his life's work with *Hier ist das Wort* (1948), singing the praises of traditional verse-forms, metres, rhymes and rhythms as the manifestations of a spirit which transcends the wretchedness of earthly transience.

The spirit of the Wilhelmine age was not conducive to the retention of true literary values: newspapers and mass journals had little respect for language, and it was the achievement of Nietzsche, some of the naturalists, the impressionists and, finally, of poets like George and Rilke, to create with the intensification of their relationship to life and nature, an intensification of the power of language. Everyday, worn-out words were excised. George revived old words (*Karde, Molke*) and romantic loanwords (*Turmalin, Karneol, Demant, Alabaster, Kristall*), while Rilke restored the pristine power of everyday words by setting them in strange new contexts. German and foreign masters of style were enthusiastically studied. Some even attempted to invent novel languages, like Rudolf Borchardt, author of the *Eranos-Brief* (1924), who translated Dante into a form of late Middle High German as a protest against the cheapening of contemporary language.

In the realm of form the neo-idealists cultivated both the rational and the irrational. Schaeffer's novel *Helianth* (1920) is constructed according to strict numerical principles, while Weinheber's *Heroische Trilogie* (1925–30) has a tripartite central section flanked by two outer sections in which the number of lines of each outer group of fifteen sonnets corresponds exactly to that of the tripartite central section. In contrast to classical and baroque influences one finds those of the irrational, of music; there is no end to the new rhythms and sound-effects, no limit to the wealth of images conjured up to express the inexpressible, in a manner like that of the European symbolists. The rational and the irrational are evenly balanced in the work of Wilhelm von Scholz, which displays a strictness of form and at the same time a romantic leaning towards the occult in his drama *Der Wettlauf mit dem Schatten* (1922) and his novel *Perpetua* (1926).

New attitudes to nature

Since the poetry of neo-idealism sought to represent the profoundest values of life, it was naturally receptive to whatever forces – physical, moral, spiritual, aesthetic, supernatural – could enrich the inner life. Certain poets tried to find their way back to nature: the travel diaries and stories of Josef Ponten (*Die letzte Reise* (1925); *Die luganesische Landschaft* (1926)) belong in this context, and in his *Wanderungen* (1924) Wilhelm von Scholz aimed to show how 'the meaning of life becomes fuller and deeper for the man who is made to confront the power of the earth in nature'. In the same mould are the lyrics of Wilhelm Lehmann (1882–1968), whose nature-poems brought hope in 1945 to a generation shattered by recent events: in poems written in the 1920s in Schleswig-Holstein he shows himself striving to discover what he called 'the inner peace of things, the changeless nature of pure existence' (*Bukolisches Tagebuch aus den Jahren 1927–32*, published in 1948). Carossa, too, living in the forests and mountains of Bavaria and by the sick-beds of his patients – he was a doctor – looked upon microcosm and macrocosm as parts of a single great organism through which the forces of life ebbed and flowed.

The new approach to history

Ricarda Huch wrote in a letter of 1942 that she had tried 'to let the dross of history pass through the sieve and retain only the gold'. This sentence touches at once the efforts of 'modern' poets of the Wilhelmine era to establish a new, creative relationship between the present and the past. Hofmannsthal proposed the establishment in Salzburg of a theatre in which the new operas and dramas of post-1918 Europe should be performed alongside the 'classics'. This was expressive of an attitude as far removed from the oppressive Wilhelminian emphasis on the legacy of the past as it was from the narrowminded dogmatism characteristic of certain revolutionary poets. It was an attitude that would have also opposed the rejection of any meaningful interpretation of the past, such as that later adopted by Gottfried Benn, to whom history was little more than a stupefying assemblage of portentous names which concealed nothing. Instead it seized on the true, great, beautiful moments of the past and brought them into the present. Anthologies and translations flourished, the former represented by Hofmannsthal's *Deutsches Lesebuch* (1923–3) and Borchardt's *Ewiger Vorrat deutscher Poesie* (1926), the latter by the work of George, Wolfskehl and Rilke. Appropriately, the essay became a highly developed form: Hofmannsthal (*Berührung der Sphären* (1931)), Borchardt, Carl J. Burckhardt and Rudolf Kassner are among those who found in it an ideal means of integrating the great figures and movements of the past into the cultural life of the present.

Rudolf Alexander Schröder (1878–1962), who around 1900 was among the aesthetes lamenting the passing of beauty, later took his place with those who sought permanent values of truth and beauty. Schröder's poetry drew its strength on the one hand from western European culture, and then, from his forties onwards, from Lutheran Christianity. He translated Homer, Virgil, Horace, Racine, Shakespeare and Persian poets, and wrote numerous essays on these and other poets of the past. His own lyrics are heavily laden with archaic strophic forms and turns of phrase, yet a number of them rise above the merely imitative in their intellectual and emotional power. Like other neo-idealist poets, Schröder opposed contemporary tendencies to formlessness, though many writers showed – witness Rilke's sonnets – that they could reconcile the relaxation of strict form with their own formal principles.

Ricarda Huch (1864–1947), an artist of varied and abundant talents, began her career with novels (*Vita somnium breve* (1903), later called *Michael Unger*) and love-poems, in which the greatness, purity and beauty of life was extolled, and over which the triumvirate of Nietzsche, Böcklin and Keller presided. After the events of World War I she turned to the search for transcendental values as a basis for life, now under the gaze of a different, religious triumvirate – that of Luther, Gotthelf and Dostoevsky. This remains the inspiration of her later historical writings such as *Im alten Reich* (1927 onwards) and the biography of Freiherr vom Stein (1925), in which latter her basic theme of the great man who overcomes the trials to which fate subjects him is perhaps most purely presented. A conservative republican, this most important woman writer of the first half of the century emigrated to Switzerland in the Nazi period and published her works there. Her final plan was for a book on the lives of various victims of Nazism: 'Such men', she wrote in 1946, 'are the soil in which the spirit grows and the heart becomes pure. They rescue us from the morass of everyday values, kindle the flame of our struggle against evil and confirm our faith in the divine nature of man.' From the novels of Enrica von Handel-Mazetti to the historical tales of Gertrud von le Fort one can see how closely linked are the Christian reform movements of the time to the powers of history.

The new irrationalism

Shortly after the turn of the century a movement arose which was to revolutionize the assumptions and the language of German literature. In this age of irresistible technical progress, economic expansionism and

European hegemony voices were raised in warning that Europe was on the point of losing its soul: so powerful had the forces of the intellect become that they were threatening to destroy that side of man which drew its strength from irrational, subconscious spiritual sources.

Among these voices were those of the so-called Kosmikerkreis in Munich, led by the archaeologist Alfred Schuler, the philosopher Ludwig Klages and the poet Karl Wolfskehl (with whom George had broken in the meantime), who opposed this intellectualization of man in the name of a new spirituality, taking their inspiration from Romantic and pre-Romantic sources, from Nietzsche and Bachofen. The Kosmikerkreis, together with those concerned with the journal *Charon* (1904–14), founded by Otto zur Linde and Rudolf Pannwitz, looked back into the primeval years of human history, uncovered primitive myths which they sought to re-create with a message of salvation for their own time, or invented myths to contain this message. Karl Röttger, who stood close to Otto zur Linde, wrote legends (*Der Heilandsweg* (1935)) to extend the meaning of the Gospels beyond the realm of Christian dogma, and Pannwitz composed new versions of myths from the Epic of Gilgamesh to the legends of classical antiquity.

There is a Faustian strain in the *Charon* writers which appears in Theodor Däubler's cosmogony *Nordlicht* (1910) and Alfred Mombert's astral myths, which aimed at a fusion of philosophy, religion and poetry. In *Der Denker* (1901), a volume of verse dedicated to the constellation Orion, Mombert evolved a free, visionary language in which, in the trilogy *Aeon* (1907–11), he undertook to describe the life of his 'eternal man' as he roamed through the world, through the ages of time, through the whole cosmos. This comprehensive mythology occupied Mombert throughout his life, but the purest artistic achievements of such writers are found in smaller forms, such as Däubler's *Sternenkind* (1914) and books on Mediterranean scenes. The failure of large-scale attempts to give man a new mythology derives less from inadequate artistic powers than from the fatal fallacy that insights into the meaning of life can be conveyed through myths which do not correspond to immediate human experience.

These early efforts in the field of modern irrationalism did, however, reveal what power of poetry resided in the unconscious, and what truth lay in the contemplation of the symbolic image, as opposed to rational language. 'The symbol stimulates intuition; language can only explain things. The symbol penetrates to the roots of spiritual reality; language only brushes the surface of understanding. Words make infinity finite; symbols waft the spirit out of the world of space and time into the realm of the eternal and boundless, and are as inexhaustible, as mysterious as religion itself.' (Bachofen, *Versuch über die Gräbersymbolik der Alten.*)

Wolfskehl's essay on darkness in *Blätter für die Kunst* III, Vol. 5, stands in this line, as does the influence of the French symbolists on George and Hofmannsthal. In Hofmannsthal's 'Die beiden' the poet holds his irrational image in firm control, whereas Rilke gives immediate expression to the creative emotion itself in a language which leaves open the associations of word and image and yet observes strict precision: the use of the word 'Schatten' in the poem 'Der Lesende' is a specific example, while poems such as 'Ausgesetzt auf den Bergen des Herzens' show how far beyond symbolism Rilke has moved.

The depth psychology of Freud and Jung also brought new stimuli to the literature of irrationalism: Hesse's novel *Demian* (1919), for instance, is a paradigm of spiritual salvation as expounded by Jung. Mention may also be made of the Swiss novelist Cecile Ines Loos (1885–1959), whose works, drawing on the esoteric wisdom of East and West, reflect the fear that the march of science will destroy spiritual values, and describe scenes which express the values of sympathetic intuition (*Die leisen Leidenschaften* (1933); *Johanne* (1946)). Such manifestations of the irrational impulse, together with those of the expressionists of 1910 and after, who proclaimed the complete domination of the fantastic, the irrational and the ecstatic, show the extent of the anti-rational movements of the time.

'It depends on what the level of the unconscious is,' wrote Musil in his diaries. And indeed one finds in this literature both a richness of spiritual and existential experience and also, as with the Dadaists and the spokesmen of pan-sexual and other neurotic conditions, displays of superficial fear and despair. The works of Hans Henny Jahnn (1894–1959) are peopled with characters whose experience covers the whole range of the irrational but who tend, as in the expressionistic drama *Armut, Reichtum, Mensch und Tier* (1948) and the trilogy of novels *Fluß ohne Ufer* (1949 onwards), to perish in their quest for salvation from the depths of what Oskar Loerke called 'lower eternity'.

New religious consciousness

'God is dead!' cried Nietzsche defiantly. And at the end of the nineteenth century many literary reforms did indeed see the end of all religions, especially Christianity. Many churches had become petrified, to their congregations a social, 'Sundays only' feature of their lives, and under attack from an atheism armed with the scientific knowledge of the age.

But the forces of neo-idealism, as mentioned above, also assembled. Among the religious writers in the neo-idealist stream are the poet Christian Morgenstern and the short-story writer Hermann Stehr. The former, a delicate, sensitive figure plagued by illness for much of his life, expressed his formula for living as the pursuit of 'the way to a purified, spiritualized religion less concerned with official churches than with the great teachers of humanity'. It was a way that took him, like the Swiss writer Albert

Steffen, to the anthroposophy of Rudolf Steiner. Stehr, on the other hand, sought inspiration in the Silesian popular mystical tradition and the works of Böhme, an inspiration that shows itself in the many God-seeking characters in his stories, particularly in the novel *Der Heiligenhof* (1917).

But the greatest poetic achievement in the religious aspect of neo-idealism is that of Rainer Maria Rilke (1875–1926). Starting as a refined and earnest practitioner in the impressionist mould and developing under the influence of Jacobsen, he discovered his real personality as a result of two journeys to Russia in 1899 and 1900 and his love for Lou Andreas-Salomé. The ecstatic, contemplative poems of the *Stundenbuch* (1906) are full of religious assurance, the modern assurance of the presence of a vague, unknown God whom the soul experiences in moments of release and who must rise again in the spirit of man in order to fulfil himself.

Rilke's second period is characterized by a new source of inwardness – that which springs from the power of earthly things. From the sculptor Rodin in Paris, who said that he would have to talk for a whole year in order to explain one of his works in words, Rilke learned to read the mysterious signs of nature and allow himself to be drawn into the inner-most recesses of reality which the world had not yet seen. This reproduc-tion of the inner world in terms of physical appearance is conveyed by the plants, animals, objects and stock human types – lovers, sufferers, those who rejoice and those who mourn – of his *Neue Gedichte* (1907–8).

The novel *Malte Laurids Brigge* (1909) goes a stage further and dwells on the forces – the powers of reminiscence, of sickness, of love and of the life-giving presence of death which loses its terrors through its eternal presence – whose creative inspiration had hitherto been passed over in the prevalent mood of existential pessimism.

The world of *Malte* is superseded by that of the *Duineser Elegien* (begun 1912, completed 1923), which, with their bold, often puzzling imagery, concentrate their gaze on the newly interpreted physical world and the new insights of human inwardness. Other-worldliness is beyond their grasp, but they for ever move outwards to the inexpressible realm symbolized by the angel, 'whose presence proves the existence in the invisible world of a higher mode of reality'. This is the immense background against which Rilke's drama of an earthly life stretching back to the beginnings of God's existence is played out, a life whose abundance he never ceases to praise, above all in the seventh and ninth Elegies and in the *Sonnette an Orpheus* (1923).

'His work is a dialogue with the possibilities of living', said a French critic of Gide. It is a statement equally applicable to Rilke. Both his poetic intentions and the richness of his range of expression far exceed anything seen before. As he drew his cultural sustenance from all regions of Europe, so in return his achievement has had a more lasting influence in

Europe than that of Hauptmann, Thomas Mann or Kafka. He un-covered a profound new dimension in life, and the emotional displays of his contemporaries pale into insignificance beside his achievement.

The new religious forces also made themselves felt in the orthodox religions. A group of progressive Catholics gathered round Karl Muth, founder of the journal *Hochland* in 1902, which sought to extend the intellectual and social range of Catholicism. An associate of Muth's between 1905 and 1920 was Konrad Weiss (1880–1940), whose urge towards trans-cendental experience led to extravagances of experience and language which culminated in *Herz des Wortes* (1928) and *Sinnreich der Erde* (1939), hermetic poems that move in their own private world. Baroque and expressionist influences are important in Weiss, who also wrote historical dramas and travelogues (*Deutschlands Morgenspiegel* (1950)).

Two Catholic converts were influential in the period after 1918, Gertrud von le Fort (born 1876) and Werner Bergengruen (1892–1964). The former, descended from a Huguenot family, proclaimed in psalm-like tones the glories of salvation (*Hymnen an die Kirche* (1924)), which she interpreted as the assumption of the individual soul into the bosom of the Church. Her novels (*Das Schweißtuch der Veronika* (1928, 2nd volume 1948); *Die Letzte am Schafott* (1931, revised 1952)) have as their heroines women who embody the mysterious supernatural power that takes hold of the soul. Her artistic attitudes have something in common with those of Claudel and T. S. Eliot.

In 1930, in the cycle *Mitte des Lebens*, Rudolf Alexander Schröder embarked on his grandest theme – the incorporation of national destiny, together with the sufferings, joys and fears of man, in an all-embracing Lutheran plan of Christian salvation. He revived poetic forms of the Reformation, baroque and Romantic periods and brought new life to the Protestant hymn in his collection *Lobgesang* (1937). Protestant ideals are also expressed by the characters of the novels of Ina Seidel (born 1885); certain of her works enter the realm of parapsychology (*Unser Freund Peregrin* (1940)), while in *Michaela* (1959) she boldly posed the question of why Nazism took hold of the minds of so many Germans.

Literature in the Weimar Republic, 1918–1933

The confused, agitated years after 1918 left deeper marks on German liter-ature than the years of the war itself. War novels range from Ernst Jünger's *In Stahlgewittern* (1920), in which the war is praised, to Erich Maria Remarque's *Im Westen nichts Neues* (1929), which shows the horrors of war; one of the noblest works is Carossa's *Rumänisches Tagebuch* (1924), while in his journal *Die Fackel* and his conglomerate drama *Die letzten Tage der Menschheit* (1922) the Viennese satirist Karl Kraus railed against all the evils and corruptions of the time.

With the year 1918 stable society and a safe, comfortable outlook on life broke down. Political parties struggled fiercely for power in a country in a state of economic collapse and military occupation, open to whatever ideas and influences appeared on the scene, whether from German sources or from abroad, and all manner of opportunists, mass-agitators and pleaders of special causes began to acquire sinister power. After the brief period of consolidation of the Weimar Republic, when inflation was brought to an end and Germany became a member of the League of Nations, the world slump set the country on the path that was to lead to the Nazi seizure of power in 1933, which brought Germany its third form of government in less than seventy years.

At first glance the intellectual scene looks to be one of utter confusion and disintegration: on the one hand lies Communism, on the other the *Stahlhelm*; on the one hand, psychoanalysis, on the other anthroposophy; on the one hand nudism, on the other Catholicism; on the one hand expressionism, on the other 'new objectivity'. And to these were added the influence of the modes of life adopted in America, Russia and the Far East.

One needs to distinguish, however, between those whose philosophy of life emerged after 1914 and those whose intellectual outlook had already been formed at the turn of the century. These latter preserved a degree of continuity and evolution which has to be set beside the over-simplified notion that 1918 meant the complete collapse of all German and Austrian intellectual traditions. The war of 1914–18 and the years that followed had little effect on the development of attitudes whose roots lay in the pre-war period – unless this effect be taken to include the general increase in productivity – which affected radical and conservative writers alike – or the temporary adoption by certain writers of new fashions (cf. the marks of expressionism on Hauptmann's epic *Till Eulenspiegel* (1927)). The multiplicity of literary activities during the years of the Weimar Republic can be gauged from any catalogue of works one cares to draw up: the brash novels of middle-class prosperity and success, written by men such as Stratz and Höcker, continued to sell in their thousands; Rilke reached his climax in 1923 with the *Duineser Elegien*; Stefan Zweig's *Verwirrung der Gefühle* in 1926 embodied the decadence of late impressionism; George's neo-classicism led in 1928 to the collection *Das neue Reich*; Karl Heinrich Waggerl's novel *Brot* (1930) showed the continued popularity of provincial literature, and the works of neo-idealism reached their apogee during the years of the Republic; in 1930 Martin Bodmer, with the support of Herbert Steiner, made the bi-monthly journal *Corona* the central organ of neo-idealist literature and thought.

In the forefront of these various movements stood the expressionists, whose concerted influence remained dominant until about 1925, and the supporters of the so-called 'new objectivity', among whom were a number of disillusioned expressionists; this latter group was in its turn pushed into the background when the Nazis came to power and promoted only such literature as served the interests of their conception of *Volk*. And not to be overlooked in the flurry of these various species of public literary activity is the activity of men of an older generation who continued to strive in their own way for a broad reconciliation of the achievements of modern times with an all-embracing ideal of humanity.

EXPRESSIONISM

The beginnings of programmatic expressionism date from 1910, when radically minded young poets, driven by an urge to reform the whole of life and literature, founded a number of periodicals for the propagation, in a novel, inflammatory style, of their views on the future of art and life: *Der Stürmer* appeared in Alsace, *Der Brenner* in Innsbruck, *Die Aktion* and the futuristic *Der Sturm* in Berlin. Not since the time of Nietzsche, Hauptmann and Dehmel had there been such a concerted revolt against the prevailing *Zeitgeist* – a revolt which continued to feed for years on the decay of true human ideals under the pressure of middle-class values of social security, the spread of technology, the continued influence of religion and the reactionary nature of much contemporary literature. The attacks of the expressionists were aimed primarily not at institutions but at those powerful individuals who lacked the vital ability to experience that sense of shock which should lead to action.

The book reviews of the young Alsatian Germanist Ernst Stadler show how dissatisfied the young poets of the time had become with the literature of the 'establishment'. With the partial exception of naturalism, this literature seemed to them to gloss over the disasters for which the age was heading and to make no effort to rouse men from their apathy. Stadler's collection of lyrics *Der Aufbruch* (1911–13), René Schickele's early poems, Franz Werfel's *Weltfreund* (1914), Reinhard Sorge's lyric drama *Der Bettler* (1912) and Else Lasker-Schüler's romantic visions in her *Gesammelte Gedichte* (1917) – these and other works express the apocalyptic visions of the young poets of the time, visions of a new humanity. The work of poets barely twenty-five years of age, living feckless lives in a world of drugs and psychedelic visions, was received as a revelation from the mysterious world beyond appearances. Such was the work of Georg Trakl, with its gentle, sombre imagery, a continual, almost pathological lament on the hopelessness of earthly life which offers only an occasional glimpse of Christian salvation. Similarly Georg Heym, whom Stadler called 'a visionary poet of the grotesque and the gruesome, a brother of

Poe and Baudelaire', filled his verses with harsh, often distorted images of decaying cities, savage wars, madmen and suicides (*Umbra vitae* (1912)) – images that correspond precisely to the contemporary paintings of Ludwig Meidner and others. Many of these young poets – Stadler, Sorge, Trakl, Engelke, Stramm – were killed in the war of 1914–18; Heym was drowned in 1912. Those who continued to follow the aims of expressionism saw their age as a battleground between a world doomed to destruction and the humanity of the future, and looked for inspiration to writers – Dostoevsky, Whitman, Büchner, Verhaeren and the others whom Kasimir Edschmid named in his essay *Über den Expressionismus in der Literatur* (1918) – who had demanded that art should transform the whole of man's being.

'Can this literature be other than chaotic', asked Kurt Pinthus in the preface to his expressionist anthology *Menschheitsdämmerung* (1920), 'since it springs from the tortured, bloodstained chaos of its age?' There are, however, certain dominant themes, chief among them being that of the man who is sustained by the forces of irrationalism and in whom all the paradoxes of the world can be resolved in a single glowing feeling of unity.

As with Bergson, intuition was valued far higher than intellect and empiricism, and those who could not transcend their early selves or sense what Gerrit Engelke called the feeling of 'total belongingness' were regarded as enemies. All barriers disappear: the individual becomes the representative, and individual identities dissolve; man outgrows his class and joins the brotherhood of all humanity, like the millionaire's son in Georg Kaiser's play *Gas* (1918) or in Werfel's poem *Veni Creator Spiritus* from the collection *Einander* (1915). The nations become a single community of peoples, as in J. R. Becher's ode *An Europa*, or in the pacifist drama *Ein Geschlecht* (1916) and the chronicle *Flügel der Nike* (1924) – the journal of his journey through France – by Fritz von Unruh. The cosmic myths of Mombert and Däubler stimulated universalist nature poems such as Oskar Loerke's *Der Strom*, while the figures of the sculptor and dramatist Ernst Barlach look anxiously upwards and outwards, waiting for a sign from the unknown God. Furthermore the urge towards an all-embracing experience led downwards as well as upwards: the ugly and the repulsive are combined with the grand and the sublime, and poetry is no longer an imitation of the world but a vision.

The expressionists were driven to the extremes of concentrated utterance, and their style was the immediate expression of visions; the ecstasy of the poet was to arouse the ecstasy of the reader; established poetic forms were avoided, metres and strophes were loosely strung together, the drama disintegrated into a series of intense, unrelated scenes enacted before a backcloth rich in forms and colours, and the novel lost its logically developed plot. Words were heaped together without syntax and without coherence: the lyrics of August Stramm show what lengths of absurdity could be reached by the aggregation of unrelated words each heavily pregnant with associations. Such excesses sometimes ended in an excessive irrational subjectivism, but the true poet could harness these forces to an new, inspired human purpose.

It was expressionism also that worked on the mood of the age to release for the first time the poetic impulse of the working class. Schiller, Herwegh and others had put revolutionary words into the mouths of the lower classes, and from Heine through Dehmel to Hauptmann there had been middle-class poets to speak on behalf of the workers, but it is only now, with figures such as Max Barthel, Heinrich Lersch (*Mensch im Eisen* (1924)) and Gerrit Engelke, that one meets real poets from the ranks of the working class itself.

The expressionists attracted a mass of imitators after 1918. Many of the poets in the anthology *Menschheitsdämmerung* betray their derivativeness, and even in the plays of Georg Kaiser the intellectually imported elements of 'ecstasy' and social criticism are stronger than the basic existential feeling – to say nothing of the caricatures in Carl Sternheim's satirical comedies such as *Bürger Schippel* (1912).

The importance of expressionism, and the reason why this importance survived into later times, is that, like irrationalism as a whole, it brought a massive extension to the range of modern poetry and encouraged the poet to express himself in new, powerful, unconventional ways. This can be observed even in those who subsequently turned away from it, like Johannes R. Becher, whose gripping lyrics from the years of his exile in Russia from 1933 to 1945 still owe their power to his mature experience of expressionism, whereas in his propaganda poems and other Communist pieces intended for the 'education' of the masses – one recalls his *Hymne auf Lenin* from the years of the Weimar Republic – his inspiration sinks lower and lower. In the later plays of Franz Werfel (*Juarez und Maximilian* (1925); *Das Reich Gottes in Böhmen* (1930)), which are preoccupied with the question of guilt and punishment, the legacy of expressionism receives a religious slant, as in the large-scale novels *Barbara oder die Frömmigkeit* (1929) and *Das Lied von Bernadette* (1941), in which man finds consolation in the concept of a merciful eternity. Oskar Loerke too, having started his career in his own idiosyncratic way with the wild, agitated poems in *Die heimliche Stadt* (1921), moved towards an art of intuitive meditation on the ultimate realities of the world, especially of nature (*Atem der Erde* (1930)), and sought for permanent values the more his contemporaries pursued shallow unrealities.

The work of Albin Zollinger (1895–1941), the most important Swiss lyric poet of the first half of the century, was influenced by Thomas Wolfe and also shows expressionist traits. In his novels (*Pfannenstiel* (1940); *Bohnenblust* (1942)) he struggles with the fundamental problems of the modern age and sees the hero as a man of passion, all-embracing in his concerns; in his lyrics (*Sternfrühe* (1936); *Stille des Herbstes* (1939)) he develops a warm sensuousness which he blends with the values of the spirit in a wealth of bold and beautiful images and vital characters.

German expressionism faded away rapidly in the early 1920s. The moments of rapture had passed, and the poet who sought to develop his humanity had to move into other fields. Contrary to his own highest aims, the writer's nature was that of a monologist, in spite of an occasional public success like that of the Communist Ernst Toller in his propaganda play *Masse Mensch* (1921), and Hanns Johst's *Schlageter* (1932), with its glorification of a Nazi hero. The more visionary poets were accused of turning their backs on tangible realities. Of the few works of lasting value, most are in the field of lyric verse; drama has little to show, and prose fiction still less. Yet it was one of the most important formative influences on life and art in the first decades of the century, and even after 1945 one finds young poets deliberately employing expressionist imagery in their works.

NIHILISM AND DADAISM

Alongside the movement of programmatic expressionism one finds a number of figures who used the same tools and launched the same attacks against the past but who would have nothing to do with ideals of community and brotherhood. Instead they often took delight in the obscene or in the destruction of even the last remnants of any faith in human values. 'The nations are full of pus', said Albert Ehrenstein, proud of his discovery. Gottfried Benn passed through a deeply nihilistic phase, and Alfred Lichtenstein, who was killed in 1914, wrote surrealistic poems reflecting in their illogicality what he saw as the illogicality of life itself:

> . . . Auf langen Krücken schief herabgebückt
> und schwatzend kriechen auf dem Feld zwei Lahme.
> Ein blonder Dichter wird vielleicht verrückt.
> Ein Pferdchen stolpert über eine Dame . . .

(. . . two lame men are crawling across the field, bent almost double over their long crutches and chattering. A blond poet may be going out of his mind. A pony stumbles over a lady . . .)   ('Die Dämmerung', 1913)

In 1916 a group of *émigré* painters and writers in Zürich – Hugo Ball, Hans Arp, Tristan Tzara, Richard Huelsenbeck, etc. – founded the Cabaret Voltaire, which devoted itself to the most extreme of all movements of disintegration in modern literature: Dadaism. 'We were made honorary nihilists,' said Arp. Nietzsche understood by nihilism the destruction of ultimate values; to the Dadaists it meant the abandonment of any attempt to make sense of the world. Dadaism represented an attempt, in an age of chaos, to express this chaos by means of correspondingly chaotic, anti-realistic artistic methods, or to mock it by striking an attitude of macabre cynicism, or to replace it with abstract montages of words and colours with an allegedly timeless significance.

Nihilism and frivolity were not far apart. The only things left from the collapse of thousands of years of cultural tradition were disembodied fragments of intuition and a one-time reality. Poetry became separated from the ordered processes of life and thought, and finally language itself disintegrated: '. . . und wie wie sie sie laden / blitz ab der leiter frieden / entwed und od und ader / als doppeltes hinieden . . .' (Arp, *Der Pyramiden-stock* (1924)). With some, like Ball, nothing remained but a senseless stuttering of vowels and consonants. For Ball, as for others like him, the painter Kandinsky had an importance comparable to that of Marc and Meidner for the expressionists.

Poetry of this kind was a starting-point for the so-called *poésie automatique* of André Breton and others around 1924, with its surrealist sequences of images from the unconscious, 'which never lies'; Arp, in particular, later sought to *épater le bourgeois* with witty exercises in this vein.

The only ones to persist in such attitudes and found Dadaist centres in Berlin and elsewhere after the war were those whose spiritual life was empty; the others sought new fields to conquer. Hugo Ball, for example, found the peace he was seeking in the cult of Mariolatry and looked back on literary irrationalism as nothing but a false scent: 'Imagery, imagination, magic itself, if they are not founded on tradition and revelation, are only a short cut to nothingness. Maybe the whole notion of associationism in art is just self-deception.' (*Die Flucht aus der Zeit* (1927).)

RETURN TO OBJECTIVITY

Expressionism was followed by a literature dominated by scepticism and sobriety – though some, like Brecht, Döblin and Bruckner, had a kind of love-hate relationship to expressionism. This new scepticism is as inseparable from the confusions of the post-war age as were the extravagances of expressionism: the intellectual scene was still one of chaos, and many young – self-consciously young – writers adopted the sceptical, disillusioned view that here was a collection of equally false beliefs all clamouring for recognition as exclusive truth. Nor did the passing of the short-lived Weimar Republic bring any change: in 1929 came the slump, the unemployed in Germany were counted in millions, and the masses were at the mercy of political propaganda from the extreme right and the extreme left. Bernhard Diebold's novel *Das Reich ohne Mitte* (1939) gives a documentary picture of life at this time.

Those who took the modest word 'integrity' as their slogan had nothing to set against these conditions but a determination to give a frank, objective account of the impoverished world as it stood, and to represent the position in this world of the man without ideals, for whom there were neither heights nor depths. Thomas Mann's *Unordnung und frühes Leid* (1926) reflects this 'new objectivity' among the young generation.

'If one is honest', said Döblin, 'one has to say that one no longer wants literature. Literature is *passé*, art is boring. What one wants is facts, just facts.' The world was presented in journalistic style as a banal and extremely dubious phenomenon: the most that could be expected of a man was to build up laboriously some brave little life for himself, like the characters in Hermann Kesten's early novels (*Joseph sucht die Freiheit* (1928)). Such works often go even lower in the social scene than did the naturalists, yet one also senses on occasion a quiet, hesitant lyricism that scarcely dares to show itself. The historical novels of Alfred Neumann (*Der Teufel* (1926); *Narrenspiegel* (1932)), with their skilful psychology and use of sources, attack the questionable aspects of the idealist view of history, and Ernst Glaeser's *Jahrgang 1902* (1928) is the chronicle of a sceptical generation.

With this 'new objectivity' the hour of Sigmund Freud had come. A number of older writers, such as Thomas Mann – in the character of the psychoanalyst Dr Krokowski in *Der Zauberberg* – and Hermann Hesse – *Steppenwolf* contains a whole psychoanalytical pandemonium – had incorporated Freud's insights into their concepts of man, but it was the younger generation that showed itself receptive as a whole to his theories, in particular that of the libido. People were looking for rational and easily simplified doctrines which would support the fashionable tendency to challenge the notion of free, unconditional intellectual impulses. The sexuo-pathological themes in Ferdinand Bruckner's drama *Krankheit der Jugend* (1926) would be unthinkable without Freud. Similarly many found in the writings of Karl Marx arguments for disillusioned pronouncements about the world, and Freud and Marx together strengthened the hand of the opponents of middle-class morality and the political establishment. The drama *Cyankali* (1926) by the Stuttgart doctor Friedrich Wolf, for example, is a protest against the abortion laws.

Hermann Broch (1886–1951), a native of Vienna, textile-manufacturer, mathematician, philosopher and, from 1928 onwards, writer, presents in his trilogy of novels *Die Schlafwandler* (1931–2) a picture of German society between 1888 and 1918, a money-grubbing, power-hungry society destructive of all human values, and ultimately of itself also. Broch was held in the grip of the defeatist mood of the years after 1925 and had at that time nothing to set against it but a sceptical and hesitant statement of freedom.

Leonhard Frank's reaction to the times comes in *Von drei Millionen drei*, a novel about the unemployed; the Bohemian cabaret-artist Joachim Ringelnatz composed satirical, parodistic songs; Carl Zuckmayer wrote coarse, popular comedies. Of particular interest is the work of the satirist Erich Kästner: the titles of his collections of poems – *Herz auf Taille* (1927); *Gesang zwischen zwei Stühlen* (1932) – show his sceptical approach, and he employed an everyday, though not insensitive language to achieve modest aims that were the very reverse of expressionist. Though forbidden to publish, he remained in Germany from 1933 to 1945, and during this time acquired fame abroad through lightweight but sensitive novels like *Drei Männer im Schnee* (1934) and attractive romantic children's stories like *Emil und die Detektive* (1929).

Bertolt Brecht (1898–1956), with Hauptmann the most controversial of German dramatists in the first half of the twentieth century, modelled his early works on Villon, Büchner and Wedekind, giving expression in his dramatic, expressionist ballad *Baal* (1922) to a crude, anarchic, challenging sensuality. Shortly after, however, leaving all individualism behind, he claimed to see only those above and those beneath, the oppressors and the oppressed, those deprived of a proper life in society – the only power that controlled their destiny: 'Those at the bottom are kept at the bottom, so that those at the top can stay at the top.' *Der Dreigroschenoper* (1928), a parody of John Gay's *Beggar's Opera*, shows the citizen as gangster and the gangster as citizen: 'Food first, morality afterwards' – one of the most cynical dicta of the age.

In Berlin, where in the 1920s Döblin, Tucholsky and Benn were also busily engaged in the savage destruction of anything and everything that savoured of human illusion, Brecht became the most sharply defined personality in the movement towards a 'new objectivity', ruthlessly attacking everything that appeared to him to be standing in the way of a new social order:

> Drum, wer unten sagt, daß es einen Gott gibt
> Und kann sein unsichtbar und hülfe ihnen doch,
> Den soll man mit dem Kopf auf das Pflaster schlagen,
> Bis er verreckt ist.

(So if anyone tells you that there's a God who's invisible yet can still help people, bang his head on the flagstones till he pegs out.)

(*Die heilige Johanna der Schlachthöfe*, 1929–30)

Brecht's involvement with Marxism dates from 1924. From that moment his one aim was revolution by means of the anti-illusionist drama which he so brilliantly exploited. His plays were dramatized parables written in order to discuss moral problems in Marxist terms, unmask the real political and social enemies in all ages, and employ his so-called 'alienation effects' – the actors addressing the audience directly from the stage, banners with slogans mounted on the stage, scene-changes in full view of the public, etc. – to force the spectator out of his intellectual and moral apathy. This 'epic theatre' was already to be found in the popular plays of India, China and the European Middle Ages, and Brecht set about hastening the destruction of the classical European drama in the same manner as he used gruesome ballads with their casual, colloquial language (*Hauspostille* (1927)) to undermine the traditional lyric.

His Communistic message was as meagre in content as it was forceful in presentation: 'When the time comes, you will no longer be yourselves – Karl Schmitt from Berlin, Anna Kjersk from Kasan, Peter Sawitsch from Moscow – but without names and without mothers: empty pages on which the revolution will write its instructions.' (*Die Maßnahme*.) It is simply the intellectual expropriation of the people so that they can be painlessly subjected to the ideology of the party.

Brecht adhered all his life to the doctrine of materialism and determinism. Yet although he was, and remained, a cunning demagogue, he also was, and remained, a skilled writer for the theatre and a man of great poetic resourcefulness. Certain of his characters – not for nothing are they the products of his years in exile – such as Mother Courage (1939) and Shen-Te, 'the good woman of Sezuan' (1938–9), have a gripping power, despite their utterly false ideology, as representatives of a helpless, suffering, persecuted mankind, and certain of his poems have a similar laconic melancholy. These poems, in fact, with their moments of powerful silence and their sometimes parodistic tone, have been the starting-point for a number of poetic movements since 1945.

Brecht returned to East Berlin in 1945, and his theories of drama are assembled in his *Kleines Organon für das Theater* (1948). His fame in the West is due to his theatrical skill and to the fact that 'in spite of a political programme that ignores the individual, he took up cudgels on behalf of the individual' (Holthusen). Denmark, Switzerland and the United States offered him asylum as a refugee from Nazi Germany between 1933 and 1945, but for various obscure reasons he spent only a few weeks in Russia, the giant empire of practical Communism. His view of the world was largely out of date before he even uttered it, and the West has found more humane ways of solving its social problems than by 'the instructions of the revolution'. But he held to his doctrine – while taking Austrian citizenship as a precaution. The late Brecht is a perfect example of the independently minded left-wing intellectual who finds himself delivered over to a Communist state.

One of the many phases in the varied career of the Berlin doctor Alfred Döblin (1878–1957) is dominated by the novel *Berlin Alexanderplatz* (1929) and centres on the intellectual metropolis of the 'new objectivity', as the earlier novel *Die drei Sprünge des Wang-Lun* (1915; written 1911–12) had shown him, an early contributor to *Der Sturm*, as a writer in the grip of the expansive ideals of expressionism. Döblin was almost always concerned, albeit in an inconsistent and sometimes careless style, with the weak, fallible character in conflict with powers that threatened to destroy him, whether in China, Berlin or, as in *Die Giganten* (1932), in Utopia, where in a mixture of soberly objective and excitedly expressionistic styles he deals with the threat to human values from the relentless march of technical progress. Using inner monologues in the manner of James Joyce, vivid, bizarre montages of advertisements, pop lyrics and statistics, Freudian psychology and Marxism, Döblin shows in *Berlin Alexanderplatz* the uncertainties confronting the ex-convict who seeks to rehabilitate himself in society. His experience in exile led to the appearance in his later works of religious elements which he had previously suppressed; also expressive of this was his conversion to Catholicism.

Elements of the hectic conditions in the 1920s, particularly from expressionism and the 'new objectivity', also manifest themselves in the work of Gottfried Benn (1886–1956) – like Döblin a native of Berlin and a doctor. He saw it as the task of his generation, as he wrote later, 'to destroy illusions and to get rid of a centuries-old reality which had become unreal'. Confronted, as a young doctor, with the ravages of the 'image of God' by disease, he embarked on the destruction of Christian and humanistic values in the same manner as Nietzsche, and the ghastly poems in his collection *Morgue* (1912) are an authentic testimony to this attitude.

Benn, the sceptical nihilist, turned his gaze on religion and history, on society and state: man was to him a rootless creature devoid of any meaningful relationship to the rest of the known universe, and this cruel theme tormented him right down to his *Ptolemäer* (1947), in which all the contradictory aspects of human existence are cynically thrown together in a single senseless mass. Taken to such extremes as this, disillusionment itself became an illusion: no destruction of values could go farther than this inferno of negations. At the same time, particularly in the volume of verse called *Spaltungen* (1925), one finds other motifs, visions of the young Hebbel, of Chopin, of Nietzsche – the loneliness of human greatness as some small source of consolation. In his search for a way out Benn also followed the paths of the irrational psychology of Jung, Klages and Lévy-Brühl, seeking in the mythical images of the subconscious 'a moment of mystic participation' and using an arbitrary, personal, 'expressionist' language to achieve this moment – the language, moreover, of a re-markably learned *poeta doctus*.

'In our efforts to find some basis, some existence, some vision of order and form, we suddenly find ourselves confronting a kind of law – the law of the formative power of nothingness', said Benn in his *Akademierede* of 1932, hinting at a third possibility of discovering some short-lived salvation in the midst of meaninglessness, the preservation of a tiny piece of existence in the form of a perfectly chiselled poetic fragment, almost like those of George and Baudelaire:

> Die Äcker bleichen,
> Der Hirte ruft,
> Das ist das Zeichen:
> Tränke dich tief . . .

(The fields grow pale, the shepherd calls; the motto is 'Immerse thyself . . .')

Poems of this kind (*Statische Gedichte* (1937–47)) exist alongside those of his earlier style and others in which he thought he could vest some degree of permanence by an independent and highly intellectual use of associative words and concepts. After the collapse of Germany in 1945 many of the young generation looked on the sixty-year-old Benn, with a fixedness born of desperation, as the one poet who expressed correctly, both in form and substance, the state of modern man, and he came to be regarded as the prophet of what he himself called 'Expressionism, Phase Two'.

An equally powerful force at that time was the work of the Jewish outsider from Prague, Franz Kafka (1883–1924). His whole life stood in the shadow of tragedy: his conflict with his father, the struggle between literature and his career, and between his pious Jewish origins and his own scepticism; he seemed certain to die young of tuberculosis, and unhappiness in love filled him with feelings of bitterness and guilt. 'The only one of the necessities of life that I possess', he wrote, 'is human weakness. This has enabled me – and in this respect it is a source of immense strength – to grasp the negative nature of my age.'

His stories, most of which were published posthumously and against his intention, are a monomaniacal set of variations on a single theme – the theme of no escape. With a relentless, agonizing logic he exposes all the anxieties that beset a meaningless human existence and drives his characters into situations from which there is no way out, making them share the feelings of a cornered animal. With a precise surrealist imagery he presents his visions of the inner life in a manner which was to make him a focus of attention and influence, not only in Germany but also among later French and English existentialist writers.

But for all the apparent clarity of their technique, Kafka's remorseless works revolve round a mysterious central point. The castle in *Das Schloß* (*c.* 1920) represents an inscrutable ultimate authority, and *Der Prozeß* (*c.* 1914) conveys in its title alone the existence of a supreme power which passes judgement on man and into whose hands, after a life spent in a tortured search for meaning, man eventually must fall.

Of post-1945 writers who show the influence of Kafka, one of the most striking is Peter Weiss (born 1916), whose surrealist, bizarre montages of terrifying images in *Abschied von den Eltern* (1961) and *Das Gespräch der drei Gehenden* (1962) present a claustrophobic picture of human hopelessness.

TOTALITY

During the 1920s, with the internal consolidation of the Weimar Republic through a more-or-less workable coalition government and the introduction of a new currency, and the strengthening of its external position through its co-operation with the League of Nations, a number of works appeared which quietly absorbed many of the literary achievements since 1885, yet presented a new appearance. At the moment when so-called 'progressive' writers were striking attitudes of nihilism and defeatism, others were devoting themselves to the supreme artistic task of presenting modern man in his totality and originality. Such writers – Hesse, Carossa, Schaeffer, Flake and others – were all in their maturity and had developed in very different ways but all sought in their later works to draw together the threads of their experience and to present, like all the great literary achievements from naturalism to expressionism, a vision of the rehabilitation of man and the world.

A sensitive awareness of the empirical world had gone far beyond the interests of the realists and the naturalists: intellectual and emotional knowledge had become more subtle, and movements such as neo-idealism and expressionism had extended the range of experience. In the novel *Kurgast* (1925) Hermann Hesse portrays the crisis of a man driven to despair by the apparent insolubility of the world's problems, by the conflict of opinions in the world and by the uncontrollable urges of his own personality, until he finds his answer in the resolution of all conflicts in unity, in an extension of the range of thought which will characterize the man of the new age: 'The supreme human utterance consists for me of those few words in which the opposing forces in the world are seen to be both a necessity and an illusion.' In *Steppenwolf* (1927) we find a similar statement: 'Instead of making your world narrower, and your soul simpler, you will become more and more universal, until eventually you will be forced to absorb the whole world into the soul whose receptivity you have so painfully extended.' This is the yardstick against which Hesse measures the man of the future in his *Glasperlenspiel*.

It is not only individual human powers themselves that were extended and refined but the whole human environment. The worker, the farmer, the citizen, the artist, the aristocrat were all seen with new eyes; the universe, the physical world and the realm of history were all drawn into modern experience, and paths to super-sensory experience seemed to open up. And in all these fields the power of language reached new heights. Twentieth-century man, in all his complexity, strode on towards the mastery of the intricate reality of his age. The movement towards totality of experience and away from one-sidedness is represented by the psychologist C. G. Jung's *Die Frau in Europa* (1929); Morgenstern had protested against what he called 'an age of cul-de-sacs', and the Austrian writer Heimito von Doderer saw it as the responsibility of the artist to seek a new universalism; Doderer's teacher Albert Paris Gütersloh (born 1887) wrote his extravagant, colourful novel *Sonne und Mond* (1962) in a similar frame of mind, depicting the complete reality presented by the old Austrian Empire. These and others in the period between the wars and afterwards show the extent of the movement towards comprehensiveness of experience, in a spirit not of definition but of heuristic participation.

The work of Hans Carossa (1878–1956) is pervaded by such attitudes. He saw man as part of a universal nature whose living power reaches from the stars to the depths of the earth. All is meaningful, including sickness, suffering and death, which brings the body back into the cycle of life – everything is a challenge to man to re-establish his unity with the cosmos. And as nature exerted her influence on man, so also did the forces of the divine and the demonic. In *Der Arzt Gion* (1931) Carossa tells the story of a doctor who lives his life in this universal context, a context created in his best poems ('Der alte Brunnen', 'An eine Katze') by the secret music of the spheres. In his autobiographical books he sought 'to cast light on other people's paths by tracing my own', and shows himself a follower of Goethe, Schelling and twentieth-century psychosomatic medicine.

Goethe is the most important of the spiritual patrons – others are Leibniz, Cusanus ('coincidence of opposites') and St Thomas Aquinas – of these writers. Thomas Mann gave a portrait of Goethe's old age in *Lotte in Weimar* (1939), which is virtually a monologue of warning against the betrayal of humane values by the Nazis. Often his many-sided characters, like Felix Krull, are without a singlemindedness of purpose, but the virtues of a universal outlook are again expressed in a document from his seventies:

> It is my belief that the best minds and hearts, over the whole world, are concerned today to evolve a conception of man which corresponds more completely than that evolved by any earlier age to the ideas of universality. There is a new feeling of humanity, in which the sinister, demonic forces in life are not mistaken or ignored but transformed, rationalized, made to serve the interests of civilization. And it is my belief that devotion to this view of man is a condition for the fulfilment of the hopes that man cherishes in this age of suffering – hopes for a better social order, for a better, more just world, for peace. (See Paul Scherrer, 'Thomas Mann und die Wirklichkeit' in *Lübeckische Blätter*, No. 7 (1960).)

The ideal of universality gave a special impetus to the novel, which revelled in the freedom to invent characters expressive of man's potential achievements. New horizons revealed the intricacies of human destiny and the *Bildungsroman* took on a new lease of life. Swiss novels like Meinrad Inglin's *Schweizerspiegel* (1934), the hero of which comes to outgrow the perversities of right-wing and left-wing ideologies, the later works of Kurt Guggenheim, Robert Faesi's historical novels and works like Arnold Kübler's *Oeppi* (1943–64), with its dream-like delight in the pleasures of the senses – these show a full-blooded joy in life and an urge to an ever more perfect understanding and delight.

Heimito von Doderer (1896–1966) drew on modern techniques of 'open form' in *Die Dämonen* (1956) in order to present events through the eyes of different characters, but preserved the ideal of 'universal man' and the assumption of a cosmic unity. In particular Doderer's novel joins the ever-increasing number of works that protest against the subjection of man to the dictates of ideology, making him an instrument of barbarism, political or otherwise. Doderer and others lay bare the immanent stupidity and narrowness of all doctrinaire attitudes, in whatever sphere they are found. 'First become a stranger to yourself, then nothing will seem strange to you', wrote Doderer, for the benefit of those trying to escape from all ideology.

The ideal world-order for such a writer is one in which there is room for as wide a range of social forms as possible but excluding all forms of drab totalitarianism. It is a quality of life described by Rudolf Alexander Schröder as 'a feeling of reciprocity, because it causes one to realise that the individual is dependent on the world, and the world is dependent on him'. This spirit underlies Otto Flake's (1880–1963) essays in *Bilanz, Versuch einer geistigen Neuordnung* (1931), and in his *Ruland* novels (1922–8) he depicts the emergence of an intellectual and political élite which would sustain the ideal of the League of Nations. The same thought inspires the novel *Die Sanduhr* (1950), which, set in Switzerland, shows the humanizing influences that can spring from social variety.

Another writer to pursue the ideal of a Germany integrated into Europe is Frank Thiess, who even dared in Nazi times to write thinly camouflaged historical novels defending justice and humanity against the forces of barbarism (*Das Reich der Dämonen* (1940)). Ideals of universality also underlie the work of scholars such as Ernst Robert Curtius and the Swiss poet and critic Max Rychner (*Zur europäischen Literatur zwischen zwei Weltkriegen* (1951)).

The world which Hermann Hesse (1877–1962) had built out of impressionistic refinement on the one hand and romantic mysticism on the other collapsed after 1914. His new total vision is conveyed in *Das Glasperlenspiel* (1943), a utopian picture of a monastic kingdom of artists and scholars who indulge in sophisticated intellectual games in order to re-establish the unified values of European and Asiatic cultures. Yet the foundations of 'the man of the future' are not complete: one member of this monastic community is driven to experience the trials and sufferings of the world outside, and only at the end does one glimpse the full meaning of totality. Hesse's spiritual and intellectual struggles to reach this position are shown in his letters (1951), a paradigm of modern thought in this direction. In the same spirit is Rilke's urge to express 'an existence full of relatedness', and the works of Albrecht Schaeffer (the novel *Helianth* (1912–13) and the epic *Parzival* (1922)) also show, in modern and medieval contexts, the fullness of personality which is the precondition for understanding and grace.

The totality with which the majority of these writers are concerned goes beyond the disposition of mere earthly phenomena. 'I shall always remain convinced of the existence of God', wrote Hesse in 1950, 'because he did not reveal himself at one time and in one place but a hundred times and in a hundred different forms, visions and languages.' Alongside this non-Christian universalism stands its Christian equivalent, represented by Ricarda Huch and Rudolf Alexander Schröder, which reached its climax in the years of Nazi tyranny and the ensuing collapse of Germany, most notably in the work of Werner Bergengruen.

LOCAL LITERATURE AND NEW PATRIOTISM

In 1900 the Alsatian writer Friedrich Lienhard wrote an aggressive essay *Die Vorherrschaft Berlins*, attacking this civic bastion of literary atheism, profiteering and feckless living: neo-idealism was criticized for having an aristocratic approach, remote from the common life of the time, while the refinements of impressionism rested on equally unreal foundations. By presenting the situation in these terms and demanding that literature should return to 'pure' German material for its subjects, Lienhard pointed the way to a nationalistic movement that rapidly gained ground. Lienhard saved himself from narrowness by taking his inspiration from classical Weimar (cf. his novel *Oberlin* (1910)), but Adolf Bartels, co-founder with Lienhard of the propaganda journal *Heimat*, based his views on a rigid racialist attitude.

Poets of this kind took as their aim the discovery, stimulation and exploitation of the strong, healthy elements in the national character, attaching themselves to Julius Langbehn and the ideas in his book on Rembrandt (1890), and to men such as Paul de Lagarde, Gobineau, Moeller van den Bruck and Houston Stewart Chamberlain. Their principles involved a belief in the racial basis of intellectual tradition and culture, and the affirmation of family ties, class, community, the landscape of the fatherland and the customs of the people. Some saw these values as part of a Christian order of things; others, like the Holstein pastor Gustav Frenssen in his *Hilligenlei* (1906), attached them to a Teutonic deity, or to a nebulous world-purpose which they claimed to hold the justification for their racialist views – 'a law', as Wilhelm Schäfer put it, 'which determined the appearance of your own ego: a law not propounded by man but decreed by a divine power' (*Rechenschaft* (1948)).

Thus, whether outward- or inward-looking, national values, both of the countryman and the townsman, which the anti-Wilhelmine literary movements had overthrown, re-established themselves, and conservative forces far more powerful than those of neo-idealism were set in motion.

One must distinguish a regional form of national literature from one concerned with the life of the country as a whole. The former embraces portraits of local life such as Hermann Löns's tales of the Lüneburger Heide, Heinrich Vierordt's stories of life in a little Swabian town, Gorch Fock's pictures of North Sea island life and Hermann Eris Busse's stories from the Black Forest. Austria and Switzerland had had a rich national literature of this kind for centuries – a literature, moreover, that is far from merely local in appeal. The Swiss novelist Heinrich Federer tells of the warm comradeship he found in St Francis of Assisi, and is as familiar with Italian scenes (*Umbrische Reisegeschichtlein* (1932)) as with Swiss (*Lachweiler Geschichten* (1911)). Among the Austrians one may note the delightfully fresh stories of the Styrian schoolmaster Peter Rosegger, with their vein of critical humour; the village stories of Wagrain by Karl Heinrich Waggerl (*Das Jahr des Herrn* (1933)), with their glimpses of Salzburg; and the stories and plays of the Styrian Max Mell. The Bavarian stories of Ludwig Thoma (*Tante Frieda* (1907)) – one-time contributor to *Simplizissimus* – deal in an often caustic, satirical manner with village and small-town life, introducing above all the oddities and misfits in the community; so polemical is his tone on occasion, especially when exposing the hypocrisies of middle-class morality (*Moral* (1909)), that one could take him for one of the naturalists. Primitive, demonic forces fill Richard Billinger's stories and plays on the lives of Catholic country folk, while the ode-like lyrics of Paula von Preradovic contain motifs from the eastern shores of the Adriatic. Of dialect works mention may be made of Paula Grogger's *Bauernjahr* (1947) from Styria, the poems of Meinrad Lienert and the stories of Rudolf von Tavel, a Berne patrician.

On the broader front, however, there developed in Germany, from similar roots as this regional literature and with the added stimulus of the events of the war, a literature which sought the essence of the German character and dealt with the spiritual problems of the German *Volk* and its destiny. The hour of this literature came with the need to cultivate the concept of a strong, singleminded nation in the disunited Germany of the Weimar Republic. The new feeling of nationalism was directed as much against the Marxist class-struggle as against liberal capitalism, and represented a protest against the left-wing revolutionary movement, gaining more and more adherents after 1930, among them Paul Ernst and Emil Strauss (*Der Spiegel* (1919); *Das Riesenspielzeug* (1934)). Wilhelm Schäfer portrayed Zwingli and Pestalozzi as archetypes of men who create a spirit of community; the best of his stories (*Anekdoten* (1928)) use a laconic style which was a deliberate protest against the decay of formal values in expressionism and the 'new objectivity'. Indeed, the whole popular nationalistic movement, in this sense, brought a return to the more compact literary forms characteristic of realism. Hans Grimm's novels (*Volk ohne Raum* (1926)) served the Nazi cause by glorifying the German pioneer troops in Africa and advocating the distribution of the countries of the world among the strong nations, and in 1930 Josef Ponten began his series of novels on the German heritage overseas (*Volk auf dem Wege*).

Quite different are the poems and stories (*Geschichten aus Altpreußen* (1926)) of Agnes Miegel (born 1879), who took her subjects from her native East Prussia and its melancholic inhabitants, holding to a pattern of life honoured by tradition. Her ballads, right down to those in which she describes in gripping style the flight of the people of East Prussia to the West at the end of World War II, are written in a strict form, with an effective use of popular material.

The most striking document of this new German nationalism is the intellectually complex and contorted trilogy of novels *Paracelsus* (1917–26) by Erwin Guido Kolbenheyer (1876–1962), in which the figure of the Faustian doctor is intended to show the German in the full extent of his potential. According to Kolbenheyer's 'philosophy', as stated in *Die Bauhütte* (1925), greatness depends on the preservation of the 'pure' plasma which determines the fate both of the individual and of whole peoples. This is the framework within which his Paracelsus rejects the allegedly 'foreign' worlds of the Church and of humanism. Certain writers used the argument of heredity to adopt a deterministic biological material-ism analogous to the Marxism they detested, narrowing their definition of 'German' to the point where its best qualities, Christian, humanistic and universal, were excluded.

There is a strange mixture of narrowness and expansiveness in the work of Hermann Burte: Alemannic stories and poems (*Wiltfeber* (1912), the tale of a Wiesental Zarathustra, and the *Madlee* poems (1923)) exist along-side an aristocratic English tendency (*Patricia* (1910)) and translations of Voltaire.

Even more striking is the dichotomy that long persisted in Ernst Jünger (born 1895). At the age of nineteen, full of Nietzschean ideas of strength, virility and everything else that seemed to stand for the opposite of narrowminded, middle-class existence, he became a soldier (*In Stahl-gewittern* (1920)) and returned triumphantly from the war with the determination to instil heroic virtues into the German people. 'When every-thing is called in question, one tends to think in terms of catastrophes' – such was the attitude behind Jünger's view of present and future as a perpetual battle against the dominating forces of technology and eco-nomics: a strong nation needed to unite in a supreme act of determination, irrespective of the suffering that resulted. The new man was worker and soldier, and Jünger welcomed him in inflammatory, nationalistic tones (*Die totale Mobilmachung* (1931)); it would only have needed a few touches of crudity for us to find ourselves in the world of National Socialism.

But Jünger was also an intellectual aristocrat, whose values were far from those expressed in collective enterprise; rather, as the precise, cool, measured, subtle prose of *Das abenteuerliche Herz* (1929) in particular shows, he was an artist looking to celebrate the presence of the rare, the fine and the beautiful. Gradually, in the face of developments after 1933, the values of *Das abenteuerliche Herz* prevailed, and in *Auf den Marmorklippen* (1939) he depicted characters who symbolized the new humanistic élite which is to resist the forces of nationalistic and scientific nihilism, and begins to evolve the elements of a comprehensive philosophy of life. His later works, particularly his diaries, which he developed to a high degree of artistry, are commentaries on the age of the atomic bomb, Russian ex-pansionism, gene-mutations and other contemporary phenomena which offered his questing spirit a perpetual challenge and, as with Teilhard de Chardin, encouraged his urge towards utopianism (*An der Zeitmauer* (1959)).

1933–1945: Literature and the Third Reich

With a single stroke of the pen the new National Socialist government laid the foundation in 1933 for its intervention in German literary life and, after the *Anschluß* of 1938, also in that of Austria: only those of 'German blood' and 'acceptable to the new German State' were to be allowed to be members of the Reichsschrifttumskammer, which controlled publishers, booksellers and librarians as well as writers; anyone excluded from this central organization faced virtual extinction in the literary world. The result was the greatest exodus that modern German history had seen, while those who stayed either bowed to party pressure and were rewarded accordingly or wrestled with their consciences to preserve something of their intellectual integrity during the years of Nazi domination.

The supreme goal of Nazi totalitarianism was the creation of a strong, unified, power-hungry German Reich under the one fanatical Führer, the one political party and the one crude ideology of the supremacy of the 'Arian' race (cf. Gerhard Schumann, *Lieder vom Reich* (1936)), and pride of place was accorded to that literature which sang the praises of the 'Teutonic spirit'. This literature reached from humble works of local patriotism, of varying degrees of relationship to Nazi ideas, to the grey mass of party literature which set out to glorify in crude emotional terms the super-masculine man 'who had ceased to distinguish between the life of a soldier and the life of a civilian' (W. Picht, *Die Wandlung des Kämpfers* (1938)), and to pour a savage, nihilistic scorn on all other attitudes – humanistic, Christian, democratic or anything that reminded one of the Jews.

The great Nazi writer they were looking for never arrived. At the same time one finds during these years writers who adopted a fanatical loyalty to the Nazi state and some, like Benn and Weinheber, who allowed themselves to be drawn along in its wake for a time. While men like Binding made light of Nazi violence and persecution (*Antwort eines Deutschen an die Welt* (1938)), others paid the price of resistance (Albrecht Haushofer (shot in 1945), *Moabiter Sonette* (published 1946)).

INNER EMIGRATION

It was easy to assume abroad that all writers of quality had left Germany under Hitler and to draw premature conclusions about the literature written by those who remained. But Nazi attitudes were not the only ones, and there persisted thoughts of true and false, good and evil, noble and base, which were a potential threat to the State yet which, possibly with an eye to reaction abroad, the authorities allowed to be expressed, while keeping them within limits and reserving the right to suppress them at any time. Open resistance was out of the question, but these writings strengthened many in their inner resistance:

> Licht ists im Schatten zu wohnen,
> Vergessen werden ist Huld, und vereinsamt werden ist Gnade . . .

> (Brightness is to live in the shadow, to be forgotten is a favour, and to be left in isolation is grace . . .)
> (Gertrud von le Fort, *Lyrisches Tagebuch aus den Jahren 1933 bis 1945*)

Although the extent of literary resistance decreased after 1933, its intensity did not. Many, like Ernst Barlach, had their works banned; Ernst Wiechert, apostle of a somewhat vague Christianity, spent months in Buchenwald (*Der Totenwald* (1946)); the Jewess Gertrud Kolmar, poetess of a broad lyrical sensitivity, from the smallest things to the greatest, was deported with her father and never seen again; Luise Rinser tells in her *Gefängnistagebuch* (1946) of her experiences after her arrest in 1944; the novelist Jochen Klepper, who judged every action in his life by the Word of God (*Unter dem Schatten Deiner Flügel: Tagebücher 1932–42*), went to his death with his Jewish wife and her daughter. Living under the sword of

Damocles, such writers converted the pressure of their external existence into meditation on the inner life.

One source of refuge from which the writers of the so-called inner emigration could not be driven was the Christian religion. Among these writers were Ricarda Huch, Rudolf Alexander Schröder and Werner Bergengruen, whose novel *Der Großtyrann und das Gericht* (1935), placed in the camouflaged setting of the Italian Renaissance, is a protest against the totalitarian state in the name of the unshakeable principles of the Christian conscience. In 1937 Bergengruen was expelled from the Reichsschrifttumskammer.

Others withdrew into their own private world and concerned themselves with what the Nazi writer Christian Jenssen scorned as 'purely private problems with no relevance to the emergence of our new Germany'. Manfred Hausmann (*Abschied von der Jugend* (1937)), who later turned to Christianity, belongs here, as does Georg Britting, writer of bright and sparkling poems of the countryside and tales of mischievous figures caught in the spell of sinister powers. Thiess, Flake, Kästner and Albrecht Schaeffer also form part of this context. In Schaeffer's novel of married life *Cara* (1936) occurs the memorable sentence of protest against official racial policy: 'For me, too, it is the human being that comes first, then his country, and whoever imagines himself to be my brother, *is* my brother.' Friedrich Schnack, like the Silesian Friedrich Bischoff in his novel *Die goldenen Schlösser* (1935), created a romantic world of nature linked to the 'world-spirit' and to the mediating role of man in the universe, while Carossa later looked back on the phenomenon of 'inner emigration' in his *Ungleiche Welten* (1951).

WRITERS IN EXILE

The writers who left Germany between 1933 and 1939 founded a number of journals and publishing houses in various European cities, but with the outbreak of war and the expansion of the Nazi occupation many sought refuge outside Europe, above all in the United States. Moving accounts of the adventures and tragedies, physical and spiritual, experienced by refugees at this time are given in Döblin's *Schicksalsreise* (1949) and Leonhard Frank's *Links, wo das Herz ist* (1952).

A persistent figure in the work of *émigré* writers is the refugee who struggles to find a new identity in the strange, new society that has given him shelter. An associated mood of melancholy finds expression in the work of Nelly Sachs (1891–1970) and in Max Herrmann-Neisse's simple poems *Um uns die Fremde* (1936). A different reaction is represented by Karl Schnog (see H. Wielek, *Verse der Emigration* (1935)), who defiantly claimed the right of the poet to proclaim his wishes and desires whatever the circumstances. But those *émigré* poets who continually adopted the familiar, negative critical attitudes, whether in a Marxist spirit or in a mood of persistent scepticism or despair at the condition of the whole world, are not those who carry the greatest conviction, and the productions of Alfred Kerr, Erich Weinert, Friedrich Wolf and others seemed to the outside world, despite their vocabulary of freedom and humanity, remarkably trivial.

'My craft was too frail for the ocean,' wrote Döblin; 'the sides were bound to give way, and the bottom, being of paper, just collapsed.' These words reflect the feelings of the refugee who, like the representative of 'inner emigration', saw it as his task to help to build a new world which would break the physical and intellectual grip of Nazism. The greatest hope lay for each poet in the pursuit of his own individual development, as proven by Musil in *Der Mann ohne Eigenschaften*, by Döblin in his *Hamlet* and by Broch in his reflections on politics as a substitute for religion, in the mysticism of his *Tod des Vergil* (1941) and, at a less profound level, in his *Der Versucher* (1954). By virtue of his novel *König Heinrich IV* (1935–7) one may also include Heinrich Mann, who, otherwise a writer whose chief delight lay in critical destruction, here portrays the French king as 'the first ambassador of reason and human happiness'.

Most Communist writers did not get farther than the reproduction of the principles of party doctrine, but there is an occasional exception. One is Anna Seghers, with her novel *Das siebte Kreuz* (1947), set in a concentration camp; another is the poet Johannes R. Becher, who emigrated to Russia in 1935 but, though tending to become more and more a propagandist, still struck an occasional personal note with poems recalling the glories of Bach and Hölderlin and touching on questions – unwelcome to party leaders – of the inadequacy of ideology in the face of individual suffering:

> . . . Habe ich vielleicht gesprochen
> Mit jenem Bauern, der den Weinstock spritzte
> Dort bei Kressbronn? Ich habe mich nicht gekümmert
> Um seinen Weinstock. Darum muß ich jetzt
> Aus weiter Ferne die Gespräche führen,
> Die unterlassenen. Fremd ging ich vorbei
> Mit meinem Wissen, und an mir vorüber
> Ging wieder einer mit noch besserem Wissen.
> O überall war besseres Wissen, jeder
> Besaß die Weisheit ganz. Doch die Liebe fehlte
> Und die Geduld . . .

(. . . Do you think that *I* talked to that farmer who was spraying his vines over at Kressbronn? I was not concerned about his vines. That's why I'm now holding the conversation at a distance which I ought to have held at the time. Aloof and full of knowledge, I passed him by, and the next moment someone with even better knowledge passed *me* by. Better knowledge was every-where; everyone was the epitome of wisdom. But there was no affection – or patience . . .)

('Das Holzhaus', in *Die Hohe Warte: Deutschland-Dichtung 1933–1945*)

'Exile has the effect either of ruining a man or of bringing him to the peak of his development,' said Jacob Burckhardt. The latter effect is only to be observed in those who were striving towards a more complete humanity – what Döblin called 'saturation with inexhaustible reality'. Thus Carl Zuckmayer, in his *Pro domo* (1938), spoke of all the noble, humanistic qualities which are the true heritage of Germany and which it is the clear duty of the German to preserve; and in the realistic drama *Des Teufels General* (1942–5), written during his exile in America, he reveals so intimate an empathy with his compatriots left in Germany to their 'inner emigration' that one would think he had never left the country.

The forces of religion are particularly in evidence in Wolfskehl, Döblin, Werfel and Nelly Sachs. Döblin's conversion in 1940 led to the story *Der Oberst und der Dichter* (1943), a protest against life which becomes rigid under the pressures of everyday existence, and the religious dialogue *Der unsterbliche Mensch* (1946). In his exile in New Zealand Karl Wolfskehl found consolation in a return to Judaism and used the figure of Job to symbolize his own sad but not hopeless existence (*Hiob* (1950)). Franz Werfel's fantastic utopian novel *Der Stern der Ungeborenen* (1945) ends with a call for the Judaic and Christian traditions to remain united till the end of time, while Nelly Sachs (1891–1970), for whom despair and grace were inseparably linked, wrote of the sufferings of the persecuted, above all of the Jews, drawing on the Psalms and on Chassidistic writings (*In den Wohnungen des Todes* (1947)).

The true spirit of Germany survived both in the 'outer' and in the 'inner' emigration, which were closer to each other than was either of them to those who threatened the liberty of man from the right or from the left. Spiritual frontiers made for different allies and enemies from national frontiers, and between a Carossa, a Bergengruen and a Ricarda Huch on the one side and a Thomas Mann, a Wolfskehl and an Urzidil on the other there remains, in spite of differences, a profound identity of interests which made itself felt in developments after 1945.

Developments since 1945

For an account of German literature since 1885 one can draw on a great deal of documentary material surrounding the literature itself, though one is at the same time hampered by the fact that many of the writings not published during the lifetime of Hauptmann, Thomas Mann, Brecht and other important figures are still not available. But when dealing with the most recent literature, one can only hope to arrange the mass of material in a manner which shows some of the basic principles at stake and something of the relationships between writers.

When the German army surrendered in May 1945, countless German cities were in ruins and much of Europe lay devastated after the most terrible slaughter in its history. This trauma continued to dominate German literature for many years after the end of the war and its effects have still far from completely disappeared. Bruno E. Werner's novel *Die Galeere* (1943–7), for example, depicts the individual caught in the treadmill of the Third Reich and the destruction of both in the conflagration of the war. Hermann Kasack, showing the influence of Kafka, symbolized the totalitarian state in surrealistic manner (*Die Stadt hinter dem Strom* (1942–6)) in his picture of a ruined city of the dead, shrouded in mist, where no one was any longer himself and just a few conspirators knew that a dying Europe could only be saved by ascetic philosophies from the East. Theodor Plievier, once one of the working-class poets of expressionism, wrote a pseudo-documentary account, in his *Stalingrad* (1945), of how masses of German soldiers had been wiped out. In 1949 appeared the first volume of *Die Sintflut*, an expansive trilogy of novels by Stefan Andres (born 1906) which describes the two worlds of the 'inner' and 'outer' emigration down to the year 1946 and presents as a model for the future the character of a young man struggling to achieve some form of Christian *humanitas*.

1945 naturally brought the end of nationalistic literature, and with the restoration of free expression the writers of the 'inner emigration' were among the first to be heard; the late works of *émigrés* such as Döblin and Thomas Mann reappeared, together with translations of Éluard, Mayakovski, T. S. Eliot, Thornton Wilder and many others, which made a deep impression on young German writers who had been cut off from progressive developments abroad. These young writers, members of a rebellious, sceptical generation born in the 1920s, described the miseries of the contemporary scene and had a deep distrust of all conventions and values based on security and reasonableness. The differences of opinion between the generation of the 'inner emigration' and that of these often self-styled 'progressive' younger writers has dominated the literary scene in German-speaking countries since 1945, more obviously so in West Germany, where conditions encouraged the adoption of extreme positions, than in Austria and Switzerland, where the moderating force of national culture has always been stronger.

In the German Democratic Republic the tone was set by the Marxist opponents of Hitler, and one dialect of totalitarianism gave way to another, this time under Communist control. Among the leading figures were Brecht, Anna Seghers, Arnold Zweig, and the lyric poets Stephan Hermlin, Günter Kunert, Johannes Bobrowski (1917–65) – all characterized by a melancholy attachment to the countryside and an aversion from everything conventional and fashionable – and Peter Huchel (born 1903), a master of laconic, objective social poetry which uses the small-scale symbols of peasant life to describe the destiny of man in general (*Gedichte* (1948)). The East Berlin journal *Sinn und Form* contains samples of work by poets who in general reflect the official policy of making the writer a tool in the achievement of a political purpose: 'Art', said Otto Grotewohl, 'must follow the direction dictated by the political struggle.' There has no more been an 'official' poet of any consequence in East Germany than there was in the Third Reich, and all signs indicate that, as in all totalitarian states, the development of 'official' literature leads to the end of development altogether.

Here belongs the figure of Uwe Johnson (born 1934), who grew up in the German Democratic Republic but came over to the West in 1959. In a cool, casual, neutral style he employs inner monologues, flashbacks and other techniques of 'decadent' Western art to compare life in the two Germanys at a moment when common human interests seemed to him to be seriously threatened (*Das dritte Buch über Achim* (1961)). The flat didactic tone of 'socialist realism' in the Soviet Russian style only becomes significant on the rare occasions when it appears as 'realistic socialism', a personal conviction that goes beyond the formulae of party doctrine. Similar to Johnson in this respect is Erwin Strittmatter (born 1912), whose novel *Ole Bienkopp* (1963) is also far from a replica of the standard party pattern.

MODERN SCEPTICISM

One of the most remarkable phenomena in the two years immediately after the end of the war was the publication of the handful of pieces by the young Hamburg actor Wolfgang Borchert (1921–47), one-time infantryman and prisoner in a concentration camp. These works were the most authentic of all contemporary protests by a young generation that saw itself as having been cheated out of its birthright by the Nazis and the war, and regarded the world as a place where human values had been cruelly betrayed. In his play *Draußen vor der Tür* (1946) Borchert's hero Beckmann, spokesman for this generation, returns from the war and throws his accusations in the faces of the powerful, the hard-faced and the exploiters who had spent the war comfortably at home.

Almost all Borchert's successors bore the scars of their age. There was nothing to resemble the ecstatic, extravagant notions of the advent of a new man which had characterized the expressionists of 1918. While new cities were rising from the ruins of the old, and the foundations of future prosperity were being laid, these poets concentrated on the significance of the year 1945 for the history of Germany and on the threat to civilization of of atomic warfare, totalitarian states and the senseless pursuit of material prosperity. Thus the hero of the novel *Der Tod in Rom* (1954) by Wolfgang Koeppen (born 1906) is a twelve-tone composer called Siegfried Pfaffrath who stands opposed to the world both of yesterday and today, and who, weary of the pleasures of the senses and disgusted with the world he knows, escapes from his *Angst* only in rare moments of aesthetic excitement and 'existential' artistic creation. Koeppen's travel-books, on the other hand, full of effective contrasts of light and shade (*Nach Rußland und anderswohin* (1958); *Amerikafahrt* (1959)), mark a release from the long years of coming to terms with the past.

Koeppen and others of his kind also rejected the language of the present – forgetting that the writers of the 'inner emigration' had preserved the German language through the ravages of the Nazi period, which, with its political and ideological claptrap, cheapened all noble concepts and all but destroyed the language itself. Under the Nazis liberation meant annexation; peace and *Volk* meant rearmament and war and the Nazis' own coterie. Words like love, faith, hope, fatherland, goodness, nobility and man also seemed to the young generation to be lies, and what had hitherto appeared unassailably real now lay in ruins.

With what they called a 'Kahlschlag', a clean sweep of traditional approaches as a reaction against highflown, idealistic phraseology, these young writers adopted a blunt, emotionless style in the manner of Brecht and others of the 'new objectivity', and took over from Kafka, Benn, Breton and Joyce the irrational, melancholy, wilful imagery descriptive of man's helplessness in the world. The result was a hybrid style born of the union of realistic precision and bizarre fantasy. Earlier and contemporary examples of this style from the literatures of other countries which left their mark on this generation of Germans were collected by Hans Magnus Enzensberger in his anthology *Museum der modernen Poesie* (1960).

Lyric poetry

> Der Häher wirft mir
> die blaue Feder nicht zu.
>
> In die Morgendämmerung kollern
> die Eicheln seiner Schreie.
> Ein bitteres Mehl, die Speise
> des ganzen Tags.
>
> Hinter dem roten Laub
> hackt er mit hartem Schnabel

tagsüber die Nacht
aus Ästen und Baumfrüchten,
ein Tuch, das er über mich zieht.

Sein Flug gleicht dem Herzschlag.
Wo schläft er aber
und wem gleicht sein Schlaf?
Ungesehen liegt in der Finsternis
die Feder vor meinem Schuh.

(The jay will not throw me his blue feather. The acorns in his cries rumble out into the dawn. A bitter kind of meal, food for the entire day. Behind the red foliage throughout the day he pecks the night out of branches and berries with his hard beak – a sheet that he draws over me. His flight is like a heart-beat. But where does he sleep, and like whom does he sleep? Unnoticed in the darkness, the feather is lying in front of my shoe.)

(Günter Eich, born 1907; from R. Grimm, *Evokation und Montage*, 1961)

This poem, published in 1955, characterizes the new direction. All emphasis is carefully avoided; understatement is the rule, a muted, prose-like, parlando style free in rhythm and without rhyme. At one moment the word conveys the object precisely, at the next it establishes bold and unexpected associations; on the one hand it conceals, on the other it confuses; and the whole poem is linked to the strange, irrational symbol of the blue feather, which at first the bird does not throw to the poet and at the end the poet does not even notice: nature, to which man thinks he is close, turns out to be a mystery. The blue feather is one of the commonest symbols of modern melancholy in *Botschaften des Regens* (1955), a collection of lyrics which at first sight seems to consist of nothing but an assemblage of grey, nebulous images of a doomed and empty existence. Yet scattered through Eich's poems are isolated moments of hope derived from the love and the suffering of man and from the greatness of the past.

A firmer call to return to the consolations of nature was made by Wilhelm Lehmann (1882–1968), whose quiet, modern lyrics had their moment of influence in 1945. His vision of nature, conveyed in a self-consciously clipped style, has a timelessness that enables him to people his landscapes with mythical rulers and spirits which share the origins of nature herself. A loose, ambivalent style similar to that of Eich appears in the stories and lyrics of Marie Luise Kaschnitz (born 1901). *Totentanz und Gedichte zur Zeit* (1947) gives a pitiless account of the inner and outer destruction wrought by the war but also sounds a note of solace with the motto 'We are not the world'; her later works, such as *Ewige Stadt* (1951) and *Dein Schweigen – meine Stimme* (1962) – the latter written on the death of her husband – retain this dual motif of the reality of suffering and the reality of conquering this suffering.

In the plain, blunt poems of Hans Magnus Enzensberger (born 1929) the modern style of the 'Kahlschlag' is used to belabour the smugness of the age with unpleasant realities and attack the falseness of contemporary society (*verteidigung der wölfe* (1957); *blindenschrift* (1964)). In his essays *Politik und Verbrechen* (1964) Enzensberger expresses himself on a broad range of subjects in independent critical style based on dialectical Marxist principles, taking his values, not from ideology but from what has survived through the ages.

Certain modern lyric poets show a return to the use of irrational images, such as the Austrian Ingeborg Bachmann (born 1926), whose rich use of metaphor expresses silence as well as action and who feels her way tentatively out of the abyss of emptiness and meaninglessness in her collections *Die gestundete Zeit* (1953) and *Anrufung des Großen Bären* (1956). Her Swiss contemporary Erika Burkart (born 1922), living a withdrawn life in the quiet surroundings of the Aargau, very different from Ingeborg Bachmann's city life, nevertheless writes poetry of a similar kind in which a stream of fresh, poetic images, without destroying the mystery of the inexpressible, points towards the union of the soul with the Great Unconscious (*Ich lebe* (1964)).

In contrast, Max Hölzer (born 1915), a pupil of André Breton, adopted the style of *poésie automatique* and abandoned himself to an endless stream of associative images from the unconscious, while the most significant poet in the surrealist line is Paul Celan (1920–70), an Austrian who lived in Paris from 1948 until his death. His collections *Mohn und Gedächtnis* (1952) and *Sprachgitter* (1959) present a visionary world of melancholy which both suffers from reality and seeks it, a world which became both alienated and intensified in his poetry.

Karl Krolow (born 1915) cultivated an extravagant, colourful metaphorical style to express his sense of fear and emptiness (*Wind und Zeit* (1954)), while Walter Höllerer (born 1922; *Der andere Gast* (1952)) and others, also devoting themselves to the technique of the inner monologue, show formal tendencies which link them to younger poets who affect a highly rational blend of realistic and irrational elements that recalls the disembodied montages of Benn. Some may well have hoped that 'profundity' would follow from such exercises as a matter of course. In fact, where montage became more and more an end in itself, and where the 'modern' poet imagined that he was dealing with 'nothing but language', the alienation of language from the objective world and the subjective ego entered its final stage. Thus poets such as Helmut Heissenbüttel (born 1921; *Kombinationen* (1954)) contented themselves with mannered typographical efforts:

ist aber ein pfahl ist aber
der stein der da war
                        der sprang nicht
der sprang im rock in der höh
schrie am licht
              war zuerst
ein mann der knab übers wasser haut
geprellt nur fünfmal
                  aber so flach
                      so leicht gelernt
so leicht zu vergessen unter der haut

In the anthology *Movens* (1960), edited by Franz Mon (born 1924), the German translator of Ionesco, one finds highflown programmes concealing a welter of montages of words, parts of words and mere groups of letters from a host of languages, all leading nowhere. Far from serving what their authors allege to be the needs of the time, they merely represent the activities of a few naïve cliques. A comparison with Joyce, Gertrud Stein, Dada, the early expressionist montages of August Stramm, or even the much-despised Hesse of *Steppenwolf* shows how far from being 'advanced' these *avant-garde* poets are. '*Avant-garde*', said Enzensberger in his essay *Die Aporien der Avantgarde* (1962), 'has become its opposite: it has become an anachronism. And as for the great hazard which besets the artist's future – the *avant-garde* cannot cope with it.'

Narrative fiction

Like the lyric, prose fiction shows varying blends of the anti-conventional modes of expression current after 1918: the sober, uninhibited, descriptive technique of the 'new objectivity', and the manipulation of creatures of the free imagination. Chronological order was deliberately confused, flashbacks were introduced, wild, unpunctuated monologues à la Joyce were strung together, and in the same breath close-ups of reality were inserted. Recollections of the past years of terror which most of these young writers had spent in work-camps, at the front, in prisoner-of-war camps, and later in the post-war conditions of hunger and despair, together with what they saw as the dubious aspects of the affluence of the rising German Federal Republic – such were the themes of their works. They all subscribed to 'opposition' of one kind or another, whether originally Catholic in inspiration, as with Böll and Schallück, or Communist, as with Andersch – opposition in particular to what Gerd Gaiser called 'the discrepancy between perfectionism and underdevelopment', façade and deception, which they found in the mad rush for prosperity.

Hans Erich Nossack found his true subject when his native Hamburg went up in flames (he described the scene in a dispassionate tone in *Der*

Untergang (1948)): it is the subject of man as a refugee from catastrophe, or as a failure in life, who has become liberated from apparently reliable conventions and embarked on a new, autonomous existence which spans the emptiness below and in which there are no conventions or guarantees (*Spirale* (1956)) – a set of motifs which led Sartre to his existentialist philosophy.

Many, like Peter Weiss and Martin Walser (the novel *Halbzeit* (1960)), had little to set against the crude descriptions of social evils but a universal scepticism; others rediscovered the authority of a passionate personal and social conscience, writing novels and short stories to show how, in the years following the war, the individual who was disillusioned with ideologies and cheated by political parties, churches and his fellow men, struggled to find his own meaning in life. This is the substance of the majority of the popular stories of Heinrich Böll (born 1917; *Und sagte kein einziges Wort* (1953); *Doktor Murkes gesammeltes Schweigen* (1958); *Ansichten eines Clowns* (1963)). Gerd Gaiser (born 1908), a former fighter pilot, painter and art teacher, used more experimental methods, seeing the image, even of the irrational and inexpressible, as a means of introducing order into the chaos of reality; his novels – *Eine Stimme hebt an* (1950), the story of a German soldier returned from the war; *Schlußball* (1958), a story of the *nouveaux riches* of the time; and *Am Paß Nascondo* (1960), written in a surrealistic style – show the true man trying, against the opposition of the false men around him, to find these principles of order. Similarly Alfred Andersch (born 1914), in *Sansibar oder der letzte Grund* (1957) and *Die Rote* (1960), presents the true man as one who escapes from the political and moral degradation of life into the unknown.

The Swiss writer Max Frisch (born 1911), partly with the techniques of impressionism, partly with those of surrealist alienation, used his novels (*Stiller* (1954); *Homo faber* (1957)) and dramas (*Die chinesische Mauer* (1946)) as scenes in which the painful dichotomy in modern man is revealed in terms of the self, of the empty middle-class world, of conventions in marriage, career and social life (*Mein Name sei Gantenbein* (1964)), of ideologies of power (*Andorra* (1961)) and of man's own eternally unfulfilled dreams of a perfect and unproblematic existence.

A few young writers, however, have been quietly turning away from the cult of 'novelty at all costs' affected by those determined to decry all the values of the modern world and adopt the fashionable aesthetic of unrelated, disembodied forms. Klaus Nonnenmann (born 1922), for example, infuses the technique of montage with a light, playful Romantic irony and uses it to describe how man can break out of the modern sense of unfulfilment (*Teddy Flesh oder die Belagerung von Sagunt* (1964)). Despite being at the mercy of the vagaries of life, man is discovered to possess a hidden greatness, and while being on one's guard against accepting premature idealistic assurances, one finds it possible to overcome the fashionable insistence on the meaninglessness of life. The Austrian Herbert Eisenreich (born 1925) looks optimistically to such a 'new man' as 'the only real chance for mankind' (*Böse, schöne Welt* (1957)), and the Swiss writer Hugo Loetscher (born 1930), who in his *Abwässer. Ein Gutachten* (1963) describes a modern city from the viewpoint of a sewage inspector, ventures to use the phrase 'human dignity' again and to make fun of the student with literary pretensions who declares that 'the age of poetry has passed and the dawn of protest has come'. Traditional modes of storytelling, but with the laconic characteristics of the 'Kahlschlag' style, are found in the tales of Hans Bender (born 1919; *Mit dem Postschiff* (1962)) as in those of Siegfried Lenz, Wolfdietrich Schnurre, Ilse Aichinger, Thomas Bernhard and others.

The full-length novel of the 'sceptical generation', however, has rarely exceeded the mediocre. The most striking success is probably that of Günter Grass (born 1927), a native of Danzig, who, after being released from a prisoner-of-war camp, became successively an agricultural worker, a jazz musician and a sculptor, and achieved world fame with *Die Blechtrommel* (1959). As in his *Hundejahre* (1962), his subject is the life of man through the rise and fall of his native Germany, to which he has a kind of love-hate relationship. From the proud Reich of 1914 through the Nazi collapse to the economic affluence of 1955 Grass describes in a disillusioned tone but with Rabelaisian gusto a series of bizarre characters of all classes and attitudes. Conventional and unconventional narrative methods exist side by side; the author's view stretches from the contemporary world situation to cheap, tasteless eroticism, but one dominant figure always re-emerges – the rabid anarchist with the small mind, inquisitive, uncouth, sometimes blasphemous, but always true to himself, the only character likely to survive modern conditions. Such a figure – one found not only in Grass – is also related to the roguish characters in challenging, exuberant novels like *Die Insel des zweiten Gesichts* (1953) by Albert Vigoleis Thelen (born 1903).

Drama

Since 1945 the German theatre has been waiting for a great modern German dramatist. Most of the plays performed were, and still are, translations of foreign works. On the one hand German playwrights like Karl Wittlinger dealt in 'realistic' style with contemporary issues; at the same time there were attempts by Hermann Moers and others to create poetic drama in the manner of Christopher Fry, and experimental, *avant-garde* montages by Peter Weiss, Günter Grass and Wolfgang Hildesheimer – the last-named a follower of Ionesco's Theatre of the Absurd. *Der Stellvertreter* (1963) by Rolf Hochhuth (born 1931), a propaganda piece which gained

great popularity, became a model for those who set out to make controversial figures from recent history into subjects for plays. An extreme
example of this kind is the conglomeration of documentary evidence from
the Auschwitz trial which Peter Weiss put together to make his *Die
Ermittlung. Ein Konzentrat* (1965).

The only outstanding modern dramatist writing in German is the Swiss
Friedrich Dürrenmatt (born 1921). In imaginative burlesque manner drawing on a variety of anti-conventional dramatic styles from Brecht to
Wilder, he passes summary judgement on man in his modern decadence,
in particular the representative, big or small, of brutal power. He is an
aggressive writer 'in the train of Aristophanes and Swift', as he once said.
The background to many of his scenes, as it is for *Ein Engel kommt nach
Babylon* (1953), could be the great nebula of Andromeda, for he measures
man by absolute standards of greatness, and thus turns many of his
characters into caricatures. His presentation of human fallibility gains in
depth from what he senses as the ultimately religious nature of the eternal
human tragi-comedy.

The revival hoped for in the drama came in an unexpected form – not
in the theatre but in the radio play. With the growth of public broadcasting
in Germany in the 1920s there arose a need for dramatic works which
depended entirely on the spoken word and the accompanying sound-
effects, and following the adaptation of established theatrical works
efforts were made, initially in England, to evolve original forms appropriate to the new medium. One of the earliest German examples of such
works is Ernst Wiechert's *Spiel vom deutschen Bettelmann* (1932).

The radio play has exerted a particular fascination on modern writers.
Since its effect depends on the word alone, it offers a challenge to combine
the irrational depth of lyric poetry with the narration of a striking event
and the dramatic characterization of men and their fate, whether in
tragedy or comedy. Since 1950 the German radio stations have published
an annual *Hörspielbuch* containing the year's radio plays; among the
authors represented are Günter Eich, Friedrich Dürrenmatt, Ilse Aichinger and Jürg Federspiel.

A retrospective view of twenty years of sceptical post-war literature
reveals many works, far in spirit from the great classical forms of the past,
created by an intelligence which freely combines the forces of the irrational
imagination with a clear-sighted realism. In contrast to this free mode of
creation, which can go to the extreme of a montage technique that pays no
heed to meaningful content, is the strictly realistic approach. 'The great
event in the life of the modern poet', said Karl Krolow in 1961, 'is the
diminution of the human image.' This approach is at its most effective
when it sets out to portray the vulnerability of man and to warn the world

in passionate tones of the dangers of basking in the enervating pleasures of relaxation.

This is the continuation of a tendency prominent in German literature since 1885. It is an emancipating desire to release man from traditional metaphysical, moral, social and all other patterns of life, even from the unity of his personality, and can be traced through naturalism, the Nietzschean school, impressionism and certain aspects of expressionism down to the 'new objectivity' and beyond.

Alongside the serious-minded writers of this kind there were inevitably large numbers of imitators who simply took over the assumptions of scepticism and despair, indulged in all manner of stylistic tricks and lowered the tone of serious poetry with their affectations. Every age has its Tartuffes. Particularly noticeable in such writers is the onesidedness of their attitude to the present. 'Modern reality is incommensurable. How can modern literature be otherwise?' wrote Wolfgang Weyrauch (see Hans Bender, *Mein Gedicht ist mein Messer* (1955), a collection of declarations by young modern poets). Walter Jens wrote in the same tone: 'Anyone who has any respect for himself remains in chaos.'

But views such as these take no account of widespread efforts to think in terms of a meaningful future for mankind – efforts which have nothing to do with attitudes of appeasement which Enzensberger regards as characteristic of all 'positive' thought – or of movements in modern biology towards a new view of nature, or of psychosomatic medicine and psychology, or of the movement in history to see past greatness in a context of universal human development, or of political visions of a community of nations, quite apart from bold attempts to link the religions of the world, or to reconcile religion and science, or religion and man's sense of meaninglessness. In fields like these the apostles of 'modern' literature are nowhere to be seen, and to call the members of the fashionable cult of alienation 'progressive' is open to question. And apart from this it is only one way of facing the challenge of the hour.

HUMANISM, CHRISTIANITY AND UNIVERSALISM

The German catastrophe of 1933 to 1948 was most convincingly withstood by those who regarded the devaluation of life affected by the 'sceptical generation' as a capitulation on the part of men who were not spiritually free. They shared a common enemy with this generation and underwent the same experiences of war, of defeat, of 'man's inhumanity to man'; but they regained a sense of the meaning of life and rescued the word 'positive' from exile, restoring man to the context of eternal truth.

A bold attempt at a religious humanism was the *Venezianische Credo* of Rudolf Hagelstange (born 1912), written while Hagelstange was fighting in Italy and published secretly in 1944. In a series of passionate sonnets against the tyranny of Nazi totalitarianism he sought, as he put it, 'to overcome the chaos of the present by dwelling on the pure, indestructible powers of man', powers that had enabled mankind in antiquity and in Christendom to overthrow more than one tyranny. Hagelstange treated this inexhaustible theme in a variety of styles in his later verse (*Die Meersburger Elegie* (1950); *Die Ballade vom verschütteten Leben* (1952)) and also wrote books on his journeys to the United States and the Soviet Union.

A historical novel drawing inspiration from Hofmannsthal, Handel and Jacob Burckhardt and seeking to preserve the creative artistic values of Europe is *Der blaue Kammerherr* (1949) by Wolf von Niebelschütz (1913–60), which sets itself up against the fashionable cult of 'the literature of misery'.

In the Amsterdam underground in 1941 a group of resistance fighters was formed, taking their inspiration from Stefan George. This led to the foundation in 1951 of the international journal and publishing house *Castrum Peregrini*, devoted to preserving George's influence and making known the work of his followers. One such was Ludwig Derleth (1870–1940), whose collection *Der fränkische Koran* (1932) exudes a heroic religiosity derived from early Christianity; another is Fritz Usinger (born 1895), who took over George's criteria of form and greatness and applied them in his Orphic poems to a huge 'universe of the intellect' which embraces the earth, the cosmos and transcendency (*Gedichte* (1940); *Niemandsland* (1957)).

The neo-classical poems of Friedrich Georg Jünger (born 1898) draw their strength from antiquity and a certain Nietzschean self-confidence; his collections of memoirs (*Grüne Zweige* (1951) and *Spiegel der Jahre* (1956)), like his essays on contemporary issues (*Die Perfektion der Technik* (1946)), reveal a mind which, like that of his brother Ernst, applies the criteria of conservatism to the problems of the present.

Johannes Urzidil (born 1896) grew up in the Prague circle of Kafka, Werfel and Max Brod, emigrated in 1939 to England and then to New York, working for a time in a leather factory. His works, which only became known in Germany after 1955, are among the richest and fullest of *émigré* productions, drawing nostalgically on his memories of the old world of Prague (*Die verlorene Geliebte* (1956)) and on his experiences in the new world of America (*Halleluja* (1959)). Everything is seen with a keen eye for human weaknesses and their expiation, and informed by a mature, generous nature that has been educated in the school of life and influenced above all by the values of Goethe and Schiller. Poets like Urzidil avoided anything that resembled the 'Kahlschlag' approach to language and literature, and returned to the values of the great traditions of the past.

The writers discussed above stand in a line of development that stretches back through neo-idealism to the roots of European humanism. From this humanism stems a second force in twentieth-century German literature, alongside that of the spirit of emancipation, namely an unorthodox conservatism concerned to re-establish man's community of interest with the past, the present and the transcendental sense of the future. Ricarda Huch, Rudolf Alexander Schröder, Werner Bergengruen and others had combined this humanism with Christianity to provide a bulwark against fear and nihilism, and their Christian successors extended the range of their verse to incorporate new and powerful tensions reminiscent of the baroque age. They praised the divine order in the universe, from the lowest to the highest of objects and living things, but warned of the dangers of seeking an ultimate refuge in the things of earth; as they gazed into new depths of evil, God became a greater and greater mystery, and they saw the devastations of the age as a harsh summons to final repentance. Man was stripped of his earthly properties, and his existence was thereby made indestructible.

Among these later Christian poets is Reinhold Schneider (1903–56; *Die letzten Tage* (1946)), who examined the course of history for moments when man's confidence in salvation was put to what seemed impossible tests. The modern Christian poet lives on the perilous borders of metaphysical security and often uses the loose, unconventional expressions of insecurity to declare his position. The work of Elisabeth Langgässer (1899–1950) shows on the one hand a passionate involvement in the world of nature and instinct and on the other an equally passionate urge for knowledge; her poems (*Der Laubmann und die Rose* (1947)) and novels (*Das unauslöschliche Siegel* (1947); *Märkische Argonautenfahrt* (1950)) show an escape from this conflict into a world governed by intense humility and devotion and inspired by Catholic miracles. Similarly Luise Rinser's characters undergo conflicting experiences (*Mitte des Lebens* (1952)) before finally submitting to the Commandments.

Edzard Schaper (born 1908), who was born into the Russian Orthodox Church and became a Roman Catholic convert in 1950, wrote a number of Christian tales of the oppression of the Slavs (*Der Henker* (1940); *Die Freiheit des Gefangenen* (1950)), while the stories of Stefan Andres, who lived from 1937 to 1949 in Positano, reflect the pagan and Christian worlds of the Mediterranean (*Die Reise nach Portiuncula* (1954)). The Swiss lyric poet Urs Martin Strub (born 1910) presents in an original style of rhythmic prose archetypal figures of modern man in the pressures of his existence (*Die Wandelsterne* (1955)), and in his poems (*Signaturen – Klangfiguren* (1964)), written in strict rhythmical and rhyming forms, he aims at a similar breadth of sympathy which embraces the true, timeless proportions of life. Equally broad in conception are the poems of the critic Hans Egon Holthusen (born 1913), which, in a neo-baroque spirit, embrace the antithesis of temporal suffering and eternal salvation (*Hier in der Zeit* (1949); *Labyrinthische Jahre* (1952)).

In Catholic Austria we find the dramatist Fritz Hochwälder (born 1911; *Das heilige Experiment* (1943)), Felix Braun (born 1885), Rudolf Henz (born 1897; the verse epic *Der Turm der Welt* (1951)) and the lyric poetess Christine Busta (born 1915). In the Protestant tradition stands the Swabian pastor Albrecht Goes (born 1908), whose works range from the smallest subjects to the largest without shirking any embarrassing questions (*Gedichte 1930 bis 1950*; *Unruhige Nacht* (1952), a story based on his experiences as a chaplain on the Russian front; *Das Brandopfer* (1954)). The novel *Der neungekerbte Wanderstab* (1959) by Emanuel Hirsch (born 1888), a retired professor of theology, is a traditional, realistic work whose hero illustrates Kierkegaard's thesis that the path of grace leads through *Angst* and insecurity, and at this point Christian literature comes close to the existentialism, such as that of Nossack, which springs from doubt and scepticism.

Werner Bergengruen overcame the chaos of the age by ignoring all orthodoxies and joyfully embracing in a Christian universalism all earthly creatures and earthly fates: all life passes, but insecurity does not exclude sympathy, and transience does not deny knowledge of the infinite. 'The world is based on principles of an everlasting divine order', is his conclusion, and in 1951 he published a volume of verse with the defiant title *Die heile Welt*. Bergengruen was the most powerful Christian writer of his age, a master of realistic techniques, and his stories – *Der Tod von Reval*, a collection of *Novellen* published in 1939; *Die Rittmeisterin* (1954) – contain an abundance of characters as varied as those of Doderer.

Bergengruen thus takes his place close to those writers who, after 1945, sought to preserve a universality of outlook by combining the objective and the subjective, the conservative and the progressive, the realistic and the speculative. Hesse's *Glasperlenspiel*, for instance, was eagerly read in Germany after 1945, as were the works written by Thomas Mann and Werfel in exile. Flake and Doderer also belong here; so does the novelist Ernst Kreuder (born 1903), author of melancholy, playful, surrealist works (*Die Gesellschaft vom Dachboden* (1946)), who wrote in 1960: 'The literary fashion of hopeless despair must be overcome: a writer who aims at epic completeness must therefore swim against the stream ... The aim of such a writer can only be expressed as a paradox – to embrace the infinite.'

There is a onesided form of current literary criticism, found in figures as influential as Heissenbüttel and Adorno, and characteristic of those who affect rigid attitudes and think in terms of immutable formulae, which sees the only 'relevant' values as those of alienation, scepticism and meaninglessness. Sometimes such attitudes are the product of philosophical embarrassment, sometimes of a desire for influence, sometimes merely of a fear of being seen to have misjudged the course of the future.

For many it has become particularly difficult to form an independent opinion since the much-publicized activities of the self-styled 'Gruppe 47'. Skilfully led by the novelist Hans Werner Richter, this free association of writers has included Andersch and Grass, Weiss and Ingeborg Bachmann, Böll and Enzensberger, and many lesser figures of the 'sceptical genera-tion', and at its annual meeting new writers are invited to read from their own works before a critical audience, with the aim of discovering like minds among the younger generation.

The agitation that surrounds these meetings is a remarkable contrast to the Group's quiet beginnings in 1945, when Richter, Andersch, Schnurre and a number of other left-wing intellectuals in an American prisoner-of-war camp planned a radical journal *Der Ruf*, in which they intended to lay the intellectual foundations of a new socialist German democracy. After the Americans had banned this journal in 1947, the group decided to name themselves after the year in question, meeting regularly from then on to criticize each other's works according to the criterion of 'relevance' to the age.

But present-day German literature extends far beyond the activities of the 'Gruppe 47' and sceptical attitudes in general. The lines that divide authentic from spurious, valuable from worthless, run not between the so-called conservative and progressive camps but through them, and what is really contemporary – that is, what deals with the great concerns of the present, and of mankind in general, in a manner that is truly relevant – is not the prerogative of one faction alone. What is genuine and aesthetically convincing will be decided by the public at large, not by a clique. It remains to be seen whether the last twenty-five years have produced any literary works which, in the words of Goethe, 'possess that remarkable quality of belonging to mankind as a whole', and to which mankind will accord that approval which will put them in the ranks of true world-literature.

Bibliography

General Histories of Literature

BIESE, A. *Geschichte der deutschen Literatur*. 3 vols. 25th ed. Munich: Beck, 1931.

BOOR, H. DE, and NEWALD, R. *Geschichte der deutschen Literatur*. Munich: Beck, 1949 ff. (in progress).

MARTINI, F. *Deutsche Literaturgeschichte von den Anfängen bis zur Gegenwart*. 14th ed. Stuttgart: Metzler, 1965.

ROBERTSON, J. G. *A History of German Literature*. 6th ed. by D. Reich. Edinburgh/London: Blackwood, 1970.

STAMMLER, W. (ed.). *Deutsche Philologie im Aufriß*. 2nd ed. Berlin: Schmidt, 1957 ff.

Histories of Individual Genres

DRAMA

ARNOLD, E. (ed.). *Das deutsche Drama*. Munich, 1925.

MANN, O. *Geschichte des deutschen Dramas*. Stuttgart: Kröner, 1960.

PETZSCH, R. *Wesen und Formen des Dramas*. Halle: Niemeyer, 1945.

PRANG, H. *Geschichte des Lustspiels*. Stuttgart: Kröner, 1967.

WIESE, B. VON. *Die deutsche Tragödie von Lessing bis Hebbel*. 2 vols. 7th ed. Hamburg: Hoffmann and Campe, 1967.

WIESE, B. VON (ed.). *Das deutsche Drama vom Barock bis zur Gegenwart. Interpretationen*. 2 vols. Düsseldorf: Bagel, 1964.

NOVEL AND SHORTER FICTION

BENNETT, E. K. *A History of the German Novelle*. 2nd ed. by H. M. Waidson. Cambridge University Press, 1961.

BORCHERDT, H. H. *Geschichte des Romans und der Novelle in Deutschland*. Leipzig: Weber, 1926 ff.

GERHARD, M. *Der deutsche Entwicklungsroman bis zu Goethes Wilhelm Meister*. Halle: Niemeyer, 1926.

KLEIN, J. *Geschichte der deutschen Novelle.* 4th ed. Wiesbaden: Steiner, 1961.

LÜTHI, M. *Märchen.* Stuttgart: Metzler, 1964.

MALMEDE, H. H. *Wege zur Novelle.* Stuttgart: Kohlhammer, 1966.

PASCAL, R. *The German Novel.* Manchester University Press, 1965.

SPIERO, H. *Geschichte des deutschen Romans.* Berlin: de Gruyter, 1950.

WIESE, B. VON, *Die deutsche Novelle. Interpretationen.* 2 vols. Düsseldorf: Bagel, 1956, 1962.

POETRY

CLOSS, A. *The Genius of the German Lyric.* 2nd ed. London: Cresset Press, 1962.

GRAY, R. D. *An Introduction to German Poetry.* Cambridge University Press, 1965.

KILLY, W. *Wandlungen des lyrischen Bildes.* 4th ed. Göttingen: Vandenhoeck and Ruprecht, 1964.

KLEIN, J. *Geschichte der deutschen Lyrik.* Wiesbaden: Steiner, 1957.

PRAWER, S. S. *German Lyric Poetry.* London: Routledge, 1952.

STAIGER, E. *Grundbegriffe der Poetik.* 6th ed. Zürich: Atlantis, 1963.

WIESE, B. VON. *Die deutsche Lyrik. Interpretationen.* Düsseldorf: Bagel, 1964.

The Middle Ages

GENERAL

BÄUML, F. H. *Civilization in Medieval Germany.* London: Thames and Hudson, 1969.

BOSTOCK, J. K. *A Handbook of Old High German Literature.* Oxford University Press, 1955.

CURTIUS, E. R. *Europäische Literatur und lateinisches Mittelalter.* Berne: Francke, 1948.

EHRISMANN, G. *Geschichte der deutschen Literatur bis zum Ausgang des Mittelalters.* 4 vols. Munich: Beck, 1922–35.

HEER, F. *The Medieval World.* London: Weidenfeld and Nicolson, 1962.

HUIZINGA, J. *The Waning of the Middle Ages.* London: Arnold, 1924.

SALMON, P. B. *Literature in Medieval Germany.* London: Cresset Press, 1967.

SCHNEIDER, H. *Heldendichtung, Geistlichendichtung, Ritterdichtung.* 2nd ed. Heidelberg: Winter, 1943.

SCHWIETERING, J. *Die deutsche Dichtung des Mittelalters*. Darmstadt: Gentner, 1932.

WALSHE, M. O'C. *Medieval German Literature*. London: Routledge, 1962.

SPECIFIC AUTHORS AND SUBJECTS

BRINKMANN, H. *Entstehungsgeschichte des Minnesangs*. Halle: Niemeyer, 1926.

— *Liebeslyrik der deutschen Frühe*. Düsseldorf: Schwann, 1952.

BROGSITTER, K. O. *Artusepik*. Stuttgart: Metzler, 1965.

BUMKE, J. *Wolfram von Eschenbach*. 2nd ed. Stuttgart: Metzler, 1966.

BURDACH, K. *Reinmar der Alte und Walther von der Vogelweide*. 2nd ed. Halle: Niemeyer, 1928.

ECKER, L. *Arabischer, provenzalischer und deutscher Minnesang*. Berne: Francke, 1934.

FARAL, E. *La Légende arthurienne*. 3 vols. Paris: Champion, 1929.

FOURQUET, J. *Wolfram von Eschenbach et le Conte del Graal*. Paris: Les Belles Lettres, 1938.

FRANK, I. *Trouvères et Minnesänger*. University of Saarbrücken, 1952.

GOLTHER, W. *Tristan und Isolde in den Dichtungen des Mittelalters und der neuen Zeit*. Leipzig: Hirzel, 1907.

— *Parzival und der Gral in der Dichtung des Mittelalters und der Neuzeit*. Stuttgart: Metzler, 1925.

HATTO, A. T. *Gottfried von Strassburg: Tristan*. English translation with introduction. London: Penguin Classics, 1960.

— *The Nibelungenlied*. English translation with introduction. London: Penguin Classics, 1965.

HATTO, A. T., and TAYLOR, R. J. *The Songs of Neidhart von Reuental*. Manchester University Press, 1958.

HUNGER, J. *Walther von der Vogelweide*. Berlin: Kongress-Verlag, 1955.

KLEIN, K. K. *Die Anfänge der deutschen Literatur*. Munich: Südostdeutsches Kulturwerk, 1954.

KOLB, H. *Der Begriff der Minne und das Entstehen der höfischen Lyrik*. Tübingen: Niemeyer, 1948.

KRAUS, C. VON. *Des Minnesangs Frühling. Untersuchungen*. Berlin: de Gruyter, 1939.

KUHN, H. *Minnesangs Wende*. 2nd ed. Tübingen: Niemeyer, 1967.

— *Walther von der Vogelweide. Untersuchungen*. Berlin: de Gruyter, 1935.

MCKENZIE, D. A. *Otfrid von Weissenburg: Narrator or Commentator?* Stanford University Press, 1946.

SACKER, H. *Introduction to Wolfram's Parzival.* Cambridge University Press, 1963.

SCHRÖDER, W. J. *Spielmannsepik.* 2nd ed. Stuttgart: Metzler, 1967.

SCHULTZ, A. *Das höfische Leben zur Zeit der Minnesinger.* 2 vols. Leipzig: Hirzel, 1879–80.

STAMMLER, W. *Das religiöse Drama des deutschen Mittelalters.* Leipzig: Hirzel, 1925.

TAYLOR, R. J. *The Art of the Minnesinger.* 2 vols. Cardiff: University of Wales Press, 1968.

WAPNEWSKI, P. *Hartmann von Aue.* Stuttgart: Metzler, 1962.

WEBER, G., and HOFFMANN, W. *Gottfried von Strassburg.* 2nd ed. Stuttgart: Metzler, 1964.
— *Das Nibelungenlied.* 2nd ed. Stuttgart: Metzler, 1964.

WECHSSLER, E. *Das Kulturproblem des Minnesangs.* Halle: Niemeyer, 1909.

WENTZLAFF–EGGEBERT, F. W. *Deutsche Mystik zwischen Mittelalter und Neuzeit.* 3rd ed. Berlin: de Gruyter, 1969.

WILMANNS, W. *Walther von der Vogelweide.* 2 vols. 4th ed. by V. Michels. Halle: Niemeyer, 1916–24.

YOUNG, K. *The Drama of the Medieval Church.* 2 vols. Oxford University Press, 1947.

Sixteenth and Seventeenth Centuries

GENERAL

HANKAMER, P. *Deutsche Gegenreformation und deutsches Barock.* 3rd ed. Stuttgart: Metzler, 1964.

MÜLLER, G. *Deutsche Dichtung von der Renaissance bis zum Ausgang des Barock.* Potsdam: Athenaion, 1927.

PASCAL, R. *German Literature in the 16th and 17th Centuries.* London: Cresset Press, 1968.

STADELMANN, R. *Der Geist des ausgehenden Mittelalters.* Halle: Niemeyer, 1929.

STAMMLER, W. *Von der Mystik zum Barock.* 2nd ed. Stuttgart: Metzler, 1950.

SPECIFIC AUTHORS AND SUBJECTS

BAINTON, R. H. *Here I Stand. A Life of Martin Luther.* New York: Abingdon Press, 1951.

BECKMANN, A. *Motive und Formen der deutschen Lyrik des 17. Jahrhunderts.* Tübingen: Niemeyer, 1960.

BRUINIER, J. W. *Das deutsche Volkslied.* 7th ed. Berlin: de Gruyter, 1927.

BURGER, H. O. *Renaissance, Humanismus, Reformation.* Bad Homburg: Gehlen, 1969.

BUTLER, E. M. *The Fortunes of Faust.* Cambridge University Press, 1952.

CATHOLY, E. *Das Fastnachtspiel des Mittelalters.* Tübingen: Niemeyer, 1961.

CLARK, J. M. *The Great German Mystics.* Oxford University Press, 1949.

CLOSS, A., and MAINLAND, W. F. (eds.). *German Lyrics of the 17th Century.* London: Duckworth, 1940.

HAYENS, K. C. *Grimmelshausen.* London: St Andrews University Publications, 1932.

MANNACK, E. *Andreas Gryphius.* Stuttgart: Metzler, 1968.

NAGEL, B. *Meistersang.* Stuttgart: Metzler, 1962.

PALMER, P. M., and MORE, R. P. *The Sources of the Faust Tradition from Simon Magus to Lessing.* New York: Oxford University Press, 1936.

STRAUSS, D. F. *Ulrich von Hutten.* 2 vols. Ed. O. Clemen. 3rd ed. Leipzig, 1938.

TAYLOR, A. *The Literary History of Meistergesang.* New York: Modern Language Association, 1937.

Eighteenth Century

GENERAL

BRUFORD, W. H. *Germany in the Eighteenth Century.* Cambridge University Press, 1935.

DAUNICHT, R. *Die Entstehung des bürgerlichen Trauerspiels in Deutschland.* 2nd ed. Berlin: de Gruyter, 1965.

HAZARD, P. *European Thought in the Eighteenth Century.* London: Pelican Books, 1968.

HEITNER, R. R. *German Tragedy in the Age of Enlightenment.* Berkeley: University of California Press, 1963.

HETTNER, H. *Geschichte der deutschen Literatur im 18. Jahrhundert.* 3 vols. 7th ed. Brunswick: Vieweg, 1925.

KORFF, H. A. *Geist der Goethezeit.* 4 vols. Leipzig: Koehler and Amelang, 1923–53.

NICOLSON, H. *The Age of Reason*. London: Constable, 1960.

PASCAL, R. *The German Sturm und Drang*. Manchester University Press, 1953.

SCHNEIDER, F. J. *Die deutsche Dichtung vom Ausgang des Barocks bis zum Beginn des Klassizismus*. 2 vols. 2nd ed. Stuttgart: Metzler, 1949, 1952.

STAHL, E. L., and YUILL, W. E. *German Literature of the 18th and 19th Centuries*. London: Cresset Press, 1970.

STRICH, F. *Deutsche Klassik und Romantik*. 5th ed. Berne: Francke, 1962.

WELLEK, R. *A History of Modern Criticism*. New Haven, Conn.: Yale University Press, 1955 ff.

WOLFF, H. M. *Die Weltanschauung der deutschen Aufklärung*. Berne: Francke, 1949.

SPECIFIC AUTHORS AND SUBJECTS
First half of the century

DANZEL, T. W. *Gottsched und seine Zeit*. 1848. Repr. Hildesheim: Olms, 1970.

FREIVOGEL, M. *Klopstock*. Berne: Francke, 1954.

KINDT, K. *Klopstock*. 2nd ed. Berlin: Schmidt, 1948.

MAHRHOLZ, W. *Der deutsche Pietismus*. Berlin: Furche-Verlag, 1921.

MICHELSEN, P. *Laurence Sterne und der deutsche Roman des 18. Jahrhunderts*. Göttingen: Vandenhoeck and Ruprecht, 1962.

PEURSEN, C. A. VON. *Leibniz*. London: Faber, 1969.

VIËTOR, K. *Geschichte der deutschen Ode*. Munich: Beck, 1923.

WEHRLI, M. *J. J. Bodmer und die Geschichte der Literatur*. Frauenfeld/Leipzig: Huber, 1936.

WILKINSON, E. M. *Johann Elias Schlegel. A German Pioneer in Aesthetics*. Oxford: Blackwell, 1945.

WOLF, H. *Versuch einer Geschichte des Geniebegriffs in der deutschen Ästhetik des 18. Jahrhunderts*. Heidelberg: Winter, 1923.

Lessing and his age

GARLAND, H. B. *Lessing*. Cambridge: Bowes and Bowes, 1937.

OEHLKE, W. *Lessing und seine Zeit*. 2 vols. Munich: Beck, 1919.

RITZEL, W. *Gottfried Ephraim Lessing*. Stuttgart: Kohlhammer, 1966.

ROBERTSON, J. G. *Lessing's Dramatic Theory*. Ed. E. Purdie. Cambridge University Press, 1939.

SCHMIDT, E. *Lessing: Geschichte seines Lebens und seiner Schriften*. 2 vols. 4th ed. Berlin: Schmidt, 1923.

HATFIELD, H. C. *Winckelmann and his German Critics, 1755–81*. New York: King's Crown, 1943.

— *Aesthetic Paganism in German Literature*. Cambridge, Mass.: Harvard University Press, 1964.

JUSTI, K. *Winckelmann und seine Zeitgenossen*. 3 vols. 5th ed. by W. Rehm. Cologne: Phaidon, 1956.

PATER, W. 'Winckelmann'. *The Renaissance*. 1873.

SOMMERFELD, M. *Friedrich Nicolai und der Sturm und Drang*. Halle: Niemeyer, 1921.

Wieland, Herder, 'Sturm und Drang'

ABBÉ, D. M. VAN. *C. M. Wieland: A Literary Biography*. London: Harrap, 1961.

SENGLE, F. *Wieland*. Stuttgart: Metzler, 1949.

BARNARD, F. M. *Herder's Social and Political Thought*. Oxford University Press, 1965.

CLARK, R. T. *Herder's Life and Work*. Berkeley: University of California Press, 1955.

DOBBEK, W. *Herders Humanitätsidee als Ausdruck seines Weltbildes und seiner Persönlichkeit*. Brunswick: Westermann, 1949.

GILLIES, A. *Herder*. Oxford University Press, 1945.

HAYM, R. *Herder*. 2 vols. Berlin: Aufbau, 1954. Reprint of original ed. of 1877–85.

HERAEUS, O. *Friedrich Jacobi und der Sturm und Drang*. Heidelberg: Winter, 1928.

O'FLAHERTY, J. C. *Hamann's 'Socratic Memorabilia'*. Baltimore: John Hopkins Press, 1967.

RÖDEL, W. *Förster und Lichtenberg*. Berlin: de Gruyter, 1960.

SCHMIDT, E. *Lenz und Klinger*. Berlin: Schmidt, 1878.

STERN, J. P. *Lichtenberg: A Doctrine of Scattered Occasions*. Bloomington: University of Indiana Press, 1959.

UNGER, R. *Hamann und die Aufklärung*. 2 vols. Repr. Tübingen: Niemeyer, 1965.

Goethe

BIELSCHOWSKY, A. *Goethe: sein Leben und seine Werke.* 2 vols. New ed. by W. Linden. Munich: Beck, 1928.

BOYD, J. *Notes to Goethe's Poems.* 2 vols. Oxford: Blackwell, 1944, 1949.

BRUFORD, W. H. *Culture and Society in Classical Weimar 1775–1806.* Cambridge University Press, 1962.

FAIRLEY, B. *A Study of Goethe.* Oxford University Press, 1947.

— *Goethe's Faust, Six Essays.* Oxford University Press, 1953.

FRIEDENTHAL, R. *Goethe: His Life and Times.* London: Weidenfeld and Nicolson, 1965.

GUNDOLF, F. *Goethe.* 12th ed. Berlin: Bondi, 1925.

MASON, E. C. *Goethe's Faust, its Genesis and Purport.* Berkeley: University of California Press, 1967.

PEACOCK, R. *Goethe's Major Plays.* Manchester University Press, 1959.

REISS, H. *Goethes Romane.* Berne: Francke, 1963.

SCHRIMPF, H. J. *Das Weltbild des späten Goethe.* Stuttgart: Kohlhammer, 1951.

STAIGER, E. *Goethe.* 3 vols. Zürich: Atlantis, 1952–9.

STRICH, F. *Goethe und die Weltliteratur.* Berne: Francke, 1946.

TREVELYAN, H. *Goethe and the Greeks.* Cambridge University Press, 1941.

VIËTOR, K. *Goethe.* Berne: Francke, 1949.

WILKINSON, E. M., and WILLOUGHBY, L. A. *Goethe: Poet and Thinker.* London: Arnold, 1962.

WITKOWSKI, G. *Goethes Faust.* 9th ed. Leiden: Brill, 1936.

ZIMMERMANN, R. C. *Das Weltbild des jungen Goethe.* Munich: Fink, 1969.

Schiller

BURSCHELL, F. *Schiller.* Reinbek: Rowohlt, 1968.

GARLAND, H. B. *Schiller.* London: Harrap, 1949.

MAINLAND, W. F. *Schiller and the Changing Past.* London: Heinemann, 1957.

MANN, T. *Versuch über Schiller.* Frankfurt: Fischer, 1955.

STAHL, E. L. *Friedrich Schiller's Drama.* Oxford: Blackwell, 1954.

STAIGER, E. *Schiller.* Zürich: Atlantis, 1967.

STORZ, G. *Der Dichter Friedrich Schiller.* Stuttgart: Klett, 1955.

WIESE, B. VON. *Friedrich Schiller.* Stuttgart: Metzler, 1959.

Nineteenth Century

GENERAL

ALKER, E. *Die deutsche Literatur im 19. Jahrhundert.* Stuttgart: Kröner, 1961.

BOESCHENSTEIN, H. *Deutsche Gefühlskultur.* 2 vols. Berne: Haupt, 1966.

BRANDES, G. *Hauptströmungen in der deutschen Literatur des 19. Jahrhunderts.* Leipzig: Hirzel, 1891.

HÖLLERER, W. *Zwischen Klassik und Moderne.* Stuttgart: Klett, 1958.

KORFF, H. A. *Geist der Goethezeit.* 4 vols. Leipzig: Koehler and Amelang, 1923–53.

MEYER, R. M. *Die deutsche Literatur des 19. Jahrhunderts.* 7th ed. Berlin: Bondi, 1923.

ROMANTICISM

General surveys

FURST, L. *Romanticism in Perspective.* London: Methuen, 1969.

GUNDOLF, F. *Romantiker.* 2 vols. Berlin: Keller, 1930, 1931.

HAYM, R. *Die romantische Schule.* 6th ed. by E. Redslob. Berlin: Weidmann, 1949.

HUCH, R. *Die Romantik.* 2 vols. Leipzig: Hässel, 1899–1902.

KLUCKHOHN, P. *Das Ideengut der deutschen Romantik.* 3rd ed. Tübingen: Niemeyer, 1953.

KORFF, H. A. *Geist der Goethezeit.* 4 vols. 2nd ed. Leipzig: Koehler and Amelang, 1949–53.

LION, F. *Romantik als deutsches Schicksal.* Stuttgart: Kohlhammer, 1947.

MASON, E. C. *Deutsche und englische Romantik.* Göttingen: Vandenhoeck and Ruprecht, 1959.

PRAWER, S. S. (ed.). *The Romantic Period in Germany.* London: Weidenfeld and Nicolson, 1970.

SCHULTZ, F. *Klassik und Romantik der Deutschen.* 2nd ed. Stuttgart: Metzler, 1952.

STRICH, F. *Deutsche Klassik und Romantik.* 4th ed. Berne: Francke, 1949.

TAYLOR, R. *The Romantic Tradition in Germany.* London: Methuen, 1970.

TYMMS, R. *German Romantic Literature.* London: Methuen, 1955.

Specific authors

BÖHM, W. *Hölderlin.* 2 vols. Halle: Niemeyer, 1928–30.

PEACOCK, R. *Hölderlin.* London: Methuen, 1938.

RYAN, L. *Friedrich Hölderlin.* Stuttgart: Metzler, 1962.

SALZBERGER, L. S. *Hölderlin.* Cambridge: Bowes and Bowes, 1952.

HIEBEL, F. *Novalis: Der Dichter der blauen Blume.* Berne: Francke, 1951.

REHM, W. 'Novalis'. *Orpheus. Der Dichter und die Toten.* Düsseldorf: Schwann, 1950.

HORST, K. A. *Ich und Gnade. Eine Studie über Friedrich Schlegels Bekehrung.* Freiburg: Herder, 1951.

SANDKÜHLER, H. J. *Schelling.* Stuttgart: Metzler, 1970.

GUNDOLF, F. *Heinrich von Kleist.* Berlin: Bondi, 1922.

SILZ, W. *Heinrich von Kleist. Studies in His Works and Literary Character.* Philadelphia: University of Pennsylvania Press, 1961.

STAHL, E. L. *Heinrich von Kleist's Dramas.* Oxford University Press, 1948.

WOLFF, H. M. *Heinrich von Kleist. Die Geschichte seines Schaffens.* Berkeley: University of California Press, 1954.

SCHMIDT, A. *Fouqué und einige seiner Zeitgenossen.* Darmstadt: Bläschke, 1958.

BRANDENBURG, H. *Joseph von Eichendorff. Sein Leben und sein Werk.* Munich: Beck, 1922.

STOCKLEIN, P. (ed.). *Eichendorff heute.* Darmstadt: Wissenschaftliche Buchgesellschaft, 1966.

GARDINER, P. L. *Schopenhauer.* London: Penguin Books, 1963.

TENGLER, R. *Schopenhauer und die Romantik.* Berlin: Ebering, 1923.

BERGENGRUEN, W. *E. T. A. Hoffmann.* Zürich: Atlantis, 1960.

HEWETT-THAYER, H. W. *Hoffmann: Author of the Tales.* Princeton University Press, 1948.

TAYLOR, R. *Hoffmann.* Cambridge: Bowes and Bowes, 1964.

GERSTNER, H. *Die Brüder Grimm.* Ebenhausen: Langewiesche-Brandt, 1952.

MICHAELIS-JENA, R. *The Brothers Grimm*. London: Routledge, 1970.

REALISM AND NATURALISM

General Surveys

BIEBER, H. *Der Kampf um die Tradition: die deutsche Dichtung von 1830–1880*. Stuttgart: Metzler, 1928.

BUTLER, E. M. *The Saint-Simonian Religion in Germany*. Cambridge University Press, 1926.

KOOPMANN, H. *Das junge Deutschland*. Stuttgart: Metzler, 1970.

OSBORNE, J. *The German Naturalist Drama*. Manchester University Press, 1971.

PETZET, C. *Die Blütezeit der deutschen politischen Lyrik, 1840–50*. Munich: Beck, 1903.

RÖHL, H. *Der Naturalismus*. Leipzig: Quelle and Meyer, 1927.

Specific authors

MARCUSE, L. *Das Leben Ludwig Börnes*. Leipzig: Hirzel, 1929.

FAIRLEY, B. *Heinrich Heine. An Interpretation*. Oxford University Press, 1954.

PRAWER, S. S. *Heine, the Tragic Satirist*. Cambridge University Press, 1961.

SAMMONS, J. L. *Heinrich Heine, the Elusive Poet*. New Haven, Conn.: Yale University Press, 1969.

SPANN, M. *Heine*. Cambridge: Bowes and Bowes, 1968.

STORZ, G. *Eduard Mörike*. Stuttgart: Metzler, 1967.

WIESE, B. VON. *Mörike*. Tübingen/Stuttgart: Wunderlich, 1950.

BAUMANN, G. *Grillparzer*. Heidelberg: Stiehm, 1966.

NADLER, J. *Franz Grillparzer*. Vienna: Bergland, 1952.

BLACKALL, E. A. *Adalbert Stifter*. Cambridge University Press, 1948.

KREUZER, H. (ed.). *Hebbel in neuer Sicht*. Stuttgart: Kohlhammer, 1963.

PURDIE, E. *Friedrich Hebbel. A Study of his Life and Work*. London, 1932.

BOESCHENSTEIN, H. *Gottfried Keller. Grundzüge seines Lebens und Werkes*. Berne: Francke, 1948.

WILLIAMS, W. D. *The Stories of Conrad Ferdinand Meyer*. Oxford University Press, 1962.

GUTMAN, R. W. *Richard Wagner: The Man, His Mind and His Music*. London: Secker and Warburg, 1968.

HOLLINGDALE, R. J. *Nietzsche: The Man and his Philosophy*. London: Routledge, 1965.

JASPERS, K. *Nietzsche: Einführung in das Verständnis seines Philosophierens*. 3rd ed. Berlin: de Gruyter, 1950.

KAUFMANN, W. A. *Nietzsche*. Princeton University Press, 1950.

REUTER, H. H. *Fontane*. Munich: Beck, 1968.

GARTEN, H. F. *Gerhart Hauptmann*. Cambridge: Bowes and Bowes, 1954.

KNIGHT, K. G. (ed.). *Hauptmann: Centenary Lectures*. London: Institute of Germanic Studies, 1964.

Twentieth Century

GENERAL SURVEYS

BITHELL, J. *Modern German Literature*. 3rd ed. London: Methuen, 1959.

CLOSS, A. *Twentieth Century German Literature*. London: Cresset Press, 1969.

DIEBOLD, B. *Anarchie im Drama*. 4th ed. Berlin: Keller, 1928.

EDSCHMID, K. *Lebendiger Expressionismus*. Vienna: Desch, 1961.

GARTEN, H. F. *Modern German Drama*. London: Methuen, 1959.

HAMANN, R., and HERMAND, J. *Der Impressionismus*. Berlin: Akademie, 1960.

HAMBURGER, M. *From Prophecy to Exorcism: The Premises of Modern German Literature*. London: Longman, 1965.

HELLER, E. *The Disinherited Mind*. Cambridge: Bowes and Bowes, 1952.

HOLTHUSEN, H. E. *Der unbehauste Mensch*. Munich: Piper, 1951.

KUNISCH, H. (ed.). *Handbuch der deutschen Gegenwartsliteratur*. Munich: Nymphenburg, 1965.

— *Die deutsche Gegenwartsdichtung*. Munich: Nymphenburg, 1968.

MAYER, H. *Zur deutschen Literatur der Zeit*. Reinbek: Rowholt, 1967.

REICH-RANICKI, M. *Deutsche Literatur in Ost und West*. Munich: Piper, 1963.

ROTHE, W. (ed.). *Expressionismus als Literatur*. Berne: Francke, 1969.

SAMUEL, R., and THOMAS, R. H. *Expressionism in German Life, Literature and the Theatre*. Cambridge: Heffer, 1939.

SOERGEL, A., and HOHOFF, C. *Dichtung und Dichter der Zeit*. 2 vols. Düsseldorf: Bagel, 1961, 1963.

SOKEL, W. H. *The Writer in Extremis: Expressionism in Twentieth-Century German Literature*. Stanford University Press, 1959.

STERNFELD, W., and TIEDEMANN, E. *Deutsche Exilliteratur 1933–1945*. Heidelberg: Schneider, 1962.

THOMAS, R. H., and WILL, W. VAN DER. *The German Novel and the Affluent Society*. Manchester University Press, 1968.

WAIDSON, H. M. *The Modern German Novel*. Oxford University Press, 1959.

SPECIFIC AUTHORS

BENNETT, E. K. *George*. Cambridge: Bowes and Bowes, 1954.

GUNDOLF, F. *Stefan George*. Berlin: Bondi, 1930.

ALEWYN, R. *Über Hugo von Hofmannsthal*. 2nd ed. Göttingen: Vandenhoeck and Ruprecht, 1960.

NORMAN, F. (ed.). *Hofmannsthal. Studies in Commemoration*. London: Institute of Germanic Studies, 1963.

GRAFF, W. L. *Rainer Maria Rilke*. Princeton University Press, 1956.

GUARDINI, R. *Rainer Maria Rilkes Deutung des Daseins*. Munich: Kösel, 1953.

HOLTHUSEN, H. E. *R. M. Rilke: A Study of his Later Poetry*. Cambridge: Bowes and Bowes, 1952.

MASON, E. C. *Rainer Maria Rilke*. Edinburgh: Oliver and Boyd, 1963.
— *Rilke, Europe and the English-speaking World*. Cambridge University Press, 1959.

KUTSCHER, A. *Frank Wedekind: Sein Leben und seine Werke*. 3 vols. Munich: Müller, 1922–31.

BOULBY, M. *Hermann Hesse*. Ithaca: Cornell University Press, 1967.

ZIOLKOWSKI, T. *The Novels of Hermann Hesse*. Princeton University Press, 1965.

ANDERS, G. *Kafka*. Cambridge: Bowes and Bowes, 1958.

GRAY, R. (ed.). *Kafka: A Collection of Critical Essays*. Englewood Cliffs: Prentice Hall, 1962.

SOKEL, W. H. *Franz Kafka*. New York: Columbia University Press, 1966.

WAGENBACH, K. *Franz Kafka in Selbstzeugnissen und Bilddokumenten*. Reinbek: Rowholt, 1964.

ESSLIN, M. *Brecht. A Choice of Evils*. London: Eyre and Spottiswoode, 1959.

GRAY, R. *Brecht*. Edinburgh: Oliver and Boyd, 1961.

GRIMM, R. *Brecht*. Stuttgart: Metzler, 1961.

WILLETT, J. *The Theatre of Bertolt Brecht*. London: Methuen, 1959.

EICHNER, H. *Thomas Mann: eine Einführung in sein Werk*. Berne: Francke, 1953.

HATFIELD, H. *Thomas Mann*. 2nd ed. Norfolk, Conn.: New Directions, 1962.

HELLER, E. *The Ironic German*. London: Secker and Warburg, 1957.

THOMAS, R. H. *Thomas Mann*. Oxford University Press, 1956.

WHITE, A. *Thomas Mann*. Edinburgh: Oliver and Boyd, 1965.

PIKE, B. *Robert Musil: An Introduction to His Work*. Ithaca: Cornell University Press, 1961.

Name Index

Subject Index